The Complete Internet Marketer

Buy This Book at:
www.thecompleteinternetmarketer.com

The Complete Internet Marketer

A Practical Guide To
Everything You Need To Know
About Marketing Online

Jay Neuman

With-A-Clue
Press

The Complete
Internet Marketer

Jay Neuman

Contents

Part III:
How To Increase Profitability
Using Web Analytics

Chapter 13:
Using Web Analytics To Measure Website Performance

Chapter 14:
Using Web Analytics To Increase The Profitability
Of Your Website

Part IV:
How To Build A Winning Website
For Your Business Model

Chapter 15:
Building A Successful eRetail Website

How To Use This Book

Four Ways to Use this Book

Use This Book as a How-To Instructional Guide

Each chapter in the Complete Internet Marketer contains easy to follow, step-by-step guides for all of the key skills needed to be successful online. You can turn to the specific skills you need to learn and simply follow the guidelines in that chapter.

If you have a job that needs to get done now, look up the relevant instructional guide. You will be able to quickly get up and running. By continuing to implement the skills you learn, you will continuously improve over time.

Use This Book as a Textbook or Self-Study Guide

The Complete Internet Marketer provides in-depth instruction for all of the major topics that make up a well-rounded Internet Marketing course. It is perfect as a university textbook or as a self-study guide for professionals seeking to jump-start their careers in the field

All of the foundational skills are covered in Parts I, II and III. After learning the skills to be a successful practitioner in the field, you will then learn insights needed to implement that knowledge as an expert. Part IV provides real-life strategic and tactical instruction for creating successful websites in the seven online business models that make up nearly all professional websites. You will be equipped to build a successful web-based business or to provide expert leadership to a business seeking to set up their own Internet Marketing program.

Use This Book as a Reference Source

The Complete Internet Marketer is filled with instructions, how-to guides and hundreds of useful tips for being successful as an Internet Marketer. It will be an indispensable reference source for your bookshelf or office. You will turn to it over and over again.

When starting a new project in an area where you are not experienced, look up that topic and learn the key skills you need to be successful. Perhaps you are just a little rusty. Maybe you need a refresher before an important meeting or interview. The Complete Internet Marketer gives you the information you need. It also gives you expert tips for getting the best results and avoiding common mistakes.

Use This Book as a General Overview

Each chapter in the Complete Internet Marketer is written so you can read the opening sections to get a general overview of the major topics covered in that chapter. As you read further, each chapter digs deeper into the nuts-and-bolts. You can dig as deep as you want.

Read the opening sections of each chapter that interests you. By the time you reach the last chapter, you will have a strong understanding of what Internet Marketing is all about. You will be able talk knowledgeably about all of the major Internet Marketing topics. If you continue to read through to the end of a chapter, you will be able to hold your own in conversation with experts in the field.

Acknowledgements

To quote the Grateful Dead, "What a long strange trip it's been." I started my career in Internet Marketing by accident. I had finished a degree in Public Policy in 1994. As luck would have it, a recession that year had forced the entire state of California to impose a hiring freeze on all public sector jobs. By my birthday, in November, I was unemployed and out of money. That morning, I was literally on my knees in prayer, asking God if he would just give me a job for my birthday. While I was still on my knees, the phone rang. It was a temp agency calling about a job with Toyota's Direct Response department. That was the start of my Internet Marketing career. So, first of all, I must thank God for his role in this adventure.

Since that first job, I have had many mentors, coworkers and friends who have taught me, given me opportunities and helped out as we all learned together in the online school of hard knocks. The lessons in this book are all lessons I could not have learned without them. The finger prints of every one of these people are on this book. I would like to thank them all. At Toyota, David Broscow, Brian Williams, Nancy Scott, June Okamoto, Jim Pisz and the rest of the Direct Response team. At the Polk Company, Jenny Fu, Pete Affeld, Shaoling Zhu, Deirdre Borrego, Tony Goetz and the rest of the team in the Long Beach and Detroit offices. At Kabang.com, Fadi Ayloush, Abder Boukour, Sam Khulusi and the rest of the team. At BizRate.com, Rod Cha, Andy Knobloch, Bob Michaelian, Haitao Wang, Keith Dutton, Igor Roizen, George Rebane, Mark Matthews, Susan Brandt, Farhad Mohit, Chuck Davis and dozens of others. At ARAMARK Uniform Services, Diana Kononenko, Jared Way, Mike Schouder, Erika Turnquist, Nicole Allen, Mike Billings, Jennifer Lupa, Pam Phillips, Judith Weiss and the rest of the Marketing team as well as Kara Tolland, Charlie Seelig, Mark Sblendorio, Tim O'Malley, Audrey Williams, Shelly Walker, Matt Scott, Brandon Kuka, JD Schwartz and A'lan Abruzzo. Besides these, there are many vendors, clients and friends who have all contributed in some way. Above all, I would like to thank my parents who have always stood by me and supported me. Thank You.

Introduction

How The Internet Changed Marketing Forever

A new marketing terrain was created at the end of the Twentieth Century. A generation of pioneering entrepreneurs set out on a great adventure. They invented new technologies and carved out new business models from an uncharted virtual frontier. Many did not understand the terrain they would have to pass through. Hundreds of failed Dot-Com startups would litter the landscape of the, so called, "New Economy." Those who did succeed figured out what the new terrain looks like. As time went by, they adjusted their business plans to meet the realities of that terrain. In the process, they forever changed the way marketing is practiced. Those days are over now. But the lessons still remain. Everyone who hopes to succeed with Internet Marketing will be following in the footsteps of those original innovators and must learn the lessons their experiences teach. This book brings you those lessons.

In the chapters that follow, you will learn how to be successful with Internet Marketing, from soup to nuts. Just a few of the things you will learn are:

✓ How to write an Internet Marketing plan for your business
✓ How to design a website that meets the needs of your business model
✓ How to bring traffic to your website and convert that traffic to sales
✓ How to continuously increase the profitability of your website by setting up proactive reporting and analysis

Before we move on to the How-To's of Internet Marketing, we should first take a few moments to put the field into context. In a few short years, the Internet has gone from being an obscure new idea to being an essential part of any marketing strategy. Something changed dramatically when the Internet came on the scene. To be successful marketing on the Internet, the first lesson is to understand what did change and the role the Internet now plays in the new marketing world.

How Did We Get Here?

In the opening years of the Twenty-first Century, we find the practice of marketing is noticeably different than it was throughout the Twentieth Century. In the decade of the 1990's, the field of marketing went through a rebirth of sorts.

It was similar to another rebirth that happened a hundred years earlier. Advances in the technology of mass production at the beginning of the Twentieth Century created a need for marketing as a strategic tool to bring products to the masses. Traditional textbooks still emphasize things such as balancing product, placement, price and promotion to appeal to the largest possible audience. Fundamental marketing needs like these *"Four P's of Marketing"* have not disappeared. However, they have been expanded. Throughout the 1990's marketing began focusing more and more on building relationships with individual customers, one at a time.

Three phenomena came together in the 1990's to make this possible. To understand today's Internet Marketing world, we must start with a basic understanding of these three.

(1)   Database Marketing
(2)   One-to-One Marketing
(3)   The Internet.

None of these are new. In fact, in one form or another they have all been around since the early 1970's. However, advances in technology prompted their explosion into the mainstream in the 1990's. As a result, the Twenty-first century finds no company insulated from the need to interact with their customers as individuals.

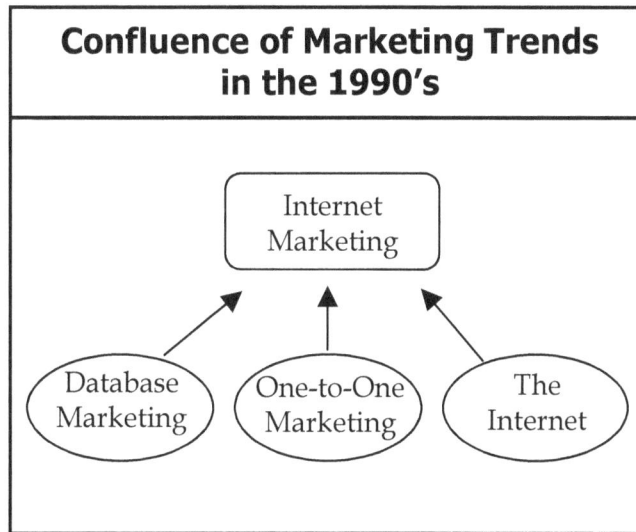

Figure 1

Database Marketing

The advent of database marketing can be thought of as the first step in the evolution of today's Internet Marketing environment. In the early 1970's, innovators began experimenting, using computing technologies to take the field of direct marketing to a new level. For the first time, companies began to put their entire customer lists into databases with the specific purpose of learning about them to maximize direct marketing efforts. These early efforts were very costly and involved huge mainframe computer systems to make them work. So only very large companies and direct marketing list vendors made use of the new technology.

In the early 1990's, microcomputers and local area networks made it possible for every company to have a customer database. Database marketing moved into the mainstream. Forward thinking companies put that technology to work to better understand their customers. In turn, they were able to target their marketing efforts to meet their customers' wants and needs. These forward thinking companies began to raise the bar for their competition by reaching out to customers on a more personalized basis. The trend which continues to drive marketing innovation today was born.

Database marketing technologies were put to use by savvy marketers to reach customers in ways they had only dreamed of before.

One-to-One Marketing

At the same time as database marketing technology was becoming popular, a little revolution in how we think about the practice of marketing itself was sparked. Writings like "The One-to-One Future" by Don Peppers and Martha Rogers (1993) changed the way we think about Marketing itself. Marketers started to think in terms of using the new technologies to build long term relationships with their customers, one at a time. As with database marketing, the basic concepts of One-to-One Marketing were not new. In fact, the basic concept is to reproduce an earlier time when shop owners got to know each one of their customers and built loyalty by meeting each one's specific wants and needs. Early examples of one-to-one marketing ideas include such things as store membership programs where customers received birthday cards, gift reminders or other personalized communications.

The revolution of one-to-one marketing was a change in perspective. Marketers traditionally focused on maximizing market share across entire customer segments. This began to change. Some began trying to maximize the share of each customer's expenditures that their company was able to capture. New technologies were to be applied to the customer database to transform it into a learning engine. This would allow companies to discover the wants and needs of each customer. Then through automated, customer focused communications that same technology was used to maximize the share of each customer's wallet that the company was able to meet. Pepper's and Rogers coined the term *"share of wallet"* as a contrast to the traditional focus on market share.

Back in the early 1990's this seemed more like a pipedream than a realistic goal. Nevertheless, the ideas were having a big impact on direct marketing and customer relationship practices at the time. We did not realize that a new technology was about to make the pipedream a reality.

The Internet

In the late 1990's the Internet brought the revolution right into customers' homes. Most marketers today know the basic history of the Internet. It first came online in 1969 as a way to share information between universities and government agencies. But, it was the invention of Hypertext Markup Language (HTML) and the World Wide Web (www) in the early 1990's that created the websites we know today.

The basic design of a website makes it an engine for collecting detailed customer information. Right from the start, there were companies applying statistical algorithms to transform that information into learning that could drive personalized marketing messages. Once again, savvy marketers started using the new technologies to do what we only dreamed of before. Today, customers themselves are raising the bar by going to those web sites which best meet their needs and wants as individual customers, rather than as generic members of a target audience.

Successful Internet Marketing strategies will combine components from all three streams.

Database marketing provides the technological backbone to capture and utilize the flood of customer information coming into your company through the Internet. It also provides the tools and techniques to transform that information into actionable intelligence and to maintain customer communications. The principles of one-to-one marketing provide practical guidelines for using technology to build and maintain customer relationships. Finally, the Internet provides technology which transforms the customer communication process into a real time interaction which takes place in the customer's home or cubicle at work. One way to think about it is that *the Internet has turbo-charged database marketing technologies to make the dream of one-to-one marketing a reality.*

The New Marketing Terrain

Traditional businesses, spend years cultivating relationships with their customers. They must now compete against businesses online to keep those customers. We live in an age when customers need to go no further than their living rooms, or offices to get satisfaction. New, virtual businesses have rushed in to occupy that space in the customers' living rooms. Still, they must offer a superior online experience if they are going to sway customers away from businesses they are loyal to.

Who will win the battle for your customers?

Businesses today have no choice except to enter the competition to satisfy the ever-increasing expectations of online customers. Even if a customer comes in person to buy a product or service, chances are they first researched it online. Businesses themselves have made this even easier for consumers. They have put high speed Internet access on their employee's desktops.

The Internet is doing for consumers in the early Twenty-first century what labor unions did for workers in the early Twentieth century. It is leveling the playing field. The old saying, attributed to PT Barnum, goes "A sucker is born every minute." Today, the Internet is turning that saying on its ears. An informed consumer is born every minute. Businesses no longer have a choice. They must use the technology available to them to meet their customers on their own terms. Otherwise those customers will go to someone else who will.

People still go to the local mall after work to shop. But today, they can take five minutes out of their lunch break to research the products they are planning to buy first. Savvy online marketers are capturing those customers before they ever take that trip to the mall.

The watershed moment for online buying was the 1999 holiday shopping season. Shoppers spent over $5 billion through the Internet. That far exceeded all expectations with a 300% increase over 1998. There were no skeptics anymore. Online buying had become a permanent fixture on the retail landscape. As we crossed the threshold into the twenty-first century, the corporate website, which four years earlier had been little more than an afterthought in marketing departments, had moved to center stage. The landscape had changed.

What does the new terrain look like?

The Internet came upon the marketing world like a flood. The rate of technological and organizational transformation that took place in it's wake was enough to make your head spin. It seemed like every couple of months the pundits were declaring a new "paradigm shift" and heralding the triumph of the latest eBusiness innovation over Old Economy dinosaurs. Now the waters have receded. We are able to see what has actually changed and what has not.

As it turns out, the Internet did not create an entirely new economy. The hype was clearly overrated, to the point of almost being comical. However, to be successful, marketers must be aware of the forces that are shaping the Twenty-first Century marketing terrain. Figure 2 shows what changed and what did not change in five areas where the New Economy was to have put to death traditional marketing practices.

The New Marketing Terrain

	What Changed	What Did Not Change
A New eRetail Sales Channel Opened	✓ An electronic retail channel opened making mail order shopping easy, convenient and popular ✓ New technology has made eRetail the channel of choice for some producers and customers	✓ Mail order is still not suited for all products and not desired by many customers ✓ The new terrain is still characterized by integrated sales & marketing channels; the Internet is one channel among many
Customers Gained an Advantage	✓ Your customers are online researching your products and services ✓ They are comparison shopping and visiting your competitors' websites ✓ Competition increased and prices were pushed down	✓ Brands are still important. People are risk-averse and rely on quality brands to help make purchase decisions ✓ Customers still want loyal relationships with businesses and products they trust
Barriers to Entry were Lowered	✓ Small stores have equal access to online customers ✓ Small and independent producers have direct access to the end customer	✓ Large, multi-channel players still realize economies of scale
Customer Expectations were Raised	✓ Customers now expect instant, online access to customer service and information about your company and products	✓ Customers still want the human touch from real people
The Value of Time Increased	✓ Research & purchase now take place at accelerated speed. If information and services are not delivered in Internet time, then	✓ Customers still behave in predictable ways. They still respond to advertising messages and marketing promotions

Figure 2

The Fifth "P" Of Marketing

We do not need to create a new economic model to successfully navigate this new terrain. But we do need to re-think some parts of our existing business models. In the 1990's, using database marketing to promote loyalty among your customers, one customer at a time, was an opportunity. In the first decade of the Twenty-first Century the explosion of Internet Marketing has made it a necessity.

The secret to understanding the new marketing terrain is found in the convergence of three marketing streams: database marketing, one-to-one marketing, and the Internet. The tried and true principles of marketing are still being used to reach a mass audience. But now, technology makes it possible to extend the reach of your marketing efforts. Marketing activities can now be personalized for each customer. You could say there is now a fifth "P" of Marketing – the *Person*.

This is how Internet Marketing has forever changed the marketing terrain. Marketing in the Twenty-first Century can be personalized for every customer.

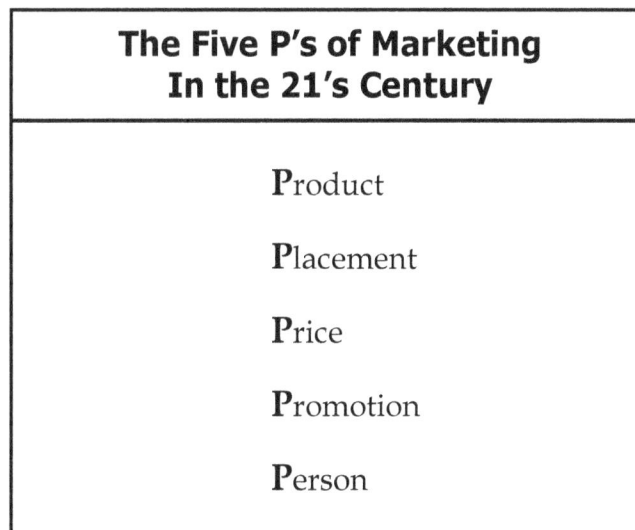

The Five P's of Marketing In the 21's Century
Product
Placement
Price
Promotion
Person

Figure 3

Personalized marketing uses technology and ideas that themselves are not entirely new. As we saw, they have been around in one form or another since the 1970's. However, personalized marketing is truly a new marketing paradigm because of at least two very critical differences:

(1)   The individual customer — *the person* — is an interactive participant in real time.

(2)   New technologies give businesses the ability to make that real time interaction a unique — *personalized* — experience for each customer.

Personalization Technology vs. Personalized Marketing

One of the major features utilized in Internet Marketing programs is "Personalization." The term usually refers to technology features that can be used on a website to modify – personalize – the content for each user. The two most common examples are customizable content and dynamic recommendations. In the first case, registered users of the site are given the ability to choose what information they see when they "log on" to the site or in email messages. In the second case, the site observes what a customer purchases over time. Dynamic recommendations are given based on other customers who have made similar purchases. Both cases involve learning about the customer. The online experience is modified to better suit his or her individual preferences.

Personalization is a tremendously important development. But, by itself, personalization is nothing more than adding bells and whistles to a website. What is needed to be competitive in your customer's living room or office is a strategic marketing outreach to each individual customer. Personalization techniques are a component of that strategy. There are many other components. Some of them are drawn from the principles of one-to-one marketing. Some of them come from the off-line world of database marketing. Some of them are entirely new with the advent of the World Wide Web.

How do you put together a personalized marketing program?

A successful personalized marketing program is somewhat like a jigsaw puzzle. There are many pieces. The secret to winning over your customers when they are visiting your business from the comfort of their own home or office is not just to have all the pieces. The secret is to be able to put all the pieces together in a way that allows each customer to have a truly personalized and rewarding relationship with your business. Your customers should not see a jumble of nice features on your site. They should see the picture that emerges when all those pieces are fit together to meet their individualized needs and wants.

The chapters in this book will show you how to put together the pieces of that puzzle.

Part I

How To Create A Successful Internet Marketing Plan

The Dot-Com Revolution took the world by storm in the late 1990's. Hundreds of new Internet businesses raised venture capital and started doing business online. Investors were in a mad frenzy to invest in the latest start-up. No one knew which was going to be the next big thing. Everyone expected many of these new businesses would fail. But, no one was prepared for the wholesale die-off of Internet companies after 2001.

Stories about pioneers of the Dot-Com revolution have since quietly faded into business folklore. Like the heroic tales of ancient China, Dot-Com stories are part adventure and part comedy. Regardless of the outcome, you have to admire the guts of those entrepreneurs. They jumped into the fray before most people even knew what was happening. They raised capital and spun out new innovative businesses as quickly as they could. Their goal was to capture the opportunity before it passed by. It turned out the opportunity only lasted a few years. Today, the rest of us can sit back and learn from their successes and their failures. Some of the mistakes seem obvious to us today – in 20/20 hindsight. We even make jokes about some of them. Do you remember Pets.com, with their sock puppet mascot? Their tag line was, "Because pets can't drive." Unfortunately, pets can't shop online either.

A common theme among those companies who are succeeding even after the crash is that they are the ones who had well thought out strategic plans. They have continued to evaluate and revise those plans on an ongoing basis. As you read the chapters in Part I you will learn how to put together a winning plan for your Internet Marketing venture.

A Step-By-Step Guide To Creating Your Internet Marketing Plan

To many people, doing business on the Internet is a mystery. I hear people say things like, "It is one thing to sell widgets. We've got that down pretty well. But when it comes to selling widgets on the Internet, we do not know where to start." It is certainly true that developing an Internet Marketing strategy takes some hard work. It is not for the faint of heart. But it does not have to be so complicated that only a few "gurus" can understand it. The chapters that follow unveil the mystery. You will learn a straightforward, step-by-step approach to putting together a strategic plan for your Internet Marketing program.

To develop a winning Web strategy for your business or organization, there are basically just four things to do.

Step 1:	Understand your online business model
Step 2:	Know your customers
Step 3:	Set effective goals
Step 4:	Choose the right tactics

The overall process can be represented by the simple diagram shown below.

You will learn . . .

✓ That there are only seven dimensions behind all online business models. By identifying which apply to your business, you will be able to easily define how you can use the Internet to make money, or otherwise support the goals of your organization.

✓ That you can understand the needs and wants of your online customers in terms of four levels of customer intimacy that all online customers experience.

✓ The key to putting together a winning online strategy is to set goals and choose tactics that match up the dimensions of your online business model with the needs and wants of your customers along these four dimensions.

The Internet Marketing Plan Made Easy

**7 Dimensions of
Online Business Models**

1. eCommerce
2. Business Development
3. Lead Generation
4. Brand Development
5. Customer Relations
6. Information Delivery
7. Cost Savings

**4 Levels of
Customer Intimacy**

Online Goals & Tactics →

- Loyalty
- Satisfaction
- Trust
- Interest

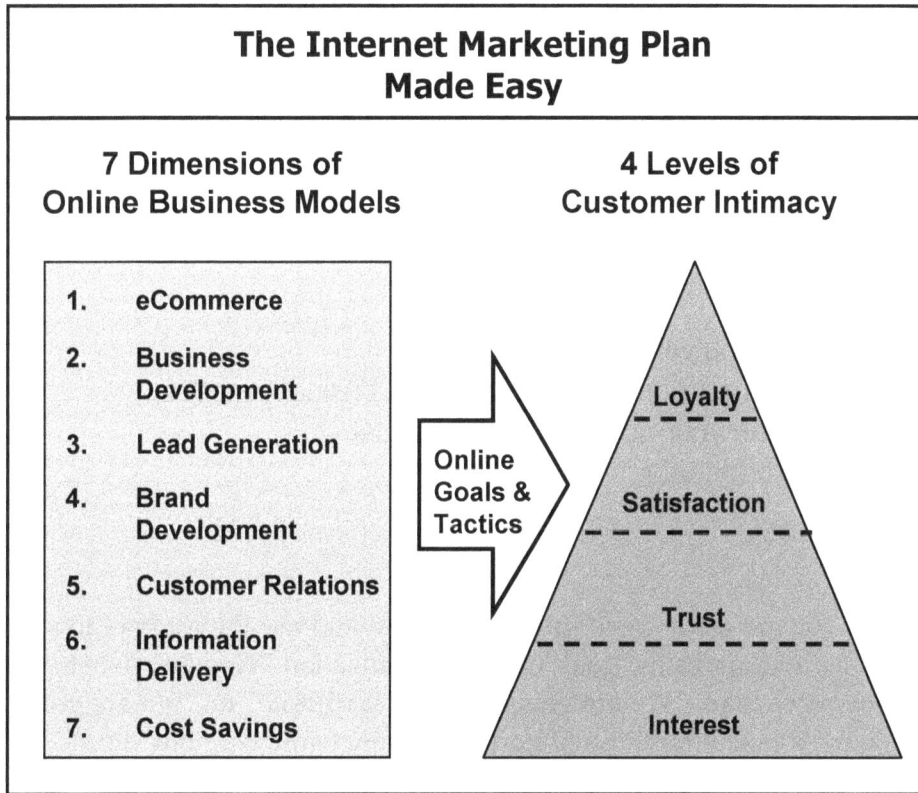

You will learn a process that anyone can follow. The basic concepts of putting together an Internet Marketing plan are presented in a way that highlights the issues especially important to marketing on the Internet. There is not time in this book to go into a complete discussion on the planning process. However, if you follow the steps presented in the following chapters, you will put together a back-of-the-envelope plan that will allow you to have a successful program. You need no formal training. Anyone can do it.

Chapter 1

Understanding Your Online Business Model

In this chapter, you will learn . . .
- The seven dimensions behind all online business models
- How to define your online business model
- How to be profitable

So you are ready to go full steam ahead and use the Internet to support the sales and marketing goals of your organization. To many people this means no more than, "We are going to build a website" or "We are going to give our website a facelift and add some new features." But simple statements like these are deceptive. They can mean many things. For a retail store, it may mean selling your products online. To a manufacturer, it may mean promoting your brand and offering customer service online. Government and nonprofit agencies are using the Internet to provide information and access to public services. The first step to effective Internet Marketing is to understand *how* you can use the Internet to help your business succeed.

Your Business Model vs. Your Online Business Model

It is important to distinguish between your company's business model and the business model for your website. Every business has a business model (although some do not take the time to figure out what it is). It is how your company makes money by selling products and/or services to a target market. In the case of government or nonprofit organizations, the business model is how to meet the objectives of the organization by delivering goods and/or services to a target population. Your online business model is simpler than this.

Your online business model is how you will use the Internet to support the sales and marketing objectives of your business model.

The Seven Dimensions Of Online Business Models

Luckily, your online business model is easier to figure out than the business model for your company. There are basically just seven ways companies and organizations use the Internet to support the sales and marketing goals of their business models. Knowing this will give you an easy way to define your online business model. Simply identify which of these seven applies to your business. These are the *dimensions of your online business model*.

Now let us take a look at the seven dimensions.

Dimension #1: eCommerce

eCommerce takes place whenever goods or services are exchanged for an electronic payment through a website. In other words, selling things online. The most basic form of eCommerce is simple transactions through an eRetail website. In this case, products are listed for sale and a simple shopping cart mechanism allows purchases to be made. We are all familiar with this type of website. More complex forms of eCommerce include such things as online auctions, where multiple buyers compete against each other in bidding for the purchase.

You have an eCommerce dimension to your online business model if a monetary transaction occurs on your website.

Dimension #2: Business Development

Business Development takes place when the website is being used as a tool to support a larger sales process. The most basic form of Business Development is simply collecting contact information from prospective customers. This could be done through a simple "contact us" form. Other ways to collect prospect information are through a needs assessment form or to offer a useful download that first requires contact information to be entered. More complex forms of business development services could include allowing prospective customers to schedule a follow up call from a sales person or submit a request for proposal (RFP).

You have a Business Development dimension to your online business model if you are collecting sales leads for your business or otherwise supporting a sales process which goes beyond transactions on the website.

Dimension #3: Lead Generation

Lead Generation takes place when the website is used as a way to collect qualified traffic who will be sent to another website, usually for a fee. We are all familiar with lead generation websites. The most common are search engines. Whenever you search for something in a search engine, you are identifying an interest you have. Chances are that someone has something they want to sell to people with that interest. If you click on a "Sponsored Link" you become a qualified lead to that website. This is Lead Generation in action.

Another common form of Lead Generation are websites who rely on revenue generated from banner ads or other online advertisements placed on their website. Perhaps the most complex of the Lead Generation models is the Business-to-Business Exchange. In these "online marketplaces," multiple sellers compete to make a sale in some form of online bidding process.

You have a Lead Generation dimension to your online business model if an important reason for your website to exist is to redirect traffic to other websites.

Dimension #4: Customer Relations

Customer Relations takes place when the website provides online services to existing customers thus enhancing their ability to do business with the company. The most basic form of Customer Relations is to provide online customer service. This could be as simple as a customer service phone number and email. It could also include self-service customer service tools, technical manuals, FAQs or online chat with a live person. Another form of Customer Relations is when service companies allow their customers to manage aspects of their service program online. An online banking website is perhaps the most common example of this. Loyalty rewards programs are also a form of Customer Relations if they are administered through the website.

You have a Customer Relations dimension to your online business model if servicing existing customers online is an important part of what your website is intended to accomplish.

Dimension #5: Brand Development

Brand Development takes place when the website is used to build customer affinity to the brand, but not necessarily to sell products and services directly to the end customer. Brand Development is especially important for companies who do not sell directly to the end consumer, but through channel partners. In this case, the website acts as an information resource promoting the products and the company. In many cases, manufacturers will use their website to provide information that will be used by their retail partners to help make sales. Another place where Brand Development is especially important is for nonprofit agencies who rely on donations. In this case, the website promotes the agency's cause and promotes the credibility of the agency to meet the needs of their target population.

You have a Brand Development dimension to your online business model if you expect people to come to your website seeking information about your company or products outside of the sales or customer relations process. Also, as a result of that information, you hope they will be more likely to purchase your products or use your services in the future.

Dimension #6: Information Delivery

Information Delivery takes place when information itself is being provided as a value-added service. Government agencies and nonprofit organizations often have information delivery as a primary part of their online business model. Personal blogs are also information delivery websites.

Online businesses with a Lead Generation business model often use information delivery as the means to attract web users to their website. In this case, when users come to the website, they self-select themselves as being interested in the targeted content they are searching for or viewing online. In most cases, the Information Delivery dimension is a free service of the website. However, there are cases where the information itself is the product being sold. These "content provider" websites may charge a fee for information ranging from teaching aids, to white papers, to syndicated news.

You have an Information Delivery dimension to your online business model if customers come to your website specifically to view information for its own sake and if providing that information is an important reason for your site to exist.

Dimension #7: Cost Savings

Cost Savings takes place when processes are performed or services delivered online which otherwise incur higher costs in another medium. The most common Cost Savings measures are when customers are encouraged to obtain customer service or make catalog purchases online. These steps save money otherwise spent on supporting call center operations and printing/mailing catalogs. Other Cost Savings measures can range from such things as online delivery of billing statements to online procurement and supply chain management.

You have a Cost Savings dimension to your online business model if revenue is being realized through your website by reducing costs in other areas of your business.

How To Define Your Online Business Model

You have learned the seven dimensions of online business models. To determine your online business model, simply identify which of these seven apply to your Internet Marketing program. Figure 1.1 gives you a simple checklist you can use. Just check the dimensions that apply to your website.

Once you have identified which dimensions apply, the easiest way to define your online business model is to put together a simple one-page summary. For each of the dimensions of your online business model, write a short description of how each applies to your business. By using this simple format, you can define your online business model on a single page. This will give focus to the rest of the planning process.

	Identifying The Dimensions of Your Online Business Model	
✓	**Dimension**	**Criteria**
	1. **eCommerce**	We sell products online
	2. **Business Development**	We capture sales leads and support the sales process
	3. **Lead Generation**	We direct qualified sales leads to other businesses, for a fee
	4. **Brand Development**	We provide value added services and information to promote loyalty to the brand
	5. **Customer Relations**	Our customers interact with the business and receive automated services online
	6. **Information Delivery**	We deliver informational content, for a fee or gratis
	7. **Cost Savings**	We reduce operational costs by performing certain actions electronically

Figure 1.1

How To Be Profitable

The main reason for defining your online business model is to figure out how to make your Internet Marketing program profitable. As you have probably guessed by now, you can do this by determining how revenue will be generated by each of the dimensions of your online business model. Once you have identified your dimensions, you will need to determine the source of revenue generated by each dimension. This will allow you to calculate a return on investment (ROI) from your Internet Marketing efforts.

The basic formula for calculating your online ROI is shown in figure 1.2. This formula is presented in its most general form to show how easy the concept really is. You will adapt the basic formula to the specific online tactic you are measuring.

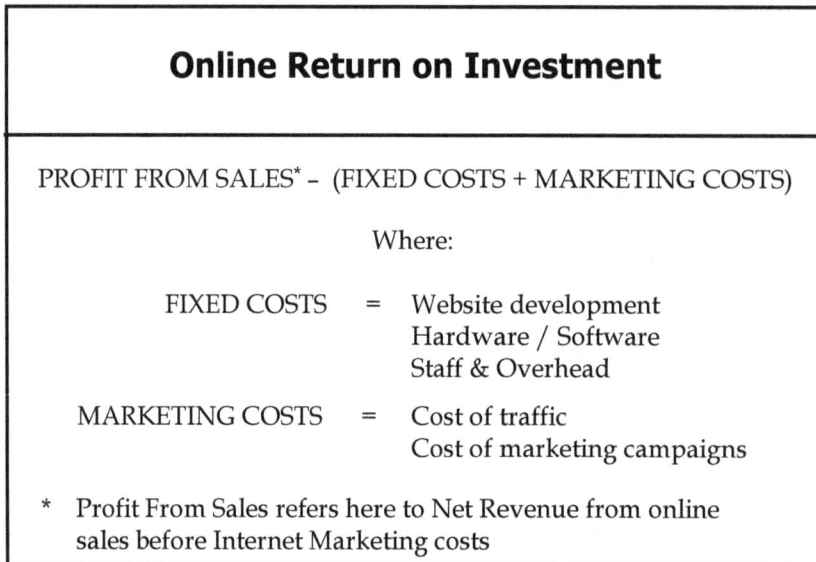

Online Return on Investment
PROFIT FROM SALES* – (FIXED COSTS + MARKETING COSTS)

Where:

FIXED COSTS   =   Website development
                              Hardware / Software
                              Staff & Overhead

MARKETING COSTS   =   Cost of traffic
                                    Cost of marketing campaigns

*   Profit From Sales refers here to Net Revenue from online
     sales before Internet Marketing costs

Figure 1.2

A simple example will show how you can use this formula to make the most out of your Internet Marketing investment. Assume you are measuring the ROI for your marketing efforts to generate sales through your eCommerce site. This example assumes the only thing that matters to your online business model is getting traffic to your website. You calculate the three metrics of our ROI formula as follows:

Profit From Sales: (Net Revenue before online costs)	Assume you are averaging one sale, yielding $50 net revenue (before online costs), for every 100 customers who click on your website. That equates to $0.50 per click to your website.
Fixed Costs:	Assume you spend $10,000 per year to maintain your website and support for online transactions and customer service.
Internet Marketing Costs:	Assume you spend, on average, $0.40 per click to bring traffic to your website (from search engines, email, and online ads)

From these three numbers, you can calculate what it will take to make your online store profitable. Figure 1.3 shows what your net revenues will be as you generate more and more traffic to your website.

➢ If the numbers remain constant, you will be earning $0.10 from each click to the website. (($0.50 net revenue - $0.40 marketing costs) = $0.10)

➢ At this rate, you will become profitable when you generate 100,000 visits to your website. ($0.10 * 100,000 = $10,000) That will cover the $10,000 fixed costs.

➢ Every sale to your website above and beyond that is profitable.

But notice that if your average cost per click goes up to $0.50, you will never be able to recover your fixed costs. ($0.50 net revenue - $0.50 marketing costs = $0.0)

If your average revenue per click is not greater than your cost per click, you will never be profitable. Your average net revenue per click is a ceiling that you cannot go over.

A common mistake is to calculate ROI using total revenue from sales instead of net revenue (i.e. profit before online costs). This will overestimate your ROI and can result in a net loss.

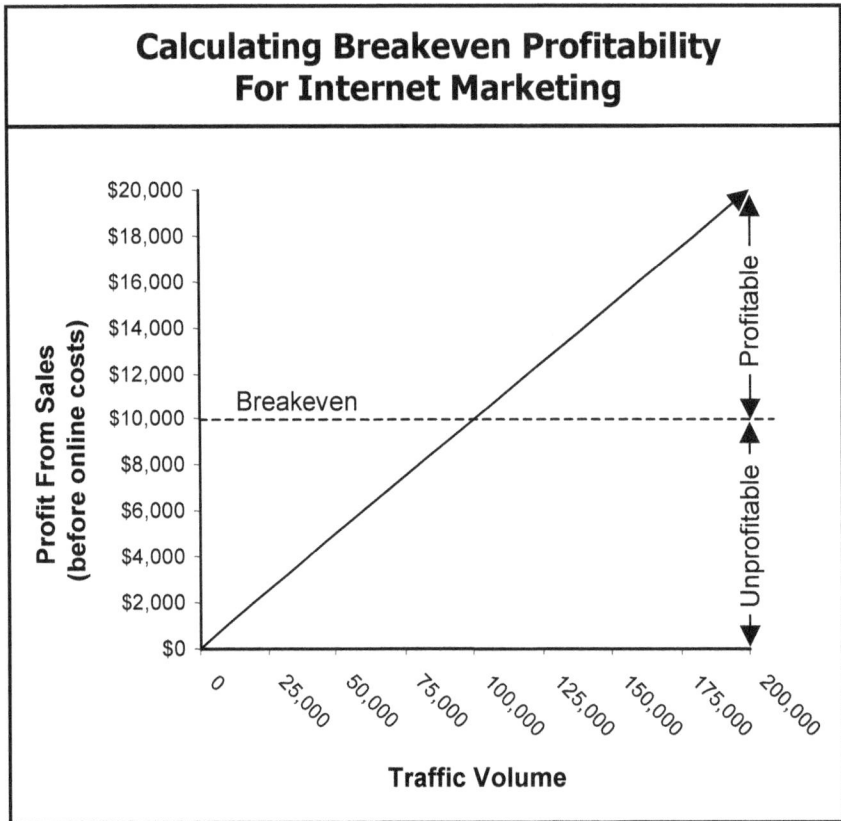

Calculating Breakeven Profitability For Internet Marketing

Figure 1.3

In actual practice, things get more complicated than this simple example. For example, you may have multiple revenue generating aspects to your Internet Marketing program. You will probably want to create an ROI calculation for each one. Then you will balance them to find the best mix of budget dollars to be invested into each one. Nevertheless, once you get this basic concept down, the exercise loses its intimidation. With a little patience, you will be able to determine the best way to turn your online investment into profitability.

As you put this into practice, you will quickly discover two of the first keys to successful Internet Marketing:

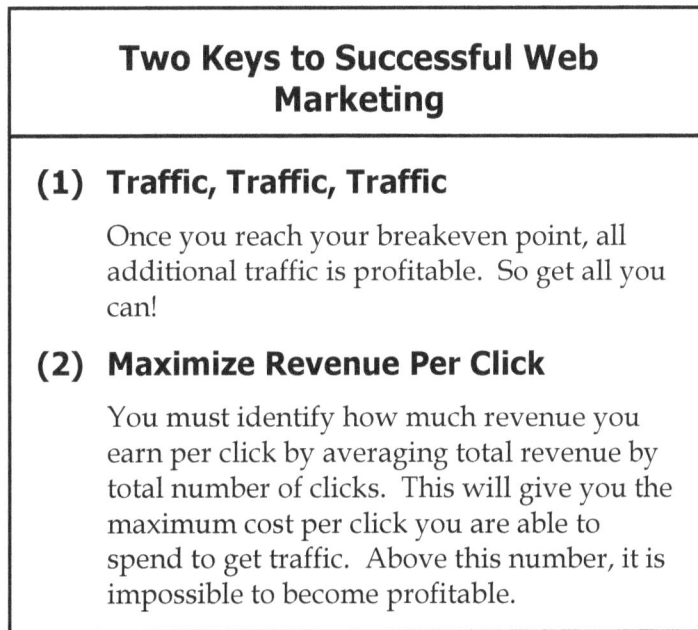

Two Keys to Successful Web Marketing
(1) Traffic, Traffic, Traffic Once you reach your breakeven point, all additional traffic is profitable. So get all you can!
(2) Maximize Revenue Per Click You must identify how much revenue you earn per click by averaging total revenue by total number of clicks. This will give you the maximum cost per click you are able to spend to get traffic. Above this number, it is impossible to become profitable.

Figure 1.4

Sources Of Internet Revenue

When you are calculating your return on investment, you will need to identify how revenue will be realized from your Internet Marketing Program. Figure 1.5 shows the most common sources of revenue from each of the seven dimensions. You can use this as a reference when you are figuring out how to calculate your ROI. The chapters in Part IV, *How To Build A Winning Website For Your Business Model*, will go into more detail about how to calculate the ROI for different sources of revenue.

	Sources of Internet Revenue	
✓	**Dimension**	**Source of Revenue**
	1. **eCommerce**	Profit from sales
	2. **Business Development**	Lifetime value of new customers
	3. **Lead Generation**	Revenue per redirect from sale of leads
	4. **Brand Development**	Protect & grow market share
	5. **Customer Relations**	Increase customer loyalty & prevent defection
	6. **Information Delivery**	Increase return visits (or a subsidized public service)
	7. **Cost Savings**	Net cost savings

Figure 1.5

Conclusion

In this chapter, you have learned how to define what your business or organization needs to be successful online. We have called this your online business model. Once you have defined your online business model, you can clearly map out what *you are trying to accomplish* online.

In Chapter 2, you will learn how to understand who your prospective customers are and what *they want to accomplish* when they go online.

Chapter 2

Reaching Your Online Customers

In this chapter, you will learn . . .
- The four levels of intimacy in online customer relationships
- How to define your target market
- How to define your online customer segments

Successful Internet Marketing is built around a partnership with the customer. In one way or another, all Internet Marketing programs put the customer in the driver's seat. In the Introduction to this book, we used the phrase *Personalized Marketing* to describe how online marketers must respond to customers who have been empowered by the Internet. This phrase is useful because it points us in the direction of what makes a successful Internet Marketing strategy tick.

The definition of the word *personalize* itself give us the first clue.

> "Personalize: 1. Put initials or name on something - to mark something as a wallet, pen, or item of clothing with somebody's initials or name. 2. Change something to reflect the owner's personality – to change or modify something showing that it obviously originated or belonged to a particular person." (Encarta Dictionary)

The promise of Internet Marketing is that it makes life more convenient for the customer. Your customers expect, and will demand, that this promise be fulfilled. Not every online service or website will offer a high level of personalization for each user. But, to be successful, each user must feel like they are getting their own personal needs and wants met. Those needs and wants may be met by providing a generic service, like a search engine, or a personalized service, like an online brokerage. *In either case, you must start by understanding who the potential customers are and what will make them want to be a user of the site.*

What Customers Need When They Come To Your Website

Online customers are as diverse as the general buying public. Web folklore used to say that typical web "surfers" are mostly male youth and techies. Those days are long gone. Web users today are business professionals and grandparents, women and men. A successful website has to appeal to the unique wants and needs of each group. However, to understand what will make them keep coming back to your site, we have to start by considering what they all have in common.

Online buyers are people, like the rest of us. In fact, they are us. When people take precious time out of their busy lives to do business online, they bring with them real or perceived needs. They come to a website hoping these needs will be satisfied. They don't want to find themselves singing along with Mick Jagger, the old Rolling Stones song, "I can't get no....satisfaction...I can't get no...no, no, no."

We don't want them to be singing, "no, no, no" when they come to our website either. But is it possible to know what customers' needs are before they come to the site?

Hierarchy of Online Needs

A variation of Abraham Maslow's "Hierarchy of Needs" (1943) gives us a way to understand how to satisfy online customers. Maslow's general theory is that our needs form a pyramid. We have to have our lower level, most basic needs met before we are even concerned about the higher level needs. The things people are looking for when they come to a website can be thought of in the same way. Figure 2.1 illustrates this idea.

A successful Internet Marketing strategy will be designed with a recognition of these needs of online customers.

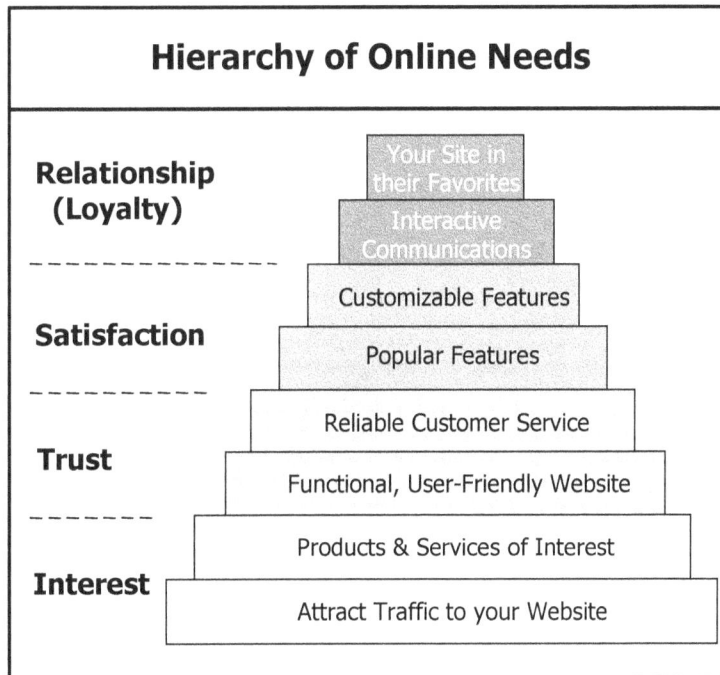

Hierarchy of Online Needs

Relationship (Loyalty)
- Your Site in their Favorites
- Interactive Communications

Satisfaction
- Customizable Features
- Popular Features

Trust
- Reliable Customer Service
- Functional, User-Friendly Website

Interest
- Products & Services of Interest
- Attract Traffic to your Website

Figure 2.1

When a customer comes to your website for the first time, they are at the bottom layer of the pyramid. Throughout their experience with your online business, they work their way up the pyramid. If they have not yet had their needs met at the level they are at, then they do not care very much if you have bells and whistles and fancy features at the higher levels. Once they are comfortable at one level, then they become more interested in the higher levels. This process may all take place in the first visit, or stretch out over numerous visits.

If, at any time in their experience on your site, they find themselves singing along with Mick Jagger, the doorway out is only one mouse-click away. Even if they have moved up in the pyramid, at any time a trap door can open and the bottom fall out at one of the lower levels. The biggest risk of this is from the customer service level. An effective site will have feedback devices in place so that the customer can tell you the bottom has just fallen out somewhere. In that case, the key to keeping them from singing along with Mick Jagger is how the customer relations staff handles their complaint or how your automated help features assist with their questions.

Four Levels of Customer Intimacy

Just like any relationship, the relationship with your online customers progresses through increasing levels of intimacy. The hierarchy of online needs diagram shows that customer needs can be separated into four distinct groupings. These can be thought of as levels of intimacy in the customer relationship. Figure 2.2 describes how intimacy is increased at each level.

The best Internet Marketing strategy will focus on the customer at every level of the pyramid. For each dimension of your online business model you will need to meet customer needs and wants at each of the four levels of customer intimacy. Only then can you expect customers to add your site to their "Favorites" list.

Levels of Intimacy in the Customer Relationship Process

(1) **Interest**

- Something about your business attracts their attention.

(2) **Building Trust**

- Implement best practices in site design and customer service.

(3) **Providing Satisfaction**

- Engage in market research activities to know who your customers are and what features or services they will want.

- Provide a variety of features and services with the ability for customers to customize them.

(4) **Nurturing Relationship**

- Implement interactive communications personalized to each customer, such as opt-in email, dynamic product recommendation, or giving customers the ability to customize what content they will see.

- Implement learning into your website, so you can continually modify each customer's online experience to better match their personal preferences.

Figure 2.2

Defining Your Target Market

Nurturing the four levels of customer intimacy addresses what all customers have in common. You also need to know about the differences. You need to know specifically what customers will be hoping for when they come to your website.

In most cases, there will be multiple customer types who you are reaching out to through your website. Each is coming to your website for a different reason. The site must be able to draw each one into a path that leads them to the things they need and want. In marketing terms, groups of different types of customer are called *segments*.

Identifying customer segments is an essential part of any marketing plan. The same is true for your Internet Marketing plan. You will use this knowledge for many things, including: what content you will include on your website, what features you will need, where you will seek to get traffic and to plan your targeted marketing efforts.

To develop an Internet Marketing program that effectively reaches all of your customers, the easiest approach is to ask the five basic questions that all news reporters know: *Who, What, Where, Why* and *How*. These are known as "the Five W's." By taking time to answer these five questions up front, you will be able to make the most effective use of limited resources, as you build a website that meets the needs and wants of all your customers.

Who Are Your Customers?

In the first question, you want to define the basic characteristics of the people coming to your website. You will ask questions like: How old are they? Are they men or women? Are they business professionals, students or veterans? In marketing lingo, this kind of information is called *demographics*. If your customers are businesses, then you will ask questions like: Are they retail stores or service suppliers? Are they Fortune 1000 corporations or mom & pop shops? Are they local or national? These are called *firmographics*. They are the same as demographics, but for firms.

You will use this information to create targeted content on your website and targeted messages for your marketing promotions.

What Are They Interested In?

In the second question, you want to identify what motivates your customers to want what you have on your website. If you are selling shoes, are your customers fashion conscious people who want new shoes to match their new outfits? Are they parents, who are buying shoes for their kids to wear when they go back to school?

You will use this information to figure out what your customers are looking for and to create targeted marketing campaigns for your most profitable groups.

Where Will They Come From?

In the third question, you want to find out where your traffic is coming from. All websites rely on traffic from search engines. But do not stop there. If you will rely on current customers visiting your site, then you may want to send email or advertise your website in their billing statements. If your customers will also be visiting specialty content websites, then try advertising on those sites. An online shoe store, for example, may advertise on a fashion magazine website.

You will use this information to create a strategy for driving traffic to your website from as many sources as possible.

Why Will They Come to Your Website?

In the fourth question, you want to know what needs and wants your customers are seeking to fulfill when they come to your website. You will ask questions like: Do they want to buy products online? Do they want to contact customer service? Will they be gathering information prior to a sale, and need to see product reviews? Will they be ready to buy, and want to see available deals and special offers?

You will use this information to design the architecture of your website to make sure people are able to quickly and easily find what they are looking for.

How Will They Use Your Website?

In the fifth question, you want to determine how people will interact with your website to do the things they want to do on the site. If they are buying products, will they want to browse through categories or search by keywords? If you are collecting sales leads, will they be more likely to fill out a needs assessment form or request a white paper requiring their contact information prior to downloading?

You will use this information to create a user interface that is intuitive and user friendly.

You will typically answer these questions through a series of interviews and brainstorming sessions prior to building your website. As you gather this information, you will begin to discover patterns that let you create a program to successfully meet the needs and wants of all your customer segments. In Web-speak, this is called, *Knowledge Discovery.*

Identifying Your Customer Segments

After you have gone through the knowledge discovery process, you will have a lot of information about your prospective online customers. The next thing to do is to start identifying groups of similar customers. These are called segments. If you have done a thorough job of recording all the information you gathered from the five questions, you will probably notice some obvious groupings. By identifying specific customer segments, you can plan content and promotions targeted to their specific needs and wants.

You will also be able to measure the results of these efforts and determine which segments are the most profitable for you. This is an iterative process. You can continue to improve the results of your Internet Marketing efforts by targeting the most profitable segments. You can also continue to research your customers to refine and improve the specification of your segments.

Naming Your Segments

It is a common practice for marketers to give their customer segments cute names that are easy to remember. That allows you to visualize a personality for each group. This helps when you go to create targeted content or marketing campaigns. Having segment names also makes it easy to measure results by segment and present the results to others who will make marketing decisions based on the data.

You will put together a brief description of each segment based on the answers to the Five W's. Then you will give each segment a descriptive and memorable name that sums up what you wrote about them in the description.

A simple example will demonstrate how easy it is to identify your customer segments. Assume you have launched an online shoe store called, "Leslie's Shoes." You have determined that there are four major types of online shopper who will come to your website. Take a look at Figure 2.3 to see how you might define your customer segments.

Notice how defining your customers this way puts a face on the people coming to your website. Once you have defined and named your customer segments in this way, they quickly take on a life of their own. You are likely to begin treating them like people you know rather than just numbers on a sales report.

Example: Customer Segments for Leslie's Shoes	
Segment Name	**Description**
Fashionistas	These are shoe enthusiasts. They love to buy new outfits and want shoes to match. They might even feel like they are getting an allergic reaction to being out of style. Sometimes they just buy a new pair to put themselves in a good mood. However, unlike their offline counterparts, online shoppers are more likely to want knock-offs of the name brand rather than the more expensive originals. This group is 75% female, between 25 and 65 years of age.
Home & Hearth	These are parents shopping for the whole family. They are practical and looking for a balance between price and quality. Some in this group are single parents who do not have time to go to the store and depend on the convenience online shopping offers. Usually selfless and pragmatic, still this group likes to treat themselves sometimes. This group is 90% female, between 25 and 55 years of age.
Working World	These are mainly people in service industry jobs who must buy footwear for their work. Of all segments, this one has the highest percentage of male shoppers, nearly 40%. This group also includes business owners who negotiate deals for their employees. This group is 60% female, between 18 and 45 years of age.
Bargain Basement	These are price shoppers. They scour the Internet looking for deals. But surprisingly, when it comes to shoes, this group is often impulsive and will respond to sales and special offers in the email. This group can be any age or gender

Figure 2.3

Conclusion

In this chapter, you have learned how to define your online customers in a way that will let you effectively market to them online.

You are now able to put together a clear picture of who your customers are and what they will be looking for when they come to your website. In Chapter 1, you learned how to define your online business model. You now know how to make money (or otherwise support the mission of your organization) by getting customers to your website. In Chapter 3, you will learn how to clearly define what results you want to achieve from your Internet Marketing program.

Chapter 3
Setting Effective Online Goals

In this chapter, you will learn . . .
- The difference between effective and ineffective goals
- How to set effective online goals
- How to set objectives to reach your goals
- How to write a vision statement

At the beginning of any successful Internet Marketing program, you must decide what it means to be successful. You do this by setting goals. Goals are essential to any plan for the simple reason that they let you know what it is you are trying to accomplish. This might sound obvious. But most people who have worked in the corporate world for any length of time realize how often programs are implemented without goals.

A fairly typical example will make this point clear:

> SpeedyClean Managed Services, Inc. provides janitorial services to businesses in a variety of industries. In an attempt to stay up with the times, the management team decided they need a website. A small web design shop was contracted to build the site. However, no direction was given as to how SpeedyClean would make money from the website. The result was a small site with about 10 content pages, giving a brief description of their services. Buried within the site was a 1-800 phone number to contact customer service. No efforts were made to bring traffic to the website nor to help prospective customers find what they are looking for once they get there. Not surprisingly, the website did not yield significant results. When additional resources were requested to upgrade the site, senior management responded by saying, "Our customers don't use the website we have, why should we invest even more?"

If you are reading this book, the chances are good that people will be looking to you for guidance on what to do online. Just as likely, you will also be pressured to just do something quickly. This is a good place to draw a line in the sand. Before you start building, first take the time to plan for success.

You will set the course of your Internet Marketing program by setting effective online goals.

Now we are ready to identify what these goals should be. You have seen that before you can have an effective program, you must first determine the dimensions of your business model. Chapter 1 showed how to do that. Next, you need to meet the needs and wants of your customers at each of the four levels of customer intimacy discussed in Chapter 2. In other words, for each of the dimensions of your online business model, you should have at least one goal for each level of customer intimacy.

What Is An Effective Goal?

An important thing to remember about goals is *you get what you measure*. This is especially important for a website. Internet solutions often have a technology focus, and rightly so. But this makes it easy to forget that a website is there primarily to accomplish business goals. To be effective, your goals must be specific enough so you can use them as a standard to measure the results of your program. There are two critical conditions that must be met for a goal to be effective:

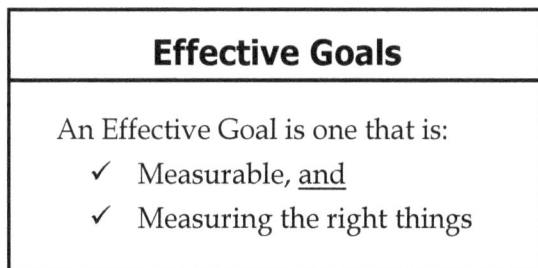

Effective Goals

An Effective Goal is one that is:
- ✓ Measurable, <u>and</u>
- ✓ Measuring the right things

Figure 3.1

Effective vs. Ineffective Goals

A simple example illustrates the difference between effective and ineffective goals.

One of the features many online stores use is product recommendations. There are a variety of software solutions that will let you make product recommendations. All of them accomplish this by matching the user's onsite behavior to other shoppers of the website. Then the store will display a message such as, "Customers who shopped for this item also have purchased these other items." Let us look at the results of different goals being set for implementing this software.

Figure 3.2 shows two common goals for product recommendations, a technology goal and a marketing goal. Both goals are legitimate. But as you will see, only one produces the desired results.

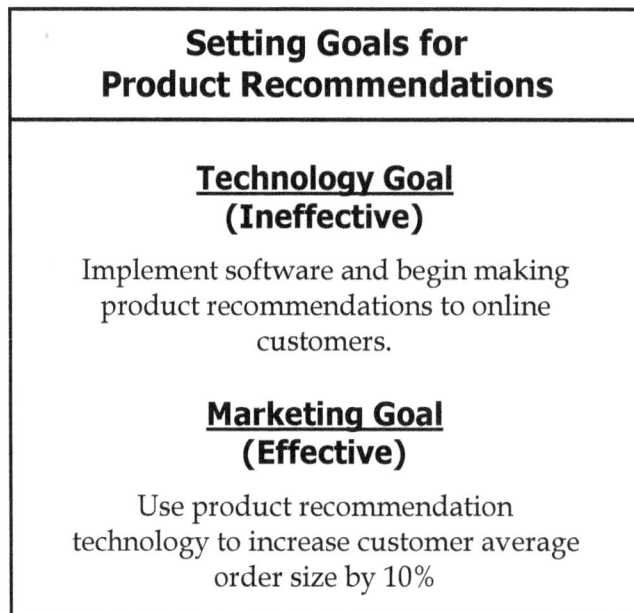

**Setting Goals for
Product Recommendations**

**Technology Goal
(Ineffective)**

Implement software and begin making
product recommendations to online
customers.

**Marketing Goal
(Effective)**

Use product recommendation
technology to increase customer average
order size by 10%

Figure 3.2

1. **Ineffective Technology Goal**

   If we are following a technology goal, we would stop measuring for success once the tool was successfully installed. There is no way to tell if it is actually producing profits or helping the company become successful.

2. **Effective Marketing Goal**

   With the marketing goal, we would measure response rates and conversion rates of people who are exposed to the product recommendations. Implementation will continue to be modified and improved until increased order size is observed. Furthermore, the marketing goal has set a target of ten percent increase in average order size. You will typically set a target like this after doing a breakeven analysis as we described in Chapter 1. In this case, you will know that anything above a ten percent increase in average order size is profit.

The results of these two goals can be summed up as follows: *If your goals focus on customers, you will get customers. If your goals focus on technology, all you are assured of getting is technology.*

This example demonstrates how effective goals can be used to both plan for success and to measure your success as you go along. This can only happen because you first take time to make sure you are setting goals which measure the things that are really important to your business's success. Then you must make sure to set goals that can be used as a yardstick to measure your progress. In this example, we explicitly set a goal of ten percent increase. You do not have to always put a numeric value to your goals. But you do have to set goals that are put in terms that can be measured. The technology goal is not effective because it is measuring the wrong thing. However, it is a valid, measurable goal even though it does not have a numeric target. You will either successfully install the software, or not. The same can be true of goals that do succeed in measuring the correct things. Whether you use numeric targets in your goals or not will be a matter of personal style combined with the needs of your specific Internet Marketing program. The key is to set goals that are both measurable and that can be measured in terms of the things that cause success or failure.

The Goal Setting Process

An easy way to set goals for your Internet Marketing program is to use the hierarchy of online needs diagram to create a visual map of the goals you need to set. For each of the dimensions of your online business model you will need to set goals for reaching each of the four levels of customer intimacy.

Figure 3.3 provides an example of how to do this for the Lead Generation dimension. Assume you are launching a referral website for housekeeping services called, "Maid2Order.com." Your business model is to provide a national portal to housekeeping service providers around the country. You expect to make money by charging local service providers for sales leads you send to their websites.

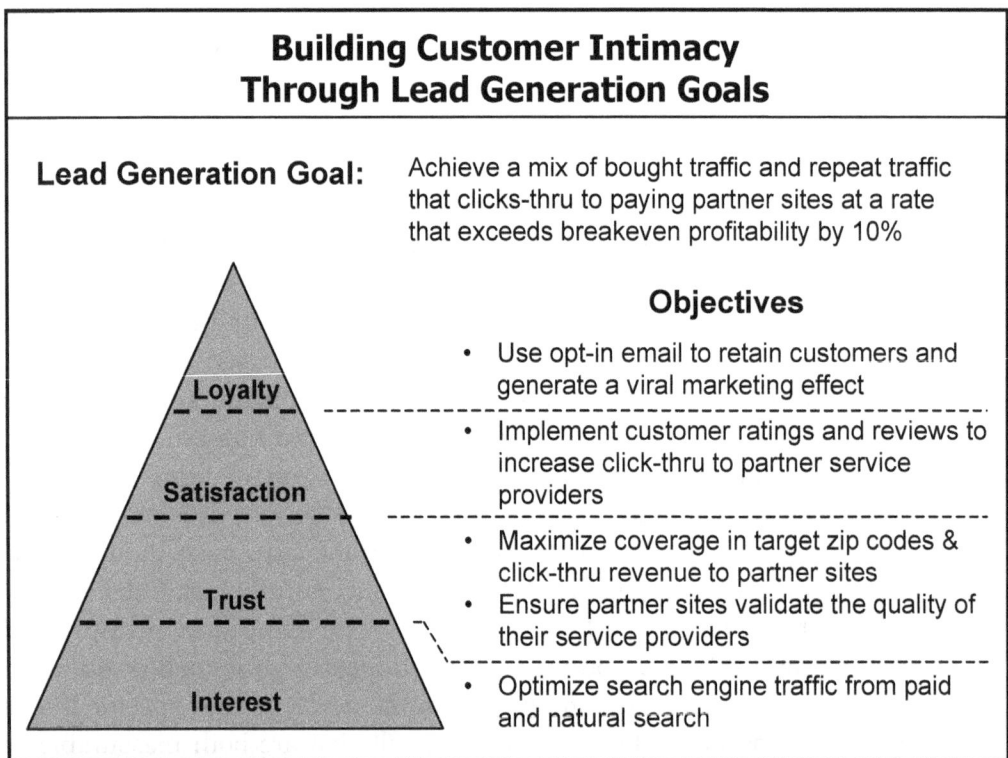

**Building Customer Intimacy
Through Lead Generation Goals**

Lead Generation Goal: Achieve a mix of bought traffic and repeat traffic that clicks-thru to paying partner sites at a rate that exceeds breakeven profitability by 10%

Objectives

- Use opt-in email to retain customers and generate a viral marketing effect

Loyalty

- Implement customer ratings and reviews to increase click-thru to partner service providers

Satisfaction

- Maximize coverage in target zip codes & click-thru revenue to partner sites
- Ensure partner sites validate the quality of their service providers

Trust

- Optimize search engine traffic from paid and natural search

Interest

Figure 3.3

There are basically two parts to the goal setting process. First, you will set one or more high-level goals for each dimension of your online business model. Then you will set goals for each level of customer intimacy that support the overall goal(s) for that dimension.

High-Level Goals

For each dimension of your online business model, you will set one, or more high-level goals. These goals will be used to set the course for the overall Internet Marketing program. They will show you what you are trying to accomplish and provide the key metrics against which the success of the entire program will be measured.

In Figure 3.3, we have stated a simple goal. The business will buy traffic and generate repeat traffic. That both new and repeat traffic will redirect to paying websites at a rate that will exceed breakeven profitability by ten percent. This is not a particularly visionary goal. Nevertheless, it is an effective goal and provides a clear measure of success.

Notice that there are actually three parts to this goal:

(1)   You must buy traffic at an optimal cost
(2)   You must generate repeat traffic
        (which is at a much lower or zero cost)
(3)   That traffic must redirect to paying websites at an optimal price

To reach your goal, Maid2Order must balance all three of these to exceed 10% profitability.

Supporting Goals (a.k.a. Objectives)

After setting high-level goals for a dimension of your online business model, you will want to set one or more goals for reaching your customers at each level of customer intimacy. These goals will be much more specific than the high-level goals, as you can see from Figure 3.3. These goals also must support the overall goal of that dimension. In other words, you will accomplish your high-level goals by meeting your supporting goals.

In business planning lingo, supporting goals like these are called *objectives*.

The result of this goal setting process is a roadmap to achieving successful results from your Internet Marketing efforts. The next step is to create a vision statement that provides overall direction and focus for the program.

Your Vision Statement

Once you have finished defining your goals and objectives, you will know what you want to accomplish with your Internet Marketing program. These will be in a set of detailed statements that can be followed and measured. But there will usually be too many details for most people to keep in focus. This is even more true when the entire plan is completed. Your vision statement puts in very clear language exactly what your Internet Marketing program is going to accomplish. In essence, it sums up all of your high-level goals into one or two inspirational sentences.

The vision statement is basically part of the header to your Internet Marketing plan. Some people think it is just window dressing. But it actually serves two important purposes.

There is an easy way to visualize why the vision statement is important. Think about how many people are going to read your entire plan? Or even, how many will read all of your goals and be able to see why they are important? There probably are not too many. For everyone else, the vision statement may be all they read. Since some of these people may be important stakeholders in the project, it is key that you capture the essence of what the program will accomplish in a few short sentences. The vision statement does that.

The second purpose for your visions statement has to do with how you will keep your project on track after work begins. Now, think about the people who do read the whole plan. Pay special attention to the people who will be responsible for implementing the various parts of it. How many of these people will remember it all six months later, when you are well into the project? More importantly, how many will change their minds about what they think the project should be doing? The vision statement sets a compass heading for the project. By crafting a vision statement and set of goals that all your key stakeholders can buy into, you will have a valuable tool to help resolve differences later in the project.

Writing the Vision Statement

When you are writing your vision statement, you want to strike a balance between being inspirational and giving clear direction. You are part cheerleader and part accountant. It is typical to start by brainstorming sentences about what you are trying to accomplish and what makes your business unique. You may get the whole team together in front of a whiteboard for this exercise. Then you will boil down this set of sentences into two to five clear and concise statements that contain the essence of what your program is all about.

The following is an example of what a vision statement for Maid2Order.com may look like:

> *Maid2Order.com will be the ultimate online source for finding quality housekeeping services anywhere in the United States. We will become profitable by building the most complete directory of housekeeping services in the country and by driving a high volume of in-market customers to their websites.*

Conclusion

In this chapter, you have learned how to set goals and objectives for your Internet Marketing program.

Now you are able to define what it means for your online venture to be successful by setting effective high-level goals for the program. By setting objectives, you are also able to define what you need to accomplish in order to reach your goals. By summarizing all of this into a vision statement, you will be able to set a compass heading for your program. In Chapter 4, you will learn how to figure out what tactics you will need to implement to achieve your goals and objectives.

Chapter 4

Choosing The Right Online Tactics

In this chapter, you will learn . . .
- How to choose tactics which accomplish your online goals and objectives
- How to ensure a successful launch by breaking your project into multiple stages

Now we come to the nuts and bolts of your Internet Marketing Plan, choosing the tactics to accomplish your goals. This is the hardest part. The specific actions you will take and technology you will implement to accomplish your goals are your tactics. This is where you put together the actual blueprint for your program. Your Internet Marketing Plan can be very detailed or provide general guidance for the program. That is a matter of personal style and the needs of your organization. What is critical to keep in mind is that the tactics you choose must produce the desired results specified in your goals. After launch, you are likely to find that the program does not meet the goals. You should be able to trace these results back to the specific tactics responsible. Then, by modifying or replacing those tactics, you can improve the results of your program.

Choose Tactics To Accomplish Each Of Your Goals

An easy way to choose your tactics is to follow the same basic process you used to set your goals. Start with the visual map you created for your goals. For each dimension of your online business model, you will have identified one or more goals for each level of customer intimacy. Then for each of those goals, you will have identified one or more objectives which will allow you to reach the goal. Now, add to this. For each of your objectives, determine the tactics you will use to meet that objective. Figure 4.1 continues where we left off in Chapter 3. The Lead Generation objectives set for Maid2Order.com are shown. Next to each objective you will find the tactics necessary to achieve the objectives.

Notice that every tactic being implemented is there to meet a specific objective. Furthermore, every objective directly supports the goal of the business model.

There is usually quite a bit of discussion, and perhaps horse-trading, between key stakeholders before the final list of tactics is agreed upon. Additionally, some type of ROI analysis would need to be conducted to help determine which of the tactics can successfully be included in the initial launch.

If the prospect of slogging through an ROI analysis including detailed mathematical calculations for each tactic in your plan seems daunting, do not worry. Although, it is definitely the right thing to do, most companies do not actually go that far. Instead, they will make a "best guess" estimate based on the information they know and put together a summary of projected costs and expected returns based on this "best guess" (although most do not actually include the word "guess" in the report). This back-of-the-envelope ROI analysis is usually good enough to make the needed decisions at this planning stage. As the project moves forward, more detailed assessments of costs and potential returns can be calculated as the need arises.

After you have put together your list of tactics, take some time to consider how each tactic will impact each of your customer segments. Go through each of your objectives and ask yourself, will these tactics meet the needs and wants of each group of customers that the objective applies to? As you are going through this process, you may need to make adjustments to your list of tactics. The chapters in Part IV of this book will go into more detail about the type of tactics that typically applied for the most common online business models.

Maid2Order.com Internet Marketing Tactics

	Objectives	Tactics
Interest	Optimize search engine traffic from paid & natural search	1. Engage an agency to perform search engine optimization and marketing 2. Hire full time staff person to continuously optimize landing pages and search terms
Trust	Achieve universal coverage in target zip codes and maximize click-thru revenue to partner sites	3. Build a database of at least 3 providers in every target zip code. 4. Utilize custom spiders to find service provider sites and auto-generate recruitment emails 5. Utilize an outbound sales staff to sign up partners
	Ensure partner sites validate the quality of their service providers	6. Establish a written quality standard and a quality seal/logo. Clearly label partners who meet the quality standard
Satisfaction	Implement customer ratings and reviews to increase click-thru to partner service providers	7. Establish a 5-star rating system in addition to the quality seal 8. Opt-in users, when they fill in lead forms, for a follow up email to rate their satisfaction 9. Allow users to enter reviews of service providers and solicit reviews in the follow up survey(s)
Loyalty	Use opt-in email to retain customers and generate a viral marketing effect	10. Periodically send follow-up email to the opt-in list, checking on satisfaction and with an incentive to Forward-to-a-friend 11. In future, use email to promote other home services (from affiliate partners) such as handyman or legal services

Figure 4.1

Roadmap To Success

When you have finished identifying your tactics, you will have a roadmap for Internet Marketing success. You can visually represent this roadmap with a tree diagram as shown in Figure 4.2.

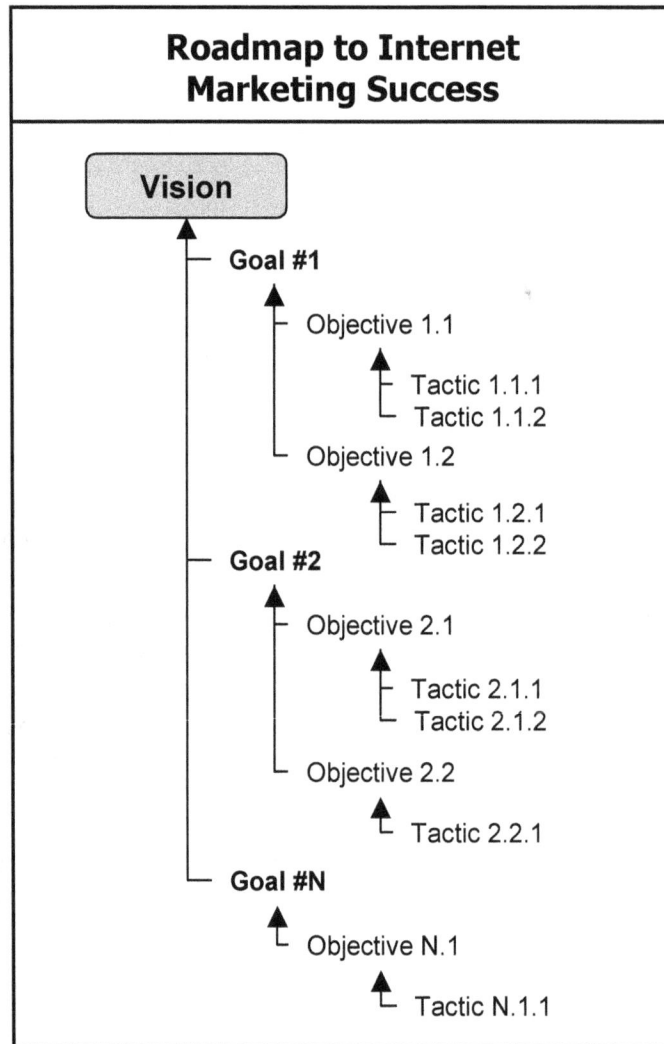

Roadmap to Internet Marketing Success

Vision
- Goal #1
  - Objective 1.1
    - Tactic 1.1.1
    - Tactic 1.1.2
  - Objective 1.2
    - Tactic 1.2.1
    - Tactic 1.2.2
- Goal #2
  - Objective 2.1
    - Tactic 2.1.1
    - Tactic 2.1.2
  - Objective 2.2
    - Tactic 2.2.1
- Goal #N
  - Objective N.1
    - Tactic N.1.1

Figure 4.2

This is no different than what you just saw in Figure 4.1. However, by showing how your goals, objectives and tactics all fit together into a hierarchy, you can easily tell what tactics are likely to be causing success or failure in each objective. This will prove to be a key to successful implementation of your program over time.

Following the Roadmap To Success

By laying out your Internet Marketing Plan in a format that lets you see the hierarchy of goals, objectives and tactics, you will be able to optimize your investment and your workload to become successful. You will quickly see which tactics are needed to accomplish each objective. In turn, meeting these objectives will lead to successfully achieving your goals. The roadmap leads to fulfilling your vision.

By taking the time to create a plan that lays out this "roadmap," you will achieve the following results:

1.   Save Money

You will be able to implement only those tactics that directly contribute to your company's success. You will therefore avoid costly investments in bells & whistles that do not help meet your core goals.

2.   Avoid Catastrophe

You will be able to identify which tactics are critical to success and make sure they remain in the program when the budget axe falls.

3.   Continuously Improve

You will be able to measure the impact each tactic is having on meeting key objectives and goals and therefore invest in improvements that will have the biggest bang for the buck.

Planning For Staged Implementation

Once you have identified the tactics needed to meet all of your Internet Marketing goals, chances are you will find that you do not have the budget or the time to complete all of them. In this case, you will need to include a plan for staged implementation. There is one thing you must keep in mind when doing this. It can spare you a lot of agony. You must realize that it will be very hard to get people to commit resources to future stages of your project *after* the initial launch is completed.

When you are putting together your plan, you may find you need to break down your project into multiple phases. There are three key guiding principles that will help you secure the buy-in you will need down the road.

1.   The Initial Launch Must Stand on Its Own

Web projects can be very exhausting and time consuming for all involved. Once you have launched the first phase of the project, the entire organization will breathe a collective sigh of relief. They will want to move on to the next thing and expect the successes to roll in from the newly launched project. For this reason, it is absolutely critical that the initial launch includes all essential components needed for a successful Internet Marketing program. This often means you will have to fight some battles. When mapping out your goals and tactics, you must clearly identify which elements of the plan will result in failure if they are left out. Then you must make sure adequate resources are provided to include all of these things in your initial launch. If you do not, you are setting yourself up for failure.

1.   Be Able to Demonstrate Success at Each Stage

The second key consideration is closely related to the first. You must be able to demonstrate successful results at each stage of the project. This is especially true for your initial launch. It is very likely that the only way you will be able to get the approval and resources needed for a Phase II is to demonstrate success in Phase I.

This can be a very delicate situation for the Web Project Manager. You will be pressured to finish and launch quickly, which means cutting corners. But you will also be held to blame if you do not show results. To be successful, you not only need to fight to include what you believe is essential for success. You also need to plan for how you will demonstrate that success after you have launched. This means determining what your metrics for success will be and being prepared to show that those metrics have been met. Part III goes into more detail about measuring the results of your Web Program.

1. Clearly Define All Future Stages

Finally, you need to clearly identify what will be needed to carry out the future phases of the project and what results you can expect from them. As far as possible, you want to get the commitment from the decision makers in your organization and the funding for all phases of the project up front. You also need to create the expectation that there will be more to come after the initial launch.

If you leave this part of your plan vague, it is more likely than not that you will find you cannot get the resources or internal support for future phases of the project when you need them. That is unless your program is an unequivocal success with support from some powerful stakeholders in the organization. On the other hand, if you have clearly included it in the project, you still may have a hard time getting the approval, but at least you have gotten tacit approval that these additional phases are needed. If you demonstrate success at one phase, you will have already created the expectation that committing additional resources will result in even greater success in the future. You will not be starting over with a plan for a whole new project, but simply asking for the resources to do the things that were already approved.

Conclusion

In this chapter, you have learned how to determine the specific tactics you will need to implement in order to meet the goals and objectives you set for your Internet Marketing program.

Unfortunately, there is no easy way to choose the tactics for your Internet Marketing program. This requires experience and research. However, you can learn from those who have gone before you. Part IV goes into detail about the major online business models and how to choose the right tactics for each. Learning about these will give you insights you can use when developing your own plan. But first, turn to Chapter 5, where we will walk through the complete process of putting together your Internet Marketing plan with a basic scenario.

Chapter 5

Putting It All Together:
The Internet Marketing Plan

In this chapter, you will see the entire process of how to put together an Internet Marketing Plan from beginning to end.

The first four chapters of this book have walked through the process of developing an effective Internet Marketing Plan. This chapter will bring all those steps together. A theme of this book has been that developing an effective plan is something anyone can do. It takes effort and attention to detail. But, the basic idea is not really that difficult. This chapter presents the whole process in a fairly simple scenario.

PathFinder GPS Devices Scenario

PathFinder GPS Devices is a fictional direct mail catalog company and an online store. They sell GPS devices to automobile owners and outdoor enthusiasts. Have-a-Clue Web Consultants were contracted to help Path-Finder GPS develop a profitable Internet Marketing strategy.

For the sake of this scenario, put yourself into the position of the Have-A-Clue consultants. It is often the case that a consultant or agency, like Have-A-Clue, will be hired to help develop the Internet Marketing Plan. In other cases, the plan will be put together by a staff member within the company or by an entrepreneur starting a new Web business. In either case, this is the process you must go through to have an effective and profitable online venture.

Let us now walk through the four steps identified in the previous chapters for developing a successful Internet Marketing plan.

Step 1: Understand Your Online Business Model

The first thing Have-A-Clue did was set up interviews with key stakeholders at PathFinder GPS Devices. Through these meetings, it was determined that the online business model consisted primarily of just one of the seven dimensions: eCommerce. Defining their online business model is therefore quite easy.

	Dimensions of the PathFinder GPS Online Business Model	
✓	**Dimension**	**Criteria**
✓	1. eCommerce	We sell products online
	2. Business Development	We capture sales leads and support the sales process
	3. Lead Generation	We direct qualified sales leads to other businesses, for a fee
	4. Brand Development	We provide value added services and information to promote loyalty to the brand
	5. Customer Relations	Our customers interact with the business and receive automated services online
	6. Information Delivery	We deliver informational content, for a fee or gratis
	7. Cost Savings	We reduce operational costs by performing certain actions electronically

Figure 5.1

Description of the PathFinder GPS Online Business Model

The PathFinder GPS team came up with the following description for their online business model.

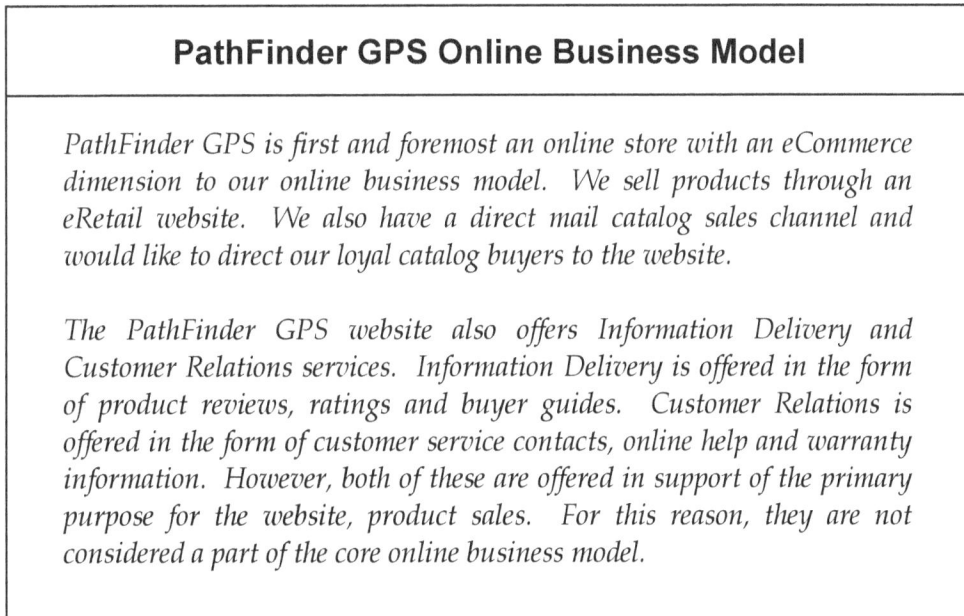

PathFinder GPS Online Business Model

PathFinder GPS is first and foremost an online store with an eCommerce dimension to our online business model. We sell products through an eRetail website. We also have a direct mail catalog sales channel and would like to direct our loyal catalog buyers to the website.

The PathFinder GPS website also offers Information Delivery and Customer Relations services. Information Delivery is offered in the form of product reviews, ratings and buyer guides. Customer Relations is offered in the form of customer service contacts, online help and warranty information. However, both of these are offered in support of the primary purpose for the website, product sales. For this reason, they are not considered a part of the core online business model.

Figure 5.2

Step 2: Know Your Customers

During the stakeholder interviews, Have-A-Clue sought answers to the Five W's. They took detailed notes from each stakeholder's answers to the *who, what, where, why* and *how* of PathFinder GPS's customers. From these notes, they were able to define five basic customer segments. They also identified the key features they believed would meet those customers' online needs and wants.

Some of the highlights from these questions are shown below.

Who Are Your Customers?

PathFinder GPS customers purchase one, or more of three major GPS product categories: Automotive, Handheld and Boating. Buyers of all these categories had, at first, been almost entirely male. Except for the boating segment, they were also mostly 25 to 45 years old. In the boating segment, there was no upper limit to the age of buyers. As the market has matured, the demographics of GPS buyers have also expanded. Now the biggest segment, automotive GPS devices, has a 50% female market and is purchased by those from 25 to 75 years of age.

The market for handheld devices has also expanded. It had been mostly males between 25 and 45 years of age. As prices came down, a new hobby, GeoCaching, emerged. People hide a package and place the latitude and longitude coordinates on the Internet. Other GeoCachers use their GPS devices to find the "treasure." This new game sparked a surge in GPS devices, not only among young techies but also among women and seniors.

What Are They Interested In?

The PathFinder GPS staff identified eight key areas of interest among their customers: daily commuting, travel, high-tech gear, boat and auto racing, backcountry sports, hunting & fishing, sailing and motorboating.

Where Will They Come From?

Like most online stores, PathFinder GPS will rely on search engines, email, affiliate partnerships and comparison shopping websites for much of their traffic. They also will generate traffic from existing customers who receive their direct mail catalogs. However, PathFinder GPS plans to differentiate themselves as the segment experts through their product knowledge. They plan to enter into content partnerships with special interest websites and generate much of their traffic from those. This will include maintaining buyer guides, reviews and product comparison charts which will be presented on special interest sites.

Why Are They Coming?

PathFinder GPS customers are expected to come to the website for one of four reasons. The highest source of traffic is hoped to be those who are in the market for a GPS product and are ready to make a purchase. After this, are those who are researching products prior to purchase. These will be looking for product reviews, specs and buyer guides. The third are price shoppers who are responding to a promotion. And finally, those looking for customer service. These will either be looking for customer service from the PathFinder GPS store, or else looking for warranty or customer service information from the manufacturers of the products they have purchased.

How Will They Use the Website?

PathFinder GPS expects their customers not only to make their purchases on the website, but to also conduct their research prior to purchase. In both cases, they will be placed on low-level landing pages most relevant to what they are interested in. If they are on the purchase track, they will be placed on a product page, a category page or a custom landing page where they can redeem a promotional offer. Customers who are on the research track will be placed on a product review page or buyer guide for the product or category they are interested in. Furthermore, there must be a seamless integration in user experience between the two tracks. Those who land on a purchase page must be able to easily see reviews, buyer guides, specs and the like. Also, those who land on a research page must be able to easily buy right from the page they are on.

A smaller percentage of customers are expected to land on the store's home page. These may or may not already know what they are interested in finding. Therefore, they must be able to quickly navigate to any of the four key areas of interest: buy, research, customer service or special offers. As with all online stores, customers must be able to browse by category or search by keywords to find what they are looking for in the fewest number of mouse clicks.

PathFinder GPS Online Customer Segments

Segment Name	Description
High-Tech Racers	These people are serious about their rides, whether they are cars or boats. They like high performance vehicles and high performance technology. Some are amateur or professional racers but most just imagine that they are. Many will also buy handheld devices for their adventures in the outdoors. This group is mostly male, 35 to 65 years old. They are the group most likely to purchase top of the line products and expect top of the line service.
Weekend Warriors	These people are hunting, fishing and boating enthusiasts. They are likely to drive their motorboat to the lake for the weekend and may hitch it to the back of an RV. While they are there, they might just hide a secret package and post the latitude and longitude coordinates online for other GeoCachers to find in their Twenty-first Century game of Treasure Hunt. This group is about 75% male and 25% female, between 25 and 55 years of age. They are most likely to buy entry level or mid-tier products in all three categories.
Day Trippers	This group makes up the bread and butter of the largest share of the GPS market, Automotive. They are daily commuters who periodically take their cars on a road trip vacation. What is most important to this group are hands free features and a fully loaded database of restaurants, gas stations and convenience stores. Hovering right around 50% female and 50% male, between 25 and 55 years old, this group will balance price with functionality for an Automotive GPS device.
Backcountry Explorers	This is the National Park set. They love hiking and bike riding. The more adventurous of them also feel the need to get out in the backcountry with their cross-country skis or on an overnight backpack trip. About 70% male and 30% female, between 18 and 55 years of age. This group is seeking a lightweight, handheld device with long battery life. They would like to save money, but are willing to spend a little more for a smaller and lighter model.

Price Shoppers	These are people searching for a bargain on a GPS device. They could be any age and have any interests. What makes them part of this group is they searched the Internet looking for a deal and found their way to the PathFinder GPS site.
	These are not high value customers for PathFinder GPS. But they represent an important ongoing source of sales. However, if these customers continue to interact with the company, it is possible to convert them to one of the other four higher value segments.

Figure 5.3

Customer Segments

After compiling the information from the knowledge discovery interviews, Have-A-Clue held a series of meetings with the PathFinder GPS team to sift through the data. One of the key outputs from these meetings was to identify customer segments. The team grouped PathFinder GPS customers into four unique segments. A fifth, generic "Price Shopper" segment was identified to capture those customers who are attracted to the site by special deals or low prices listed on comparison shopping sites. Figure 5.3 shows the five customers segments the team came up with.

Step 3: Set Your Goals

The next step was for Have-A-Clue to help the PathFinder GPS team set the goals, objectives and vision statement for their Internet Marketing program. This was done during the same working sessions where the customer segments were identified.

Goals and Objectives

The four levels of intimacy diagram was used to provide a visual map of the goals and objectives for the website. These are shown in Figure 5.4.

Take a few moments to review these goals and objectives. Look back at the answers to the Five W's. See if you can think of ways information about PathFinder GPS customers can be matched with the needs of the online business model to lay out a roadmap for the company's online venture.

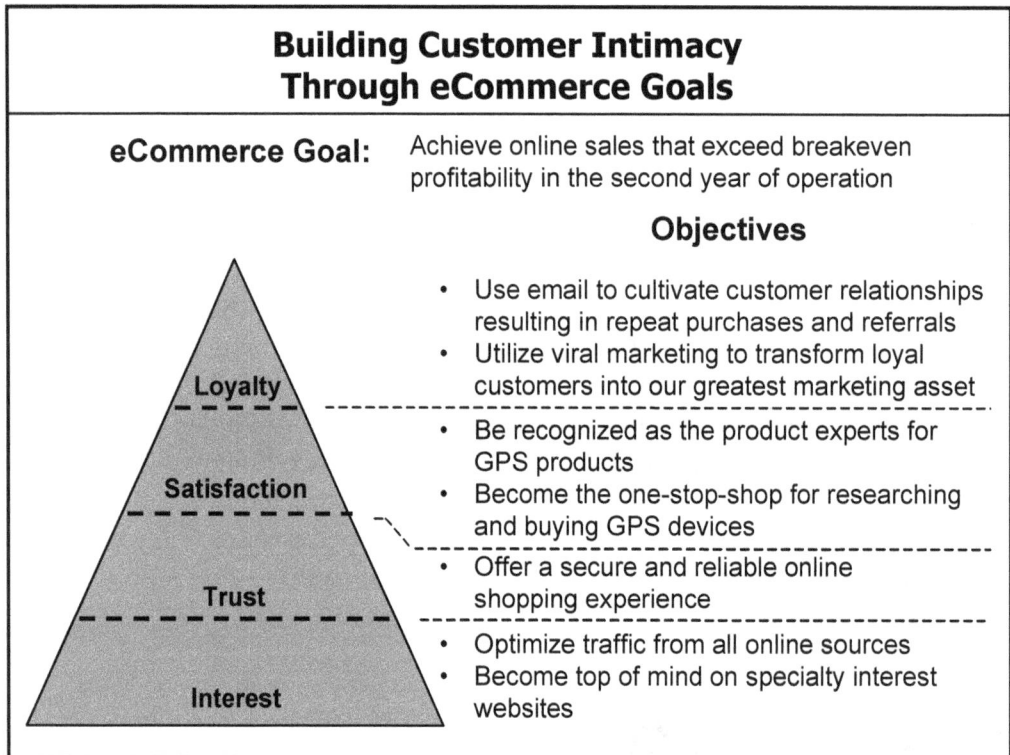

Building Customer Intimacy
Through eCommerce Goals

eCommerce Goal: Achieve online sales that exceed breakeven profitability in the second year of operation

Objectives

Loyalty
- Use email to cultivate customer relationships resulting in repeat purchases and referrals
- Utilize viral marketing to transform loyal customers into our greatest marketing asset

Satisfaction
- Be recognized as the product experts for GPS products
- Become the one-stop-shop for researching and buying GPS devices

Trust
- Offer a secure and reliable online shopping experience

Interest
- Optimize traffic from all online sources
- Become top of mind on specialty interest websites

Figure 5.4

Vision Statement

PathFinder GPS management agreed on the following vision statement for their online sales and marketing channel.

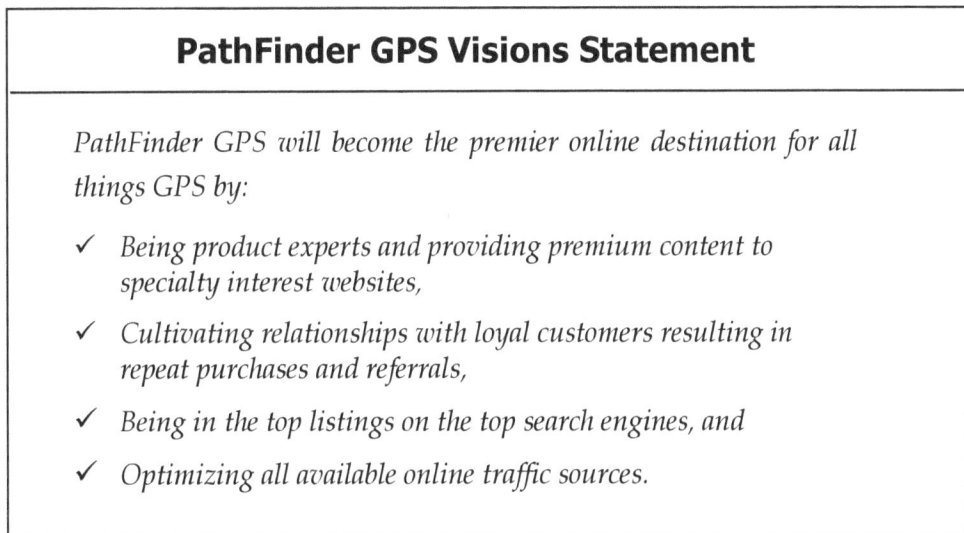

PathFinder GPS Visions Statement

PathFinder GPS will become the premier online destination for all things GPS by:

✓ *Being product experts and providing premium content to specialty interest websites,*

✓ *Cultivating relationships with loyal customers resulting in repeat purchases and referrals,*

✓ *Being in the top listings on the top search engines, and*

✓ *Optimizing all available online traffic sources.*

Figure 5.5

Step 4: Choose Your Tactics

The final step was to choose the tactics needed to achieve the program goals. At this point in the process, Have-A-Clue relied on their experience in the field to recommend a set of features, services, content and marketing campaigns they believed would allow PathFinder GPS to achieve the goals they had agreed on in the working sessions. In this scenario, we will go no further than to show some of the recommended tactics to give an idea of how the process works. If this were a real life program, PathFinder GPS would still need to reach agreements with key stakeholders as to the final set of tactics. This may require some kind of ROI analysis, budget justification and the occasional political battle.

Figure 5.6 shows Have-A-Clue's recommended tactics. Each tactic is grouped under a corresponding high-level goal and supporting objective. That allows the entire plan to be seen as a roadmap for achieving the PathFinder GPS visions statement.

PathFinder GPS Internet Marketing Tactics

	Objectives	Tactics
Interest	Optimize traffic from all available online channels	1. Hire an agency to do search engine marketing and optimization
		2. Set up an affiliate program and get listed on all comparison shopping and other shopping sites
	Become top of mind on specialty interest websites	3. Advertise online with specialty websites such as Car & Driver and Backpacker.com
		4. Provide sponsored content to specialty sites, including: articles, reviews and buyer guides
Trust	Offer a secure and reliable online shopping experience	5. Outsource web hosting and eCommerce processing to a state-of-the-art provider with guaranteed security
Satisfaction	Be recognized as the product experts for GPS products	6. Employ an industry expert to review GPS products, write articles and buyer guides, and post a regular column online
		7. Employ a PR specialist to get PathFinder GPS content on as many specialty sites as possible and create positive PR to be used in online ads
	Become the one-stop-shop for researching and buying GPS devices	8. Create a robust sub-site for researching products: with reviews, buyer guides and side-by-side comparisons
		9. Aggressively drive traffic to research pages
		10. Set up robust cross-linking between purchase pages and research pages
		11. Utilize ongoing usability testing to continuously improve conversion rates

Loyalty	Use targeted email to cultivate customer relationships resulting in repeat purchases and referrals	12. Create a large opt-in email list. Send a regular newsletter and seasonal offers 13. Send follow-up surveys to rate customer satisfaction <u>and</u> respond to negative feedback
	Utilize viral marketing to transform loyal customers into our greatest marketing asset	14. Include Forward-to-a-friend links on all content (reviews, buyer guides, pricing, special offers, etc.) 15. Use outbound email to solicit user reviews and ratings. Include an incentive to forward to others, who will participate and opt-in

Figure 5.6

Putting Together The Internet Marketing Plan

Once, Have-A-Clue had finished leading PathFinder GPS through the planning process, then came time for the final deliverable, an Internet Marketing Plan for the PathFinder GPS website. If all of the previous steps have been completed, this is the easiest part of the process. All of the components of the plan have already been done. All that is left is to basically cut and paste it into a formal document. There are many ways to format your plan. A method that has come into popularity in recent years is to present the plan in a Microsoft PowerPoint presentation. This is perhaps the easiest way to put together the final document. It also makes presenting the plan to managers and key stakeholders easy.

To put together your Internet Marketing Plan using MS-PowerPoint, all you need to do is put the key information into a set of slides. We have already formatted the information so it lends itself to such a presentation format. All that is left is to cut and paste. In this scenario, the Have-A-Clue consultants put together a simple presentation with just eight slides.

Outline of the PathFinder GPS Internet Marketing Plan	
Slide 1:	Title slide
Slide 2:	Vision Statement (Insert from Figure 5.5)
Slide 3:	Description of Online Business Model (Insert from Figure 5.2)
Slide 4:	Customer Segments (Insert from Figure 5.3)
Slide 5:	Goals and Objectives (Insert from Figure 5.4)
Slides 6-8:	Tactics (Insert from Figure 5.6)

Figure 5.7

Conclusion

In this chapter, you walked through the complete process of creating an Internet Marketing Plan. If you have never done business planning before, it may seem somewhat overwhelming. However, the chapters in Part I have shown you an easy way to do each of the pieces. It requires time, effort and attention to detail. There is no way around that. But, by taking it step by step, you will find that you have a clearly thought out strategy that gives you an edge over your competition. The next time around, you will be the guru on the project. It will start to be second nature.

Part IV goes into detail about how to go through this process for seven of the most common online business models. But first, turn to Part II, where you will learn practical how-to steps for bringing traffic to your website.

Part II

How To Bring Traffic To Your Website

A Spy In The House Of Links
The Gator Story

The Gator Company was founded in 1998. They offered an electronic wallet as a free download. This little tool would fill in forms for you when you checked out of online stores. It was a convenient service to many online shoppers. It made the process faster and easier. They called it the Gator Toolbar, because it installed an extra set of icons in your browser, displaying the Gator tools. Toolbars like this are common today. Google and Yahoo both offer toolbars that provide helpful utilities. The Gator Toolbar was one of the first. In exchange for receiving the free toolbar, the user also agreed to let Gator serve ads while they were surfing the Net. This was the true business model. They offered a free software that would be funded through ad revenues generated by its use.

The Gator Toolbar contained computer code that would read every web page viewed. It scanned the information on the page and then served ads related to the content it found. Since these ads were served in the context of the user's online experience, they were called *contextual ads*. Being good marketers, the people at Gator knew they could do better than that. They also recorded all of the information about each user's online behavior in a database. This let them apply statistical algorithms to further target ads. They could serve ads based not only on the current page being viewed, but also on the user's entire history of web browsing. Since these ads were served based on the user's online behavior over time, they were called, *behavioral targeting*.

To get a better idea of what the Gator Toolbar did, consider visiting the Yosemite National Park website. Based on this visit, the Gator Toolbar might serve ads for an outdoor living magazine or an online sporting goods store. Now, let us also say that you subscribe to a newsletter from a website called SeniorLife.com and click-thru to articles on their website. You also regularly make purchases from Drugstore.com. You make that same visit to the Yosemite website. This time, the Gator Toolbar might display ads promoting travel discounts for seniors and estate planning services.

It was a great business model. Gator was pioneering new technology. They had one of the best methodologies for delivering highly targeted online ads directly to the individual web user. All that was needed were users to download the toolbar (to deliver website traffic) and website visits (to deliver ad real estate). In these, Gator was also a pioneer.

Gator entered into distribution agreements with software vendors who included the Gator Toolbar along with the download of their software. This brought in millions of users. The only problem was those users did not always know they had downloaded the toolbar along with their software purchase. You can imagine the surprise when they started getting pop-up ads on every website they visited.

The technology allowed much more than just pop-ups. The Gator Toolbar would also recognize online stores and it would pop-up offers from competing stores. Many online stores jumped at the chance to advertise directly on their competitors' websites. It did not stop there. The Gator Toolbar used JavaScript to read the HTML code generating the web pages being viewed. That same code also allowed them to re-write the HTML of a web page before it displayed in the user's browser. If they saw banner ads appearing on a web page, they would replace them with banners being served by Gator. Well, that obviously did not make those websites happy. Website owners had hoped to earn revenue from clicks to the banner ads on their website. Instead, Gator captured that revenue by serving their own ads in place of the original ads. Many websites complained. Some went further. They charged that Gator was stealing the ad space on those websites. In fact, some of the largest advertising organizations in the business sued them. Among the plaintiffs were the New York Times and the Internet Advertising Bureau.

At about this same time, the general public was becoming more concerned about online privacy. The average person did not use terms like contextual ads and behavioral targeting. They started using new terms like, *adware* and *spyware*. Gator was seen as a pioneer and champion of both. In 2003, after multiple lawsuits and a flood of public scorn, Gator decided to change their company name to Claria -- a change they hoped would present a new face and new company direction to the public. They replaced their senior managers. Then in 2006, they decided to drop their adware business altogether. In its place, they have decided to focus only on opt-in behavioral targeting.

As Claria, the company has turned from its bad boy role in the early days of online advertising and is seeking to take the high road. With opt-in behavioral targeting, the end users are fully informed about how the technology will be used to provide them with targeted ads based on their online behavior. Users receive targeted content in a personal assistant type interface rather than having ads appear while they are browsing other websites. Time will tell if the public will accept fully disclosed behavioral targeting as a valuable service or if they will still consider the amount of personal information collected as too much an invasion of privacy.

Gator started out with a good idea. They realized that to be successful, all website owners must make use of the technology available to bring qualified traffic to their websites. It is the job of technology innovators to create opportunities for connections between Web users and the websites that may be of interest to them. However, the Gator experience teaches a more fundamental lesson. That is one of discovering the ethical limits of online privacy. They started out showing the way for effective use of technology. In the end, those who remember the Gator Toolbar will remember it, in infamy, as a company who helped define where the public wants the limits of online privacy to be drawn. They found that line as they were crossing over it.

The chapters in Part II dig into the details of how to bring customers to your website. Step by step instructions are provided for the six most important ways to drive traffic to your website. In addition, a seventh chapter shows you how you can make money from your content website or blog, by sending traffic to other websites who will pay for it.

In Part II, you will learn how to:

Chapter 6   Get listed on search engines
Chapter 7   Send email
Chapter 8   Advertise online
Chapter 9   Set up an affiliate program
Chapter 10   Use viral marketing
Chapter 11   Use blogs
Chapter 12   Make money from your content website or blog

The need for traffic is at the very heart of an Internet Marketing strategy. Just building a great online program is not enough. You have to get people to use it. You have to literally go out and beat the bushes to bring people in. One thing is common to all successful Internet Marketing programs. They all succeed in driving traffic to their web-based features and services.

Chapter 6
Getting Listed On Search Engines

In this chapter, you will learn . . .
- What Natural Search and Paid Search are all about
- How to be successful with Search Engine Optimization
- How to be successful with Search Engine Marketing
- How search engines work under the hood

Earning Your Cool Sunglasses
The Yahoo "Cool Sites" Story

In 1995, the most coveted honor a website could get was to have a pair of cool sunglasses displayed next to their search results on Yahoo. This was Yahoo's way of designating the website as a "Cool Site." That little pair of dark sunglasses told the world, "Check this site out!" Cool sites would also be displayed at the top of search results listings for relevant keywords.

Search engines, as we know them today, had been a part of the World Wide Web since 1993. By 1995, the combination of irreverent nerdiness and relevant search results had propelled Yahoo to the head of the pack. The Cool Sites ratings made them indispensable. The Internet was still new to most people. Every week, websites would pop up with something useful or unusual. People relied on those cool sunglasses at Yahoo to tell them which ones were worth checking out. It was a day to celebrate when your website got those cool sunglasses and became a "Cool Site."

The idea of using search engines as part of an overall Web marketing strategy was not clearly understood until then. Those cool sunglasses brought it into focus for everyone wanting to have a successful website.

Search engines held the key to the popularity of your website. The technology powering search engines was still primitive, by today's standards. But, the lesson Yahoo's cool sunglasses taught marketers has become a truism of Internet Marketing. To be successful online, you must be successful with search engines.

The ABC's Of Search Engines

If you are like most web users, a search engine is the first place you go when you are looking for something online. Entering a word, or phrase into a search box has become so much a part of our everyday lives, we do not even think about it anymore. You click, "Search." Then a long list of websites comes back. Sometimes over a million sites are listed. You also see sponsored links at the top and right side of the page. To be successful with search engines, you want your link to show up on the first page of search results when people enter terms related to your products or services. Preferably, you want to be near the top of that page. There are two ways to do this, *natural search* and *paid search*. Successful search engine strategy will usually employ a combination of both.

Natural Search

Search engines use computer programs, called *spiders*, to read the text they find on web pages. Then they index those words and phrases to be searched in the future. After you click the search button, the search engine matches the terms you entered with the indexed values to return a list of web pages. Because it is based on finding information naturally occurring on existing websites, this process is sometimes called *natural search*. Another term often used is *organic search*. These terms are interchangeable.

Paid Search

Natural search is a free service. Search engine companies do not make money from the free service. To make money, they also display sponsored links which are paid for by websites being listed. Sponsored links are displayed by matching the term you entered with a list of terms other websites have submitted. Every time a sponsored link is displayed and then clicked on, the submitting company or organization is billed. Because it is based, not on existing web content, but on paid listings, this process is called *paid search*.

Being Successful with Search Engines

To be successful in driving traffic from search engines to your website, you must optimize search results listings from both natural and paid search. In both cases, this comes down to three things:

1.   Get Listed

First, you have to make sure your website appears at the top of the search results listing. When people search for the words and phrases relevant to content on your website, they should see your site in the first few results. This is done by optimizing your web pages and by buying sponsored links on search engines. Both of these will be discussed in detail later in this chapter.

2.   Get Clicked

Once people are seeing your website in their search results listing, you must get them to click on your link. This is done through good copy writing. The displayed search results listing will contain a title and a short description. For natural search, this information usually comes from the web page's meta tags or from the first text found on the page. For paid search, you will submit a title and description to be displayed. This should be thought of as your advertising copy. Take as much care writing this copy as you would with any other form of advertisement.

---

3.   **Convert Clicks to Actions**

Finally, after a customer sees your link and clicks on it, you want them to perform some action when they get to your website. What that action is will depend on the goals of your website. It may be to buy something from your online store. It may be to subscribe to your service or newsletter. It could be any number of things. Whatever that action may be, it is up to you to get customers to perform that action after they have clicked on your link. This is done by designing the web page they land on to elicit the desired action.

The first page a web user sees after clicking your link is called the *landing page*. For natural search, users will land on whatever page the search engine indexed and listed in the search results. For this reason, every web page on your site should be designed to draw customers to the desired action that is relevant to that particular page. For paid search, you provide the search engine company with a URL to the page web searchers will land on. You want to make sure customers either land on a page designed to generate the desired conversion or create a custom landing page specifically for that web listing. Do not leave this up to chance. Clicking on your link is only the beginning. It is up to you to continue marketing to them after they get to your site.

Now let us look at the two ways you can get your website listed on search engines.

Search Engine Optimization (SEO)

Being found when people search for terms related to the information your website is offering is the single most important thing you can do to drive traffic to your website. The simple truth is, people use search engines to find what they are looking for online. An absolutely critical part of designing your website is to make sure search engines find it and list it at the top of search results for relevant terms. This is done by finding out what the major search engines are looking for and then making sure your web pages are organized so they can easily be found. Optimizing your web pages to be found, and listed by search engines is called, *Search Engine Optimization,* or SEO for short.

As you read through the rest of this chapter, you will learn more about how SEO works and how to successfully optimize your web pages.

Search Engine Marketing (SEM)

Another way to get your listing in front of web searchers is to pay to be a sponsored link. Search engines typically have sponsored listings at the top of their search results page or along the right side of the page. Buying paid search listings is called *Search Engine Marketing,* or SEM for short.

Purchasing placement on search engines is done by "buying keywords." Keywords are single words or phrases people enter into the search box when they perform a search. You pick the keywords you think are relevant to your product or service. Then you pay to have your listing appear when those keywords are searched for. More popular keywords will cost more than less popular ones. You will pay a per-click fee each time your link is clicked on. In some cases you may also pay a listing fee that guarantees your listing will show up on the first page of web searches for the keywords you select.

Since multiple sponsored links can be displayed for any given keyword, most search engines use a bidding process. You will place a bid for how much you want to spend for each click. Then the listings with the higher bids will appear higher in the search results listings. You can also tell the search engine what your maximum budget is. They will only display your listing until your budget has been met.

It is a good idea to test a number of keywords on a number of different search engines. Then stick with the ones that perform the best for you.

Successful Search Engine Optimization In Seven Easy Steps!

Search Engine Optimization is the most important thing you can do to bring traffic to your website. In the "Search Before the Purchase" report of 2005, DoubleClick and ComScore Networks found that roughly half of all online buyers perform a related search before they make their purchase. If your website does not show up in their search results, then you have missed the opportunity to reach that customer. But how do you make sure your website gets listed? It does not have to be a mystery.

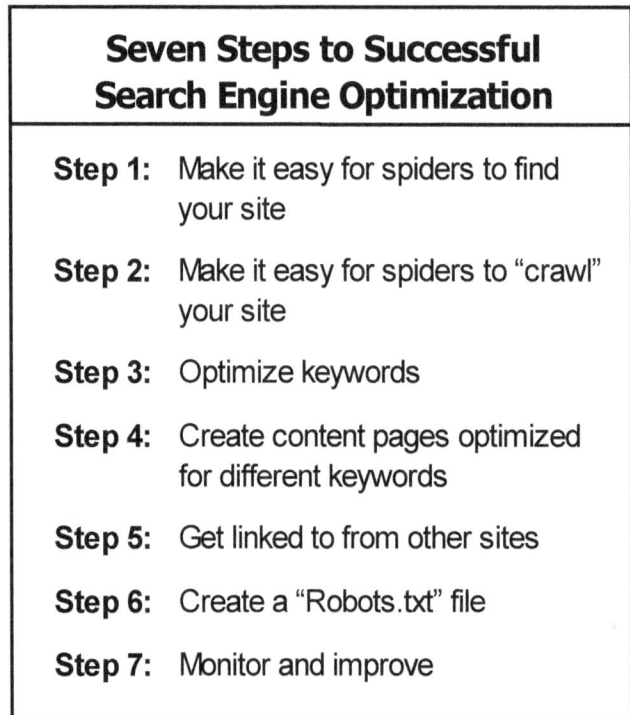

Seven Steps to Successful Search Engine Optimization
Step 1: Make it easy for spiders to find your site
Step 2: Make it easy for spiders to "crawl" your site
Step 3: Optimize keywords
Step 4: Create content pages optimized for different keywords
Step 5: Get linked to from other sites
Step 6: Create a "Robots.txt" file
Step 7: Monitor and improve

Figure 6.1

Search engines have programs called *spiders* that scour the Internet looking for web pages to list in their search results. *Search Engine Optimization* is web-speak for organizing content on your website so the spiders will find your web pages and list them in the top search results. Professionals in the field usually just call it *SEO* for short.

The secret to successful SEO is found in following these seven easy steps.

Step 1:
Make It Easy for Spiders to Find Your Site

The first step in getting listed by search engines is to make sure they find your website to list it. Luckily, search engines help with this. They will allow you to submit your website to them to be spidered. The easiest way to be found by a search engine is to submit your site to them. Identify the search engines you want to be listed on, go to their websites and find out their submission requirements.

Submitting your website to search engines will get you listed. But, it can sometimes take a long time. In addition to submitting your web pages to search engines, it is also important to optimize your website so it is easy for search engines to find it. There are really two things that search engines do that affect them finding your site. First, you must have URLs that are easy for spiders to read. This is discussed in the next section. Second, you should try to get your website linked to from other popular websites. Since spiders find websites by following links, they will find your site as they are crawling other sites.

Step 2:
Make It Easy for Spiders to "Crawl" Your Site

Once a spider finds your home page, it will follow the links on the page to other pages on your site. Then it will evaluate each of those pages. This is called *crawling*. An easy way to make sure the spiders crawl the pages you want listed is to create a site map page linked to the home page. If this page contains links to all the pages you want crawled, then each page is only two links away from the home page.

In addition to having a site map of links that spiders can follow, it is also important to have URLs that spiders can read. Many websites dynamically generate URLs for some of their web pages that rely on information pulled from a database. This is a very good idea for efficient website design, but it throws up a roadblock for spiders trying to crawl your website. Spiders are designed to read words and phrases. They often will completely ignore parameters that appear in dynamically generated web pages. For large, dynamically generated websites, this can be a complex issue. However, if you follow two simple rules, you will be ahead of the game:

✓ A fixed path is easy to read. Dynamically generated URLs with parameters are hard for search engines to read.
✓ English words are easy to read. Numbers and alphanumeric codes are hard for search engines to read.

Step 3:
Optimize Keywords

People find what they are looking for on the Internet by entering keywords into a search engine. The search engine finds your web page by matching those keywords to words and phrases on your site. The next step to getting your web pages listed is to learn what keywords people are most likely to use to find your site. Then make sure those words and phrases are strategically placed in places the search engines look. Optimizing keywords on your web pages is the heart of search engine optimization.

There are three critical things you must do with your keywords, once you have decided what they are:

1.   Keyword Density

Keywords should appear more than once on your web page to get a high ranking by the search engines. However, if they appear too often on the page, the search engine will see it as a way to trick the search engine and will push the page into a lower ranking. Search engines look at the amount of times the keyword appears on your page as a percentage of total words on the page. This is called *keyword density*.

2.   Meta Tags

Each web page can contain a title, keywords and a page description. These are placed in hidden locations on the web page called *Meta Tags*. They do not show up on the page, but the search engine can see them. The Title, Description and Keywords meta tags give web developers a way to categorize their own web pages. So, this is the first place search engines look to determine what words are most relevant to the page. The keywords that are most relevant to the web page should appear in these meta tags.

Many people try to trick search engines by loading their meta tags with keywords that are not directly related to the content of the page. As with keyword density, putting too much into your meta tags will push your search results listing down. Your search engine ranking may also be reduced by having words in your meta tags that do not also appear in the body of the page.

The Title and sometimes the first few words in the Description will show up in the search results listing. These two meta tags should be considered as advertising copy. Care should be taken to provide wording that people will want to click on.

3.   Position on Page

Third, search engines look for the location of words on the page to determine how relevant they are to that page. The HTML code on your web page can identify titles and subject headers. Keywords appearing in these are considered important to the page. Also, keywords appearing closer to the top of the page are considered more important than words appearing lower on the page.

By identifying which keywords you expect your target audience to be searching for and then following these three guidelines, you will obtain high search result rankings for your most important keywords.

Step 4:
Create Content Pages Optimized for Different Keywords

You may want your website to appear in the search results for many different keywords. If you have an online store, you would probably want to appear for all of your best selling products. If you offer a service to business clients, you may want to appear in listings for all of the target industries you service. The challenge is that you cannot optimize one web page to rank high for all of these different keywords. The answer is to create content pages relevant to each of these keywords. Then optimize these content pages to rank high for their targeted keywords.

An online store could create buyer guides for each of their top product categories. A business-to-business supplier could create custom pages tailored to the needs of each target industry. Another common practice is to create an area on your website for archived articles you have written. These pages will be rich in keywords related to the topic at hand. If you further optimize these pages for those keywords, search engines will direct traffic to them. Then, design the layout of your article pages and other custom pages to draw people from those pages into the main areas of your website.

Step 5:
Get Linked to from Other Sites

Getting other sites to place links to your site is another essential part of your search engine strategy. Search engines look at the amount of times your website is linked to from other sites when ranking your web page. In general, the more links you have coming to your site the better it is for your ranking. If your site is linked to from other high ranking sites, that will do even more for your ranking.

When you are thinking about getting links from other sites, the basic rule is to have content that users on other websites will find useful. Then, find those websites where your content will make a contribution. Once you find those sites, you will pursue getting both *reciprocal links* and *one-way links*.

1.   Reciprocal Links

Reciprocal links are links from websites that you also link to. This is a tit-for-tat situation. When you have compiled your list of websites, look for websites that have content you would like to link to from your website. Then place a link to their website on your own site. After you have linked to them, then contact the owner of the website directly and ask to have your link placed on their site. All websites are in the same boat. They all need to be linked to in order to get higher rankings. So most will be open to your request. There are also services that specialize in helping you find reciprocal links.

2. One-Way Links

Reciprocal links are important. However, to get a high ranking, you must also have one-way links. These are links from sites that you are not also linking to. Search engines look for both types of link when determining their ranking. The basic rule applies. Have web content that is worth being linked to. If you are targeting your website to a niche audience, then create content that is especially useful to that niche. Other sites serving the same niche will want to link to your site. It helps them serve their customers. This process can take time, though. As your site obtains higher search ranking, more sites will find you and want to link to your content. But, of course, you need to get those links to get the higher ranking. To get beyond this, you can look for websites that allow you to submit content to them that will contain links back to your site.

A good way to get one-way links is to find websites that publish and archive articles related to the content on your site. Once you find these, submit articles to them. When they publish your article and store it in their archive, you will get a link back to your site.

Also, look for websites that act as information clearinghouses, with links to other sites. Find business directories that cater to your industry or niche issue. Then submit your website to be listed by them. If you have created content that can be offered as a free download, you can submit it to download sites. If you have a blog on your website, submit it to be listed in blog directories.

It used to be a common technique to try and trick search engines by creating a variety of websites, then having them all link to each other. This is called *crosslinking*. As with most ways people have tried to trick search engines, this one has been found out also. Crosslinking is not prohibited by search engines. It is only natural for a family of websites to link to each other. However, too much crosslinking will be noticed and hurt your ranking.

Step 6:
Create a Robots.txt File

The main reason for search engine optimization is, of course, to get search engines to find and list your web pages. However, there are often pages that you do not want them to find. You may have an area of your website for customers, that you do not want the general public going to. You may have pages that simply serve as redirect pages which record click stream information on the way to other content pages. Some websites have pages that run interactive software which do not work with automated robots. There are many reasons why you may not want a particular page listed.

Well, the search engines do not want to go to these pages either. They would like for you to tell them which pages they can skip. You can do this by creating a small text file called the *robots.txt* file. This file sits at the root directory of your website. It is the first thing search engines look for when they arrive at your website. The robots.txt file contains instructions to search engines on which pages to skip over.

Some search engines will not spider a website if a robots.txt file is not present. You should create one even if there are no pages to exclude. Search engines will see the blank file and proceed to spider all of your web pages.

Step 7:
Monitor and Improve

Getting your website to show up in search results does not need to be a mystery. By following these seven steps, your web pages will appear in your customers' search results. It is an iterative process. Your first pass at it may not yield the results you were hoping for. Keep at it. Think of these seven steps as seven levers you keep adjusting until you find the right balance. When you find that balance, your site will consistently appear in the first page of search results for relevant keywords. Then, keep tracking your results. Things will change over time. SEO is a process you should expect to repeat periodically. It is a relatively small investment in time that will yield big results.

Each search engine has things it looks for when finding and ranking web pages. Things like the format of your URLs or the optimal keyword density vary from engine to engine. Research what the search engines you want to be listed on are looking for. Optimize your site for those search engines. This changes over time, so you must repeat this exercise periodically.

Successful Search Engine Marketing In Seven Easy Steps!

Search Engine Marketing is the most effective way to advertise online. When people want to find something online, they start with a search engine. Getting a link to your website and a few words of promotional copy displayed on the first page of their search results reaches them at the most opportune moment. Customers have just described what they want by entering the search term. They are actively seeking something they can respond to. It is the best case scenario for targeted marketing.

Buying sponsored links on search engines is easy. Some search engines have automated bidding tools to make buying keywords as easy as placing a bid on eBay. On the other hand, very small

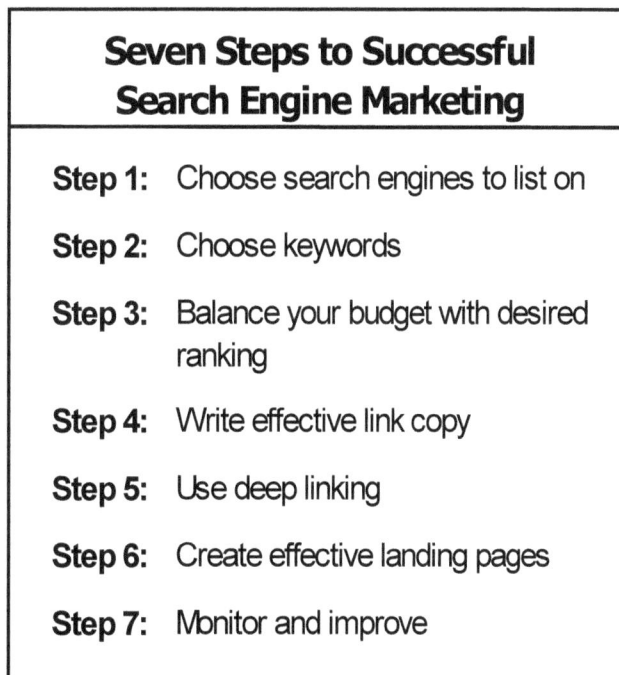

Seven Steps to Successful Search Engine Marketing

Step 1: Choose search engines to list on

Step 2: Choose keywords

Step 3: Balance your budget with desired ranking

Step 4: Write effective link copy

Step 5: Use deep linking

Step 6: Create effective landing pages

Step 7: Monitor and improve

Figure 6.2

differences in your click-thru rates and conversion rates can make the difference between positive and negative return on your investment. It is a balancing act.

The secret to successful search engine marketing is found in following these seven easy steps.

Step 1:
Choose Search Engines

Which search engine should you advertise on? This is the first decision you must make once you have decided Search Engine Marketing is right for you. The simple answer to this is start with the big ones. As of the writing of this chapter, 73% of all online searches in the United States are performed on two search engines, Google and Yahoo. If you do nothing else with search engine marketing, you should advertise on these two. After Google and Yahoo, there are two more that account for another 15%, MSN and AOL. Almost 90% of all searches are performed on these four search engines. (source: Nielsen NetRatings July 2006)

After you have bought keywords on the big search engines, you can look into specialty search engines that focus on the niche you are targeting. For example, if you have a restaurant or live music venue, you may want to get listed on Citysearch.com. If you are a Business-to-Business supplier, you may want to list on Business.com.

Step 2:
Choose Keywords

The second, and most critical step is to determine which keywords you will buy. There are two parts to this decision. First, you must identify the words and phrases that best describe the content on the web pages where you want to direct traffic. Next you must identify what words and phrases web users are most likely to enter as search terms when they are looking for content related to your web pages. The basic rule is to find as many variations as you can on the words and phrases you identified as being relevant to your web page. Then try to figure out which are the most likely variations web users will search for. These are the keywords you want.

Some search engines will show you suggested variations to the terms you've selected. They also may be able to tell you which terms are most popular.

Now here is an important point. You do not necessarily want the most popular search term. If the term being searched most is a very general word or phrase, then you may get a lot of clicks on your link (which you pay for), but they may not convert to sales. It is better to be more specific in your keyword choice. This way you will get clicks from searchers who are more likely to be interested in the specific things you offer on your site.

For example, you may have a business offering legal assistance for small businesses. You could advertise on the very popular search term, "legal services." However, this would be likely to bring a lot of clicks from people who did not need help with their small business. You could also advertise on the popular term, "small business." But then you might get clicks who do not need legal services. On the other hand, if you advertise on the specific phrase, "small business legal services," you will get clicks from searchers who are in the market for your specific services. You will get fewer clicks, but they will convert at a higher rate.

It is not possible to tell exactly what the right keywords for your business will be up front. The best approach is to start with a larger set of keywords as a test. Measure the results in clicks and conversions. Then stick with the ones that yield the best results.

Step 3:
Balance Your Budget with Desired Ranking

Once you decide where you want to advertise and what keywords you want, the next step is to decide how to make the best use of your available budget. You will pay more money for a higher rank in the search results. The top listing will cost more than the second listing, which will cost more than the third, and so on. The general rule is that you want to be *above the fold* on the first page of search results. The fold is the area of the page displayed without scrolling down. However, having the number one listing does not necessarily gain that much over the number two or three. You will only know by testing. You may also find that you get better overall results by paying less for a listing below the fold, or even on the second page.

The best way to proceed is to start with a test using only a small budget. Test a large number of different search terms, on different search engines and at different list order. Run this test for a few weeks and see how your various options perform. Pay special attention not only to click-thru rates but also to conversion rates. With this information, you can run your full program with those terms, search engines and rank orders that performed the best for you.

Step 4:
Write Effective Link Copy

The best keywords will only work for you if people want to click on your link when they see it. The next step is to write effective link copy. You have only a few words to make people interested enough to click. This is critical advertising copy. Make those words count.

Link copy should be closely related to the keywords the user entered. Generic sounding links are not very good at enticing clicks. Separate copy should also be written for different variations of your search terms.

Link copy should match the needs or wants of users entering the given search term. When writing link copy, consider why a person might be entering one term versus another. Then tailor your copy to that. Take the example of small business legal services above. Someone entering the term, "small business law" may be looking for general information. On the other hand, someone entering, "small business lawyer" may be looking to hire a lawyer. Both may be good prospects for your business. But they will respond to different messages.

Link copy should be clearly related to the content of your website without turning off potential customers. This is a balancing act. Your link should act as a filter that draws in only people who are likely to convert on your website. On the other hand, you may also want to bring in potential customers who do not know yet that they want what you are offering. Once again, you will only find the right balance by testing a variety of options and sticking with the best performers.

Step 5:
Use Deep Linking

When people are looking for something on the Internet, they are impatient. They want to be sent directly from the search results to information related to the topic of their search. If people find themselves dropped onto a home page they are likely to just leave and go to the next search result listing until they find what they want. In other words, they expect to be linked from the search results directly to a page deep in your site where they can instantly see what they are looking for. This is called *deep linking*.

Deep linking is especially important when you are buying keywords. Make sure the listings you put out there go directly to the content on your site related to the keyword being searched.

Step 6:
Create Effective Landing Pages

In some cases, deep linking is not enough. You may want to create custom pages for people coming from your link. You customized the copy of your link to match specific needs and interests of people who would be entering a given search term. You may also want to customize the content on the first web page they see. Custom landing pages like this are sometimes called *doorway pages*.

Making a copy of your web page with alternate versions of the messaging, images or offer is easy and inexpensive. This can greatly increase conversions from your search engine traffic.

Step 7:
Monitor and Improve

Finally, it is absolutely essential that you monitor the results of all keyword spending and continuously improve your program. This is easy to do. The search engine will provide simple reports showing all keyword buys with details about the results each generated. You can then fairly easily set up a report from your Web Analytics software to show the conversions resulting from each.

Behavior on the Internet is constantly changing. Keywords and copy that perform well this month may not next month. You should be constantly monitoring for drops in performance and make adjustments. Also, continue to try new search terms. Slight changes in click-thru or conversion rates can make a big difference in your bottom line.

There are seven critical metrics for Search Engine Marketing campaigns.

Key SEM Metrics and Typical Areas for Improvement

1.	# of Impressions	→ Measure the reach of your ad spend
		Optimize spend for most effective keywords
2.	Keyword Ranking	→ Measure results by rank to optimize budget
3.	Click-thru Rate	→ Targeting the right keywords
		Effective copy
4.	Conversion Rate	→ Targeting the right keywords
		Effective landing pages / deep linking
5.	Cost Per Conversion	→ Optimize spend for most effective keywords
6.	Variable Results (by keywords)	→ Targeted versions of link copy
		Custom landing pages by source
		Eliminate non-productive keywords
7.	Decreasing Results	→ Freshness of keywords targeted
		Updated content on landing pages
		Broken links

By collecting information about these seven metrics, you will know what is working and what is not working. You can then use this information to continuously improve future Search Engine Marketing efforts.

The next section goes into detail about how search engine technology works. If you do not want to dig this deep into the details, feel free to turn ahead to the next chapter.

Bonus Section:
How Search Engines Work Under The Hood

The key to successfully getting listed on search engines is to understand how natural search works. How do search engines find things people are looking for and how do they choose which results to list first? When you understand this, you will be able to make sure people find your website.

To understand how search engines work, there are really just two key things to learn: *spiders* and *ranking web pages*. Everything else revolves around these two things. Spiders are automated computer programs that *crawl* the Web and read all of the words on web pages they find. These words are then put into a database. The words in the database are organized so it is easy to search in the future. For each word in the database, web pages will be *ranked* to tell which will be listed at the top of search results.

The process of organizing the database to allow future searches is commonly called *indexing*. This is a little bit of a jargon shortcut. Indexing and ranking web pages are actually two separate actions that occur in the database. These will be described below.

Being successful with search engines is a matter of knowing how to get spiders to find your web pages, what the search engines are looking for when they rank order pages, and how to use that knowledge to get your pages listed at the top.

Spiders Crawl the Web

It all starts with those digital creatures that could only exist on the World Wide Web. *Spiders* are small, automated computer programs that search for web pages and read all of the text on each page they find. To make more sense out of just what this means, we need to take a dive into the world of Internet jargon. This is where it starts to get pretty thick.

First, spiders are a type of program known as a *robot* or *bot* for short. Robots are automated programs that are designed to carry out some kind of action on the Web. Usually, this involves searching for some type of information on web pages and then performing some action based on the information it finds. They are called robots, because once they are turned on, they will keep doing what they are programmed to do without human intervention. For example, shopping bots search online stores and can be used to find the best prices on products you are looking for. Search engine spiders simply read every bit of text they find on each page they go to.

So what do spiders do? Well, of course they *crawl* the Web. Here is how crawling works. A spider goes to a particular website. The search engine will send it to the URL of a popular site to start on. The spider reads every bit of text on that web page. Also, the spider will collect some information about that text. For example: is it in a meta tag, is it in the page title or a section header, is it close to the top of the page? Once it has collected all of the information it was programmed to get, the spider follows every link on that page. This way, it will go through all of the pages on that website. It will also go to all of the other websites that are linked to from that site. Once it gets to another website, it will follow the same processes. In this way a spider continues to go from website to website, picking up all of the words on each one as it goes. It is crawling through the World Wide Web.

Filling the Database

What happens to all of that information the spiders collect? It gets sent back to the search engine computers and stored in their database. You can think of the database as being a gigantic list of words. To make sense out of all the information collected, it has to be organized in some way.

Every word on the Web is in there, at least all the ones found by the spiders. For each word, it stores the URL of the web page where the word was found. It also has information about that word as it appeared on the page. Was the word in a meta tag? Then it will show which meta tag it was in (Meta tags will be discussed in a later section). Was it in a subject header on the page? How close was it to the top of the page? Each word, with its corresponding URL and information is a row in the list. If the word appears ten times on a given page, then there will be ten rows for that word with that URL.

There is one more important piece of information that will be stored in the database. For each web page, the search engine will record all of the external websites which link to that page. Remember, the spider gets to a website by following links on other websites. Each time a link takes the spider to a given website, that is recorded in the database. So the search engine knows how many times your website is being linked to from other websites. This will become important when it comes to rank ordering your web pages. Websites being linked to from many external websites are considered more popular than those with few external links.

Ranking Web Pages

Now the spiders have filled the search engine database with a list of words found on web pages. The next step is to organize the information in the database so it will return relevant listings. All of the URLs associated with each word in the database are rank ordered, so ones where a given word is particularly important to the content of the web page will be listed higher than those where the word just happens to appear there. This is done by assigning weights to the web pages.

Every search engine has its own algorithm for ranking web pages. In general, they all assign weights based on certain information about the word as it appears on the page. Think of it as a point system. The web page gets points, or loses points based on the algorithm. There are four key factors considered by search engines in assigning these points.

---

1.   Meta Tags

Every web page contains sections in the HTML code set aside to give information about what is on the page. These are called *meta tags*. This is where the website creator can tell what the page is about. Information in meta tags is not displayed on the page, but it is read by search engine spiders.

Three meta tags are especially important for every web page: the *Title*, *Description* and *Keywords*. These three tags allow you to categorize your own web page. So it is also the first place search engines look when figuring out which words are most important on that page. There is also a fourth meta tag important for search engines. That is the *Robots* tag. This meta tag allows you to instruct search engine spiders to skip over your web page altogether.

Of course, people are going to look for ways to trick the system. Sometimes websites will load a lot of popular terms into their meta tags that do not really have that much to do with the content of the page. To account for this, search engines will take away points from pages that have the words in the meta tags but not in the body of the page. Search engines also take away points from pages that simply have too many words of any kind in the meta tags.

2.   Keyword Density

The second thing search engines look for when ranking web pages is how often the word appears on the page. This is called *keyword density*. In general, the more often the word appears on the web page, the more relevant the word is to the overall content of the page. Therefore, it will receive a higher weight.

However, search engine companies know that some websites try to trick the system and load their web pages with text that is just there to be found by search engines. To get around this, the search engines will start taking away points if the word appears too many times.

3. Position on Page

Another way web pages rank the relevance of words to the pages they are on is by where the word appears. The HTML code for the web page identifies subject headers and titles on the page. These will usually be displayed in a larger font, in bold or in a different color. When a word appears in a title or subject header that gives the page more points.

Also, when people design web pages, they want the most important information to be displayed at the top of the page, where people will see it without scrolling down the page. This is called being *above the fold*. Words that appear above the fold are considered more important than those below. But there is no easy way to tell exactly where the fold will be for each page. Instead, search engines give more points for how close the word appears to the top of the page.

4. External Links

Finally, if all else is equal, search engines want to list more popular web pages above pages that are not very popular. They estimate how popular a web page is by how many times it is linked to from external websites.

Once again, search engine companies know that people will try to work the system. A common trick is to set up a lot of useless or redundant websites and have them all link to the main site. Search engines have ways of identifying this trick.

Indexing the Database

As we said above, organizing the database to be searched is often referred to as indexing, or creating the index. *Indexing* is a technical database term. It means to physically re-organize the information in the database. Some advanced mathematical algorithms are used to allow very fast search and retrieval of data records. There are a variety of indexing methods available. Search engines have massive amounts of information that must be searched and retrieved in a matter of seconds. So you can imagine they use some of the most complex algorithms available. Luckily, you really do not need to know about them. What is important to understand is how web pages are ranked in the database. It is just a nice thing to know that the database is also indexed to make it run faster. Anyone who actually needs to know about indexing will be a database professional and already familiar with the concepts.

The main reason for discussing indexing at all is to avoid confusion. In the common web jargon, the terms indexing and ranking are often used together. You should be able to know what the two terms actually mean.

Performing Searches

The search engine has an indexed database full of words. All of the web pages where those words appear are rank ordered based on relevance. Now it is ready to be searched. So what happens when you type those words into the search box and click on the "Search" button?

It is easy to see what happens when you enter just a single word. Let us say you want to find information about the Kodak Corporation. You type the word, "Kodak" into the search box and click "Search." All of the web pages where the word Kodak appears have been weighted. So the search engine basically just returns web pages with the highest weight first. But what happens when you enter more than one word? That is when it gets interesting.

To search for more than one term, the search engine uses what is called *Boolean logic*. Boolean logic connects multiple words using connectors such as *and, or, not*. These are known as *Boolean operators* in computer programming speak. By stringing together multiple words into a phrase, using these connectors, the search engine is able to find results based on the combination of all the terms being searched. Doing this basically involves searching for all of the words and then using some kind of algorithm to calculate a weight based on the combination of all of the words. Once again, each search engine will use their own algorithms for calculating weights for the combined search term.

Most people do not use Boolean operators when submitting their searches. They just type in all of the words. The search engine then has to decide how to construct the Boolean expression before submitting the search. Typically, a search engine will try an expression where all the words are present (connected by *and*) first. Then it will look for pages where some of the words are present (connected by *or*). If you want to narrow your search beyond this, you can enter your own expression.

Submitting Web Pages to Search Engines

Now spiders are crawling web pages to build their database of words to be searched. What do you do if you have a small website that isn't being linked to by popular sites? Do you just have to wait and hope the spiders find your website? Luckily, most search engines will allow you to submit your website to be spidered.

Each search engine has its own submission procedure. To submit your website, just go to the search engine where you want to be listed. Their submission guidelines will be posted on the website. If you are using a Search Engine Marketing firm, they will usually be able to do this for you.

Blocking Robots

In most cases, you want spiders from the major search engines to find your web pages. But sometimes you do not. There are a variety of reasons you may not want some of the pages on your website to be crawled. You may have pages on your website that are still under construction or are simply intended as doorways from specific links. Also, robots look like web users coming to your web pages. They perform actions (e.g. following links) just like web users. They also leave a record in your web logs like regular users. But, robots are not web users. They are little automated computer programs. What if your web pages are running some kind of software that is triggered by the actions of users on the page? The actions of spiders on the page could throw a wrench in your works. Perhaps you just do not want your traffic logs being cluttered with robot traffic. Is there anything you can do about it? Luckily, yes.

Robots usually identify themselves. In most cases, the robots are benign. They are there to perform a legitimate service. Companies have nothing to gain by hiding them. In fact, they want websites to know they are coming. That makes it easier for the websites to optimize their pages to be searched by the robots. This also helps if you do not want to be searched by the robots.

The first good thing about this is it lets you automatically filter out robot traffic from your traffic reports. They are easily identified as robots and can simply be taken out of the calculations.

The second good thing is you can instruct the robots to skip your web page altogether. There are two ways to do this. First, you can instruct spiders to skip a specific web page by including a special meta tag called the *Robots* tag. This simply tells the spider to skip that page.

A better way to block robots is to include a *robots.txt* file in the root directory of your website. This is a simple text file that lists all of the pages you do not want spiders to crawl. You can also instruct specific search engines not to crawl pages on your website in the robots.txt file. By putting this file at the root directory of your website, robots can easily find it. It is the first thing they look for. Some search engines require a website to have a robots.txt file or else they will not crawl the site. It is, therefore, a good practice to have the file present even if there is nothing in it.

Conclusion

In this chapter, you have learned how search engines work and the difference between natural search and paid search. You know how to be successful using Search Engine Optimization and Search Engine Marketing to drive traffic to your website.

Now turn to the next chapter and learn how to be successful with Email Marketing.

Chapter 7
Sending Email

In this chapter, you will learn . . .
*   What email marketing is all about
*   About Spam and Privacy Regulations
*   How to be successful with email marketing
*   How email marketing works under the hood

A Direct Marketer's Epiphany
The Story Of A Crazy Dream

In the early 1990s, direct marketers started reading a new generation of books with titles like "Relationship Marketing" (1993) and "The One-to-One Future" (1993). These books talked about a brave new world. Direct marketing techniques would be used to interact with customers as individuals, not just as members of a target market. You would use your customer database to learn enough about each customer to focus your communications on just what they are interested in. You would engage your customers in two-way dialogue. Some marketers even started using terms like "real time." When customers responded to a marketing campaign or submitted personal information, it was going to be automatically updated in the customer database. You would be able to respond back to them in real time.

Well, of course, this was all just crazy talk.

In 1993, direct marketing was a time consuming and labor intensive process. It took months to execute a single direct mail campaign. The cutting edge of direct marketing technology at the time was to apply statistical algorithms to a marketing database. This would allow marketers to target messages to those most likely to respond. Marketing databases were created by pulling data extracts from the company's main transactional databases. This required a lot of computer processing. The marketing database was usually maintained by a direct marketing vendor. Updates were performed by extracting company information onto a computer tape. That tape was then physically mailed to the vendor. They would merge the updated customer data with information collected from previous direct marketing campaigns. This process was typically only performed monthly. Weekly updates were an expensive luxury most companies wanted, but few could justify the budget to have. Sometimes, a supplemental extract was pulled just before a mail piece was sent. That way the vendor could match the list of names to be mailed with updated addresses and eliminate people who no longer wanted to receive mail. This might delay the mail by a day or two.

After the mail was sent, the vendor would collect responses from those who received the mail. Some stragglers let the mail piece sit before responding. So the direct marketing agency would continue to collect responses for up to a month before reporting final results of the campaign. It was not until the next database update cycle that those responses were added into the marketing database. Only then could the company respond back to the customer.

In the mid-1990's, time delays were an accepted reality direct marketers lived with. Communicating with customers and updating their information took days, if not weeks or even months.

Then along came the Internet. By the end of the 1990's, real time one-to-one marketing was not only possible but also commonplace. It should have come as no surprise that some of the first online businesses to become profitable were those who had been successful with direct mail catalogs. These companies knew how to make direct marketing work online. They also made good use of the new electronic direct mail, *email*. Catalogers knew that getting customers to their online store was only the beginning. The goal was to get them to opt-in to a mailing list. That way, each customer could continue to be promoted to over and over again. Besides, email was far less costly and time consuming than direct mail. Customers could express their preferences one day and receive an email promotion for those products the same day. If they made a purchase that day, you would know it immediately. The dream, once spoken about in awe around the water coolers, had become a reality.

Direct marketers realized something that all Internet Marketers need to know. Email is one of the most effective tools to transform one-time shoppers into loyal customers. At a relatively low cost, mailing to an email list will bring these customers back to make purchases over and over again.

The ABC's Of Email Marketing

Email is the electronic version of direct mail. There are some new bells and whistles you can use with the electronic version. You can also save some money on printing and postage costs. These new wrinkles on the old classic open up some exciting opportunities for email. Nevertheless, at the core, it is still basically the same thing. To demonstrate how to be successful using email, we must first show how successful direct mail campaigns work. Then we will move on to show how the added functionality offered by the Internet can be used to turbo-charge your email efforts.

A Direct Mail Primer

Of all the marketing activities being carried out online, email is the one that most closely parallels its offline counterpart, direct mail. Direct mail is effective because of its ability to send messages focused on a targeted group. Direct marketers start by targeting their mail list to only those most likely to be interested in their product or service. Then they create a mailer tailored to what those people will respond to. For this reason, direct marketers often refer to their craft as *targeted marketing*. Email is the electronic form of targeted marketing.

There are two basic types of direct mail campaign. The classic mail campaign is aimed at generating immediate sales. These are usually sent to a large list of both customers and prospects. They have a promotional offer aimed at eliciting an immediate response. In the old days, before technology allowed much targeting of mail lists, these were called *mass mailers*. Marketers hate this term today. It brings to mind another hated term, junk mail. Today, much effort is taken to target mail pieces so those who receive it are likely to be interested in what they get in their mail. So we call this type of mail campaign a *targeted mailer*.

The second type is a *customer communications mailer*. These are sent to existing customers and are usually offered as a service, or value-added benefit to the customer. Customer communication mailers include things such as service reminders from your car dealership, birthday cards from your favorite restaurant, or notification of frequent flyer rewards from your preferred airline. These mail pieces also contain a call to action and usually an offer. But, it is a soft sell. The goal is to keep you as a satisfied customer and provide incentives to keep purchasing from the company. The return from customer communication mailers goes beyond immediate sales. It also includes the future purchases you make as a loyal customer, plus the positive word-of-mouth they generate among your friends.

Both types of direct mail campaign include the same five basic elements. *Being successful with direct mail requires mastering each of these five elements.*

1.   The List

Direct mail starts with a *list*. The direct mail list is the group of people who receive your marketing message. These people are selected by using a targeting method that chooses people or businesses who are most likely to respond to your message.

2.   Opening the Envelope

After receiving the message, recipients in the mail group must *open the envelope*. This is the first hurdle. You can probably think of many mail pieces you have thrown away without opening. We all do it every day. To overcome this, direct marketers have devised many methods aimed at getting people to open their envelopes.

3. The Marketing Piece

If your recipient does open the envelope, he will see your *marketing piece*. This piece will always contain a *marketing message* and a *call to action*. It will usually also contain a *promotional offer* to incentivize people to respond to the *call to action*.

4. The Response

The next hurdle is for recipients to *respond* to your marketing piece. This could entail calling a 1-800 phone number, returning a business reply card, or many other possible actions. Not surprisingly, this is called a *response*. Recipients who go the extra step of responding are called *responders*.

5. The Conversion

The final hurdle is for responders to actually make a purchase (or carry out some other desired end result). When they do, it is called a *conversion*. In some cases, the conversion takes place as part of the response. The call to action could be, for example, "Return this card and start your subscription to Today's Internet Guru." In cases like this, the act of responding is also the conversion event.

In addition to these five components, there are two other parts of direct mail programs that are particularly important for understanding how email offers significant improvements over its predecessor: *pre-program testing* and *post-program evaluation and improvement*.

6. Pre-Program Testing

Direct mail campaigns can be costly to implement. Printing, postage and list rental costs can easily run to more than a dollar per mail recipient. It is not hard to see how costs run up quickly. It is not unusual for a large direct mail campaign to send mailers to tens of thousands or over a million people. For this reason, companies do everything they can to generate the greatest response possible.

One way to increase the effectiveness of a direct mail campaign is to send test mailers first, before mailing to the entire list. A variety of different messages, offers and creative designs can be sent to a small audience. Then those that produce the best results will be used in the final mailer. This kind of pre-program testing can save a lot of money with large mailers. Thousands, or even tens of thousands of dollars can be saved by eliminating ineffective mail pieces. But, it also adds valuable time. A pre-program test requires printing the mailers, sending them out, waiting for response and calculating results. This can take weeks, or even months to complete.

7.   Post-Program Evaluation and Improvement

A second way direct marketers increase the effectiveness of their direct mail programs is to evaluate results after the campaign is complete. Then the findings are used to improve results of future campaigns. For example, a direct mail campaign promoting a new luxury car could be evaluated to see how well recipients of different income brackets responded. If it is observed that households with incomes below $75,000 did not respond at profitable levels, then these households could be removed from future campaigns promoting that vehicle.

Post-program evaluation and improvement of this type is theoretically an important part of every direct mail campaign. However, there can be significant costs to compile and analyze the results. Doing so also adds time to the end of the project. Subsequently, it is not uncommon for companies to skip this step. It is human nature to trade the future benefits of improved results for the immediate benefits of time and money saved today. Sometimes marketers are just ready to move on to the next project and do not want to bother with following up on the last project.

It is easy to see that costs can be very high for traditional direct mail. By using the Internet, email cuts these costs dramatically. There is another, even more dramatic consideration than the costs. The process described above for a traditional direct mail campaign can take months to complete. Email, using Internet technology, cuts this time from months to days.

Being Successful With Email

Now we will see how an email campaign follows the same process as the classic direct mail campaign.

1.   The Opt-In Mail List

First, you start with a list. Your email mailer is sent to an opted-in list of customers and potential customers. The most important part of a successful email campaign is the list. So far this is pretty much exactly like direct mail.

2.   Effective Subject Lines

The first hurdle you cross is for your email recipients to actually open the email. Once again, this is very similar to opening the direct mail envelope. With email, the "envelope" is your subject line. People will decide to open an email or not based on two key aspects of the subject line. First, they will look at who sent the email. If they trust the sender, they will likely open the mail. Second, they will look at the subject line itself. If it catches their attention (in a good way) they are likely to open it. If your subject line fails on either of these two tests, the email will most likely be deleted.

There is also another important factor in getting your email opened. It must actually make it through to the recipient. Most email systems have filters to block unwanted Spam from ever getting into the inbox. These filters look at words and phrases in the subject line that are commonly used in Spam emails. Care must be taken to make sure your mailer does not get blocked by these filters or else they will never be opened.

3.   The Email Promotion

When the recipient does click on the subject line and "opens your envelope," they will see your email message. That message is equivalent to the first promotional piece they pull out of the envelope. This email message will contain your promotional copy, call to action and offer.

4.   The Click-Thru

The second hurdle is for the recipient to respond to your email by clicking on a link in the email document. After clicking on a link in the email, the recipient is taken to a landing page with the opportunity to complete some kind of conversion action. This could be an eCommerce page, with the opportunity to buy. It could be an application form with the opportunity to subscribe for a service or become a sales lead. It could also be another promotional page with multiple options for further responses.

At this point, the email campaign differs from offline direct mail in an important way. Every action that occurs on after clicking thru on the subject line is an electronic event that can be immediately recorded. Therefore, all responses and conversions to your email campaign can be automatically tallied and reported.

5.   Conversions

Conversions are the ultimate action you want your email recipient to take as a result of your email. It could be a sale. It could be a subscription to your service or online newsletter. It could be a download of your white paper or free software. The most important consideration in gaining conversions is to design the user experience from start to finish. From their first mouse click on your subject line, every step should lead them to another click which brings them to a page designed to generate the conversion. This whole process should take as few clicks as possible.

Testing, Evaluation and Improvement

With offline direct mail, pre-program testing and post-program evaluation are important steps, but costly and time consuming. One of the greatest advantages of email over its offline predecessor is that it removes these cost and time constraints.

With email, it is a relatively easy thing to send multiple versions of your mailer to a test audience. Creating multiple versions of HTML documents is relatively inexpensive. The mail is delivered and responses (clicks) start being recorded the day email is delivered. Therefore, with email, an effective test can be conducted in a couple of days instead of weeks.

It is also relatively easy to set up automated tracking and reporting of email results. Responses take place as clicks to your (or your vendor's) web servers. They can be immediately recorded and updated results reported. Conversions can also be tracked by recording the session cookie of each click-thru from the email campaign and following the visit through to a sale. (This is explained in Part III). All of this means you can have real time, or at least same-day results from your email campaigns. Changes to HTML documents can be made fairly easily as well.

The whole process of testing, evaluation and improvement is a fairly easy process with email.

Five Ways To Use Email

Email follows a fairly simple formula that was pioneered and perfected by direct marketers before the advent of the World Wide Web. The Internet added some bells and whistles that make it easy and cost effective for anyone to be successful with it. As marketers spent time mastering the use of email in reaching out to their customers, five unique types of email campaign emerged. Today, these five types of email form the backbone of almost all email marketing programs. As you take time to develop your own email marketing program, you will probably want to make use of one, or more of these.

Promotional or Seasonal Mailers

The first and most basic type of email is the one-time promotional mailer. These campaigns are the most like a classical targeted direct mail campaign. You start with a reason to send a promotional message to your opt-in list. It could be a sale. It could be the arrival of the new seasonal line of products. It could be a holiday. For nonprofit organizations, promotional mailers could be sent to promote an annual fundraising event or to influence an election. Anything that will give customers a reason to come back to your website can be turned into a promotional mailer.

Newsletters

The next way businesses use email is to send a newsletter. Newsletters are not promotions. They are offering a service to your subscribers. If you have something useful or of interest to your customers, that they will want to see on a regular basis, then you could send them a newsletter.

Newsletters come in all shapes and sizes. They could be as short as a "Tip of the Day." They could be as long as a collection of articles related to your customers' selected interests. You could send out a monthly description of upcoming events with "member pricing" offers. You could simply collect online articles posted by others and send ones you think will be interesting to your subscribers. The idea is that you continue to keep your business at the top of your customers' minds and give them opportunities to return to your site.

Basically, newsletters are not waiting for customers to come back to your website. They bring the website to the customer. Once they have opened the newsletter, they are only one mouse click away from returning to your website. Of course, within the newsletter, you may have promotional content designed to entice customers to make that mouse click.

Customized "Alerts"

The first two types of email can be targeted to the specific interests of different segments on your opt-in list. But they do not have to be. The third type of email, on the other hand, makes extensive use of the Internet's ability to provide customized information to each person.

Your website may contain useful information that changes on a regular basis. If your customers have reason to need, or want the updated information, you can send it to them in the form of *alerts*. A comparison shopping website could offer weekly "deal alerts" with coupons found that week on various eRetail websites.

Now, emails are basically just web pages. They contain blocks of content that can be dynamically filled in for each recipient. In other words, a deal alerts mailer could be filled in with different deals based on the category preferences filled in by each person on the mailing list.

You can also allow users on your website to enter a search criteria for information that interests them. Then you can send email alerts to them with updated results of their search query. This is very common. There is a good chance you are receiving one right now. Dating services send updates of new matches meeting their members' search criteria. Real estate websites offer alerts of new homes. Career websites send job openings. eRetail stores send alerts with products on sale or clearance.

With customized alerts, the website is doing the work for the customer. If the search results are relevant, customers will appreciate the service. It will build loyalty and positive word of mouth. Even more, you are taking your products and services right to the customer. You continue to give them more reasons to buy from you. You also stay on top of their mind until they are ready to make a purchase.

Loyalty Rewards

The most famous loyalty rewards programs are the frequent flier miles programs with the airlines. Each time you fly, you get one point per mile. Then you can redeem the points for future flights. The point of a program like this is to give you an incentive to keep using the airline. But the bigger reason is to give you an incentive NOT to use a competitor airline. After all, you are not getting a bonus for using them are you?

It is not only the airlines who use frequent buyer points. Almost any business selling a product or service can find a way to offer rewards to loyal customers. Coffee shops give you a punch card for one free cup with every ten. Car washes, barbershops and tanning salons all do the same. Your favorite restaurant may give you a free desert after you have spent more than $75 with them.

These rewards are meant to be used. When customers return to the coffee shop to claim their free cup of coffee, they may also buy a pastry. They may also bring their friends. The loyalty rewards really only work if people use them. So these businesses may also collect their customer's email address and send them a reminder.

You can do the same thing with your online business. It works basically the same way as customized alerts. You will create a series of email messages that correspond to different point levels. Then, each day or week, the campaign will run. It simply goes through your email list and reads the amount of points each customer has. Then it sends the email corresponding to that point level (or no email at all).

Loyalty rewards emails not only keep customers coming back. They also get more and more invested with your business every time they do.

Viral Marketing Emails

Viral marketing emails are meant to be passed along. With viral marketing, you are creating something of value to your customers, such as an eBook, an article, a video download or a game. If you succeed in creating a viral marketing message that your site users like, they will pass it along to their friends. When you send it to your mail list, it does not stop there. They send it to their friends. And they send it to their friends. And so on. And so on. The email takes on a life of its own. Along with the main object of the email (the fun or useful thing) the email will also contain a promotional message for your business along with a special offer or an incentive to click thru to your website.

Viral marketing is discussed in detail in Chapter 10.

Spam and Privacy Regulations

The first thing that comes to many people's minds when they hear the word "email" is Spam. We all get unwanted emails almost every day. I am sure you can picture your inbox filled with unwanted Spam. You usually do not know who it came from or how they got your email address. The chances that you will actually click on their link and respond to their message are pretty slim. More than that, if you do recognize who sent the Spam, you will become angry at them. You may even take some kind of action, like submitting their website to your ISP as a Spammer. This will lead to future email coming from them being filtered out and blocked by your ISP servers. This is called being *blacklisted*. The ISP will not deliver email from a blacklisted source.

The first thing to know if you are thinking of using email for your business is DO NOT SPAM! People hate Spam. If you have a legitimate business, it is not only ineffective, but will actually hurt you. It damages your reputation and you will lose customers. It is also illegal.

If you have decided to send email from your business, you must be concerned about Spam and customer privacy. It is good business practice. It is also the law. Gone are the days when you could just collect email addresses and send out emails. You must take care only to mail people, or businesses, who have asked to receive your email. You must take measures to secure the privacy of any information you collect as part of your email list. Failure to do so can result in large fines. You may also find your emails being blacklisted from major ISP servers.

You may never send out an email campaign by casually sending it to some of your customers. You could still find yourself being labeled as a Spammer, if you are not careful to get their permission first.

Anti-Spam Law

The most important thing you must know about Spam is the law. Spam is illegal in the United States. At the federal level, email is regulated by the Federal Trade Commission (FTC). As of the writing of this book, the law being enforced is the CAN-SPAM Act of 2003 (Controlling the Assault of Non-Solicited Pornography and Marketing Act). Before beginning any email campaign, it is a good idea to familiarize yourself with the requirements of this law.

You may be planning to send email to wireless devices, such as PDA's (personal digital assistants) or cell phones. If so, you may also be subject to laws regarding telephone privacy. This is regulated by the Federal Communications Commission (FCC). As of the writing of this book, telephone privacy is regulated under the Telephone Consumer Protection Act (TCPA).

You can find the most current federal laws at **www.ftc.gov** and **www.fcc.gov**.

You should also check to see if there are any additional laws regarding email in your state.

Email Best Practices Resources

Following the minimum requirements of the law will keep you out of jail. It may not, however, be enough to keep your customers happy. The Direct Marketing Association (DMA) is the main organization in the United States that supports the direct mail and email industry. The DMA has published guidelines for email best practices. These should also be considered as required reading prior to beginning any email marketing activities.

You can find guidelines for responsible email practices at **www.dma.org**.

Successful Email Marketing
In Seven Easy Steps!

Email is the most effective way to build online relationships with a group of loyal customers who will return over and over again to your website. An often quoted marketing statistic is that it costs five times as much to gain a new customer as it costs to retain an existing customer. It is a tried and true rule of marketing success to nurture relationships with existing customers so they will

Seven Steps to Successful Email Marketing
Step 1: Build your opt-in list
Step 2: Target your list
Step 3: Get your email opened
Step 4: Create effective email documents
Step 5: Create effective landing pages
Step 6: Respect your customers' privacy -- Do Not Spam
Step 7: Monitor and improve

Figure 7.1

continue to buy from you. Another rule of marketing says that prospective customers do not always buy on their first visit. Often, it takes repeated contacts before a new customer makes their first purchase. In both of these cases, effective use of email will keep your customers interested until they make the purchase. By opting-in new and existing customers to your email list, you can maintain communications that build the customer relationship over time. This will result in sales and repeat sales.

Every email campaign has seven things in common. Whether you are sending your message to a list of prospects or to your loyal customers, the secret to email marketing success is found in following these seven easy steps.

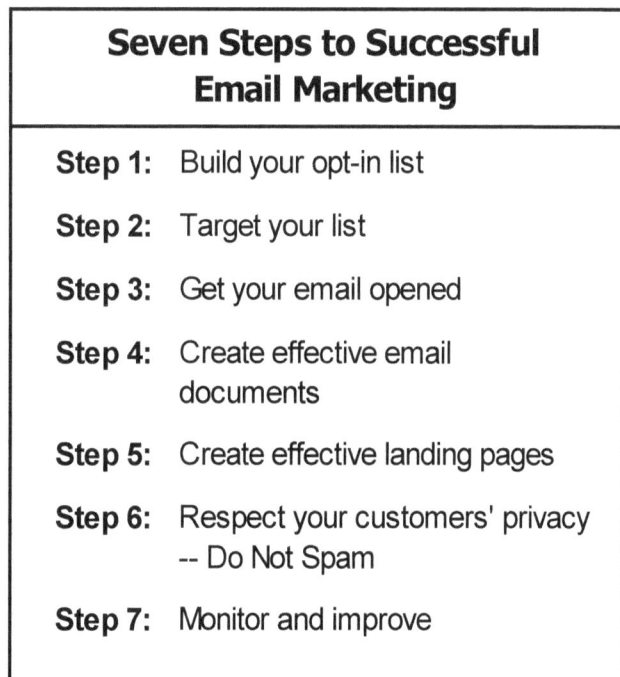

Step 1:
Build Your Opt-In List

The first and most important thing you must do when setting up an email program is to build your list. An opt-in email list is one of the most important marketing assets an online business has. These are people who can continue to be drawn back to your website over and over again.

Winning email strategies start with people who have expressed interest in your products or services and have asked to receive email from you. The only way to get a group of people like this is to ask them to opt-in to your email list.

Building your opt-in email list is not that difficult.

1.   **Make It Easy to Subscribe**

First, you must make it easy for people to find and subscribe to your list. There are many ways to recruit subscribers to your email list. You can set up an affiliate program to recruit subscribers from other websites. You can create a viral marketing campaign with a newsletter opt-in promotion. You can have a sweepstakes that requires an email address to be entered, with the option to opt-in to your newsletter. The place to start however, is to make sure it is easy for users on your website to opt in for your email list as part of their site visit. A few basic guidelines will help attract email subscribers from among your site visitors.

✓ Have your subscription form prominently displayed throughout your site
✓ Include subscription options at checkout or site registration
✓ Have a compelling graphic and call to action in your subscription content block
✓ Do not ask for any more information than needed

This last point requires a little explanation. You may want to provide customization options in your email program. Do not do this on the first form. Asking a lot of information up front will turn people off. Rather, simply ask for an email address and maybe their name. Then you take them to a second, confirmation screen where you can ask them to qualify their interests. But make sure this is presented as a service to them. Let them know that this information is optional and will only be used to send them emails that are of interest to them.

2. Give People a Reason to Subscribe

Second, give people a reason to subscribe to your list. It really cannot be said enough. People hate Spam. You must let your audience know what they will receive in your emails that will be a benefit to them. Will you offer free tips and advice? Will you give updates or news about something that interests them? Will you have coupons and special deals? Whatever it is, let them know as part of your call to action.

Beyond this, you can have a special offer to entice people to subscribe. You can offer a free eBook or a sweepstakes entry. Any freebie that you think your target audience will like to receive can be used. However, keep in mind that your goal is to sign up subscribers who really want what you will offer in your emails. A list for list's sake is not your goal. Conversions resulting from emails sent to your list is the goal.

3. Ease Their Fears

Third, assure your subscribers' privacy. Even more than people hate Spam, they are afraid of identity theft. Assure people right up front that you will take care to ensure their privacy. The issue of privacy is discussed in more detail below. The important point here is to make sure people feel confident enough about their privacy when viewing your opt-in opportunity that they will subscribe. This may include:

✓ Stating up front how you will protect their information
✓ Providing a link to your privacy policy
✓ Using a double opt-in method (described below)
✓ Not asking for more information than needed

Step 2:
Target Your List

Now you have a list of people who want to receive email from you. The next thing you must do is to match your message and offer to the needs and interests of the recipients. You may have a variety of products or messages you will be promoting to your customers. It is likely that all of your customers will not be interested in every message. If you send every email to your entire list, you run the risk of burning out your audience. They will get tired of receiving emails that do not interest them and will simply stop opening emails from you. You can avoid doing this in two ways.

1.   List Targeting

First, you narrow the selection of people who will receive your email message to only those who are likely to respond to it. This is called *list targeting*. An easy way to target your emails is by simply asking people their interests when they opt in for your list. Then simply respect people's preferences and only email them messages related to those self-identified interests.

2.   Segmentation

Second, you can divide your list into different groups, or *segments*, that will receive different versions of the email message. In this way you target the message and/or offer to the specific interests of the sub-groups. This is called *segmentation*. You can create mail segments using the same set of interests customers identify when they opt in to your list. You can also segment your lists using any other useful information you have about them. A common technique is to send different messages to current customers than the ones sent to those who have not yet purchased from you. Another common technique is to create different messages based on how much business they have done with you.

Step 3:
Get Your Email Opened

After having a good targeted list, the next most important thing you must do is make sure people open the email. People get a lot of email in their inbox. They do not open many of them. There are three keys to getting people to open your email.

1. Be Someone Reliable

First, be someone reliable. When people are deciding whether to open an email, the first place they look is to see who sent the message. You can create customized "From" labels that sound more appealing. Instead of just saying "XYZ Company," you could address your emails from, "Bonus Rewards from XYZ Company." Still, the most important thing is to make sure the first thing recipients see is the name of a business or organization they know and have opted into.

Notice, the point is to "be" someone reliable. This does not include "pretending to be" someone reliable. It is not good business practice to cover up your identity. It is also against the law.

2. Have a Compelling Subject Line

Second, have a compelling subject line. The second thing people do is to look at whether the subject line is something that is of interest. You only have about 30 characters of space to be exciting or important enough for them to think your email is worth their time.

Once again, it is both good business practice and the law to be honest in your subject lines. Care must also be taken to create compelling subject lines that avoid using words or phrases that will be filtered out as Spam from your recipients' ISPs. For example, avoid using phrases like, "FREE" or "BUY NOW." These can cause your email to be dumped into the "bulk email" box or blocked altogether.

3.   Send Email When People Will Open It

Third, timing is critical with email. Most people tend to read their emails during the workweek. The worst time to send your email is Friday night. It will arrive on Saturday and probably sit in their inbox until Monday morning when they look at email again. By then, their inbox has filled up with emails and they do not have time to read them all. The best time to send your emails is Monday night or Tuesday. That way, they arrive in your customers' inboxes mid-week when they have the most time to read and respond to them.

Step 4:
Create Effective Email Documents

Once people have opened your email, you have to grab their attention with an email document that is both interesting enough to read and compelling enough to generate a response. Of course, a big part of this is writing good advertising copy and creative design. In addition to copy and creative design, all effective email documents must follow four key considerations.

1.   Fit Inside Their Email Browser

First, it is important to understand how your email message will appear on the recipient's computer screen. Most email clients block off a large part of the top and left side of the computer screen for navigation. Your email documents must fit in the width that remains. People hate to scroll to the right when they are online. Equally important is the height of the document. All of your key messaging, call to action and offer should be displayed in the area the recipient can see when they first open the email documents. This is called being *above the fold*. It is perfectly okay to have more content below the fold. But readers will only scroll down to find it if what they see above the fold is compelling enough to keep their attention.

2.   Have an Offer

The second important consideration is having an offer. People respond to offers. You usually do not have to offer something big or expensive. But you usually do have to provide an offer. Offer an incentive that will be of value to your email recipients. Test different offers to see which ones get the best response. Then stick with the best ones.

3.   Have a Call to Action

Unless your email is purely informational, it should have a call to action. This is the third consideration. Craft the main message to have as little text as possible. Get them excited. This short message should lead them right to the call to action. Along with the call to action they should prominently see the offer they will receive if they take that action.

4.   Have a Way to Respond

Finally, your call to action must include the ability to click thru directly to a page where they can complete their response. You may have a great product and a great offer, but if you do not make it easy for them to respond, they probably will not. When you design your email campaign, you must have prominently displayed links and design the pages your links will take responders to. These are called *landing pages*.

Step 5:
Create Effective Landing Pages

What result do you need to get from your email campaign? Do you want immediate sales? Do you want to sign up potential customers to a new service? Do you want potential customers to fill out a form for you to follow up with them later?

The immediate result from an email message is the *click-thru*. All emails have links to your website that can be clicked. Is this all you want, for people to see your site? No! You want them to do something when they get there? Based on what you want them to do, you must design the path they will take after the click. Lead them to that action in as few clicks as possible. This will typically be done by creating a special landing page for the email campaign or deep linking directly to a page on your site where they can carry out the desired action.

A critical part of an email campaign is the landing page. The email message should have a prominently displayed link, or clickable graphic image. Clicking on the link is only the first step. Once the readers do, they should be dropped onto a landing page that also has a compelling message and opportunity to carry out the call to action. If you want them to buy a promotional item, then they should land directly on a page where they can make the purchase and claim the offer.

An email message that lands on your home page or a generic product page will be a roadblock on the path to your call to action. People may click on the link, but then abort before the pay-off.

Step 6:
Respect Your Customers' Privacy -- Do Not Spam

Before you begin email marketing, you must make sure to reference the most current laws regarding email marketing and Spam. In the United States, email is regulated by the Federal Trade Commission (FTC). As of the writing of this book, the law on the books is the CAN-SPAM Act of 2003. You must be sure to read the requirements of this law and make sure you are in compliance with it. It can be found at **www.ftc.gov**. You should also check to see if there are any applicable laws in your state and check **www.fcc.gov** if you plan to send email to wireless devices.

In addition to the law, all email marketers should follow the Direct Marketing Association (DMA) guidelines for email best practices. These are published by the DMA Council for Responsible Email. They can be found at **www.dma.org**.

The general requirements for responsible email can be summed up in the following five points. This is meant to give you an idea of what to expect, and should not be taken as a substitute to learning the law and DMA best practices for yourself. The laws and accepted best practices can also change over time. Therefore, you should always verify the most up to date requirements before beginning your email program.

1.   Use a "Double Opt-In" Method to Build Your List

Before you send any marketing emails to an email address you have collected, you must receive permission to do so. You may have collected an email address as part of creating a customer order. That does not mean you can use that email address. You cannot, unless the person tells you it is okay.

One way of obtaining permission to send marketing emails is by offering an email subscription. In this case, you have a content block promoting your email. Users know they are opting in, because they are being asked to enter their email address for this service. Another way of obtaining permission is to offer email options with checkboxes next to them. This could be done if the email address is being collected for some other purpose, when becoming a customer for example. When the user checks any of these boxes, they are opting in for the associated email. It used to be a common practice to have the box pre-checked. Then the user would have to actively un-check the box or else they would be opted-in. This is called *negative opt-in*. Today, negative opt-in is not considered a legitimate form of gaining permission. It should not be done.

After you have received permission to send marketing email, you should confirm that permission. This is called *double opt-in*. The most common form of double opt-in is to immediately send an email to the address you collected. Within that email, notify the user that you have just received an opt-in for their email address. In order to activate their subscription, they must take some action. This confirms their opt-in. The action should be as simple as returning the email or clicking a link to confirm their opt in. By receiving this confirmation of an opt-in, you offer an added measure of security and privacy to your opted-in email recipients. It also will help to make sure your list only contains people who want to receive email from you. If they do not want to confirm their opt-in status, then they probably will also not want to respond to your emails. They may consider them as Spam.

2.   Provide an Easy Way to Opt-Out

Not only must people opt-in to your list, they must also be able to opt-out of it. This is the law. This is also good business practice. An email program is all about building profitable relationships with your customers. If you make it hard for them to stop receiving your emails, you will just make them mad at you. This is exactly the opposite effect from what your program is trying to do.

Every email you send should have a link at the bottom allowing customers to "unsubscribe" from your emails. Clicking this link should take them to a page on your website where they can confirm their opt-out. This will then record the action in your marketing database. You should also auto-generate a confirmation email letting them know that their opt-out has been processed. If you are using an email service, they should have a built-in unsubscribe feature.

3.   Be Diligent About List Hygiene

If you send email to someone who has either not opted-in or has opted-out of your email program, that is Spam! Many people will become very angry at this and will report you to their ISP. That will result in your being blacklisted from being able to send email to any email address hosted by that ISP. It could result in legal penalties. Most businesses have no intention of doing this. Nevertheless, it happens anyway. Mistakes are made. People who are not opted-in may get emails anyway.

The most common cause of emailing those who do not want to receive your email is poor list hygiene practices. Your email list is stored in a database. Often, the opt-in is recorded simply as a single field in the database being set to "yes" or "no." It is possible for email to go out to them anyway. This could happen for a number of reasons. In some cases, the opt-out may generate an auto-response confirmation to the user. However, the change may not be recorded in the database. Another common error occurs in defining the campaign. Your campaign may look to your total email list, and then filter out those who do not have an active opt-in. Sometimes, this little piece of code in your campaign software is left out. The way to avoid this is to set up a process that prevents this from happening. Make sure your back-end systems are set up to check for these type of errors, and correct them BEFORE email goes out.

The best practice for list hygiene is to maintain a separate list of email addresses for those who have opted-in. If you collect email from all of your customers, keep those who have opted-in to your marketing campaigns in a different database. When someone opts-out, delete them. This way, it is impossible to email someone who has not opted-in. Beyond this, you should delete entirely from your system any email addresses that you do not need for a business reason. The best way to prevent inadvertently sending email is to not have the email address in the first place.

4. Identify Yourself

At the core of the CAN-SPAM law is to let email recipients know who you are and where you can be found. Any deception regarding these two issues is against the law. At a minimum, you must provide the following:

✓ Your headers must accurately identify who you are along with the originating domain name and email address.
✓ In the body of the email, you must have a valid physical postal address where you can be found.

The point behind these requirements is obvious. Businesses who are not willing to let people know who they are and where they can be found are probably up to no good.

5. Be Honest About Your Intent

Finally, you must not be misleading in your emails. To risk being repetitive, this is not only against the law, it is bad business practice. Successful email is all about building long term relationships with your customers so they will keep coming back. If people feel as if they have been manipulated into opening an email or clicking on a link, they will just get angry. The minimum requirements for honesty in email are:

✓ You cannot be misleading in your subject lines. They must reveal the actual contents of the message.
✓ If your email is promoting a product or service, it must clearly state somewhere in the body of the message that it is an advertisement and that the recipient can opt-out of any further commercial solicitations.

Step 7:
Monitor and Improve

Did your email result in new sales? Did your email result in new subscriptions? Did some segments of your email list do better than others? Did some offers do better than others? The power of marketing through the Internet is that you can track and measure everything.

When someone clicks on a link in your email message, you can attach a code that gets passed with them to your landing page. This way you know exactly who has clicked your link. You can then pass that code along with every subsequent action they take on your site. This way you can measure your click-thru rate and the resulting actions taken on your site.

There are four critical metrics for an email campaign.

By collecting information about these four metrics, you will know what is working and what is not working. You can then use this information to continuously improve future email campaigns.

Key Email Metrics and Typical Areas for Improvement	
1. Deliverable Addresses	➔ List Hygiene
	Blacklisted
2. Open Rate	➔ Effective Subject Lines
	Effective segmentation & targeting
3. Click-thru Rate	➔ Effective email documents
	Content relevant to subject line
	Content relevant to targeted mail segments
4. Conversion Rate	➔ Effective landing pages
	Broken links
	Unmet expectations

The next section goes into detail about how the technology behind email marketing works. If you do not want to dig this deep into the details, feel free to turn ahead to the next chapter.

Bonus Section:
How Email Marketing Works Under The Hood

To understand how the Internet has turbo-charged direct mail, we must first take a quick look at how email works under the hood. In the next section, we will focus on two key areas where email has advanced beyond its offline print roots: (1) mass customization and (2) real time relationship marketing. These two areas of advance are made possible by the technology platform underlying email campaigns. An understanding of that platform reveals how all of this is possible. However, it may get a little technical. Technical jargon will be kept to a minimum.

This section discusses how email marketing systems work. If you have read up on email before, you might notice something is conspicuously missing from this discussion. There is no attempt made here to describe how the technology behind physically delivering email works. Instead, this section only shows how the technology behind creating an email marketing campaign works. The assumption is that marketers really do not need to know about how the mail physically gets there, just so long as it gets there. However, you do need to know about the technology that allows you, as a marketer, to engage in real time one-to-one marketing with your customers. That is the topic of this section.

There are four components to the typical email system. These are shown in Figure 7.2. The interaction of these sub-systems allows the direct marketing process to be automated and significantly enhanced. These four components are software systems, each handling a different part of the process.

Email systems come in various shapes and sizes. It is technically possible for all four of these sub-systems to run on the same physical computer (server). For some smaller systems, that is exactly what happens.

For larger scale systems, these four components are always separated. Each component runs on one or more separate machines to optimize the performance of email delivery. For a small business, you can send email to your customers and prospects without needing all of this hardware. You can outsource your email program to an email vendor (recommended approach) or you can buy an email system where all of the components run on the same machine. As you are successful, your email program will grow. By understanding how these four components of the email system work, you will be better prepared to scale up your systems as needed to accommodate growth.

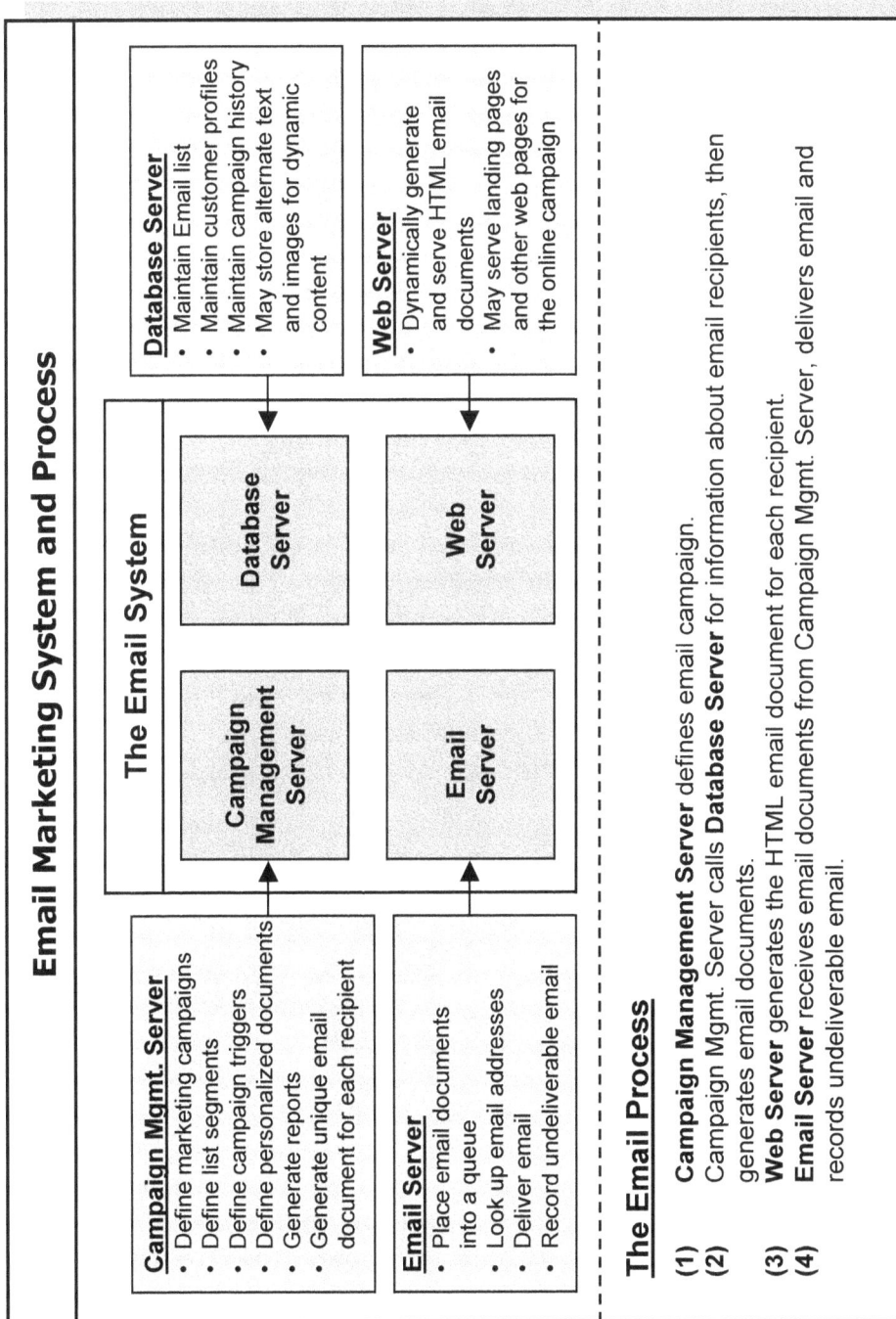

Email Marketing System and Process

The Email System

Database Server
- Maintain Email list
- Maintain customer profiles
- Maintain campaign history
- May store alternate text and images for dynamic content

Web Server
- Dynamically generate and serve HTML email documents
- May serve landing pages and other web pages for the online campaign

Campaign Mgmt. Server
- Define marketing campaigns
- Define list segments
- Define campaign triggers
- Define personalized documents
- Generate reports
- Generate unique email document for each recipient

Email Server
- Place email documents into a queue
- Look up email addresses
- Deliver email
- Record undeliverable email

Campaign Management Server

Database Server

Email Server

Web Server

The Email Process

(1) **Campaign Management Server** defines email campaign.
(2) Campaign Mgmt. Server calls **Database Server** for information about email recipients, then generates email documents.
(3) **Web Server** generates the HTML email document for each recipient.
(4) **Email Server** receives email documents from Campaign Mgmt. Server, delivers email and records undeliverable email.

Figure 7.2

The Campaign Management Software

The heart of any email system is the campaign management software. This is where email campaigns are created and executed. There are five major functions of the campaign management software.

1.   Define Your Email List and Customer Segments

The first part of setting up an email campaign is to tell your email system who will receive the email. The campaign management software will allow you to address your email to the entire mail list or to specific addresses on the list. It will also let you send different versions of the email to different segments of the list. This is the main purpose of the campaign management software.

One of the powerful features of email is the ability to send targeted communications to different recipients. You do this by defining customer segments in your campaign management software. When you set up your campaign, you will also choose the criteria for inclusion in the campaign. The simplest case is to select everyone who has opted in to receive your email. This could come from a checkbox on your customer registration page agreeing to receive a newsletter.

However, you will often want to create targeted mailings for specific groups. You may have a bi-weekly newsletter. On your registration page, you could include checkboxes for a variety of interests. Then you could create different versions of your newsletter based on the interests customers identified. You will use your campaign management software to define which customers get which version. This is done by setting up customer segments when defining your campaign.

Since your campaign management system is linked to your marketing database (discussed below), you can create targeted segments based on any information in the customer profile. You could send different promotions to women versus men. You could give a different offer to loyal customers versus one-time shoppers who signed up for your newsletter.

More advanced email systems allow you to go beyond simply sending different versions to targeted segments. You can define parameters that will identify content elements to be inserted into the email document. Perhaps you are an art broker and have an online store selling fine arts. You could ask your customers what type of art they are interested in: sculpture, painting, mixed media, etc. Then you could create a single email campaign that notifies customers of new art in the categories they selected. When the campaign runs, it will check the marketing database for each recipient, to identify their interests. Then it will search the product database to see if there are any new products in each category they selected. If there is, it will insert the products for those categories into the email document.

2.   Load the Email Document(s)

The next step is to load the email documents themselves into the campaign. This is a fairly straightforward process. The campaign management system will have an option to load your document and identify which segment of the campaign it applies to.

At this point, you must know about different email formats. First is text versus HTML email. Some people do not have the ability to open HTML documents on their home or office computer. Also, with dial up modem connections, it can take a long time to open an HTML email document. This is not as big an issue today as it used to be. However, there are still many users who either cannot or do not want to receive HTML documents in their email. So how do you deal with this situation?

One answer is to offer an option on your email opt-in page where users can choose HTML or text versions of your email. Then you include this as a parameter in your customer segmentation. However, this does not address the case where users log in from different systems. In some cases they will be at a computer that can read the HTML document. In other cases they will not. The answer to this question is to create what is called a *multi-part MIME* document.

MIME is a standard for how documents are formatted when they are transmitted over the Internet. A multi-part MIME document includes multiple formats in the same document. When the recipient opens their email, the browser opens the version that is appropriate for that browser. If the user can only read text, it will open the text document. If they can read HTML, it will open the HTML document.

In addition to text versus HTML, some people will want to receive email on a wireless device. It is very common now for people to receive email on their cell phone, PDA (personal digital assistant) or BlackBerry device. Wireless devices such as these use the Wireless Application Protocol, or WAP, to display documents in their browsers. WAP browsers cannot display HTML files. Instead, they read files written in the Wireless Markup Language (WML). This creates the same basic scenario as text versus HTML. You must create another version of your email document that can be displayed by wireless browsers.

3. Set Up Campaign Timing and Triggers

The next part of your email campaign is to define when it will be sent. When you send an email from your personal email account, you will just hit the "send" button. The email goes out. With an email campaign, this is not such a good idea. We can all remember times when we hit that send button and then regretted it. With email campaigns, you will set a time when the email will start sending. You will usually want to send a test campaign to a few recipients within your business first. That way you can make sure there will be no problems when you send it to the full list.

There are basically two ways to time an email campaign. The first is to send the email out to the entire list all at once. The second kind is sent out in response to triggers. We will start with the simplest case.

For a one-time campaign being sent to your list, you will simply define the campaign and set a time when the campaign will be launched. This is pretty straightforward.

The next case is a campaign that goes out automatically on a given schedule. In our example of the fine arts dealer, the new product announcement could be set up to run automatically. In the campaign managements system, you could set the time to every Monday at 11:00PM, for example. That way, your customers would get the email in their inbox the first thing in the morning every Tuesday. This same technique applies to birthday emails. If you want an email to go out on your customer's birthday, you would have a campaign run every day. It will go through your email list and send an email to everyone whose birthday matches today's date (or some number of days before their birthday).

Next comes an email campaign that is triggered by an event. The most common example of this is an auto-response to some event that occurs on your website. For example, when someone submits a customer complaint through a form on your website, you could trigger a response notifying the customer that their issue was received and they would be contacted within a given period of time to resolve it. There are a couple of different ways email systems can set up triggers. The key thing is the ability to set up campaigns that can be launched dynamically based on triggering events.

4.   Capture Results and Maintain Campaign History

In addition to defining campaigns to be sent, the campaign management system will also maintain a record of all campaigns that have been run. This is called the *campaign history*. When you send out your email, a record is created in your marketing database for every person who the email was sent to. So you will have a record of everyone who you sent email to and when. But this in itself is not very useful. You want to know how effective your email was.

When you set up your campaign, you will also identify a number of metrics that will be recorded in your campaign history, along with the fact that an email was sent. The most basic metrics are bounce-backs and responses. This is one place where all four components of your email system work together. The email server (discussed below) will try to send out every email. If it is unable to deliver one, or more of those emails, it will record it as an undeliverable email address. This is known as a *bounce back*. Some campaign management systems will receive this information from the email server and write it into the campaign history.

For emails that do get through, you want to know what happens when people receive them. This is where the web server (discussed below) comes in. For HTML emails, when a recipient opens the email, it can be set up to call your web server to serve a tiny, invisible image into the HTML page. The web server records this. Some campaign management systems will also record it in your campaign history. You will have a metric for opened emails. Next, when someone clicks on a link in your email, a web page is served. In some cases, that page will also be served by the email system. This event is also recorded and can be put into the campaign history. This gives you a metric for responses. By using the web server associated with your campaign management system, you can set up a variety of things to record in your campaign history. This will be discussed below in a section on the web server.

5.   Generate Reports

Finally, your campaign management system will generate reports. Basically, anything that has been captured into the campaign history can be reported on. How much reporting is available will be a function of your campaign management system. Some provide very little reporting. Others let you to build elaborate customized reports.

The Marketing Database

Behind the campaign management software sits a marketing database. This is the database where you store your customer list and all the information about your customers that is needed to run campaigns. There are three core components in the typical marketing database.

1.   **Customer List(s)**

Your marketing database is fundamentally a database of customers and prospects. At the core, it is a list. The simplest version of a marketing database would be a simple list of everyone who opted in to your email list and their email addresses. However, this would not allow much flexibility with your email program. Most marketing databases will also include a lot of information about each customer on the list. The general rule is that everything you might need to know to effectively market to your customers should be in the marketing database. This information is sometimes called the *customer profile*.

2.   **Customer Profile**

The customer profile refers to a set of fields in the database with information about each customer. Perhaps you have an email program for your company consisting of a weekly newsletter and birthday rewards. When customers sign up for your email, you give them the opportunity to choose which of these they want to receive. You also ask them some basic product interests that you will use to target the newsletter content. A fairly basic marketing database will contain the name and email address of each recipient plus fields for each of these options.

This basic customer profile will be quite sufficient for many email programs. However, if you want to get more sophisticated, you can include almost anything you want in the customer profile. You could include demographics such as age and income. You could create custom segmentation codes based on how much money they spend with your company or how long they have been a customer. For almost anything you can conceive, you could probably find a way to get it into the marketing database. Once there, you can use it to create targeted email campaigns.

Another important thing stored in your marketing database is information that will be used as triggers for relationship marketing emails. This could be your customer's birthday. It could be special days they identified when they need to make gift purchases. If you offer financial services, it could be the stock value when they want their stock to be sold. Once again, almost anything you can think of can be stored in the database.

One caution about your marketing database is to take special care with information that may be subject to your privacy policy. Websites and email programs are subject to strict enforcement of privacy concerns. In other words, people do not want their personal information being made public. Now most companies do not willfully violate their customers' privacy concerns but accidents do happen. We have all heard news stories about organizations who have had their computers hacked into or accidentally released information about their customers. You must be vigilant against this happening to you. The first line of defense is to take care to ensure the security of your customer data and the computers it sits on.

3.   Campaign History

The marketing database will include a record of every campaign that is sent out. This was discussed above. You will have a record of each campaign, of each recipient of those campaigns and a variety of metrics you have chosen to measure. By having this information, you will be able to measure the success or failure of your email campaigns. You will also be able to measure trends and continuously improve your email program.

A simple way to understand the campaign history component of your marketing database is to think of it as consisting of two tables. A *table* is basically the same thing as a spreadsheet with rows and columns. In the first table, you have one row for each campaign. It shows the basic details of the campaign, including the name, description and timing of the campaign. In the second table, you have a row for each recipient of each campaign. Clearly, this is the bigger table. In fact, it can get quite huge. There will be one row for each person on your email list every time they receive an email. It will record the campaign they received plus all of the metrics you set up to be measured for that campaign.

By having all of this information in one place, you will be able to do analysis about both campaigns and customers. You can see how well campaigns work with different types of offers. You can see if your emails are more likely to be opened if they are sent on different days or have different subject lines. You can see if different customer segments respond better than others. Having all of this information in one place allows you to easily create a set of reports that can be used to continuously monitor and improve your email program.

The Web Server

For any given email campaign, one or more HTML documents will be created and loaded into the campaign management system. When the email is sent out, an HTML document is sent out to the recipient. This is actually an HTML web page that is served by your web server. The web server loads the HTML document plus all images and other files to be displayed, just as if it were serving a page on your website. The only difference is the page is served into the email document. The web server will generate a complete email document for each recipient as the email is being sent out. A common technique is to also include in the document a call for a tiny, invisible image to be served from the web server when the user opens the email. This allows an *open rate* to be calculated for the email campaign.

In more advanced systems, the web server will sometimes be used to also generate the landing pages for links in the email document. This gives you more flexibility in customizing landing pages based on parameters in the email campaign. The campaign management system can recognize the customer identifier carried by the email link and tell the web server exactly what landing page to serve. (This can still be done without linking the web server to the campaign management system, but it requires extensive use of parameters in the linking URLs from the email message.)

An even more significant reason for serving web pages through the email campaign itself is that it allows the campaign management system to track every action that occurs after the customer clicks thru. Some companies will include copies of all the key pages, all the way through the conversion event. In addition to ease of tracking results, content on the pages can be tailored to reflect the marketing messaging in the email campaign.   This capability of more advanced campaign management systems also allows email agencies to offer a much more robust service to clients who want to outsource a larger integrated marketing program.

The Email Server

The final component to the email system is the email server itself.   This system does nothing except send out emails.

When the campaign management system starts running the campaign, it creates a separate document for each and every recipient on the mail list. This includes at least a minimum of personalization in the email address and the opening greeting. In some cases, there will be customized documents generated for each customer based on preferences they entered when subscribing to the email.

These email documents are queued up in the email server. They are then sent out one at a time. The email server checks the email address and attempts to deliver the email. It will record all of the successful deliveries. Unsuccessful deliveries (called *bounce backs*) are also recorded. The list of bounce backs is usually used to purge the email list of bad email addresses. For example, if an address cannot be reached in three successive campaigns, it may be tagged as a dead email address. By removing it from the list, you will reduce the load on your email server in future campaigns.

Now let us see how all four components of the email system work together.

Mass Customization

One of the most powerful features of email is the ability to customize messages to each subscriber. Most email documents today are in HTML. That means your email message is a web page. All of the customization that you are able to do on a web page can also be done with email. We saw how this works above. You can ask your subscribers to provide information about themselves and their email preferences. This information can then be included in their customer profile. When the email is sent out, the campaign management software searches the marketing database for the parameters associated with each subscriber's profile. Then content is inserted, by the web server, into the HTML page based on those parameters.

You may receive emails like this yourself. A common type of customized email is to allow users to enter a search criteria for information that interests them. For example, a real estate website could allow users to enter search criteria for the type of home they want to purchase. Then an email could be sent out with new listings matching that criteria. This could be a weekly email. Or it could be sent out only when new listings appear that match their criteria. In this second case, the campaign could actually run every day, but only send email to those where search results are found meeting the user's criteria.

Real Time Relationship Marketing

The last section has shown how the email system can create a customized email for each subscriber. Now let us see how it also allows you to use triggers to send out those emails at times that are customized to the needs of your relationship with each customer.

We saw above how a subscriber's search criteria can be used as a trigger to send email to them. They simply enter the criteria for information they want to receive and the email system sends an email whenever that search returns results matching their search. There are also other ways to trigger email based on needs the customer identifies within their customer profile. These can include:

✓ Reminder programs (for example, it is time for an oil change)
✓ Emails based on triggering events (for example, a product that interests them appears in current inventory)
✓ Emails based on special events on the calendar (for example, their birthdays)

Next, is email triggered not by information defined in the user profile, but by events that occur on the website or with the online business. Examples of this type of triggering event include:

- ✓ Customer reaches a certain level in their reward points program
- ✓ Customer exceeds a certain sales volume and qualifies for a discount, or a loyalty reward
- ✓ Customer buys certain items and receives coupons for other related items
- ✓ Customer fails to return to make a purchase after a certain amount of time and receives an incentive to return or an inquiry about the customer service experience.

Message for Email Managers

For the general reader, the preceding discussion about back-end email technology is helpful. It lets you better understand some of the things you can do with email. However, if you are responsible for running an email program, this section can save you a lot of headaches.

If you have anything more than a very small business, there is a good chance your email program will quickly outgrow the original system you set up. This brief description of the back end technology will give you a good idea of how to scale up your system when you begin to encounter bottlenecks.

There are three typical bottlenecks you may run into. Maybe you already have?

First, you may have so many emails to send out, they do not all get out fast enough. Perhaps you have an email newsletter that goes out once a week. It is not unheard of, when your list grows quickly, for it to take longer than a week for your system to get all those emails out. In some cases, it may even crash your system. This is a rude awakening when first it happens. The first place to look for a solution is your email server. It is likely that your email queue is just too long. There are probably settings on your system that can help optimize the speed of this system. But you may still just have too many emails. You can fix this bottleneck by adding more email servers.

If you are not having problems with long email queues jamming up your email server throughput, then you may have a problem in how you configured your campaigns. This is the second common bottleneck. It is very tempting to use a lot of customization in your emails. You can literally make a unique email document for each customer. However, doing this requires your campaign management system to take a lot of extra time processing each and every message. It will have to make database calls to your marketing database to find the correct parameters for each customizable element on the email. If you have used a lot of customization, it may just be taking too long to generate each email before it gets sent to the queue. One way to fix this is to simply scale down the amount of customization you put into each email. If this is not an option for you, then you can buy a faster machine to house your campaign management software and perhaps also for your marketing database.

A third common bottleneck is for your large campaigns to so overload your system that your smaller campaigns never get out. Perhaps you have a weekly email newsletter with special coupons and offers. This email takes three days to send to the entire list. But you also have a birthday campaign where you send a special message to each customer on their birthday. You may find that while the weekly campaign is running, none of the birthday greetings are getting out. Well, you don't want people getting a Happy Birthday message two days after their birthdays. What do you do? This one is usually pretty easy. Most campaign management systems will have priority settings that regulate which email gets sent out first. You can set your birthday mailer at a higher priority than your weekly mailer. That way, it will make sure the birthday mailer gets out, even if it is in the middle of sending out the larger campaign. Another part of the solution to this problem is often to buy a separate email server dedicated just to these time sensitive campaigns. If you keep running everything off the same email server(s), your campaign management software will send out the time sensitive email in the middle of the larger mailing. Still, it has to wait until the entire queue ahead of it gets through the email server. This may be okay for a daily birthday reminder. But it may not be okay for an auto response for a customer service inquiry.

There are other bottlenecks and problems that may arise. This section by no means gives you all the answers. Hopefully, though, you will at least have an idea of the kind of issues you may encounter and where to look for the solution. When you do get to the point of needing an email system that runs on multiple servers, you will need a system administrator who is familiar with these systems. This may be adding a level of complexity you do not want to take on yourself. A better option for many companies is to outsource your email program to an agency specializing in email marketing.

Conclusion

In this chapter, you have learned how email marketing works. You know how to be successful using email to reach out to an opt-in mail list, bringing them back over and over again to make purchases from your website.

Now turn to the next chapter and learn how to be successful with Online Advertising.

Chapter 8
Advertising Online

In this chapter, you will learn . . .
- What online advertising is all about
- How to be successful with online advertising
- How online advertising works under the hood

And Then There Were Click-Thrus
The HotWired Banner Ad Story

The first *banner ad* appeared on the HotWired website on October 25, 1994. Clickable online ads had first been used the previous year, by a website called Global Network Navigator. But it was HotWired (the content website of Wired Magazine) who gave them a name. HotWired coined the term "banner ad." It was HotWired who first sold banner ads on a large scale. It was HotWired who first reported ad results in terms of a "click-thru rate." This was the birth of what quickly became a multi-billion dollar Online Advertising industry.

Online Advertising exploded between 1994 and 1999. Many Dot-Com fortunes were made by the revenue from banner ads in those years. Then the bottom fell out. Starting in 2000, the numbers started coming in. Click-thru rates dropped as the novelty of online ads gave way to annoyance. It also became clear that actual conversions resulting from click-thrus were dramatically lower than had been expected. The resulting collapse of cost-per-impression and cost-per-click ad revenues was one of the major factors leading to the general collapse of the Dot-Com revolution. It spelled the end of the so called, "New Economy."

For a while, it seemed as if the emperor had no clothes. As it turned out, he did after all. It took a few years, but eventually advertisers discovered that the rules of direct marketing rather than general advertising held the key to successful online advertising. Today, online advertising is healthy and growing, even if the giddy excitement of its early days has been replaced by pragmatic realism.

The crash, and slow recovery of online advertising in those days teaches lessons that must be learned by everyone hoping to bring traffic to their websites by serving online ads. Online advertising must be approached as a direct marketing medium, not as general advertising. Online ads are successful for the advertiser when they result in conversions on the website. Click-thru and conversion rates must be vigilantly monitored otherwise money is being wasted.

The ABC's Of Online Advertising

Online advertising is the online equivalent of placing ads in a magazine or newspaper. As with everything on the Internet, though, this is just the beginning. The Internet provides opportunities to go beyond simply placing ads and hoping people respond when they see them.

In some ways, a website is very much like a magazine. It has a fixed amount of real estate. Some parts are set aside for content. Other parts are set aside for advertisements. You advertise on websites that attract the same kind of people who will be interested in your product or service. On the other hand, a website is very much like a targeted direct mail list. Users on the website can be segmented by what actions they take on the site. Also, as with direct mail, online ads produce an immediate and measurable response, the click-thru.

The first and most important key to being successful with online advertising is to recognize that, in spite of its name, what you are really doing is direct marketing.

Being Successful with Online Advertising

Online ads should be treated as the envelope of a direct mail piece. Your goal is to get it opened – for people to click thru to a promotional landing page. This may seem counter-intuitive. Online advertising starts with ad real estate on websites. So far, this is just like offline print advertising. You place ads in magazines whose readership you think will also be interested in your products or services. You also place ads on websites whose viewers you think will be interested in your products or services.

You can see the difference between online advertising and print advertising by the expected results advertisers have for the two. With print advertising, as with all general advertising, advertisers pay for *impressions* rather than *responses*. That is to say, they want their ad to be seen by as many people as possible. But, they do not expect an immediate response from each ad. Creating awareness is as important as eliciting immediate action. Companies may place ads in magazines, newspapers, television and radio. The expected results are not necessarily generated by any one ad. Instead, the cumulative effect of repeated exposure to the marketing message creates a change in behavior.

By contrast, online ads tend to be fairly ineffective at generating brand awareness. People are much more likely to "tune out" banners on a website than ads in traditional offline media. Awareness is still a goal for some online advertisers, but a secondary goal. Instead, online ads are most effective when people click on them. This is why online advertising is more a form of direct marketing than a form of general advertising.

This requires a little explanation.

Opening a Virtual Envelope

Online ads are more like the outside of a mailer you receive in your mailbox than like a print advertisement in your favorite magazine. Think of a banner ad. This is typical of what online ads do. The goal of a banner ad is to get you to click on the ad – open the envelope. Once you do, all of the other aspects of a direct marketing campaign come into play. You will be directed to a marketing piece presented on the landing page. It will have a call to action and maybe an offer. All responses and conversions will be tracked and evaluated. Based on these results, future online media buys will be modified and improved.

The key metrics for online advertising are measured in click-thrus and conversions not in number of impressions.

Successful Online Advertising In Seven Easy Steps!

In 2005, advertisers spent $12.5 billion on online advertising. It was an increase from $9.6 billion in 2004 and $7.3 billion in 2003 (source IAB PwC report Q2 2006). On-line advertising is an important part of the Internet Marketing strategy for so many companies because it works. It can work for you. However, it must be approached with care.

The Internet is a collection of highly

Seven Steps to Successful Online Advertising
Step 1: Define your target
Step 2: Choose how you will serve your ads
Step 3: Choose what type of ads to serve
Step 4: Choose how you want to pay for your ads
Step 5: Create your ads
Step 6: Create effective landing pages
Step 7: Monitor and improve

Figure 8.1

targeted websites with even more highly targeted web pages. Placing your ad on the right web pages will get your message in front of motivated buyers who are interested in your products and services. But, paying to

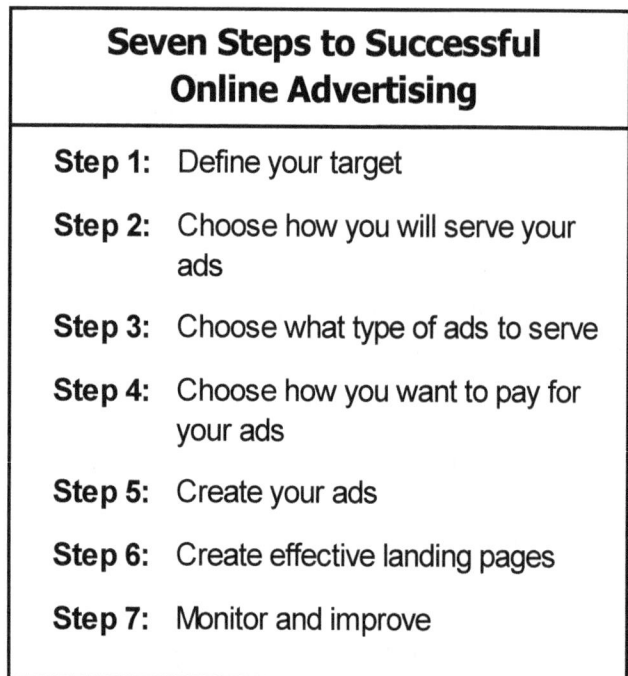

place your ad on the wrong web pages can be like throwing confetti in the wind. You might not get clicks to your website at all. You might get clicks, but once on your site, they may not convert to sales.

The secret to successful online advertising is found in following these seven easy steps.

Step 1:
Define Your Target

When placing online ads, you are looking for websites where people go who are likely to respond to your marketing promotion. To do this, you first have to identify the type of people who will be interested in your products or services. In marketing terms, you will be identifying the *demographics* and *psychographics* of your target market.

1.   Demographics

Demographics are descriptive characteristics of those who are your potential customers. Included are such things as their age, income and marital status. Whatever descriptive information that will help figure out who you want to reach should be researched.

2.   Psychographics

Psychographics relate to what motivates your potential customers. The basic psychographics marketers collect are interests and life-styles. In other words, what do your customers do and how do they live their lives?

Once you identify the demographics and psychographics of your target market, you can find websites that reach people with those same profiles. These are the sites where you will want to advertise.

Step 2:
Choose How You Will Serve Your Ads

The second step is to decide how you will go about getting your ads placed. You have two choices. You can do it yourself or you can have someone else do it for you.

1.   Buy Media with an Ad Server Network

The most common way to buy online ads is to go through an *Ad Server Network*. These companies keep an inventory of available ad placements for websites across the Internet. They also maintain profile information about the kind of users who go to the websites with available ad space. This information allows you to target who sees your ads. By working through an ad server network, you can buy ads with one company and have your messages appear on a large variety of websites.

Ad server networks offer a service to both ad buyers and sellers. If you have available space on your web pages, you can let the ad server network manage that real estate for you. You give them the specifications of the type of ad that can be placed. When a user visits that web page, there is a piece of programming code that tells the page to ask the ad server network to supply the image or text that should appear. The ad server network tracks how many people click-thru, provides reporting and manages billing for the ads.

2.   Place Your Own Ads

Buying ads yourself is a tricky and time consuming process. It should be undertaken with caution. If you have a very targeted market for your website, then it might be worth doing your own research to find other websites who cater to the same audience. Then you can find out from them how to buy ad space on their sites.

Step 3:
Choose What Type of Ads to Serve

The third step is to choose what type of online ad you want. Online ads come mainly in four varieties.

1. Banner Ads

The most well known form of online ad is the banner ad. Banner ads are a square or rectangle on the target website where your ad is placed. In the early days of Internet Marketing, banners came in only three shapes. You could get a horizontal box about one inch tall and three inches wide somewhere inside the page. You could also get a box at the top or bottom of the page that was about one inch tall and six inches wide. Finally, you could get a "button" that is about half an inch high and one and a half inches wide. The problem with these banners is people learned to tune them out.

Now banners come in a variety of shapes and sizes. A very popular size is the "skyscraper" banner that is a tall vertical box, usually along the side of the page. Even in the new shapes and sizes, people will often tune out banner ads on a web page. Still, they can be effective if the match is right between what is being offered and the interests of the people viewing the page.

2. Pop-Ups and Pop-Unders

In the ongoing effort to make online ads effective, web marketers started opening a new window right in the middle of your screen. It just pops up there with an advertising message in it. That is why they are called *pop-ups*. These ads can actually be very effective. But, they also can make people very mad. As with all online advertising, the key to making pop-ups work is how well you tie together the interests of the people viewing the website with the content in the pop-up window. What makes pop-ups work is that you can not just ignore them. You have to either close the window or respond to the ad.

A variation of the pop-up ad is the *pop-under*. The same basic thing happens. When you are on a website, a new window opens with the ad in it. In the case of a pop-under, though, the window does not pop-up in your face. It opens underneath the existing window. The idea is that people will not get mad because this window interrupts them. However, they will see it when they close their existing window, and then have to make the choice of closing it or responding to it.

Pop-ups and pop-unders are also called *interstitial ads*. They are called this because they interrupt your user experience and force you to make a choice about the ad you are being exposed to.

3.   Rich Media Ads

Pop-ups and pop-unders have their drawbacks. As with banners, people have learned to tune them out. Many free "pop-up blocker" software programs have also become available. So web marketers came up with yet another way to get people's attention. Rich media ads are like banners, but they move and do interesting things.

Some rich media ads are like banners except they have movement and you may be able to do things inside the ad. You could have a bouncing smiley face that moves when you roll your mouse over it. Other rich media ads work like pop-ups. They display right over top of other content on the web page. You cannot perform actions on the page under the ad until you click on the ad itself.

4.   Text Links

The final type of online ad is a simple text link. As the name implies, text links contain no graphics. They are just some words and a hyperlink to the target website.

Far and away, the most prevalent use of text link ads is in paid search results. Paying for sponsored links on a search engine is also called *Search Engine Marketing*. This form of online advertising was discussed in detail in Chapter 6.

Step 4:
Choose How You Want to Pay for Your Ads

Fourth, you must choose how you want to pay for your ad. You can pay a low price for just getting your ad out there. You can pay a higher price for some kind of measurable action being taken by those who see your ad. Pricing for online ads come in three varieties.

1.   CPM -- Cost Per Thousand

With CPM pricing, you pay for your ad to be viewed by website visitors. In other words, every time a web page is downloaded with your ad on it, you pay. A single downloaded web page is called a *page view*. If your ad is on it, it is called an *impression*. In web-speak, impressions are also called *eyeballs*. You are not paying for any action being taken. You just pay for people seeing your ad.

This is the typical way to price offline ads. However, it is not usually done online. It is easy to track how many people actually click on the ad. This is a much better way of telling if your ad reaches people interested in your product or service. So why not charge for that?

Another problem with CPM pricing is that it does not count for people who set their computer to block ads. Even if the end user does not actually see the ad, the ad server still sees it as being shown on the page. It still counts it as an eyeball.

2.   CPC -- Cost Per Click

With CPC pricing, you only pay when people actually click on your ad. This is by far the most common method of payment for online ads. It does not guarantee that people will actually buy your product or use your service. But at least you only pay for people who are interested enough to click on your ad.

3.   CPA -- Cost Per Action

CPA is what most of us would like to have. Unfortunately it is not always so easy to do. With CPA, you only pay when the end user actually performs an action online. That action could be filling out a survey, subscribing to your newsletter or actually making a purchase. It is difficult because you have to set up a way to measure when an action has been taken that both you and the ad server can see.

In contrast to online advertising, CPA is the norm for affiliate programs, which are the topic of the next chapter.

Step 5:
Create Your Ads

An online ad has only one purpose. It is a call to action designed to generate clicks to your landing page. A useful way to think about it is as the envelope to a direct mail piece. On any given day, you may receive ten or twenty pieces of mail. Some of it is important: bills, news from family. Some of it is interesting, letters from friends or magazines you subscribe to. Then some of it is advertisement. The advertisements have to catch your attention in those few seconds while you are sorting your mail. Otherwise, they end up in the trash.

A web page is like that stack of mail. There are many things on the page. Some of it is important. Some of it is interesting. Some of it is advertisement. Your ad has to catch the viewer's attention and entice them to click on it before they move on to the next page.

Effective ads use a combination of creative design and advertising copy to get clicks.

Step 6:
Create Effective Landing Pages

An absolutely critical part of successful online advertising is to create effective landing pages. Your ad may have been successful in generating clicks to your website. In marketing terms this is called a strong *response rate*. That was just the beginning. Your goal is not just getting people to your website. Your goal is for them to perform some type of action on your website that is of value to your business. That action could be a sale. It could be an email subscription. It could be a sales lead for your sales force to follow up on. These are called *conversions*. Successful online advertising does not only generate responses. It generates conversions. Now here is the critical part.

The online ad itself can only generate responses. Conversions can only be generated by what happens after the click. This is the job of the landing page.

Effective landing pages have four key elements:

- ✓ Compelling copy and creative design
- ✓ A call to action
- ✓ A way to convert (e.g. Put the product in a shopping cart or fill out a subscription form)
- ✓ A way to claim the promotional offer (if there is one)

A common mistake is to allow the online ad to send potential customers to the home page or some other page that is not designed to generate a conversion. By doing this, you put obstacles in the way of your customer making it harder for them to convert. As a result, many of them will leave before they do.

Step 7:
Monitor and Improve

The final step is to monitor results and improve.

The return on investment for online advertising can be very small when you measure it on a per-ad basis. It is very easy for that ROI to become negative. For this reason, it is critical to constantly measure the performance of your online ads. Even ads that are very effective can lose their appeal over time. You will only know this by monitoring the results closely.

It is important to monitor both click-thrus and conversions. If you see a drop in clicks, then try different ad copy or creative design. If you see a drop in conversions (or you just want to create a higher conversion rate) then try new landing pages. In some cases, you will find conversions from one traffic source are lower than from others. This may mean that you are drawing a different type of responder from that source. That website may have users with a different demographic or psychographic profile. Try creating different versions of the landing page for that traffic source. Then stick with the one that performs the best.

There are five key metrics for online advertising. By collecting information about these five metrics, you will know what is working and what is not working. You can then use this information to continuously improve future online advertising campaigns.

Key Online Advertising Metrics and Typical Areas for Improvement

1. Click-thru Rate → Targeting the right websites, or pages
   Effective creative design or ad copy

2. Conversion Rate → Effective landing pages
   Product assortment / service offering

3. Cost Per Conversion → Cost effective media buys
   Effective landing pages

4. Variable Results → Targeted versions of ads
   (by traffic source) Custom landing pages by source
   Eliminate non-productive sources

5. Decreasing Results → Freshness of ads
   Updated content on landing pages
   Broken links

Results from online advertising campaigns can swing quickly from being profitable to losing money. Always measure. Always test different versions to find the highest response rates and conversion rates. Always improve.

If you use an ad server network to place your ads, they will provide you with detailed reports about how well your ads are doing at generating responses (clicks). You can use this information to tell which websites are giving you the best results. You can also tell which versions of your creative design or copy are doing the best. There are a variety of similar questions you will be able to answer. However, you will not be able to measure conversions resulting from your ads. To measure conversions, you will need to set up reporting using Web Analytics software. The chapters in Part III will discuss in detail how to use Web Analytics to measure results for your online advertising campaigns.

The next section goes into detail about how online advertising works. If you do not want to dig this deep into the details, feel free to turn ahead to the next chapter.

Bonus Section:
How Online Advertising Works Under The Hood

The first key to understanding how online ads work is to understand how HTML pages are different from print pages. With print media, the ad is laid out on the page. Then the whole thing is printed as a single document. With HTML pages, every graphic object is a separate file. The HTML page is a text document that contains the location of each separate graphic file to be inserted when a user views the page in their browser. Now here is the important point. The files to be inserted can be stored anywhere on the Internet. A graphic image, such as a banner ad, could be stored on a separate computer in the same location. Organizations often optimize the speed of their website by putting all of their images on a separate computer from their HTML files. This division of labor allows one computer to generate the HTML pages while another computer does the heavy lifting of serving image files. These specialized computers are called *image servers*.

Serving Ads

It is also possible for an image to be stored on a computer in a completely different location, anywhere in the world. It could even be stored on the computers of a company who specializes in serving online ads. Companies who do this are called *ad server networks*.

Furthermore, the HTML document does not need to include the actual file name of the document to be displayed on a web page. It could, instead, include a set of parameters that allow different images to be served to different web users. For example, the HTML file could include a call to the database to retrieve the user's customer ID number or cookie. Then you could display different ads to users based on their previous buying behavior, demographics or any other information you have collected about them. The ability to target your ads in this way is one of the most powerful aspects of Internet technology. You are able to increase the response rate of your ads by incorporating the direct marketing principle of targeting your marketing messages. This is also one of the clearest examples of how the line between general advertising and direct marketing has been erased on the Internet. All advertising is direct marketing when you are online.

Alternating ads based on user information is only one advantage the Internet offers over traditional print media. The most important is the ability to rotate ads being displayed so different advertisers can advertise on the same web page. This dramatically increases the efficiency of online advertising. Both the advertiser and the website win. Online advertisers can receive only as many impressions as they are willing to pay for. Also, the website can sell ad space to multiple advertisers on the same web page. This requires a little explanation.

Online Media Buying

With traditional print media, a piece of advertising real estate is laid out on a given page. Only one buyer can purchase this spot because only one ad can be printed in that spot on the page. When determining available ad real estate, the magazine or newspaper identifies all the available spots in the book. To calculate a price for an ad, the total circulation of the magazine or newspaper is used to estimate how many people will see the ad. Then the ad real estate is priced on a cost per thousand impressions basis. Cost per thousand is abbreviated as *CPM* ("M" is the roman numeral for thousand).

With online advertising, we have seen that multiple ads can be served in the same spot on any given web page. When determining available ad real estate, the website calculates both space on the web page and number of times that page will be viewed. These are sometimes called *eyeballs*. Multiple advertisers can pay to have their ads served only up to the point that they are willing to pay for. If there are still additional page views to the web page above and beyond the number of ads that have been purchased, then this is available real estate. The website could serve their own promotional ad, give the space away for free or do something else with it. As you can imagine, finding ways to monetize excess eyeballs is an important issue in the online advertising industry.

Measuring Results

The final step is measuring results and improving. This is another way in which advertising and direct marketing come together online. With online ads, every response generates a click which can be measured. Furthermore, once that click occurs, the responder can be assigned a cookie which allows their following actions to be measured as well. This allows advertisers to measure the three critical metrics behind all direct marketing success:

1.   Impressions

The first metric for all direct marketing campaigns is *impressions*. Impressions are simply the amount of times your marketing message is seen. For direct mail, impressions are the number of mail pieces sent out (minus those that were undeliverable). For an online ad, they are the number of times the ad was served to a user's computer.

If you are using an ad server network, they will provide you with a report of how many impressions were served. There is one drawback however. Many computer users have pop-up blocker software enabled on their computers. If you are serving pop-up or pop-under ads, then your reported impressions will be overstated. You will only know how many were served, but you will not know how many of those were blocked before the user had the chance to see them. This is a problem, but not really a big one. It is just part of the territory.

2.   Responses

The second key metric for direct marketing is *responses*. With online ads, response to the ad is measured in clicks. Every click to the ad is a response. Your ad server network will report how many times the ad was clicked. The effectiveness of the ad in generating traffic is measured by calculating a *response rate*. The response rate is simply the number of responses divided by the number of impressions.

Clicks to your website will also be recorded in your web logs. A common way to measure responses to your online ads is to create a separate landing page for each ad. These can be just blank pages that are quickly redirected through. They are there to do one thing, record the click for measurement purposes. These pages are known as *redirect pages*. Using this device allows you to calculate the response from your ads for yourself. This can be useful as a double-check against the numbers reported by your ad server network. But an even more valuable use for this technique is it lets you know exactly which ad the user saw before coming to your site. That lets you correlate all of their future actions on the site to the ad that referred them.

3.   Conversions

The third, and perhaps most important direct marketing metric is *conversions*. Conversions are the completion of a desired action resulting from the ad. The most common conversion event is a sale on the website. However, it could be anything from subscribing to a newsletter to claiming a free gift and submitting a lead form. Conversions are a little trickier to measure than responses. But it can be done easily.

When a user comes to your website from the online ad, you can assign a cookie to their session. Also, by using the technique described above you can record their first click to your site on a custom redirect page. This way the user's cookie is associated with the exact ad they clicked on. When a sale or other conversion event takes place it will be associated with the user cookie. That cookie is also associated with the ad they clicked-thru from. Voila! Divide the number of conversions from each ad by the number of click-thrus from each ad. Now you have the conversion rate.

Conclusion

In this chapter, you have learned how online advertising works. You know how to be successful using online ads to bring traffic to your website from other websites reaching your target audience.

Now turn to the next chapter and learn how to be successful with Affiliate Marketing.

Chapter 9
Setting Up An Affiliate Program

In this chapter, you will learn . . .
• What affiliate programs are all about
• How to be successful with affiliate programs

You Scratch My Back. . .
The Amazon Associates Story

The story is now a legend in Web folklore. Jeff Bezos, as the legend has it, was talking to a woman at a cocktail party. She mentioned that she would like to sell books about divorce on her website. This sparked a thought in the mind of the founder of Amazon.com. He could let customers on her website link to Amazon to buy the books and she could get a commission on the sale. In 1996, Amazon.com launched their now famous Associates Program. This woman's website was the first partner. It was a win-win for all involved. Web users are able to buy books being recommended by websites they trust. The partner website gets to offer a value-added service to their customers and get a commission in the process. Amazon.com opened up a huge new sales channel for its products.

Amazon's Associates Program was not the first *affiliate program* on the Internet, although, they would like to think so. However, it was the first one to make a big splash. After Amazon showed the way, it was only a matter of time before the rest of the World Wide Web would learn the lesson Jeff Bezos learned at that cocktail party. The Internet creates a natural partnership between targeted content websites and online merchants who have products and services they would like to sell. When one website's products reach the same audience as another website's content, well nothing more needs to be said. . .

The ABC's Of Affiliate Marketing

The concept behind affiliate programs is simple. You have a product or service and need traffic. Another website has traffic but needs a source of revenue. Maybe they need to supplement the content on their site by offering their users some of the products that you are offering. You would gladly give them a little of your revenue for some of their traffic. It is a match waiting to happen. But, how do you find each other? This is where affiliate programs come in.

Affiliate programs are all about partnerships. They are one of those things perfectly suited to the Web. You can think of affiliate programs as the reverse of online advertising. With online advertising, another site has real estate and asks you to pay them to basically go fishing for traffic there. With affiliate programs, you have some kind of value-added content on your site and offer to pay other sites if they send some of their traffic your way. It is the partner sites who go looking for relevant affiliate programs to promote on their websites.

If you decide an affiliate program is right for your business, then you are going to build a network of online partners. These partners will become an online sales force for your products and/or services. You will be making some of your products and services available to the users of their websites. As their site users purchase things from your website, you pay a commission on those sales. This also means you must make an ongoing effort to keep your network partners and their customers satisfied.

Affiliate programs are a win-win-win-win. There are four parties involved. Ultimately all benefit.

> ➤ *Users* on a content website find interesting opportunities they may not have been aware were available. The partner site is, in essence, providing a referral to the merchant site.

> ➤ *Affiliate partners* get a double win. They are able to provide resources and opportunities to their site users. This allows them to offer added value to their customers. For example, buying the product being reviewed in an article. Also, and more importantly, affiliate partners gain a source of revenue that requires very little effort on their part.

> ➤ *The merchant* gets a new traffic source. Often, traffic from affiliate partners is highly targeted, because it is coming from a website tailored to those interested in what the merchant is offering. Plus, once the initial setup costs are covered, there is no risk. The merchant only pays for traffic that converts.

> ➤ Finally, *the affiliate network* benefits by getting a percentage of the commission paid on each transaction.

What makes the Internet such a powerful force in our world is the power to make connections. Affiliate programs are successful because they let mutually beneficial connections happen.

Now let us take a closer look at the role each of the four parties plays to make affiliate programs work so well.

The Merchant Sets Up a Program

First, the company or organization seeking traffic sets up an affiliate program allowing other websites to generate conversions to their website. Websites setting up affiliate programs are often called *merchants*. This goes back to the original Amazon.com model where affiliate programs generated only sales to the website. Since then, affiliate programs have sprung up generating conversions of all sorts. However, the name, "merchant," stuck.

Setting up the affiliate program will include determining how conversions will take place. It will also include the method to track and pay for conversions when they do take place. There are a variety of devices used to generate conversions to an affiliate website. Three are most common.

1.   Banners or Links

The simplest method is to give visitors to your partner sites the ability to click through to your website. This could be by banner ads or text links placed on the referring website.

2.   Lead Submission Form

The next method is to allow users to fill out some kind of online form and submit it to your site. This could be a simple lead form with contact information and some basic questions. Or, it could be a complete application. For example, home loan approval applications or auto insurance applications could be completed in full on the partner site for these services.

3.   Complete Transaction

Finally, you could allow a complete transaction to occur. Usually, this will involve the site user being sent to your website to carry out the transaction. However, there are ways to do this while maintaining the user experience on the partner site.

A common practice is to create branded eCommerce pages. In this case, the merchant site sets up custom versions of their eCommerce pages that reflect the partner's branding. Usually, these pages will include a limited product set, relevant to the partner site's content. Sometimes, the merchant will actually mirror the look and feel of the partner's website altogether, including navigational links back to the partner site. This way the site user on the partner site will likely not even be aware that they have been sent to another site. The only indicator is the URL displayed in their web browser.

Another technique, is to actually include a window to the merchant website in a frame embedded in the partner's website. In this case, the site user never actually leaves the partner site. Instead, the merchant's eCommerce page displays within the partner site's page. A drawback to this method is the use of frames on your website can cause a roadblock for search engine spiders indexing your site.

After setting up the affiliate program, the merchant must go about the process of recruiting partners. Some of this work will be done by the affiliate network provider. The merchant's program will be listed in the network's affiliate directory. That way, websites looking for affiliate programs to display on their websites will be able to find it. However, this should not be the only method of recruiting partners. The merchant should also pursue their own methods. This will typically include having a sign up web page promoting the program. This page should be optimized to appear in search engine results for people looking for affiliate programs. They may also initiate communications promoting their program to niche websites with compatible interests.

Partner Sites Participate in the Program

After the merchant has set up the affiliate program, then other websites choose to participate in their program. They sign up and agree to use the merchant's conversion devices to send traffic to their website. It is, however, up to them how and where they display those materials on their site.

Since partners are only getting paid for conversions, it is in their interests to do everything they can to generate those conversions. This is one of the great win-wins on the Internet. If the merchant has done a good job of creating their conversion devices, then partners will do the hard work of getting their customers to respond to those devices. This is a source of revenue for them, so they will be willing to invest some of their resources to realize that income. Some small websites make much, or even all of their revenue this way.

The Affiliate Network Provider Processes Transactions and Monitors Results

The third piece of the affiliate process is to track and report on results from the program. Based on these results, partners are paid and improvements can be made to increase conversions. This can be a complicated technical process. Luckily, a number of businesses have been set up to provide this service for you. They are called *affiliate network providers*. They are some-times also called *affiliate solutions providers*.

Affiliate network providers have everything you will need to easily set up your affiliate program. They have both the technology and the legal expertise to set up a winning program. Affiliate programs can be simple link-share programs sending clicks to your website. They can also be fairly complex, involving complete transactions with fairly in-depth reporting and analysis. In some cases, affiliate programs provide a commission not only on immediate sales, but also on future sales from the customers referred by partner sites. Different affiliate network providers offer different levels of complexity in their services. There is one available for every program.

The Customer Finds Things of Interest

The fourth party in this process is the customer on a partner website. The customer is viewing content on a website that interests her. While she is there, she finds an interesting opportunity and responds to it. She may be reading product reviews on an outdoor magazine's website. While there, she finds the opportunity to purchase the latest backcountry gadget. She may be reading someone's blog about Italian cooking and have the opportunity to apply for cooking school. The possibilities are endless.

In all cases, the customer is doing what people love to do online. They are following links from one interesting thing to another.

Successful Affiliate Marketing In Seven Easy Steps!

Affiliate marketing is one of the most popular ways content websites earn revenue. No matter what the niche appeal of your products or services, there are thousands of websites already reaching those people. Most of those websites want to earn money by participating in affiliate programs.

It is a match waiting to happen. Starting an affiliate program gets your word out to a highly targeted audience of potential customers.

Success with affiliate marketing starts by having the right perspective. Starting an affiliate program is, in essence, recruiting an online sales force to sell your products or services for you. This is unlike online advertising, where you simply pay for clicks from your ads. Affiliate marketing is about nurturing relationships with your partner websites who are helping you sell your products and services.

Seven Steps to Successful Affiliate Marketing
Step 1: Choose an affiliate network provider
Step 2: Create marketing materials for your partners
Step 3: Determine your commission and incentive structure
Step 4: Create an affiliate partners area and sign-up page
Step 5: Recruit affililiate partners
Step 6: Provide ongoing support
Step 7: Monitor and improve

Figure 9.1

The secret to successful affiliate marketing is found in following these seven easy steps.

Step 1:
Choose Your Affiliate Network Provider

Running an affiliate network takes a lot of technology on the back-end. You must track transactions, calculate commissions, make timely payments to your partners and provide reporting of key metrics. Fortunately there are a number of vendors providing these services. The first step is to choose an affiliate network provider that meets the needs of the program you plan to set up.

Affiliate network providers vary in the services they offer. Make sure to do your homework. As you work your way through these seven steps, find out what services and technology you will need to be successful with your affiliate program. Then choose a vendor that has the right mix of services and features to meet your needs.

Step 2:
Create Marketing Materials for Your Partners

When partners sign up for your affiliate program, they must have the means to deliver traffic to your site. The second step is to create banner ads, text links and other marketing messages for your network partners to use on their websites. These should all contain links to the pages you have set up on your site for affiliate traffic.

Your marketing materials should be thought of as resources to help your online sales force to make sales. The easiest way to get started may be to just create a few banners in different shapes and sizes along with some text links. Then let your partners select which ones fit into their site layout. But, this is not the most effective approach. Investing some extra time to maximize the effectiveness of your marketing materials can dramatically affect the success of your program. There are four basic things you should do.

1.   Research Your Partner Sites

First, you should do some research into how your partner sites reach out to their audience. That way, you will be better able to design your marketing materials to complement what they are already doing. For example, you may have an online store selling personal electronic devices. Your affiliate partners may include blogs that write about the latest such devices. Instead of just providing a simple banner ad to your site, you could create a dynamic banner that displays your newest or top selling products. People who read these blogs every day may get tired of seeing your banner. But they will be happy for the chance to buy the latest products from your store.

2.   Give a Variety of Options

Give your partners a variety of ways to sell your products and services. That way they will be better equipped to tailor their sales efforts to their own website. This will also give them the ability to test different approaches until they find the best one.

3.   Provide Guidelines

Nobody knows how to sell your products better than you do. Instead of just providing materials to be placed on your partner sites, also give them guidelines on how to use those materials in the body of their web pages.

4.   Seek Feedback

Ask your partners for their input about how your marketing materials are working for them. Ask for things you can do to make your program work better. By engaging your partners this way, you will continually improve the quality of your marketing materials. Your partners will also feel a greater sense of ownership over your program. Both will result in them putting more effort into your program than with their other affiliate partners.

Step 3:
Determine Your Commission and Incentive Structure

Your affiliate partners are a field sales force. As with any salesperson, a key to results is aligning commissions and incentives with desired performance. With online advertising, you simply negotiate a cost per action (usually a click-thru). Then, your ads are served, and you pay for the clicks. With affiliate partners, on the other hand, your goal is to incentivize them to make as many sales for you as they can. The third step to creating a successful affiliate program is to set up an effective commission and incentive structure. To do this, you must balance the financial needs and realities of your business with that of your partners. There are five key questions you must ask.

1.   What Will You Pay For?

First you must ask, what will you pay partners for. Most commonly, affiliate programs pay for three types of result: clicks, sales leads and sales.

The answer to this question will be related to your business model. In other words, you must first ask, how do you convert traffic into sales? If you are an eRetail business, you convert traffic directly into sales. You will want to pay for those sales. For a business-to-business service provider, you may need to take potential customers through a needs assessment process leading to a long term contract. In this case, it may be a better approach to pay for qualified sales leads.

2.   How Much Will You Pay?

After you determine what you will pay for, the next question is how much you will pay.

The answer to this question must be determined by a calculation of profitability. Chapter 1 showed how to calculate return on investment for bought traffic. This same basic calculation should be used here. It essential that you calculate both your expected profit per lead and your conversion rate. This will give you a breakeven threshold. You cannot pay more than this.

3.   Will You Continue to Pay After the Fist Visit?

Some affiliate programs continue to pay partners for sales made by their referred customers after the initial visit. The number of days affiliates will continue to be paid beyond the initial visit are called *return days*. You may decide, for example, to pay commissions on sales made by affiliate traffic for a full thirty days after the initial visit. In this case, you are allowing thirty return days. The third question you must ask is, will you allow return days? If so, how many?

The answer to this question is determined by assessing the typical sales cycle for customers coming to your website. This is partly a matter of fairness and partly a matter of practicality. You want your partners to share fairly in the revenues generated from customers who they send to your business. If the typical sale to your website only takes place after a number of visits, then you should allow for those extra visits when calculating commissions for your partners. If you do not, your partners will not get paid for their traffic. They will then stop participating in your program. On the other hand, you may find that new customers to your website continue to return and make purchases over and over again. The value of that initial visit is much more than the first purchase they make. By continuing to pay partners for those future sales, your affiliates will get a bigger bang for the buck from traffic they send to your site. They will, therefore, devote more effort into making sales for you than they do for another affiliate program that does not pay for return days.

4. Will You Offer Additional Incentives?

Fourth, will you offer additional incentives above and beyond the basic commission structure?

You will answer this question by determining if some partners offer a higher value to your business than others. If the answer is yes, then you may want to offer incentives that reward becoming one of those higher value partners.

5. Will You Have a Multi-Tiered Program?

Finally, will you allow your partners to sign up other partners for you, and get paid for it? This is the network marketing model. Companies like Amway and Mary Kay have successfully used this sales model for decades. Some affiliate marketers use this model for their affiliate programs also. When it is done with an online affiliate program, it is called a *multi-tiered affiliate program*.

The answer to this question is determined mainly by whether there is enough profit margin in your commission structure to pay a multi-tiered commission. Then you must determine if your product or service is one that affiliate partners will want to promote as their own. If you can answer, yes, to both of these questions, you must decide if you want the added complexity of a multi-tiered program.

Step 4:
Create an Affiliate Partners Area and Sign-up Page

When you set up an affiliate program, you are adding a new component to your online business model. You must create an area on your website making it easy for partners to participate in your program. At a minimum, this area will include program rules, payment options, contact information and a way to download marketing materials. The details of your partners area will vary depending on what you are offering to affiliate partners.

You must also set up an online sign-up form that will appear on your website and be reachable from search engines and other off-site links. The sign-up page should be considered as a piece of marketing collateral, promoting your affiliate program. It should include promotional copy and a call to action. This page should make it as easy and desirable as possible for potential affiliates to join your program. You may also want to create different versions of this page for different potential partners.

Step 5:
Recruit Affiliate Partners

Once you have an affiliate program set up, the next step is to get people to participate in it. In other words, you have to drive traffic to your affiliate program. There are four basic ways to reach potential affiliate partners. Successful programs will employ a combination of all four methods.

1. Recruit Partners Through the Affiliate Network Provider

Affiliate network providers will include partner recruiting as part of their service offerings. People who are looking for affiliate opportunities can look up programs with your affiliate provider. They will find your program listed there and be able to sign up. But do not rely only on this method. Chances are there are some unique aspects to your program that appeal to a specific niche of potential partners. You will need to reach out to them yourself.

2. Optimize Your Sign-Up Pages for Search Engines

Search engine optimization is the most important way to get traffic. This is just as true for your affiliate program as for your website. Make sure companies who are searching for affiliate programs to participate in will find yours. Optimize your sign up pages with the same amount of care you put into optimizing your home page.

3. Promote the Affiliate Program on Your Website

Tomorrow's affiliate partners may be today's site users. If your business is a good match for another business, there is a good chance they are already on your website. Make it easy for them to find that opportunity when they are visiting your site.

4. Seek Out Complementary Websites

You may have a product or service that reaches a specific niche. Look for other websites that reach that same niche. Then communicate with them directly and ask them to participate in your program.

Step 6:
Provide Ongoing Support for Your Affiliate Partners

After you have set up your affiliate program and have some partners, the temptation will be to let it sit there and make money for you. Imagine how your salespeople would react if you treated them this way? They would give their least effort, when you want their best effort. The same is true for your affiliate partners. Businesses will keep working with those affiliate programs who make them successful. They will also want to keep working with those who just simply treat them well and make them feel good about being in the partnership. It is up to you to help them succeed and to build a positive rapport with them.

1. Pay Them

The most important thing you must do to retain your affiliate partners is make sure they get paid. Work with your affiliate network provider to make sure all affiliate transactions are recorded and all commissions are calculated and paid on a timely basis.

2. Provide Fresh Marketing Materials and Guidance

Your marketing materials are sales collateral for your online sales force. You must keep these materials fresh. Otherwise, visitors to your partner sites will start to tune them out and stop clicking on them. Periodically update the creative design of your materials. Change your offers from time to time. If it works for your business, offer seasonal or holiday promotions. The relatively small investment you make in updating your materials and keeping them fresh will pay off in more sales. It will also pay off by making your affiliates happy.

Do not stop at merely providing fresh marketing materials. Also, give your partners tools to help them make the best use of those materials. Give them tips on how to best promote your products or services. Suggest the most effective places to put your banners or text links. You may want to include success stories from other partners that they can imitate.

You can be sure there are other affiliate programs that miss out on this point. By providing this added level of service, your program will stand out as one to do business with.

3. Communicate with Email

Third, use email to maintain ongoing communications with your partners. If you are proactively reaching out to your partners, they will appreciate it. Also, by keeping your program top of mind, your partners will be more attentive to it.

As a general guideline, think of what would help you if you were the partner. Then go ahead and email that to your partners. Send notifications when you post new marketing materials. If you have new tips or success stories, send those. You may want to send them eBooks on how to succeed with online marketing. Of course, if you offer incentives for reaching certain targets, encourage your partners to win those incentives.

What we are talking about is setting up a customer communication email program for your affiliate partners. All of the same things apply as was discussed in Chapter 7, for creating successful email programs. You must first opt-in your partners before you send any email to them. You should also let them know how often they will be receiving your emails. That way, they can look forward to them rather than see them as Spam.

4. Make It Easy to Contact You and Respond to Questions

Finally, your affiliate partners are likely to have a lot of questions and problems trying to make your program work for them. Make it easy for them to send emails to you. When you get those emails, be sure to respond quickly to them. The little bit of TLC (tender loving care) you give to your partners will result in their being successful with your program. You may also find that your responses to questions and concerns raised in these emails can be turned into tips or guidelines you send out to all of your partners.

Step 7:
Monitor and Improve

With an affiliate program, the key performance measures you need to analyze relate to how well your commission structure, marketing materials and partner support are aligned with the goals of your business model. This means that both your business and your partners are being successful in generating revenue and profits from your program.

There are five key metrics to measure for a successful affiliate program.

Key Affiliate Program Metrics and **Typical Areas for Improvement**	
1. Click-thru Rate	➔ Reaching out to the right partners Effective marketing materials Providing guidance to partners Are partners making money
2. Conversion Rate (in addition to above)	➔ Effective landing pages Product assortment / service offering
3. Partners not making money	➔ Effective commission structure Need to add return days
4. Decreasing Results	➔ Freshness of marketing materials Updated content or featured products Broken links
5. Shrinking Profit Margins	➔ Focusing on giving incentives to larger partners at the expense of building a base of smaller but solid performers

By collecting information about these five metrics, you will know what is working and what is not working. You can then use this information to continuously improve your affiliate program.

Conclusion

In this chapter, you have learned how affiliate programs arise from the natural partnerships that exist when many websites are all reaching out to the same targeted audience. You know how to be successful creating and supporting a network of affiliate partners who will continue to drive qualified traffic to your website.

Now turn to the next chapter and learn how to be successful with Viral Marketing.

Chapter 10
Creating Viral Marketing Campaigns

In this chapter, you will learn . . .
- What viral marketing is all about
- How to be successful with Viral Marketing

Who Wants Free Email?
The Hotmail Story

Before Yahoo Mail and Google's Gmail, there was Hotmail. Hotmail was the first free email service to become popular. After its launch on Independence Day 1996, Hotmail literally exploded into cyberspace. A small startup company, Hotmail offered a free email service to anyone who wanted it. This is commonplace now. But at the time it was a new idea. The only catch was you would have an ad for the free Hotmail service at the bottom of every email you sent. That was not such a big price to pay. As a result, everyone who received an email from someone's Hotmail account also got an advertisement for the service. To sign up for their own free account, all they had to do was click on the link. It spread like a virus.

Within weeks there were tens of thousands of Hotmail users. By December 1997, there were over 8.5 million users. Two years later, there were over 30 million Hotmail email accounts. This innovative approach to spreading the word about their product was so successful it spawned a new term in the Internet jargon lexicon. *Viral marketing* was born.

The Hotmail experience teaches an important lesson to all Internet Marketers. When people find something that they like on the Internet, they will spread it around. The principle of word-of-mouth becomes word-of-email and spreads at Internet speed. Savvy marketers are able to include a marketing message along with those fun things people love to pass around.

The ABC's Of Viral Marketing

Viral marketing is simply creating something worthwhile that people will pass around. As they pass it around, your marketing message gets passed with it. When it works well, each person who receives the viral marketing object passes it to many other people. Your message spreads exponentially.

The term viral marketing was coined because the message spreads like a virus. This is not like the ugly kind of computer virus we all hate. People like what they get and choose to pass it along. This is a good virus. A quick look at what made the Hotmail viral campaign so successful will demonstrate the key ingredients to any successful viral marketing program.

Something Worth Sharing

First, Hotmail had something genuinely worth sharing. Free email services were a new thing at the time. It was, in fact, a very significant benefit to a large percentage of Internet users. People needed free email accounts and would be happy if they were told about a way they could get one.

The message about the good thing being promoted will usually take the form of some kind of advertisement or advertising copy. With Hotmail, it was at the bottom of every email sent from a Hotmail account. This can be called the *viral message*.

A Viral Object

Second, Hotmail had a vehicle to transmit the message about the good thing they had to share. They had something which offered a benefit that people would naturally want to pass around to others on the Internet. For Hotmail this was the email itself. People sent email for its own sake. Contained within each email message was Hotmail's viral message, the advertisement for the free email service.

This *viral object* was something that could stand on its own, separate from the viral message it contained. When people received the viral object, they also received the message. The viral object must be something of benefit in and of itself. This is what people are forwarding.

There are two other significant things about the Hotmail viral object. The viral object was something that people were happy to receive. Everyone likes to receive email from their friends. Also, it was something that would stay with the recipient. They would keep emails from their friends in their inbox. Plus, additional emails would keep showing up with that same Hotmail ad attached. This way, recipients of the viral object would continue to be exposed to the message until they were ready to respond. Once they were ready, they would be only one mouse click away.

A Receptive Public

Third, the Hotmail email and ad for its free service were targeted to an audience who was ready and willing to respond to its message. The Hotmail folks knew there was a large market for free email. They devised a viral object that was designed to both appeal to that target audience and to be passed around by the target audience.

For Hotmail, the receptive public was a huge, untapped market. Their campaign did not really require that much targeting. Since they were basically the first to offer a free email service, it was like throwing meat to hungry lions. This is not usually the case. Care must be taken to research the target audience for your viral message and to design a viral object that is tailored to their specific needs and wants.

Trusted Carriers

Fourth, the Hotmail viral object was transmitted by trusted carriers. Word of mouth is the most powerful form of marketing. People rely on advice from people they trust to help make decisions. In the case of a free email service, there was no better referral than someone's friend who already had the service. Nothing needed to be said. The fact that you just received an email from your friend's Hotmail account told you that they were using the service. If they also told you they were happy with it, that was just a bonus.

Finding trusted carriers does not happen by chance. Having a successful viral campaign requires a strategy to get the viral object out to those who will be most effective in transmitting it to the target audience.

A Way to Pass Along the Viral Object

Fifth, the Hotmail email had a built in mechanism to be passed along. In their case, email can only be sent to others. It is the perfect viral object.

However, not all viral objects will automatically be passed to others. Most will be useful things people want, but must be actively passed. Common viral objects include things like eBooks, games, software programs or web content. Included in these objects should be some device and/or incentive for people to forward it along.

A Way to Respond

Sixth, the Hotmail ad at the bottom of each email contained an easy way for people to respond and sign up for the service. People just needed to click the link at the bottom of the email.

On the Internet, people require things to be easy. They will be upset if they have to use three mouse clicks to do something that could take two. It is absolutely essential that the viral message, the advertisement or promotion, contain a clear call to action and require a single click to respond.

A Method to Convert Responders

Finally, clicking on the Hotmail ad would take you directly to the sign up page to open a Hotmail account. There were no intermediate steps that could hinder people from completing this all-important action.

The response mechanism in the viral object should be directed to a page designed specifically for the viral campaign. It is usually a mistake to send links from a viral marketing campaign to the home page. Most responders are likely to become disoriented. Many will probably leave without taking any action.

More Ways to Spread Your Virus

Hotmail was the classic example of a viral marketing campaign. It was not only the first; it also had the ultimate viral object – a free mail service before free email was commonplace. Well, Hotmail is a model that can never be repeated. The cat is out of the bag. Everyone already has free email. Yes, those free services are still being used as viral objects. But, they will never have the impact Hotmail was able to have when it was all new. Still, never fear! Free email may have been the original and ultimate viral object, but it is by no means the only one.

There are many ways you can provide content that Web users will be happy to receive, happy to keep with them and happy to send along to others. Here are a few common examples of viral objects that can be very successful.

- ✓ Articles and white papers
- ✓ eBooks
- ✓ Screensavers
- ✓ Free software or games
- ✓ Free music or video downloads

Successful Viral Marketing
In Seven Easy Steps!

Viral marketing can be a very powerful force. It is rooted in the deepest parts of our biological make-up. People are social creatures who are wired to spread the news and to respond to people they trust. It is fundamental to the survival of the species. We spread the word about good things that will help us. We warn others about things that can cause us harm. The Internet has created a vast social network where people love to pass things around. If you can create something of value, and make it easy to pass along, it will spread.

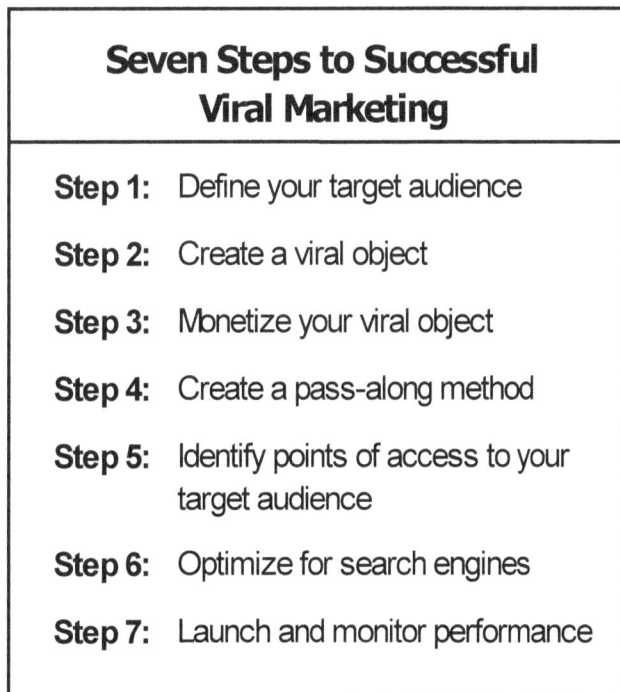

Seven Steps to Successful Viral Marketing

Step 1: Define your target audience

Step 2: Create a viral object

Step 3: Monetize your viral object

Step 4: Create a pass-along method

Step 5: Identify points of access to your target audience

Step 6: Optimize for search engines

Step 7: Launch and monitor performance

Figure 10.1

In one sense, viral marketing takes place any time your actions facilitate positive word of mouth about your company. Word of mouth has been the most important form of marketing ever since the first sale in pre-history. When the Internet came along, the relatively slow pace of spreading the word from person to person was accelerated to Internet speed. On the Internet, thousands of people can get the word in the amount of time it used to take to reach dozens.

The secret to successful viral marketing is found in following these seven easy steps.

Step 1:
Define Your Target Audience

The first step in creating a viral marketing campaign is to identify your target audience. Who will be receptive to your virus? This is not different from the market research you have to do for any marketing campaign.

The important thing to keep in mind is that your virus is the message of goodwill you are trying to spread. Also, the goal of your viral program is for people to respond to that message and then pass it along to others.

The first question you must ask is, "Who are the people who will be the most receptive to the virus?"

Let us say you have a nonprofit organization providing resources on how to prevent global warming. You want people to subscribe to your free newsletter. They will learn easy things they can do in their own communities to make a difference. You also want to sign up sponsoring members who donate funds to aid your research and lobbying efforts. Your first question is, "Who will be receptive to one or both of these actions?"

The second question you must ask is, "What will these people respond to?"

With viral marketing, you are going to give away a freebie. Within that freebie will be a call to action to subscribe to the newsletter and/or become a sponsoring member. What kind of freebie will your target audience want? Will they want an eBook of "Ten Things You Can Do to Slow Global Warming?" Will they want a screensaver with images of wildlife habitats affected by climate change? Perhaps they will want a free music download from a famous performer who sponsors your cause?

Once you have defined your target audience and what they will respond to, then you can create a viral marketing program tailored to that audience.

Step 2:
Create a Viral Object

The second step is to create a freebie based on what you have learned about your target audience. This is your viral object.

There are three things to consider when creating the viral object:

1.   The Viral Object Must Stand on Its Own

First, the viral object must be something people want for its own sake. With viral marketing, you are giving away something for its own sake. It is not an advertisement. It is something that offers a genuine benefit. People in your target audience should want it and be glad that they got it. Your object will contain the opportunity to respond. But that is secondary to the value of the object itself.

2.   The Viral Object Must Be Something Worth Passing Along

Second, your viral object must be something people will want to pass along. There should be something compelling about your object that makes people want to share it. Think of things you have gotten in the email from friends and then passed along to others. What was it about those things that made them worth passing along?

3.   The Viral Object Must Be Worth Keeping

Third, your viral object should be something people will hold onto and keep referring back to. That way, they will be exposed to your message and call to action over and over again. They may not be ready to respond to your opportunity the first time they see it. However, there may come a time when they are. Then your offer will be right there for them.

You may be thinking that you want to use viral marketing to promote your products or services, but you do not have anything you can offer as a viral object. There is help. Many people have created online content that they are willing to share with others, for free. You may be able to find free eBooks, articles or downloads that are a good fit for your target audience.

Sometimes, they are offering their content for free as part of their own viral marketing program. The free content may include links to their own website. It could also include sponsored links that will generate revenue. By allowing you to send it to your target audience, they are also increasing their own viral audience. If your two target audiences are compatible, then this can be a win-win for both of you. Of course, you can do the same thing if you are creating original content for your viral object(s).

You can find free viral objects by typing terms like, "free web content" into your search engine.

Step 3:
Monetize Your Viral Object

The third step is to include a method for generating revenue from your viral object. This is sometimes called *monetizing* the viral object. Of course, this is the whole point.

Basically, monetizing your viral object means including a way to respond to one or more offers that will generate revenue.

In the example above, of the global warming organization, you would include an easy way to become a member, subscribe to the newsletter or make a donation. Now you might be thinking, "Hey, in this example, you are not just trying to make money, but also generate a non-monetary increase in awareness and social action." Yes, that is true. Unfortunately, we do not have a Web jargon term for that.

Another way to monetize your viral object is to include paid ads in your viral object. If you have an eBook for example, you could include sponsored links to websites with related content. You could also include promotional links from affiliate programs with related content or product offerings. Some people create viral content that generates all of its revenue this way.

Step 4:
Create a Pass-Along Method

The fourth step is to make it easy for people to pass your viral object along to others. This is what makes it viral.

The most direct way to do this is by placing a "Forward-to-a-friend" link both on the email containing the viral object and on the viral object itself. This is most effective if you send out the forwarding email from your email system. The Forward-to-a-friend link can be set up to open a web page. There, the forwarder can enter the email address of one or more people to forward the message to and their own name. It should also include a place for them to enter a comment. Then, you will send out the email with the viral object to the email addresses they have entered.

Step 5:
Identify Points of Access to Your Target Audience

You have created your viral object. It is monetized and ready to be passed along. The next step is to determine *where* you will introduce it to your target audience.

1. Your Email List

You own customer list is of course an important place to introduce your viral object. Not much needs to be said about this. They are already in your target audience. If they are loyal to your brand, then they will be very receptive to receiving it from you and will gladly pass it along.

2. Opinion Leaders

Malcolm Gladwell's popular book, *The Tipping Point*, describes factors that cause social phenomena to spread like an epidemic. One of the critical factors he describes is when the message gets picked up by a special kind of person, who he calls a "connector." These are people whose lives touch and influence a disproportionately large number of other lives. In viral marketing, these people are simply called opinion leaders.

The goal of viral marketing is to get your viral object passed around to as many people as possible. Taking some time at the start to identify those people who will reach the largest number of people is time well spent. You began this journey by defining your target audience. Now, you will find out who is reaching that target audience. Then you will try to convince those people to pick up and pass along your viral object.

3.   Free Download Sites

If your viral object is something that can be downloaded you should get it posted on free download websites. There are many of these. There are websites to download free software, screensavers, games or funny videos. If your download is something people will want, there are sites that will post it for you. If the download site is a popular one, then it performs the same function as an opinion leader.

Step 6:
Optimize Your Viral Object for Search Engines

Effective viral objects are targeted to a niche audience. They are offering a benefit that members of that niche will like so much they will pass it along. They are closely related to the interests of the niche audience. These people will also be using search engines to find things related to their interests. If they find your viral object in their search results, they will download it and pass it along. In other words, search engines are one of the most important ways to introduce your viral object to your target audience.

The next step is to make the most of search engine traffic by creating a web page for your viral object. Then optimize this web page for the keywords your target audience is likely to enter into search engines. This will bring search engine traffic to your viral object just the same way you do for your website.

If you have a variety of keywords that relate to your viral object, you can create multiple web pages. Optimize each one for a different set of keywords. Let us assume our global warming nonprofit decided to make an eBook with things normal people can do to make a difference in their communities. They might make one web page optimized for keywords such as "global warming" and "climate change." Another page could be optimized for keywords like, "community impact" or "volunteer."

Step 7:
Launch Your Viral Object and Monitor Performance

The final step is to launch your viral object and monitor its progress. There are four fundamental metrics for a viral marketing campaign.

Key Viral Marketing Metrics and Typical Areas for Improvement	
1. Email Open & Download Rates	→ Effective outreach to the right audience Viral object is something they want Effect messaging promoting the object
2. Click-Thru Rate	→ Presentation of marketing message in object Ability to click-thru from viral message
3. Conversion Rate	→ Effective landing pages
4. Increasing Results	→ Effective outreach to opinion leaders Easy to be passed along Viral object worth being passed along

By collecting information about these four metrics, you will know what is working and what is not working. You can then use this information to continuously improve your viral marketing campaign.

Conclusion

In this chapter, you have learned that viral marketing works because it is based on the basic human drive to pass things along by word of mouth within a social network. The Internet has created a vast turbo-charged social network. You know how to be successful creating and launching a viral marketing campaign that will exponentially expand its reach to drive traffic to your website.

Now turn to the next chapter and learn how to be successful with Blogs.

Chapter 11

Reaching Your Customers With Blogs

In this chapter, you will learn . . .
- What blogs are all about
- How to be successful with business blogs

The Year Of The Blog
The Grassroots Journalism Story

2004 was the year of the blog. In December, "blog" was dubbed as the "Word of the Year" by the Merriam-Webster Dictionary. Immediately after this, ABC News added to the honors by declaring "bloggers" as the "People of the Year." Clearly blogs had arrived.

> The Merriam-Webster definition reads: *"BLOG noun [Short for Weblog]: A website that contains an online journal with reflections, comments and often hyperlinks provided by the author."* ABC News added to this: *"...that cover topics ranging from daily life to technology to culture to the arts."*

Blogging had been an almost unknown phenomenon since the term was coined in 1997. That all began to change in 2002. Bloggers became famous for scooping the Fourth Estate on allegedly racist comments made by Senate Majority Leader Trent Lott. The major news outlets picked up the story only after a firestorm of blog entries had made it national news. As a result, one of the most powerful political leaders in the United States was forced to resign. By 2004, the lesson was learned. All political candidates that year included blogs as part of their campaign strategies. Then it happened again. In December, a powerful earthquake in the Indian Ocean caused a tsunami to wreak havoc from India to Indonesia. Once again, bloggers scooped the news media with up to the minute stories, pictures and video clips.

A new phenomenon was discovered. It became known as *grassroots journalism*. As always, there were pundits who began to claim that the news media as we know it was coming to an end. They would never be able to compete against millions of individual reporters with instant access to their audience. This is not likely to happen. However, the balance of power had shifted. Professional news outlets no longer held a monopoly on what information the public would hear about. As people continue migrating towards the Internet as their source of information, the blogger community will become an increasingly powerful force for shaping public opinion.

The lesson was clear to anyone who was hoping to use the Internet as a way to reach out to a targeted audience. Blogs are an effective way to reach and influence large numbers of people almost instantaneously. Politicians and businesses alike realized that, whether they like it or not, bloggers are already reaching their target audience. Of course, everyone started jumping on that bandwagon.

The ABC's Of Business Blogging

To understand what blogs are all about, it is helpful to change our terminology. Do not ask, "Should I have a blog?" Instead, ask, "Should I participate in social media?" One way to think of the Internet is as a collection of overlapping communities. Each community is a network of people connected by common interests. Blogs are one way people in these communities communicate with each other.

The best way to describe what blogs are all about is to walk through the steps followed by a successful business blogger. You can be the star of this story.

Participating in a Virtual Community of Interest

Let us say, as an example, that you have an interest in photographing wildflowers. This is a pretty specific interest. Nevertheless, you can be assured there are thousands of other people with the same interest. Many, if not most of them are going online searching for information about wildflower photography. This is a naturally occurring community of interest. The Internet acts as a social medium that allows members of this community to find each other. It is not a formal community, although these do exist online. Rather, it is just people who have a similar interest, and they cover the same virtual ground when they go online. Most may not even be aware they are part of a community. They just have an interest and realize there are others online with the same interest.

Some members of this virtual community probably have information they want to share with the rest. Maybe they have advice on the best cameras or lenses to use. Maybe they know good spots to find rare species of flower. Maybe they just have interesting or funny stories about their experiences in "the field." There is a very good chance members of this virtual community will appreciate the information. They will want to keep coming back to see what new tidbit has been posted. *This is a potential blog that should happen.*

Creating a Business Blog

Now, let us also say you do not only have an interest in wildflower photography. You also have a business selling your artwork. Is there any reason why you should be disqualified from posting to your community just because you make money from your common interest? No! Of course not! As long as you are honestly contributing something of value or interest, the community will not think so either. In fact, if they like your blog, they will be glad to buy from you. They would rather buy from you than someone who has no connection to them at all. If your blog postings are interesting or useful, they will also forward them on to others who might share your mutual interest. Word about your blog and your artwork for sale will keep spreading.

Now, let us pick up the story with Bob, an amateur photographer. Bob loves the tips you post. He reads them regularly. When he sees especially good tips, he forwards them on to his friends, Mary and Rosa. Bob loved your story about falling in the creek while trying to get a good shot so much, he sent it to all his friends and family. He even sent it to the ones who do not own a camera.

Then, one day, Bob's boss says she is looking for some new artwork to hang in the reception area at the office. Bob scores some points with the boss by recommending your website. Now you have a new business client for your art.

Getting Linked into the "Blogosphere"

Eventually, Bob decides to start his own blog. He is so happy with your "Tip of the Day" that he includes a link to it on his own daily blog. Now all of Bob's friends and fellow photographers are being linked to your blog.

You should be getting the picture of how this blog thing works (pun only slightly intended). Before you started your blog, you were just another photographer out there selling your artwork online. Now, you are a trusted and valued member of an online community who are passionate about the very thing you specialize in. You have built goodwill. You have contributed that goodwill to the online community. As long as you continue to earn their trust, they will take it from there. People will spread your message of goodwill around the Internet. As a result, you will gain a large and loyal readership. This can convert into a growing number of loyal customers.

Blogs do not stand on their own. They are part of a social network of blogs that are all linked to each other. This is how word spreads so fast and reaches so many people. Bloggers refer to the universe of all blogs as the *blogosphere*.

Setting Up an RSS Feed

Well, you saw how popular your tip of the day was with Bob's readers. Now you want to get those tips out to more people. You decide to syndicate your tip of the day using *RSS*. RSS stands for "Rich Site Summary" or more commonly known as "Really Simple Syndication." It is a fairly simple technology to use. You publish a part of your content in an *RSS feed*. This is basically a headline that gets pushed out to people who subscribe to your feed. They read your RSS feed with an *RSS Reader*. You allow people to subscribe to your "Wildflower Photography Tip of the Day" feed by putting a button next to your tip of the day post in your blog. Once people have subscribed to your feed, they will get your headline pushed to their RSS reader every day. If they want to read more, they just click on the link and will be sent to your blog. Then you make your tips even more available by including a "Forward-to-a-friend" link with each daily tip. Traffic to your blog increases dramatically.

Monetizing Your Blog

Now we will move one step farther. Your wildflower photography blog, with its loyal readers, has become a highly targeted source of traffic. As an additional revenue stream, you may decide to place ads on your blog. People have come to trust you. If you put ads on your site for products, services or other websites that you honestly believe in, then your readers will be glad for the recommendation; just like people were glad when Bob placed your tip of the day on his blog. As long as the links you post take your readers to someplace worthy of your recommendation, they will not have a problem with it. They will actually be more likely to become loyal customers of those businesses than people who click thru from less targeted sites.

However, if you post an ad for something unrelated to your topic or for an inferior product or service, then you risk losing the goodwill you were so careful to build. You will turn off your readers. More than that, you will turn off a group of readers who are passionate about your mutual interest. They will be sure to spread that bad news about you to others in the community.

Advertising on Social Media

There is just one more part to the blog story we must tell. You may determine that your website has something of value to contribute to a certain niche within the blogosphere. However, you do not want to invest in creating your own blog. There is a good chance bloggers are already out there reaching your target community. It is likely they are looking for revenue. If you contact them, they may be willing to post your ad in their blogs. If you are genuinely offering a significant value to the community, they may even write about your business in their blogs.

Again, here is a place for caution. If you do not offer a significant benefit, they may still write about your business. But, you may not like what they write. The same could happen if you just approach a blogger in a way that offends them.

Considerations for Business Blogs

In the example above, you have seen what a blog is and how it can help a very small business. But what about larger businesses? Can a blog help a corporation with over a hundred employees? Over 10,000 employees? The answer is yes. However, there are some considerations you must be aware of if you are planning to have a blog for your larger business.

First of all, if you have something to contribute to the communities you serve, then by all means create a blog. The same rules apply as for small blogs. However, you must remember that your blog represents your business just like any other published public relations material.

Content on your blog must go through the same scrutiny. Do not be fooled into thinking that blogs are supposed to be informal, so you can just let your employees make postings to the blog. It is worth remembering that anything posted on the Internet is there for everyone to see and will stay there forever. This is especially true of the Blogosphere where people love to spread gossip and love a good joke. You do not want your company to be the brunt of either. To avoid this, you simply need to set up official guidelines for blog postings, appoint qualified personnel to write your blog entries and involve both your Legal and Public Relations departments in the project.

A blog is a strategic outreach to a community of customers, investors and possibly the press. In the best case, they will be passionately supportive of your products and services. As such, they will value the content on your blog postings and share it with others. In the worst case, they will be critical of your company. Still, if you do a good job of it, they will see your blog as an attempt to reach out an olive branch as a good community citizen. In either case, a blog well done will help your company.

Even if you do not intend to publish your own company blog, still it is important to keep tabs on what is going on in the blogosphere. People are talking about your company. If your company reaches a significant number of people, then there is a good chance someone is writing about your business in a blog. News travels fast on the Internet. If you find that a particular story is being circulated that hurts the image of your company in some way, you will be able to respond quickly to it.

Successful Business Blogging In Seven Easy Steps!

Blogging has become an important part of the Internet Marketing strategy for businesses of all sizes. You will find blogs from the largest Fortune 500 corporation down to an individual artist or craftsman selling their work online. A well-executed blog can build positive word of mouth for your business. If need be, it lets you communicate directly with your customers to counteract negative word of mouth already being spread. By being conscientious about your business blog, you will become a valued member of a virtual community interested in the same needs and wants your business exists to satisfy.

Additionally, doing these things allows your business blog to become a powerful means to reach your target market and attract qualified traffic to your website. Many of these people will become loyal customers of your business.

Your business blog can do all of these things, and more, but only if you are genuinely contributing something of value to the communities of interest your blog reaches out to.

Seven Steps to Successful Business Blogging
Step 1: Identify community of interest
Step 2: Stay focused on your purpose
Step 3: Follow Web usability best practices
Step 4: Present products and services with tact
Step 5: Optimize for search engines
Step 6: Do not become complacent
Step 7: Advertise on other blogs carefully

Figure 11.1

The secret to successful business blogging is found in following these seven easy steps.

Step 1:
Identify Your Community of Interest

When you decide to create a blog, you become a participating member of a community. Your blog will be providing a service to a group of people who are united by a common interest. The first step to creating an effective blog is to identify the target audience for your blog. This starts by determining what it is you have to offer. Then ask, "Who wants or needs what we have to offer?" *An effective blog is focused on a specific topic that is of great importance to a specific community of interest.*

Before you start to do anything, identify what positive contribution you have to make through your blog. Does is meet these two criteria:

(1)   Is it specific?
(2)   Is it of great importance to someone?

When you can answer, "Yes" to both of these questions, then you can have a successful blog.

Your blog must be on a specific topic because you want to gain a loyal readership who continue to return to your blog. If you have a variety of topics and information on your blog, then the chances are great that your readers will not be interested in much of it. Reading your blog becomes like a crap shot for them. Some days they like what they find. But most days they do not. Eventually, they will become tired of coming to your blog and finding things that do not interest them.

Your blog also must be of great importance to your target community. This does not mean it is a matter of life or death. It does not mean your blog is of great global significance. It just means, that for some small niche of people, this topic matters enough for them to keep coming back. It relates to a part of their lives that they feel strongly about.

Now, what if you have more than one topic of great importance to more than one group of people? The answer is to have more than one blog. If you do not have the time or manpower to maintain more than one blog, then the answer is to choose one. Choose the most important topic or the topic that reaches the audience that is most important to your business. Remember, it is better to be successful satisfying a part of your target audience than to fail in satisfying all of them.

Step 2:
Stay Focused on Your Purpose

You have defined what your blog will contribute and your target community of interest. Next, you must meet or exceed their expectations. That is the only way you can build a loyal readership who will spread the word about your blog. To do this, your blog must have a purpose. You must stay focused on that purpose.

You began to define your purpose in Step 1. What is the specific thing you have to contribute to your community of interest? This basically is your purpose. But, to develop your focus, you must take it one step further. Before you begin your blog, do some research. Find other blogs that are reaching the same community of interest. Read the topics they address and the type of postings they are putting up. Then read the comments posted by readers. See the kind of topics that generate responses. Also look at the things people say in their responses – both positive and negative. Use this information to craft the details of your blog. In other words, match up the specific things you have to contribute with what your target audience needs and wants.

This does not mean copying the blogs already there. You should have something unique to offer. But it will help to know what is already going on in that slice of the Blogosphere you intend to enter.

Once you have staked out your territory, remain true to it. What you want is a loyal following. You want them to come to see your blog as a part of their lives. To do this, they must have clear expectations of what they will get out of your blog. Those expectations must be constantly met. If they find themselves not being sure whether they will find something useful or interesting, or at least relevant to their interests, they will eventually stop coming back. If you are successful in creating an emotional bond with some of your loyal readers, they could even feel betrayed by a change of focus.

Step 3:
Follow Web Usability Best Practices

Consistently delivering content focused on your purpose is only the beginning of building a loyal following. Your blog must also follow website usability best practices. A common misperception is to think, "Blogs are supposed to be informal. After all, they are like an online diary, aren't they? Therefore, it should be okay to just write an informal entry each day." This is only true for personal blogs that nobody will read except your family and close friends. Nobody else cares about rambling journal entries.

Blogs intended for public consumption are websites. They are small websites, with fewer bells and whistles. They are easier to maintain, because there is less creative design involved. But they are websites. Your blog must follow the same rules of good web usability as any other website. The following are some basic usability issues that should be followed on every business blog. (These are adapted from a posting by the Web usability guru, Jacob Nielsen.)

1. Write for the Web

Write scannable page copy. People are impatient when they are online. They need to be able to go directly to what is important. Then they must quickly learn what there is to be gained from the information on the page. Be brief and to the point. Have clear posting titles and sub-headers within the body of the post.

2. Provide User-Friendly Navigation

Your blog is a resource. Make it as easy as possible for people to find old posts that were useful to them. It will keep them coming back. It will also give them more reasons to forward your blog posts to other potential readers. Categorize your blog posts in a way that makes sense to your readers. Provide an easy way to navigate through old posts based on these meaningful categories.

Make it especially easy for people to find your best postings. These can continue to draw people to your blog long after they have been first posted.

3. Publish on Time

One of the most important goals of your blog is to give people a reason to keep coming back. They will only do this if they know when to expect new content and if they actually find new content when they expect it. Set a schedule for publishing to your blog. Diligently keep to your schedule.

It is good to have a daily post. However, it is more important to keep to your schedule than to have new content every day. If you will only have content ready to post once a week, then make that your schedule. Declare right up front, "this blog is updated weekly."

One trick to keeping on your schedule is to stockpile content. If you have a lot to say on one given day, hold back some of it. That way you will have something to post on days when you do not have anything to say, or do not have time to write.

4. Be Professional

Your blog represents your business to the world. You must take care to ensure it presents the image you want the world to have of your business. Most of your readers may be informal bloggers who revel in the occasional indiscretion. But, some of your readers are your investors, business clients, the press, and law firms of disgruntled customers.

The basic rule to follow is "Do not put anything on your blog that you do not want to find printed in the newspaper." This does not mean you cannot take a more informal tone in your blog entries. It simply means, take care not to embarrass yourself or expose your business to legal liability.

5. Don't Hide

A well-executed business blog will build a personal bond between your business and your loyal following of blog readers. Give them something to build that personal bond around.

Provide pictures and a brief bio of the people writing your blog posts. (Never have fictional characters write your blog, unless you are creating a work of fiction. People will find out and become upset about it.)

Provide an "About Us" section with information about your company. Be sure to include your vision for the service provided by your blog and the guiding principles you follow in publishing your blog. Give them a reason to want to be a part of what you are doing.

Step 4:
Present Your Products and Services with Tact

If the truth be told, the most important reason for many business blogs is to bring traffic to the website. You want to generate positive word-of-mouth for your business. You also want to bring people to your blog who will continue on to your website, where they become customers. However, the blog itself is there to be a public service. So how do you reconcile these two competing purposes?

Simply said, be classy about it. Make your own promotion clear and easy to respond to, but do not make it look as if you are being pushy to make a sale on your blog. In addition to having a link to your website, you could offer value added services that draw people back to your site. Offer a subscription to your free newsletter or a subscription to your RSS feed. (RSS is a way to push your blog postings directly to your reader's computer without them having to come to your site.) These things are services. Presented with class, they will be perceived as such.

Step 5:
Optimize for Search Engines

Now you know how to create a successful business blog. Your blog is designed to bring traffic to your website. But how do you bring traffic to your blog? As with all things Web, the most important traffic source is search engines. In fact, optimizing your blog pages to be found by search engines is an important part of the overall search engine strategy for your website.

One of the major benefits of business blogs is they add a lot of pages to your website that can be found by search engines. Blog entries are rich with keywords targeted to your specific niche. If you do a good job of optimizing these pages to be found by search engines, the very presence of these pages will provide additional search engine traffic to your website.

Additionally, having a blog that provides a valuable service to your community of interest will also result in other websites linking to your blog pages. This also will help to elevate the search result listings for your website.

Chapter 6 provides instructions on how to optimize your web pages to be found by search engines.

Step 6:
Do Not Become Complacent

After you have been running a blog for a while, what do you do if you cannot keep maintaining it? There are many reasons why this could happen. You may just not have the time any more. You may not have the budget to keep paying a staff member to write the blog. It may just be a business decision that the blog is not needed.

If you are not going to continue posting to your blog on the expected schedule, you must announce that fact to your readers!

It is much better to announce that you will no longer be posting to your blog, but still provide access to previous postings, than to let it slowly fade away. In the first case, you maintain contact with your loyal followers. You send them off happy for the blog, even if they are sad to see it go. Still, they are positive about your company and the goodwill you have built up with your previous blog postings.

On the other hand, what happens if you just stop posting? What happens if you let posting dates slip, and eventually trail off altogether? You will send your loyal readers (read this as "customers") down a spiral of disappointment and frustration. Some will feel the need to take out their frustration with you. They will post nasty comments about how you let them down in other blogs reaching your target audience. They may even start their own blog just to express their frustration with you. All of this can be avoided by simply letting them know there will be a change.

Step 7:
Advertise on Other Blogs Carefully

Finally, you may also want to advertise on other blogs who reach out to your target market. This is perfectly fine, as long as you are genuinely offering a benefit to the communities served by the blogs where you seek to advertise. As with promoting your own website on your blog, the key is to be classy about it. Honestly seek to be a contributing participant in the communities of interest where your products or services apply.

Make sure you have something worth offering. Research blogs you want to advertise on. Then approach them tactfully. Some will already be actively seeking advertisers to add supplemental revenue. These will be more receptive. In fact, generating ad revenue from blogs has become a cottage industry of sorts. To support these blogs, there are services that aggregate blog traffic to make it easy for advertisers to find them. This is a good place to start. However, if you truly feel you have something of value to offer, do not stop there. Do your own research to find the blogs that are most influential in reaching your target audience. Then approach them personally. By being a good community member, you may not only get your ads placed, you may even find influential bloggers willing to write positive things about your business in their blogs.

Conclusion

In this chapter, you have learned how blogging is a social phenomenon that is already reaching the target audience for your products and services. You know how to use business blogging to become a valued member of the communities of interest who your business is serving. By being conscientious about offering true value through your blog, you reach new customers and build loyal relationships with your existing customers.

Now turn to the next chapter and learn how to earn money from your content website or blog.

Chapter 12

Making Money From Your Content Website Or Blog

In this chapter, you will learn . . .
- How people make money from their website or blog
- How to be successful serving ads on your website or blog

The Million Dollar Man
The Jeremy Palmer Story

In 2005, Jeremy Palmer claimed to have earned over $1 million in twelve months by participating in online affiliate programs. He was still in his twenties. Jeremy is now known as the Million Dollar Affiliate. Of course, he went on to write a book about how he did it.

After trying a few web ventures, Jeremy discovered affiliate programs in 2003. Affiliate programs give you ads and text links to place on your website, or blog. Then they pay you a commission on sales made by people who click on those ads. One of Jeremy's secrets was that he started by finding affiliate programs he thought he could be successful with. Then he built highly targeted content websites aimed towards the target market for those products and services. By providing useful content, he was able to attract to his websites visitors who would be interested in the affiliate offerings he presented there. He constructed his content around drawing people towards the products and services being promoted on the page they were viewing. This not only generated click-thrus, but delivered customers who are ready to make a purchase when they get to the merchant site. Jeremy had developed a highly effective way to deliver high quality traffic through his content websites.

The next ingredient to his success was to become an expert in working with search engines. He optimized his web pages to get high rankings in search results. He also learned how to make the most effective use of sponsored links. He focused on finding highly targeted keywords that were also not very popular. That way, he would pay a low amount for each click-thru to his content websites, but would also get highly targeted traffic.

After two years, Jeremy had built over 100 content websites. He was earning over one million dollars a year in affiliate commissions. Along the way, he earned accolades from Yahoo, Google and Commission Junction, one of the Internet's largest affiliate solutions providers.

Jeremy Palmer learned the lessons everyone wanting to earn money from their content website or blog must learn. A content website must be focused on a specific topic. It must provide something useful to people interested in that topic. Monetized links and ads on the website must be presented in the context of page content, in a way that attracts people to the products and services being offered. Then, it takes an aggressive search engine strategy to draw traffic to the content website or blog.

The ABC's Of Making Money From Your Content Website Or Blog

One of the great things about the Internet is that it taps into the collective genius of us all. Everyone is an expert in something. With the Internet, you can share that expertise with everyone else. Millions of people have created small content websites that deliver information about topics they care about. Even more have created blogs. If you are reading this chapter, there is a good chance you are one of them.

For most people, their website or blog is a passion. They care deeply about communicating their passion to the world. For others, the Internet is a way of using their expertise to earn extra income. Many hope to achieve the goal of financial independence. You have probably heard stories about people just like you who are earning big money from their sites. Maybe you already have created a content website or started writing a blog. Perhaps you are just thinking about it. In either case, you want to earn money from it. Earning money from your content website or blog takes hard work and persistence. Still, the concepts are simple. Basically, it is a matter of placing ads that are targeted to the needs and wants of your target audience.

Some of the ways to generate revenue from your website or blog have already been discussed in previous chapters, in Part II. This chapter brings it all together into one place to provide you with an easy to follow guide.

Create Content

By definition, content websites and blogs are built to reach a target audience. For some, that audience is just friends and family. These are not the ones that will earn ad revenues. To earn revenue from ads, a content site or blog has to reach a large audience. To do that, the site must offer content that is of value to its target audience.

Effective content websites research their target audience and provide content tailored to their needs and wants. This is a leap for many individuals who have created their own sites. People often start a content site or blog because they feel strongly about something. Then they present the information they feel is important. It is not uncommon for those early attempts at a website to sound like self-serving ramblings or a hodge-podge of disconnected facts. Effective websites move beyond this. The site owner invests time to focus the content of his or her website to match the specific interests and needs of a *niche* audience. By doing this, the content becomes highly valuable to a relatively small audience. This is much better than being barely valuable to a very large audience.

Serve Ads

If a content website or blog is effective at reaching its target audience, and is perceived as valuable to them, then site visitors will respond to ads placed on the site. The first key to being successful is to serve ads for products and services that appeal to the same target audience as the content of the website. When this is done well, visitors will value the content as a resource provided by an expert or opinion leader. The site owner becomes a trusted source. Ads presented on the site will be seen as having been recommended by the trusted site owner. This introduces an element of responsibility. To be effective, the website must genuinely offer a service to its audience. The ads served must offer products and services that are genuinely useful to them as well. By doing these two things, site visitors will continue to return to the website and will see ads presented there as a resource as trustworthy as the site itself. Thus they will continue to click on those links and provide revenue to the site owner.

Combining website content with a means to generate revenue is called *monetizing* the content. Earning money from your website or blog is done by monetizing the content on your web pages.

Distribute Content

Finally, if the website owner is able to develop useful content, there is no reason it must stay on the website. Monetized content on the website itself can only generate revenue when people choose to visit the website. However, if the content is valuable to the target audience, there are other ways of getting that monetized content to them.

Monetized content can be distributed to its target audience by delivering it directly to them, or by making it easy to be passed along to others. In the first case, people opt-in to receiving content delivered to them.

A very common and easy method of delivering content directly to a target audience is through an email newsletter. The site owner may write a weekly article about a topic of interest to the niche audience. That article can be emailed to a list of opt-in subscribers as a weekly newsletter. Perhaps it also includes useful tips and links to other articles and resources. Along with the newsletter content are included ads, just like on the website itself. The newsletter content is monetized. By sending content to the target audience on a regular basis, the frequency of clicks each user makes on monetized links is dramatically increased.

To allow site content to be passed along, it is easy to add a Forward-to-a-friend link on each page of content. The content on that page, along with its ads, can be formatted as an email that is automatically sent along to friends and colleagues. Or a simple link to the web page can be sent. Newsletters also can have Forward-to-a-friend links attached. By making it easy to forward content to others, the monetized content reaches a much larger audience than would have come to the website itself.

Make Money From Your Content Website Or Blog In Seven Easy Steps!

Earning money from your content website or blog is easier than you might think. Being successful at it is a matter of creating partnerships. Companies are offering products and services for sale over the Internet. For them, one of the most effective ways of reaching potential customers is to get their message out on highly targeted websites and blogs. For most of those businesses, their products and services are offering a genuine benefit to customers who purchase them. There are many people and businesses out there who need what they have to offer.

Seven Steps to Making Money From Your Website or Blog
Step 1: Reach your niche
Step 2: Optimize for search engines
Step 3: Choose ads to serve
Step 4: Optimize site content for pre-selling
Step 5: Create a newsletter or RSS feed
Step 6: Create a viral marketing campaign
Step 7: Monitor and improve

Figure 12.1

This is where your content website or blog comes in.

In most cases, a content website or blog is providing information, resources and advice on a very specific topic. Internet Marketers call this *content*. That content is being delivered to a highly targeted niche audience. The same niche audience is very likely to need or want products and services related to the topics being discussed on the website or blog. As a website owner or blogger, one of your jobs is to create partnerships between the visitors to your website and the companies who offer products and services they need or want. When you can do this successfully, you will be offering a benefit to both. You will earn sales commissions in the process.

This is how you make money.

The secret to successfully making money from your content website or blog is found in following these seven easy steps.

A blog is actually a bare bones content website. To make it easier to read, the term "website" will be used in the remainder of this guide to refer to both.

Step 1:
Reach Your Niche

The first step to making money from your website is to define who your target audience is. Then you must design your content to reach that target. This can be summed up in one word: Focus! Content websites are effective when they are highly targeted and focused.

This requires some further explanation.

1.   Define Your Target Audience and Focus on Them

First, if you intend to make money from your website, you must realize that the website is not for you. It is for your target audience. This may be old news to some. But for many, it is something they just never thought about. You are passionate about something and decide to create a website about it. It is only natural that you will write it from your perspective and include things of interest to you. That does not mean other people will be interested in it. You must do some research into who will be interested in your website. Find out what topics they are interested in. Find out what will keep their interest and what will turn them off. Then develop content and write articles targeted to their needs and wants.

As a general rule, the more targeted the content of your website is, the more useful people will find it.

2.   Make a Good First Impression

Second, you must win them over on the first impression. When people first find your website, it will likely be because they were searching for a topic that your website seemed to address. If you are successful in getting them to click through to your website, you will only have a few seconds before they decide if it is what they want. You must grab their attention and prove your value to them with the very first content they see. You can only do this by knowing who your target audience is and what they will want.

3.   Have User-Friendly Navigation

Third, you must make it easy for people to find things on the website. Once again, this is part of the change in perspective that takes place when you go from building a site for yourself to building one for a target audience. You know where information is on the website. But your audience probably does not. You must take some time to design a user-friendly navigation that makes it easy for people to find the information that interests them.

4.   Bring Them Back

Fourth, you must give them a reason to keep coming back to your website. For a blog, the most important thing you can do is to post new entries on the schedule you set. If your blog is interesting to people, they will keep coming back if they can trust that a new post will be there. For content sites, having fresh content of course is important. Just as important is to have a set of informational resources your site users find useful. They will come back when they have a need they think your resources will help them meet.

Step 2:
Optimize for Search Engines

Once you have deigned your website to meet the needs and wants of a targeted niche audience, then you must get them to your website. The most important way to do this is through search engines. To make money from your website, you must have a strong search engine strategy. Reaching your target audience through search engines is done in two ways: *Search Engine Optimization (SEO)* and *Search Engine Marketing (SEM)*. See Chapter 6 for a detailed discussion on search engines.

1.   Search Engine Optimization

Every content website that hopes to make money by serving ads must optimize the website for search engines. Search engine optimization (known as SEO) is organizing the content on your web pages so search engines find them and list them at the top of their search results. The most important thing to do is to find out what terms your target audience are likely to be searching for, then make sure those words show up on your website. SEO is discussed in detail in Chapter 6.

2.   Search Engine Marketing

Search engine marketing (known as SEM) is paying to have sponsored links appear on search engines. Many profitable content websites advertise on search engines to get traffic to their website. SEM can only be a profitable means of gaining site traffic when you make more money by the paid click-thrus to the ads on your site than you pay for the search engine click-thrus. The most important thing is to calculate the breakeven point where you earn more from conversions than you pay for search engine traffic. Then only pay for sponsored links where you exceed your breakeven number. SEM is discussed in detail in Chapter 6. Calculating your return on investment is explained in Chapter 1.

Step 3:
Choose Ads to Serve

The way you are going to make money from your website is to place ads on your site that your target audience will respond to. The next step is to decide what ads you want to place. To be successful, this requires some research. The key to success is to find ads for products and services that are complementary to the content on your website. Think of your website as offering advice or information about a topic you are an expert in. When people come to your website, they look up to you as a trusted source of help. While they are on your website, they will be receptive to suggestions you make about products and services that are related to the topic of your site.

For example, you may have a website about maintaining an active life as a senior citizen. People coming to your website may be interested in things like senior discounts on travel packages. In fact, if you can give a personal recommendation about a specific travel company, they are likely to become loyal customers of that company, based on your recommendation. On the other hand, there is no particular reason they would be interested in buying a new computer. You may get a high per-click payout or affiliate commission from the computer store. But, you will not get a high response to the ad. In fact, displaying the ad will cause your site to lose credibility in the eyes of some of your customers. They will think you are just trying to sell things and are not really serious about providing genuine advice.

You also need to decide what type of ads to serve. In general, you will want to choose between serving *paid search listings* from one of the major search engines or *participating in an affiliate program*. These are the most effective and easiest ways for a small website owner to monetize their website. You can also simply sell ad real estate on your website through an ad server network. This requires much more effort to be successful. For a small website it is not recommended.

1.   Serve Paid Search Listings

The major search engines have made it very easy for small websites to display paid search listing on their websites. The idea is a simple one. Search engines make their money by displaying sponsored links along with their search results listings. Companies have their links displayed when certain terms are searched and then pay for clicks to those links. The reason they pay for these links is because their products and services are related to those terms. They expect the people searching for them to be interested in the ad.

When someone is visiting a highly targeted, niche website, they also are demonstrating an interest in the topic of that website. If sponsored links are displayed that are related to the topic of the website, then the visitors on the website are also likely to be interested in the ad.

Search engines let you chose keywords that are related to the content of your website. Then, they will display, on your website, the same sponsored links that would be displayed when people search on those terms. For the sponsoring company, the result is the same. People who are interested in their products and services see the ad, and click on it. You will be paid a percentage of the revenue the search engine gets for each click-thru.

Displaying paid search listings is extremely easy to do. It is undoubtedly the easiest way for a small website or blog to earn money.

2.   Participate in Affiliate Programs

A second way to earn money from your website or blog is to participate in affiliate programs. Affiliate programs offer the opportunity to make much higher revenues than paid search listings. They also require more work.

Affiliate programs are discussed in detail in Chapter 9. There are many variations to affiliate programs. The basic idea is that websites will pay a commission on sales generated from traffic on your website. You will research companies offering affiliate programs who have products and services that are complementary to the content on your website.

In the example above, "MySeniorDiscountTravelSite.com" may have an affiliate program offering commissions on sales. To participate,

"MyActiveSeniorsSite.com" simply displays banner ads or text links on their website. When a customer clicks on the link, it is recorded that they came from "MyActiveSeniorsSite.com." When the customer eventually makes a purchase, a commission will be paid to the referring website.

Affiliate programs typically offer commissions on sales. So potential revenues can be much higher than cost-per-click earned from paid search listings. That also means that the participating website must do more than just get clicks. You must also prepare visitors on your site to make a purchase after they click-thru. This is sometimes called *pre-selling*.

Step 4:
Optimize Site Content for Pre-Selling

To be effective with the ads on your website, it is not enough to just display the ads. You must integrate them into your site content so people respond to them. Web users have a tendency to tune out advertisements on the websites they are visiting. You must get past this barrier. The way to do it is to build the product/service promotion into the content of the website, so it is part of the user experience. In essence, you are creating for your site visitors a user experience that introduces them to the products and services being promoted on your website and that invites them to make a purchase. This can be called *pre-selling*. There are three key things you must do to optimize your website content for pre-selling.

1.   Relevance

First, ads must be relevant to the content on the page where they are displayed. The closer you can align the ad to the content, the higher your click-thru and conversion rates will be.

Consider a web page that contains a review of the Canon Rebel digital camera. What kind of ad would be most successful there? You could include an ad for a consumer electronics store like Circuit City. That would be pretty good. It would be even better if you included an ad that said something like, "Buy Digital Cameras at Circuit City" and the ad sent customers directly to a category page dedicated to digital cameras. Better still would be an ad that says, "Buy the Canon Rebel XT at Circuit City" and the ad lands customers directly on the product page for the specific product. Of course, this assumes the review is a positive one.

2.   Context

Second, ads should be built into the context of the web page where they appear. The more closely the ad is integrated into the informational content of the page, the more likely readers are to see it as something being recommended by the website as a complementary resource to the article itself. This will result in both higher click-thrus and conversions.

In the example of the Canon Rebel product review, let us assume that the review begins on the bottom half of the page. You could place a banner ad at the top of the web page. It would be much more effective, though, if you place the ad on the right column of the web page directly next to the product review. That way people see the ad while they are reading the review. Including ads in the right hand column is a common approach. Ad real estate is separated from page content by placing it in a separate column.

You could improve your click-thru rate by inserting a content element, that does not look like a typical banner, inside the content of the review. The text of the article would then wrap around the ad. The ad, in a sense, becomes part of the product review. By taking this approach, you are giving a stronger endorsement of the product and store than if you clearly separate the ad from the review. If you have done your research and believe this store truly offers a good deal for your readers, then this is a perfectly ethical thing to do. An even stronger approach is to include a text link for the store directly in the actual body of the review. Once again, you can increase your click-thru and conversion rates, but are taking on a higher level of responsibility for the products and stores you are recommending.

3.   Promoting the Product/Service

Click-thru and conversion rates can be increased even further by actually promoting the products and services within the content of the page itself. In this case, you are clearly giving your endorsement and recommendation for the products or services being advertised. This is pre-selling. You are consciously writing the content of your page content with the intent of leading readers to buy the products or services you are advertising on the page.

In the example of the Canon Rebel, a positive review of the camera is already pre-selling the product. If you go farther and say that you researched prices and found the best price at Circuit City, then you are also pre-selling the store. It is not hard to see how this prepares your site visitors to become customers of the partner store.

By taking this approach, you will send prospective customers to the merchant website with the intent to purchase. Your website is a trusted source of information and advice. Readers will follow your advice by purchasing the products you endorse. You are acting as an online sales person for the store you are promoting. This will produce the highest sales commissions for you.

This also represents the highest level of responsibility on your part. If you are actively promoting a product or company, you must also make sure your website readers have a good experience when they take your advice. If they do not, you will experience a backlash. They will not only stop coming to your website, they will spread bad news about your site to others.

Step 5:
Create a Newsletter or RSS Feed

If your website content is particularly valuable to your target audience, there is no reason it has to stay stuck on your website. Send it out!

Many content websites are offering information, education or guidance that people would like to receive on a regular basis. If you are able to provide valuable information on a regular basis, then give your customers the opportunity to receive it on their own computers. Do not make them have to come to your website to get it.

For content websites, a common way to do this is to create a newsletter. You can send out a monthly, or weekly email with articles, tips or other useful information for your target audience. If it is truly useful, they will be glad for it. Along with the content, you can include ads, just like you do on the website. If you are careful to only advertise relevant and worthy companies, then your customers will be happy to click on the ads and buy their products.

Another common technique for getting your word out is an RSS feed. This is especially popular with blogs. An RSS feed is basically a small snippet of information that gets sent to your customers' computers. You can think of it as a ticker tape headline. If they like what they see, they can click-thru from the RSS feed to your website. RSS feeds are discussed in more detail in Chapter 11.

Step 6:
Create a Viral Marketing Campaign

Is your content good enough that people will want to pass it around to their friends and colleagues? If so, you can turn it into a viral marketing campaign.

Viral marketing is simply creating something worthwhile and then giving people the ability to forward it on to others. If it is good, people will keep forwarding it. It spreads exponentially, like a virus. It is not a bad virus. It just spreads like one. Thus the name.

Let us say that you have a website offering advice to Internet Marketers. You have written an article called, "Make Money from your Website or Blog in Seven Easy Steps!" You have posted the article on your website and monetized it with related ads. Well, this article turns out to be pretty popular. You can put the article into an email with a Forward-to-a-friend link. This is a basic viral marketing campaign. People who get your email love the article and keep sending it around to their friends and colleagues. Each time someone gets your article, she also gets the ads that you included along with it. Bingo! You not only make money from people coming to your website. You also can make money by sending your content out as a viral marketing campaign.

If your article is particularly good, you may want to turn it into an eBook. Then you can put it on free download websites. People will download the eBook and be able to forward it along to others. You reach an even larger audience. Of course, this only works if your eBook is good and people want to forward it to their friends. This works the same way as your website. If your eBook is worth reading, then people will value you as a trusted source of information. If you include recommendations for products and services, they will be likely to click on them.

If your motivation is to genuinely provide something useful, then you will also check out the companies who you are advertising. If you believe they are worthy, then the entire experience you offer your readers is a positive one. This generates goodwill with your audience. As you continue to offer benefits to both your audience and your advertisers, you will also be creating opportunities for yourself to continue reaching out to them in the future.

Viral marketing campaigns are discussed in detail in Chapter 10.

Step 7:
Monitor and Improve

The final step is to monitor results and improve.

The key to continuously increasing your website revenues is to identify the levers that impact the success of your efforts. Then you can measure performance related to those levers and make adjustments to them. It is a balancing act. You will learn to do it better and better as you work with it.

We have already discussed what these levers are. Your site content must be highly targeted and useful to your target audience; otherwise people will stop visiting your site, or never come in the first place. Your ads must be closely matched to the needs and wants of those interested in the content of your website. Otherwise, they will not respond to them. The companies you serve ads for must pay a commission that provides you with a rate of return that meets your revenue goals. If they do not, you may need to switch what you are promoting. You can also increase the response to ads on a page by pre-selling them through relevance, context and promotion. Finally, if you are buying traffic to your website, through search engine marketing, you must more than cover the cost of traffic bought through commissions earned.

There are five key metrics related to earning revenue through serving ads on your website.

Key Onsite Advertising Metrics and Typical Areas for Improvement

1.	Low website traffic	→ Effective search engine optimization Effective search engine marketing
2.	Short visit lengths	→ Content not of interest to audience Freshness of content Effective site navigation & site search
3.	Click-thru rates	→ Choice of ads Relevance & Context of ads Freshness of ads
4.	Low affiliate commissions	→ Effective pre-selling Choice of affiliates Effective partnership with affiliates (eg. Effective landing pages & product assortment on affiliate site)
5.	Low or negative profits	→ Effective search engine marketing

By collecting information about these five metrics, you will know what is working and what is not. You can use this information to continuously improve the return from monetized links on your website or blog.

Conclusion

In this chapter, you have learned how to successfully earn money by serving ads on your content website or blog.

Now turn to Part III to learn how to use Web Analytics to measure the performance of your Internet Marketing efforts and continuously increase your profitability.

Part III

How To Increase Profitability Using Web Analytics

Tale Of Two Click-Streams
WebTrends vs. WebSideStory

Websites, as we know them today, first came online in 1993. Just two years later, by 1995, business leaders already began to recognize that having a website would be a requirement for doing business in the future. Thousands of companies had gone online. Still, nobody really knew how to tell if they were having an impact, or not. Two companies launched products that year to answer the question: WebTrends and WebSideStory.

WebTrends came first, with their "Log Analyzer" product. Their software read information stored in the log files of the web server to report activity on the website. As it turned out, a lot of information was stored there. Actions taking place on the website are recorded as lines in the log file. These came to be known as *hits* to the website. By stringing together all of the log entries, Log Analyzer was able to paint a picture of what was happening on the website. They could show how many people came to the site each day, which pages they looked at, how long they stayed, and more. They could also tell if a page was not loading properly or if a link was broken. For marketers and webmasters it was like removing the blinders. Reading log files quickly became the method of choice for reporting website metrics. The WebTrends product offered easy to use, standard reports that anyone could understand. They offered it at a low price. Other companies developed similar solutions. Still, WebTrends held the largest share of the market.

WebSideStory took a completely different approach. In 1995, they also launched a tool, HitBox. Their approach was to place a small piece of computer code on each page. This little program, called a *page tag* would execute when the page loaded in the user's web browser. These page tags would record information about the page view and send it back to a database hosted by WebSideStory. This meant the client did not have to buy extra hardware or install the software. They just had to apply the page tags and pay for the service. By executing the computer code within the user's browser, page tagging also allowed HitBox to capture activity that was not being stored in the web server's log file. For example, when a shopper checks out at an online store, the log file will record that the confirmation page was served, showing that a sale took place. It will not show what was purchased. Page tagging offers the ability to read what items were purchased. By piecing together all of the information captured by the page tags, HitBox painted a picture of each user's experience on the website. WebSideStory built a small and profitable business. Still, it was largely ignored by the industry as a whole. Analyzing log files had won the day.

WebTrends and other log file based solutions took off with the Dot-Com boom. Then the Dot-Com industry crashed in 2001. Web Analytics, as these tools came to be called, crashed with it. When the dust cleared, many companies no longer wanted to invest in hardware and software to be housed on-site. The pay-per-use model offered by page tagging solutions looked much more attractive. An even bigger change also took place. Companies had moved beyond simply measuring basic metrics, like number of visits and page views. They wanted a way to measure what users were doing during the visit. Page tagging offered a superior solution.

All of the sudden, unknown WebSideStory was the belle of the ball. HitBox became one of the leading tools in the industry. Companies developing strategic Internet Marketing outreaches could now measure results in terms of business metrics marketers understood. Plus, there was no costly installation.

WebTrends continued to offer a solid, low cost log analysis solution. They also introduced their own page tagging solution, called WebTrends Live. The combination of these two kept WebTrends in a dominant market position. All of the other log analysis solutions have faded away into the quiet obscurity occupied by WebSideStory during the boom years.

WebTrends and WebSideStory are both success stories in the Internet Marketing drama. WebTrends gained early success when log file based solutions were in fashion. They were also able to adapt when they realized the advantages of page tagging. WebSideStory started small and persevered until the tides turned in their favor. Both have had customer-focused business models from the beginning. They have succeeded because they consistently helped their customers succeed.

In Part III, you will learn how to use Web Analytics. Both log file and page tagging play an important part in Internet Marketing success. The following chapters show how to use both to measure performance and to continuously improve your Internet Marketing efforts.

You will learn:

Chapter 13   How to use Web Analytics to measure website performance
Chapter 14   How Web Analytics can be used to improve the profitability of your website

Chapter 13

Using Web Analytics To Measure Website Performance

In this chapter, you will learn . . .
- What Web Analytics tools are and how they work
- The strengths and weaknesses of log file parsing tools
- The strengths and weaknesses of page tagging tools
- How to derive the fundamental website metrics and what they mean

From Clicks To Customers
The Evolution Of A Metric

The years from 1995 to 2001 have been described as the "Wild West" period of Internet Marketing. They were exciting times! Innovators spun out new businesses and new technologies at a rate previously unheard of. During this time of experimentation, it was not unusual for start-ups to change their entire business models multiple times a year in pursuit of their "mother lode." Finding that right formula for success could make a fortune overnight. Missing it made for even more dramatic headlines.

Behind the scenes of this virtual free-for-all was the need to measure whether the business models were actually working, or not. How to do that was not exactly clear. After all, figuring out how to measure online success was itself one of the new experimental business models. The new technology to accomplish this became known as *Web Analytics*.

As Internet Marketing grew into a stable industry, the metrics for measuring website success grew up with it.

It all started with the *hit*. Back in 1995, when it came to the Internet, all most business managers talked about was how many hits their websites were getting. Most really did not know what a hit was. But getting a lot of them must be good. To most people, a "hit" meant the same thing as a "click" on the website.

That year, Web Analytics was born. Companies started getting detailed reports of their website traffic. It quickly became clear that a hit is a pretty bogus measure for a website's success. Marketers discovered, to their chagrin, that a hit was just one line in their website's server log. Since many things could cause a log file entry, the number of hits did not really tell anything. All you knew was that getting more of them was better than less.

By 1997, companies were relying on new metrics. *Page views, sessions* and *session length* became the measures of success. These were created by grouping hits together into complete actions taking place on the website. Companies could measure how many times people came to their website (sessions). They also looked at how many pages a web user viewed during their session and how long they stayed. Once again, to most business managers, this simply told them that more was better than less.

By 1998, the Internet Advertising boom was coming into full swing. Many companies were pursuing online advertising and email marketing campaigns to drive activity on their websites. The *click-thru* became king of web metrics. A banner ad or email was considered successful if it brought a lot of click-thrus to the website. Most businesses, however, stopped measuring at the click-thru. They were happy to get traffic, but they did not know what that traffic did when it arrived at the website. In other words, they did not know if shoppers became buyers. This disconnect allowed extraordinary fees to be charged for banners and other online ads. It was a trend that helped fuel the Dot-Com boom which really took off at that time. Many fortunes were made selling online advertising.

By 1999, it became a common practice to use the "cookie" to track a click-thru all the way to a sale. The *conversion* became the new metric of choice. "Oh Noooo, Mr. Bill!" Companies discovered that all of those click-thrus were not resulting in sales. This triggered a collapse of online ad revenues, which began in 2000.

By the end of 2000, it was clear that online ad campaigns, aimed at generating immediate results, were not living up to the hype. Companies stung by disappointing conversion rates began trying to understand their interaction with online customers over time. The *customer* had finally moved to center stage in the Web Analytics drama. By registering site users, or relying on persistent cookies, companies could begin to understand what happened over a series of visits from the same customer. This may seem obvious today, but that is always the case with 20/20 hindsight.

Internet Marketing had finally defined a set of basic metrics for measuring website performance.

All of these metrics most commonly used up through 2000 could be derived directly from the website server logs, using a method called *log file parsing*. Consequently, vendors offering Web Analytics based on log file parsing dominated the market. But marketers wanted more. Websites had grown up. They went from being a nice add-on to being an integral part of doing business. Companies needed to measure the business activities taking place on the website. But server logs do not show that. Server logs show the basic actions taking place during a website visit. But they do not show actual customer behavior.

Starting in 2001, companies started to realize that the basic set of website metrics was not enough to plan for business success. More and more, they begun turning to Web Analytics software that did not depend on log files for their data. *Page tagging* became the Web Analytics method of choice. With page tagging, a small piece of computer code is placed on each web page. It can be set up to record almost any action taking place on the website. The basic website metrics are still the foundation for measuring website performance. However, creating custom metrics, using page tagging, now allows businesses to go beyond website performance. Custom metrics can be set up for each company to measure business success.

When Web Analytics tools came on the market in 1995, both log file parsing and page tagging methods were available. Both offered the ability to measure website activity. Both would provide reporting of key metrics. At first, only log file based tools received widespread acceptance in the marketplace. After 2001, however, page tagging gained prominence. It has continued to be the method of choice for marketers. Still, both methods are widely used. Each offers benefits over the other.

In this chapter, you will learn about the two types of Web Analytics tools: log file parsing and page tagging. You will learn how they each derive and report the metrics used to measure the performance of your Internet Marketing program.

The ABC's Of Log File Parsing

Log file parsing software dominated the Web Analytics market from 1995 through 2000. During this period, all of the fundamental website metrics were defined in terms of information that can be obtained from web server logs. The terminology developed at that time focused on the technical aspects of serving web pages and tracking user sessions. This technological (versus business) focus set the tone for Web Analytics jargon, which continues to this day.

Web servers collect information about visits to your website in log files. These are called *web server logs*. Every time a visitor enters the website an entry is recorded in the log file. Every time a link is clicked an entry is recorded in the log file. The web server log provides you with a history of every click that happens on the site.

In its raw form, the log file is a big text file. It does not really mean much to look at it. That is where Web Analytics comes in. The software will splice up the log file into discrete pieces of meaningful information and store it in a database. Once the key information is in the database, the software is able to analyze it to identify patterns in the data and generate reports. The process of slicing up a text file into meaningful chunks of information is called *parsing*.

The chief advantage of log file parsing, over page tagging, is in its ability to accurately report on website diagnostics. Diagnostic information, such as failed page loads, is found in the web server logs. Page tagging does not have access to it.

Since it is reading information from your web server logs, log file parsing software must be installed on-site.

Key Data Collected in the Web Server Log

The first step to understanding how log file parsing works is to look at the information that is collected by your web server. Figure 13.1 shows the most important information collected by your web server. These are the building blocks of your reports.

Key Data Collected in the Web Server Log	
Each "hit" on the website records an entry in the log file	
Time / Date	The time and date of the hit
IP Address	The physical address of the user's computer or Internet Service Provider (ISP)
User Cookie	Information in the cookie placed by your website onto the user's computer
Referring URL	The URL of the page the user was on before the page being recorded, if the user clicked on a link to get to the page being recorded.
Filename / Path	The name of the file being served to the user's computer (The HTML page and every image or other file on the page each receives its own log entry)
Browser	The type of browser on the user's computer that made the request to the web server
Bytes	The amount of information (in bytes) served by the web server
Error	Failed attempt to serve the page or file

Figure 13.1

With these basic pieces of information, the Web Analytics software is able to calculate a tremendous amount of information about your website visitors and their activity on the website. Some of the most important things log file parsing allows you to accomplish are:

✓ Provide basic site diagnostics, to keep your website functioning properly
✓ Identify the sources and volume of web traffic, to target marketing efforts
✓ Identify usage patterns, to optimize site content
✓ Measure click-thru from marketing efforts, to increase ROI

Problems with Log File Parsing

Log file parsing provides a tremendous amount of information to support your Internet Marketing program. However, there are some challenges that limit the effectiveness of this method. The four biggest issues are as follows.

1.   Dynamically Assigned IP Addresses

The first problem companies had with log file parsing was a difficulty identifying unique users. The original method for identifying a user on the website was to use the IP address of the user's computer. However, most people are not connected directly to the Internet. They connect to the Internet through an Internet Service Provider (ISP) such as AOL. So the IP address is coming from AOL not from the actual user. Additionally, the ISP will dynamically assign a new IP address with each click. This is good for the ISP, but it makes it very difficult to identify unique visitors on the website.

There was a solution to this problem. It was to make user cookies a standard practice for websites. When a user enters the website, a cookie is placed on his computer. Then, with each subsequent click on the site, the web log records both the IP address and the cookie. That allows all of the hits during the visit to be associated with that specific user. However, this method still does not work for people who have disabled cookies on their computers. For these cases, the imperfect method of using IP addresses is all that can be done using the log file information.

2. Page Caching

The second problem encountered with log file parsing would prove to be even more difficult than the first. As soon as a company's website becomes popular, they start experiencing performance drains on their web servers. During periods of high traffic, this means customers may have to wait a long time for pages to be displayed, because the server is also processing the requests of many other customers at the same time. In order to optimize the performance of their websites, companies started saving copies of pages being served in a virtual memory storage, called a *cache*. That way, if the same page is requested again, it will be served from the cache. This results in tremendous performance gains which both improves user experience and saves money. So page caching quickly became an indispensable practice. However, when a page is served from the cache, it does not record an entry in the log file. Therefore, it is impossible to accurately record site visits when page caching is being used.

3. Outsourcing Web Analytics

The third challenge confronting companies using log file parsing was the desire to have another company perform their analytics for them. Web analytics is a somewhat technical endeavor. Not all companies are able to dedicate in-house staff to it. On the other hand, it is a fairly straightforward process that could easily be done by an outside vendor. However, with log file parsing, the software must directly access the web server logs to work. That means the software must be installed in-house on the company's web servers. This makes it difficult to outsource.

4. Measuring Business Objectives

The fourth problem companies had using log file parsing was that it is difficult to directly measure whether you are meeting your business objectives online. The log file records which pages are being served. It does not necessarily tell you what the customer was doing while they were on that page. For example, you can measure whether a sale took place on the website, by checking to see if a confirmation page was served. But it is difficult to tell what they actually bought, or how much they spent. That information is not typically recorded in the log file.

The ABC's Of Page Tagging

The second method of performing Web Analytics, page tagging, became the method of choice for marketers after 2001. Companies were still reeling from the recession that followed the Dot-Com crash. Many were looking for a pay-as-you-go outsourcing solution for their Web Analytics. Businesses were also learning how to tie website activity more directly to their marketing objectives. They wanted a solution that reported marketing results rather than just the technical activity on the website.

Page tagging allows companies to overcome the challenges experienced with log file parsing. With page tagging, you identify all of the actions you want to measure on the website. Then you put a small piece of programming code (usually Java Script) on every page where those actions occur. This is called *tagging* the page. When an identified action occurs, the *tag* will send a message to the Web Analytics software recording the action in a database. As with log file parsing, analytics is then performed on information in the database to report on key site metrics

Page tagging is only offered as an outsourced solution.

Going Beyond Log File Parsing

Page tagging has some significant advantages over log file parsing. For these reasons it has become the method of choice for companies who are using Web Analytics as a strategic tool to measure and increase the profitability of their Internet Marketing programs. Page tagging overcomes three of the four major challenges faced by log file parsing. Identifying unique users still relies on cookies being enabled on the user's computer.

1.   Overcomes Page Caching Limitations

With page tagging, the action is recorded by programming code on the web page itself. When the web page loads on the user's computer, the script file runs and records the identified actions. This allows companies to overcome the problem of caching web pages. Whether a page is served from the web server or the cache, it will still be recorded when it is loaded by the user's browser.

Nevertheless, this method has its drawbacks also. The data collected by page caching depends on the user's browser running the script file contained in the page tag. This will fail with some percentage of users on the website. Those users will then be lost in the reported site metrics. Those users whose computers do run the page tag scripts, though, will be recorded accurately. So, even though there is missing data in the report, the trends reported will be accurate.

2.   Enables Outsourcing

As important as overcoming the caching limitation is the ability to outsource Web Analytics. Page tagging sends information over the Internet to the Web Analytics software. One of the great things about the Internet is that the software can be literally anywhere in the world. That means Web Analytics can be installed on your company's website without needing to install any software at all. You just need to put the tags on your website and direct the output to your Web Analytics vendor. Their software will process the information and provide all the reports for you.

3.   Measures Business Objectives

Since page tagging records actions occurring while a user is viewing the web page, and not just the log file entry recorded when the page loads, this method is able to capture more information about the user's visit. You can capture information entered into forms contained on the web page as well as data pulled from a database into the page view. Examples of some of the information you can record with page tagging is:

✓ Responses submitted in online forms
✓ Items put into the shopping cart
✓ Actions taking place within a Flash content element
✓ Behavior occurring within a page view, such as scrolling down or accessing an onsite utility

Problems with Page Tagging

It would be nice if there was a perfect world of clean data. Unfortunately, there are always tradeoffs. As with log file parsing, there are also shortcomings to page tagging.

The biggest shortcoming of log file parsing is caused by the source of information used to generate reports. Analytics is limited by what is captured in the web server logs. In the same way, the shortcomings of page tagging are also caused by its source of data. Page tagging only records information sent from the user's browser once a page loads. There are two significant drawbacks:

1. Missing Visits

The first drawback to page tagging was already discussed. It relies on information captured by a script file running while the page is active on the user's computer. Therefore, it will be missing data from users with browsers that fail to run the script file.

2. Unable to Run Site Diagnostics

A second, and more significant problem with page tagging is the inability to run certain site diagnostics. Page tagging can only report successful page loads for computers that successfully run the script file contained in the tag. Therefore, it is unable to record failed requests, such as broken links. It also is unable to provide the complete picture of site traffic provided by the web server logs.

Because of this drawback, it is not uncommon for companies to set up a basic log file parsing solution to measure site diagnostics, while using page tagging to measure their business objectives.

Website Traffic Metrics

You now know how the two methods of Web Analytics work. These methods both start with basic data coming from a user's visit on your website. That data is then assembled into meaningful information that can be compiled into reports measuring the success of your website. The only thing remaining to understand how Web Analytics works is to see what the basic building blocks of a web traffic report are. We conclude this chapter with a brief overview of the basic metrics used to create Web Analytics reports. In the next chapter, we will take a look at how these building blocks can be assembled to create your website usage reports.

1.   Hit

A *hit* is the very first metric used to measure website activity. It is also the simplest metric to calculate. A hit is simply one entry in the web server log. In the very first websites, each web page might be no more than a simple HTML page with text on it. In this simple page, there are no images or other files associated with the web page. So each web page has only one single entry in the log. That translates into one hit for each page viewed on the website.

That quickly changed. Today, there are very few web pages that contain nothing except HTML code and text. As we've seen above, you may have pictures, graphic images, movies or other media on a single web page. Each one of these will record a separate entry in the log file. Therefore, each time a page is viewed, there will be many "hits" recorded in the log. For this reason, a hit is not really a useful metric any longer.

2. Page View

A *page view* is one complete web page loaded to a user's browser. In the web server log, a page view consists of the HTML file for the web page plus all the associated graphics and other files associated with that page. A page view is made up of one or more hits.

3. Visit / Session

The words *visit* and *session* are used interchangeably. It refers to all of the pages viewed by a single user at one sitting. The session is identified by finding all of the hits for a given user that occur within a specified period of time from each other. Typically, a half hour is used as the cutoff. In other words, a session is calculated by stringing together all of the hits for a given user, where each hit occurs no longer than 30 minutes from the one immediately before it. The result is a complete session.

4. Unique Visitor

A *unique visitor* is a visitor to the website who can be uniquely identified. That way if the same visitor returns multiple times, you can measure his activity over time. Unique visitors are typically identified by the user cookie. As discussed above, the older method of using the IP address is not a reliable method for measuring unique visitors. It is possible that a unique visitor can actually be multiple persons. In the case when a family or multiple employees at a company are using the same computer, they will all have the same user cookie.

5. Authenticated User

If the user is required to log in to the website at the start of the visit, they become an *authenticated user*.

6. Referring URL

The *referring URL* is the web page where the link that sent a visitor to your website is located. If the user types your URL directly into her web browser, she will have no referring URL. These are sometimes called *walk-ins*.

7.   **Entry Page**

The first page in a unique visit is called the *entry page*.

8.   **Exit Page**

The last page in a unique visit is called the *exit page*.

Conclusion

In this chapter, you have learned what Web Analytics is and how to use it. You know how to use both log file parsing and page tagging methods to measure the basic website metrics. Web Analytics solutions come in many varieties. There are solutions for small businesses that provide basic reporting at a low cost. There are also solutions for large businesses that provide in-depth, customized reporting and analysis for a much larger cost. Whatever size business you have, there is a Web Analytics solution for you.

Now, turn to Chapter 14, and learn how to proactively use Web Analytics to increase the profitability of your website.

Chapter 14

Using Web Analytics To Increase The Profitability Of Your Website

In this chapter, you will learn . . .
- How to use Web Analytics to achieve your website's business goals
- How to use basic website diagnostics
- How to optimize website content
- How to improve the results of Internet Marketing campaigns
- How to increase website sales

Why Would They Do That?
The Google Analytics Story

In 2004, Google purchased the Web Analytics company, Urchin. The software was at the lower end of the market, in terms of functionality. It offered a basic page tagging solution for measuring website performance. At the time of purchase, Urchin was selling for $400 per user license. Google shocked the Web Analytics industry later that year, when they announced they would offer it for free. The new name for the product became Google Analytics.

This caused many to question, "Why would they do something like that?"

To some pundits, this move by Google represented a watershed moment. Had Web Analytics software become a commodity? If so, we should expect to see a dramatic shift in the industry. The emphasis would shift from a software focus to a business solutions emphasis. In other words, Web Analytics companies who succeed will be those who help companies use the tools to proactively improve their profitability. Companies who merely offer product features will become a commodity.

This was something of a doomsday prophesy for Web Analytics firms. On closer inspection, though, it is overstated. The move by Google did reflect a watershed moment. However, it was a moment five years in the making. The Web Analytics industry had long since shifted from a software focus to a business solutions focus. It was that shift which helped drive the popularity of page tagging over log file parsing tools. All of the major vendors were already helping businesses use the tools to practically improve their profitability. But these solutions cost in the multiple tens of thousands of dollars. Small to midsize businesses could not afford them. Larger businesses require more complicated business solutions than a free tool by Google can offer. The established vendors did not feel very threatened by the Google offering.

What the Google Analytics move actually represented was a drive to make Web Analytics solutions available and popular with small to midsize web-based businesses. To Google, this move made perfect sense. The businesses most likely to use Google Analytics are those who participate in Google's online advertising network. Helping them increase the results they realize from serving Google ads will also increase Google's own ad revenues.

By offering a Web Analytics solution, Google is teaching small to midsize web-based businesses a lesson all Internet marketers must know. Proactively using Web Analytics will increase the profitability of your website. By offering the tool for free, Google simply took away one of the reasons some had for not doing it earlier.

Goal Oriented Analytics

By the end of 2002, Internet Marketing had left its "Wild West" days behind. A year of recession and two years of disappointing revenue numbers had left hundreds of Dot-Com's pushing up daisies on the virtual frontier. At the same time, "bricks and mortar" companies from the "old economy" were learning how to be successful doing business on the Internet. The manic days of burning through venture capital gave way to a new mood of sober practicality. Those businesses left standing were the ones who had learned to practice sound business judgment. It was only natural that they would turn to Web Analytics to devise measurements that could be used to proactively increase a website's profitability.

Forward thinking companies had been using Web analytics this way for years. However, most businesses had simply monitored the performance of their websites. They did not use the tools at hand to drive improvements to their online businesses.

Using Web Analytics to proactively increase your website's profitability takes a change in perspective. Quite honestly, it takes more work. The rewards are worth the effort.

This "new" way to use Web Analytics can be called "Goal Oriented Analytics." The most successful online businesses do not just measure website metrics. They design customized reports that measure the specific factors which drive their business's online success. They use those reports to continuously make improvements. And they use those metrics to test if those improvements work.

The idea is not complicated.

- ✓ *First*, define your business goals.
- ✓ *Second*, define website actions that cause or hinder attainment of those business goals.
- ✓ *Third*, define website metrics that measure those actions.
- ✓ *Fourth*, create customized reports that present those metrics.
- ✓ *Fifth*, use the reports to make improvements.

Chapter 13 gave an overview of what Web Analytics is and how it works. In this chapter, we will look at how Web Analytics can be used to increase the profitability of your Internet Marketing program. In other words, now that you have learned what the tools are, you are ready to learn how to use them.

There are many ways to increase the profitability of your website. Most of them include some kind of measurement to identify the areas for improvement. This chapter will demonstrate how Web Analytics is used effectively by showing four of the most common uses. Through these examples, you will learn the most important techniques behind successful use of Web Analytics.

These examples could be used as a blueprint for setting up your own goal oriented analytics. However, they should, instead, be viewed as a starting point. You can build on the principles presented here to create reports tailored to the specific needs of your business.

Preventing Lost Opportunities With Website Diagnostics

We start with the most fundamental use for Web Analytics, general site diagnostics. This is the easiest use of the tools. The basic diagnostic reports have all been perfected and canned. You basically just have to turn them on and use them.

Every website should have basic site diagnostic reports generated and reviewed at least daily. As far as possible, you should never allow for greater than a 24-hour turn-around time to fix problems with your website. The following diagnostic reports are a must for every website.

Broken Links

Broken links are one of the most common errors to occur on a website. The most common cause for broken links is making changes to a target page but neglecting to change all of the links that point to that page. The second most common cause appears to be gremlins. Sometimes links just become broken and nobody can figure out how it happened. Whatever the reason, broken links are a major cause of user dissatisfaction with your website. They must be detected and fixed as quickly as possible. For this reason, virtually all log file based Web Analytics packages include a broken links report as a canned report.

The broken links report is derived by compiling a list of failed requests with referring URLs that are located within your website. Those referring URLs are pages with broken links on your website.

Bad Referrer Links

Bad Referrer Links are essentially broken links coming from another website. The causes of a bad referrer link are the same as a broken link. A typical cause is changing the filename or deleting a target page but failing to send an updated link to the referring website. These could be banner ads, sponsored links on search engines or links from affiliate partners. Another common source is online promotions or email campaigns that have expired. You may have already removed the landing page for the campaign but are still receiving traffic from the links you had previously sent out. If you notice a significant amount of traffic coming from these old campaigns, it is a good idea to keep the target URLs pointing to a live page that can still convert traffic or at least maintain a positive user experience.

This is one of the most critical errors to fix immediately. Usually, you have only placed links on referring websites if they point to some revenue generating area of your website. If those links are broken, you are losing money.

The bad referrer links report is derived exactly the same way as the broken links report. A list of referring URLs from failed requests is compiled. The only difference is the referring URL is located on another website.

Bandwidth

The Bandwidth report tells you how much data is being sent from your web servers to users viewing your website. Another way to think of it is measuring how much data is flowing through your pipeline. The most important use of the bandwidth report is to tell you what your peak load usage is. This lets you effectively manage the hardware requirements of your website by ensuring you have sufficient hardware to support your peak load traffic.

Another use for the Bandwidth report is to provide an indicator that something has gone wrong with your website. If your total bandwidth drops dramatically below normal levels, that is a red flag that you have a problem. Perhaps your website went down or one of your major sources of traffic may have dropped your link from its site. Problems like these will also be indicated by reports showing number of site visits.

The bandwidth report is derived by summing the number of bytes across all log file entries for a given period of time. Then the total bandwidth usage is reported as a trend line. A typical report is bandwidth per hour over a twenty-four hour period.

Average Page Load Time

The Average Page Load Time report lets you know how long it takes for each page on your website to load on the users' computers. This report is most useful in two situations. The first occurs when you are adding new pages to your website or making changes to existing pages. This statistic gives you an indicator of whether you have included too much content on your pages. If a page takes too long to load on the user's computer, she will abandon the page before it has finished loading. This is both a source of dissatisfaction and potentially lost revenue.

The second use for this report is as a red flag telling you that something has gone wrong. If the average page load increases dramatically above normal, there is likely some technological error that must be fixed.

The Average Page Load Time report is derived by averaging, across a given period of time, the load statistics for each page on your website. Page load time is not recorded in the server log. This statistic can be derived by using page tagging. It can also be derived by running a utility that calls up pages on your website and measures the load time.

Increasing Profitability By Optimizing Site Content

A second common use of Web Analytics is to optimize website content. Maintaining content on your website and keeping it fresh can be an expensive proposition. But failure to do so will result in decreasing results and a loss of credibility with your target audience. It is important that you know which content is working and which is not. Only then can you efficiently allocate budget resources to content changes that will have the greatest impact.

There are four main ways Web Analytics can help increase the profitability of your website content.

Content Popularity

The first measure of content success is *popularity*. This can be measured with a simple report showing number of page views for each page on the website. Pages that are not getting many clicks should be reviewed to determine options for improvement. The most obvious conclusion is that people just are not interested in it. If it does not serve a critical purpose on the website, you may want to remove it. However, there may be another reason. Perhaps the page is not properly optimized for search engines. The links from referring pages could also be broken.

A content popularity report can be calculated by summing the number of page views per day by web page.

Content Freshness

A second measure of content success is *freshness*. Freshness is basically a measure of popularity over time. It can be measured with a report of page views over time for each web page. If the popularity for certain pages is decreasing over time, then the content is losing freshness. At a certain point, the content has reached a threshold that requires the page(s) to be replaced or updated. They have become *stale*.

The exact threshold for stale content will vary, depending on the needs of your website. However, some trigger level should be set. That way, you will simply need to generate a daily or weekly report of web pages that have reached the threshold level and review those pages for potential changes.

A content freshness report can be calculated by summing page views per day by web page. Then this statistic is reported as a trend line over time. A staleness report can also be set up to list all web pages that have gone below the threshold level.

Additionally, a measure of overall freshness for your website can be calculated by measuring the frequency of repeat visits by your site visitors.

Click-Thru Rate

A third measure of content success is the *click-thru rate*. Each content element that is designed to motivate an action will have one or more opportunities to click on a link leading to the desired action. When that link is actually clicked, it is called a *click-thru*. The first measure of content results is how many click-thrus you are getting. The easiest way to measure click-thrus is to set up a unique URL for each link. Then you can measure page views to each of these target pages and sum the number of page requests from each referring URL. This way, you can count the number of clicks to each link and also which web pages those clicks came from. That will tell you how many times users clicked on each content element.

Knowing the total number of clicks resulting from a given content element is very important. However, a web page that is viewed one hundred times but gets five clicks is not performing as well as one that is viewed only ten times but gets five clicks. You will also want to measure how many times the link was clicked as a percentage of how many times the content was viewed. This is called the *click-thru rate*.

If you fail to get the desired click-thru rate, you should not automatically assume the content is a failure. You should first look for other possible causes. The most common is an ineffective call to action. Either the wording, the graphical treatment or the placement of the link on the page could be resulting in a user experience that does not lead to a click-thru.

The click-thru rate is calculated by dividing the total number of clicks on a given link by the total number of page views to the page containing that link over a given period of time.

Conversion Rate

A fourth measure of content success is the payoff resulting from web content. The first two metrics were measuring popularity of content. The third measures response to website content. This metric is measuring the actual payoff. On many websites, the content is expected to serve as a sort of funnel, leading visitors to a desired action. The action could be filling out a lead form, subscribing to an online newsletter, making a purchase or any number of other favorable outcomes.

In addition to measuring clicks, you will also want to measure how many times the click resulted in the desired outcome. This is called a *conversion*. The term conversion is usually used to refer to a sale resulting from some type of marketing message. However, the same calculation applies not just to sales, but also to any type of action resulting from a marketing message. In addition to a sale, the conversion could be a completed survey, a subscription, a lead submission, or any other desired outcome. The *conversion rate* is the measure of how many conversions occurred as a percentage of how many times the content containing the marketing message was viewed.

Measuring conversions is a more complicated process than measuring click-thrus. With conversions, you must be able to capture a record of the conversion event and be able to match it back to a page view that may have occurred more than one click earlier. This is a fairly straightforward process to set up with page tagging. However, with some effort, you can also set up basic measures of conversion using log file parsing. In both cases, the user cookie is used to match the conversion event to the initial action.

The conversion rate is calculated by dividing the total number of completed actions by the number of page views to the page containing the link that leads to the opportunity to complete the action. You can also measure conversions resulting from responses, rather than impressions. This is done by dividing the number of conversion events by the number of clicks on the content element, or link.

Increasing Profitability By Improving Internet Marketing Campaigns

Another common use of Web Analytics is to measure the success of Internet Marketing campaigns. A campaign can be defined as anything you do online to drive traffic to your website or to result in a specific action, such as a sale. The most common are email campaigns, online advertising and paid search listings. With all of these, Web Analytics is used in basically the same way. A potential customer views the promotional message. That message includes a call to action with a link to your website. The campaign could be an email newsletter promoting the latest holiday sale. It could be a banner ad or a sponsored link on a search engine. It really does not matter. The basic way to measure the success of online promotions is the same as we described above for measuring the desired actions resulting from website content. You measure the click-thru rate and the conversion rate.

The biggest difference between onsite promotional content and offsite marketing campaigns is that marketing campaigns are usually targeted to specific customer groups, called *segments*. In the case of your holiday sale, you may have different versions of an email campaign for young people, parents and grandparents. In addition to email, you may also promote your holiday sale by banner ads and links on affiliate partner sites. You will want to measure which target groups (segments) are responding well and which ones are not.

We already discussed how to measure click-thrus and conversions in the last section. There is no need to repeat that here. However, there are some additional techniques to learn. For online campaigns you will need to collect information that allows you to measure results separately for each campaign and for each targeted segment. There are two commonly used techniques for doing this.

Using Custom Landing Pages

The most common and easiest way to measure the success of an online campaign is to create a custom landing page. Using this method, each online campaign will have its own distinct web page that traffic will be sent to. Since all traffic from the campaign is sent to the landing page, it is an easy task to measure the total number of click-thrus from the campaign. All you need to do is count the number of times the landing page is viewed.

There are two basic kinds of custom landing page used to measure the results of Internet Marketing campaigns.

1. Custom Promotion Page

A custom promotion page is a web page created specifically for a single online promotion. It will usually include promotional content and a call to action that are designed to appeal to the type of customer expected to respond to the campaign. These pages serve two purposes. They act as the counter page to record campaign results. They also are content pages on your website which should be evaluated for effectiveness, the same way we described for all content pages.

2. Redirect Page

A redirect page is simply a blank page that contains a link to another page on the website. Redirect pages serve as counters allowing you to measure traffic from a given source.

Redirect pages are often used together with custom promotion pages. If your promotion is going to be viewed by multiple audiences, you can use redirect pages to record traffic from each source before they are sent to the promotion page. Let us go back to your holiday sale promotion. Perhaps you promote your holiday sale by email, banner ads and links on your home page. You could have one promotion page for the sale, but have a different redirect page for each of the three traffic sources.

Redirect pages can also be set up to pass parameters to the target page. Parameters are alphanumeric codes added to the end of the URL that links to the target page. These codes are ignored when the target web page is being located. However, your web server can read them and trigger actions based on the parameter values. For example, parameters can be passed that identify the traffic source. These parameters could then trigger dynamic content on the target page based on which web page the user came from. This same result can be accomplished by including the parameters on the links placed on the source pages. However, there are two advantages to including them in the redirect page. By including parameters on the redirect page, instead of the source page, you can avoid cluttering up your referring URLs with messy parameters that are ugly to the user. More importantly, by including the parameters on the redirect page, you can make changes to the parameters after you already placed your source links. This provides added flexibility to make changes to your online campaigns.

You will often want to create a custom promotion page for your Internet Marketing campaigns. This is the most effective way to put up targeted content designed specifically to convert traffic from a targeted source that is known to have viewed your promotion. It is also very easy and inexpensive to create as many blank redirect pages as you like. Once these two have been created, you can directly measure the results of your campaign by simply counting up clicks to the promotion page(s) and redirect pages. It is not hard to see why this method is so popular.

Segmenting Traffic by Referring URL

We have already seen how easy it is to use custom landing pages to identify your target customer segments. However, there are still times when you will want to rely on the old fashioned method of referring URLs.

Before marketers started using custom landing pages, they would identify traffic sources directly from the referring URL in the server log entry. When someone clicks on a link to a page on your website, a log entry is recorded for the first hit to your website. This is the log entry that records the *entry page* for the user session. Also recorded in that log entry is the page where the referring link was located. This is called the *referring URL.*

There are two parts to the referring URL that allow you to measure information about your website traffic. These also will let you gather information about responders to your online campaigns.

1.   Referring Domain and Web Page

The first part of every URL is the website domain. This is essentially the name of the website.

It will look something like www.mywebsite.com.

Once you get below the home page of the website, you will also have a file path ending in the specific web page the URL is pointing to.

It will look something like:
www.mywebsite.com/firstleveldirectory/mywebpage.html.

By looking at this information, you will be able to tell where each individual responder to your marketing campaign is coming from. You can create reports that segment your responders by referring website

2.   URL Parameters

In addition to the website domain and path to the web page, you are also able to put parameters at the end of a URL. At the end of the URL proper, you can enter a special character that indicates everything coming after it is to be ignored when locating the web page referenced by the URL. In this commented area, you can place special codes that your website understands. These are called *parameters*.

URL parameters can serve basically any function you want them to. In the case of online campaigns, they are often used to identify targeted customer segments. In the case of your holiday sale email campaign, you could include a parameter at the end of the URL in the link back to your landing page. This parameter could indicate which of the three targeted customer segments the email is being sent to: Youth, Parent or Grandparent.

Both custom landing pages and referring URLs can be used to identify traffic sources. It is not uncommon to use both methods together. For example, you may have one custom redirect page for all responses coming from a banner ad placed on your affiliate partner sites. But you may use the referring URL to determine which affiliate site each responder came from.

Optimizing ROI by Traffic Source

You now know how to identify traffic coming from different customer segments and traffic sources. Next, you will learn how to use Web Analytics to report on the results generated from each of these segments and traffic sources. In this section, we will show how to use three simple calculations to compare the return generated from each of your traffic sources. This, in turn, will let you optimize your Internet Marketing spend.

The key to optimizing the return on investment (ROI) from your Internet Marketing campaigns is to compare the results across all segments and traffic sources. Then continue to invest in those segments/traffic sources that are the strongest performers.

There are three key metrics that measure the success of your Internet Marketing segments:

(1)   Response rate
(2)   Conversion rate
(3)   Cost per conversion

By creating a report that measures these three metrics for all segments, you can easily identify which segments are doing the best. This report is sometimes called a *performance report*.

First, let us look at the three performance formulas for online marketing campaigns. These are shown in Figure 14.1.

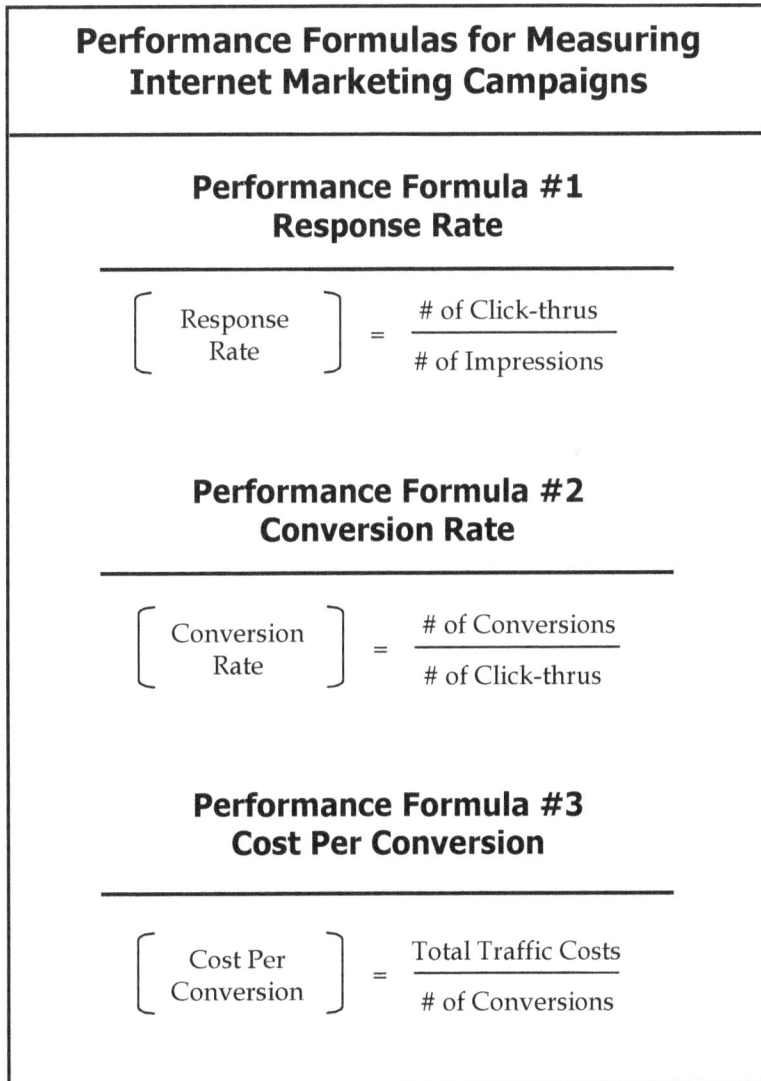

Performance Formulas for Measuring Internet Marketing Campaigns

Performance Formula #1
Response Rate

$$\left[\begin{array}{c}\text{Response} \\ \text{Rate}\end{array}\right] = \frac{\text{\# of Click-thrus}}{\text{\# of Impressions}}$$

Performance Formula #2
Conversion Rate

$$\left[\begin{array}{c}\text{Conversion} \\ \text{Rate}\end{array}\right] = \frac{\text{\# of Conversions}}{\text{\# of Click-thrus}}$$

Performance Formula #3
Cost Per Conversion

$$\left[\begin{array}{c}\text{Cost Per} \\ \text{Conversion}\end{array}\right] = \frac{\text{Total Traffic Costs}}{\text{\# of Conversions}}$$

Figure 14.1

Next, we will see how to create a performance report with two examples: paid search and an email campaign. In these examples, we will assume you have an eRetail store. For the holiday shopping season, you pursue both paid search and an email campaign to bring traffic to your website.

Example #1:
Measuring Results from Paid Search

With paid search, you will typically agree to pay a certain amount per click for a variety of search terms (also called keywords). You choose keywords that are related to your product or service offering. However, you do not know how they will perform until you see the results. Figure 14.2 shows how to set up a performance report for your paid search campaigns. This report shows which terms are working for you and which are not.

Web Analytics Performance Report **Paid Search Results**							
(a)	(b)	(c)	(d)	(e)	(f)	(g)	(h)
Traffic Source (keywords)	# Impressions*	Cost Per Click	# Entry Pages	# Conversions	Response Rate (d/b)	Conversion Rate (e/d)	Cost Per Conversion ((c*d)/e)
Holiday sale	20,000	$2.00	2,000	30	1%	1.5%	$133.34
Holiday toys	18,000	$1.50	1,800	36	1%	2%	$75
Toys for grandson	3,000	$0.50	900	45	3%	5%	$10

* # Impressions will be provided by search engine provider

Figure 14.2

In this report, notice that the popular terms, like "holiday sale" and "holiday toys" are much more expensive than the less popular term, "toys for grandson." Also, the less popular term is more specific than the other terms. As a result, the less popular term performs better. It yields both a higher response rate and conversion rate. There are less overall site visits from the less popular search term. But those visits yield much better results.

Take a moment to review the results in Figure 14.2. Notice, especially, the cost per conversion reported in Column (h). The final results show a dramatic difference in the cost per conversion from the different search terms. This type of result is not uncommon. It is not hard to see, from this example, why closely measuring your paid search results is so important.

Many companies never bother to set up their own reports to measure actual conversions resulting from their traffic buys. They just look at click-thru reports provided by their Search Engine Marketing vendor. This short example shows how neglecting to measure results all the way through to conversions is flying blind when it comes to maximizing your paid search results.

Now, we turn to measuring results for an email campaign.

Example #2:
Measuring Results from Email

With an email campaign, you will often divide the mail list into segments. Each segment represents a different type of customer. Sometimes you send the same email to each group. In that case, you just identify the groups to see how they each perform. Often, however, you will send different email messages to each segment. In the case of the holiday mailer, we have three segments: Youth, Parents and Grandparents. Each of these groups could have received a different message and a different set of featured products. They could also receive different offers. You can probably think of different things you would like to say to each of these groups, and different gifts that might entice them to make a purchase.

This report, shown in Figure 14.3, works exactly the same way as the paid search report. Each mail segment is reported on a separate row. The key metrics for measuring performance are listed across the columns. Once again, notice the difference in results. Even though each mail piece cost exactly the same amount to send, the different segments produce very different results.

Web Analytics Performance Report							
Email Campaign Results							
(a)	(b)	(c)	(d)	(e)	(f)	(g)	(h)
Traffic Source (mail groups)	Mail Volume	Cost Per Email*	# Entry Pages	# Conversions**	Response Rate (d/b)	Conversion Rate (e/d)	Cost Per Conversion ((b*c)/e)
Youth (18 – 25)	10,000	$0.05	1,000	20	10%	2%	$25
Parents	10,000	$0.05	200	20	2%	10%	$25
Grandparent	5,000	$0.05	500	25	10%	5%	$10

* Does not include cost of incentive / offer (e.g. 10% off purchase)
** Does not indicate average order size per mail group. This would be an important metric to have.

Figure 14.3

The first thing you might notice is that, as with paid search, grandparents are the most productive customer segment for your holiday season email. You will also notice that the Youth segment was very responsive to the email, but they did not convert at a high rate. On the other hand, parents were the least likely to respond to the email, but once they did, they were the most likely to make a purchase. In the end, both Youth and Parents produce the same final results. But, their actual behavior was very different.

What these results do not tell you is *why* these segments performed the way they did. On the surface, you might explain the results as just indicators of customer preference. You might think that Youth spend a lot of time online and will read most of their emails, so they have a higher response rate. However, they do not have much money, so they purchase less. On the other hand, Parents are busy and are not as likely to respond to an email. But, if they do respond, they are more likely to be ready to buy. This could be the case. However, you can only answer that question by testing different things and comparing the results. It is very likely that the results you achieved could have been improved by making some small modifications to the email campaign. Consider the following scenarios.

1.   Different Email Versions

It may be that you sent the same email to all of your target segments. This email may have included pictures of X-Box and MP3 players with a message saying that these are the most popular gifts this year. Youth open the email because they are interested in the products for themselves and their friends. Grandparents open the email because they have teenage grandchildren and are impressed by the "most popular gift" message. However, Parents only open the email if they have teenage children.

Now, what if you sent different email versions. You send a version to parents with a selection of toys for all ages. This results in Parents opening the email at the same rate as Youth and Grandparents. Since Parents actually purchased at five times the rate of Youth and twice the rate of Grandparents, this would result in a dramatic increase in campaign results.

2. Different Landing Pages

Now let us assume that you also directed the links on all of the emails to the same landing page. This page did not contain the X-Box and MP3 players displayed in the email. Instead, it was a generic holiday shopping category page. Furthermore, the messaging on the page was targeted towards parents buying presents for their children. Parents and Grandparents were both able to find gifts they wanted to buy from this page, but Youth were not impressed.

You could create different landing pages targeted to each of these groups. For the Youth landing page, you present the items on the email. Plus you present gifts for adults, with messaging about buying gifts for Mom and Dad. As a result, this landing page brings the conversion rate for Youth up to the same levels as for Parents. Once again, this will have a dramatic impact on overall results.

3. Different Offers

Finally, you may also have given the same offer to each of the mail segments. Maybe the offer was for 10% off any purchase over $100. By analyzing the average purchase amount, you find out that the Youth segment was much more likely to spend less than $100 on their purchases. You have decided that you cannot afford to give 10% off orders less than $100.

Let us assume you were able to enter into a co-branded promotion with a music download website. For the Youth segment, you offer a free music download instead of the 10% off. This increases your conversion rates for youth.

Notice that upon first glance, the results of your email campaign make sense. It seems that your three segments just have different behaviors. You could be satisfied with those results and just assume that your strongest target market are grandparents. You might even use these results to justify launching more campaigns towards grandparents. However, by testing different versions of your email messages, your landing pages and your offers, you would find completely different results. Small changes to your campaign could make a dramatic difference.

The Performance Report is not limited to measuring the results of marketing campaigns. The process of measuring performance metrics by different user groups or traffic sources is an important technique for improving results towards any action you hope users will take on the website.

Increasing Profitability By Maximizing eCommerce Sales

A fourth common area where Web Analytics plays a critical role is eCommerce. Everything we have learned so far in this chapter will be put to use with the eCommerce site. In the previous sections, we discussed optimizing website content and increasing conversions by traffic source for online marketing campaigns. The same principles apply to increasing eCommerce sales. In addition, there is one thing we have not yet learned how to measure: *abandonment*.

The concept of reducing abandonment is easy to understand. If you know in advance the path a user must take to reach a desired action, you will be able to tell at what point they leave the process before the conversion event.

Then you will be able to evaluate what is happening at that point and see if there are things you can do to keep people from dropping off. With eCommerce, the final step in a conversion event is the confirmation page that is returned to the shoppers after they have completed their sale

A quick review of how a typical eCommerce transaction takes place will show where Web Analytics can be used to improve results. See Figure 14.4.

(0)   First, web traffic is brought to the eCommerce site. Most sites will use a combination of multiple online channels: search engines, email, online ads and affiliate programs.

(1)   Once a user reaches the website, he will typically land on one of three places: the home page, a product or category page, or a custom promotion landing page. Then he can begin his shopping visit.

        If the customer arrives at the home page, or category page, he will usually have to search or browse for products before purchasing.

(1a)   If the customer enters a search, this adds an extra step. He will be served a search results page, and have to choose from the search results to continue the visit.

(1b)   When the customer clicks on menu options or navigational tabs that link to category pages, this is called *browsing*. In this path, he may browse through any number of category or sub-category pages before eventually clicking to a product page.

(2)   Product Page

(3)   Shopping Cart

(4)   Checkout

(5)   Confirmation Page

eCommerce Website Visit Process Flow

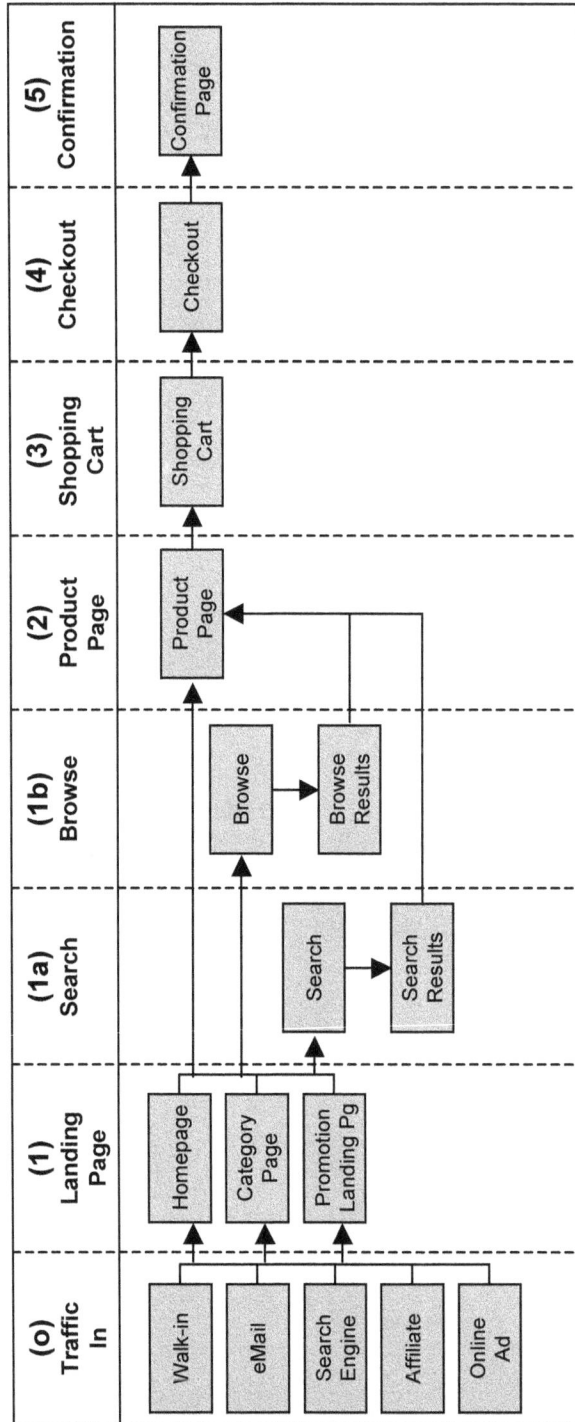

Figure 14.4

Reducing Abandonment

The key to using Web Analytics to reduce abandonment is to increase click-thus at each step in the process. The ultimate goal is to increase conversions (i.e. sales). To do this, you have to keep them moving forward in the shopping visit, until they reach the confirmation page after checkout.

You can track the user's visit using the *entry page* and the *exit page*. The entry page shows you the source of traffic. This lets you create separate reports for each targeted segment and each traffic channel. The exit page tells you if the visit results in a conversion or at what point the user abandons the visit.

You can set up a report to measure abandonment fairly easily. First group all of the eCommerce pages on your website into one of the buckets shown in Figure 14.4. These are the steps in the eCommerce process. Put each step in the eCommerce process into its own column on your report. Pick a time period you want to measure. It could be a single day, a week, month, quarter or year. Then add up all the exit pages occurring in each bucket and record that value in the corresponding column. Then add up all the entry pages that arrived on your website which resulted in an exit in one of the steps you have already recorded. Put this value in a new column. You can call it "Traffic In." Now split each of the columns for steps 1 - 5 in two. Divide the number of exit pages in the column by the total number of entry pages. Record this rate for each step in the second column. For steps 1 - 4, this is your *Abandonment Rate*. For step 5, the confirmation page, this is your *Conversion Rate*.

Now you have created a report with a single row. It shows the overall abandonment rate at each step of the eCommerce process and the overall conversion rate for your eCommerce site.

You can expand this report by creating a new row for each traffic source. You could have separate rows for: walk-in traffic, search engine traffic, email traffic, etc. This report will let you determine if there are different abandonment patterns from different traffic sources. See Figure 14.5 for a sample report format.

Web Analytics Abandonment Report eCommerce Shopping Visit																
	(0)	(1)		(1a)		(1b)		(2)		(3)		(4)		(5)		
Traffic Source	Traffic Volume	Landing Page		Search Results		Browse Results		Product Page		Shopping Cart		Checkout		Confirm- ation		
		#	%	#	%	#	%	#	%	#	%	#	%	#	%	
Walk In																
Search Engine																
Email																
Affiliate																
Online Ads																

Figure 14.5

The abandonment report will show you the general patterns of where abandonment is happening on your website. Your goal is to increase click-thrus from each step to the next step. Once you identify the pattern, you can drill down to identify specific pages with high abandonment rates. Then you can look for ways to increase click-thrus from these pages to the next step in the process.

You can also create an abandonment report that measures abandonment at each step as a percentage of users who reach that step. This provides more insight into which steps may be causing a problem. But, it requires a little more calculation. If you have followed the process to this point, you will be able to figure out how this report can easily be set up.

Some typical issues that may contribute to high abandonment rates at each step in the eCommerce process are as shown in Figure 14.6. This table shows how to diagnose potential problems that might be causing people to abandon their shopping visit and things you can do to improve.

Possible Causes of Abandonment

Step	Drop Off Point	Possible Contributing Factors	Possible Solutions
Step 1	At Home Page or Category Page	✓ May not be able to find what they are interested in.	✓ Try deep linking to a relevant product page or custom landing page
Step 1b	At Search Results Page	✓ Search engine may not be yielding useful results ✓ Search results page may not be user friendly	✓ May need to upgrade internal web search ✓ Perform usability testing on search results page
Step 1b	At Browse results / Category Page	✓ Product taxonomy may be confusing (i.e. customers have a hard time finding what they want) ✓ Category page may not display products of interest, or have old content	✓ Reconfigure taxonomy and/or perform usability tests ✓ Display different products & content
Step 2	At Product Page	✓ May be insufficient information for customers to make a purchase decision (e.g. no product image or product specs)	✓ Usability testing ✓ Add images or other needed content
Step 3	At Shopping Cart	✓ May be poor usability on the shopping cart (e.g. unable to remove items, reduce number of items to lower total price or view shipping charges) ✓ May have broken links to shipping costs or checkout	✓ Usability testing of shopping cart ✓ Repair broken or ineffective functionality
Step 4	At Checkout	✓ May be privacy concerns (e.g. ask more than needed personal info, or pre-checked email opt-in, or not a secure transaction) ✓ If unable to check price earlier, may have gone to checkout to check price, not intending to make a purchase.	✓ Usability testing of checkout page ✓ Make easier to complete the process ✓ Display proof of secure transactions

Figure 14.6

There will always be abandonment. It is not possible that every visitor on your website will make a purchase every time. The key to using the abandonment report to increase eCommerce sales is to identify trends that can be improved. By continuously monitoring your abandonment report and making incremental improvements to your pages, you will be able to gradually increase your website sales. A common example of this is to continuously improve the functionality of your product pages. It is normal when an online store first launches to have fairly minimal functionality on the product pages. Perhaps it just shows a picture and a price. This may not be enough for some customers to make a purchase. Over time you add product descriptions. Then you add product specifications. Perhaps you add user reviews or price comparisons with similar products. Each of these gives customers added information they need to make their purchase. You should expect to see a reduction in abandonment rates.

On the other hand, if you notice a particular step, or specific page, that is showing a higher than expected abandonment rate, that indicates there is a problem. The abandonment report will work as a diagnostic tool to identify issues that need to be fixed. A common example of this occurs when a website neglects to change site imagery and promotional content after seasonal promotions. A spike in abandonment right after Mothers' Day, for example, may be an indicator that you forgot to replace your Mothers' Day promotions. The same situation can occur any time content becomes out of date on the website.

The Abandonment Report is not limited to eCommerce visits. This process of mapping out the path a typical user visit will follow, and then measuring actions that occur at each step is an important method to improve the performance towards any goal you have for user activity on the website.

Conclusion

In this chapter, you have learned how to use the most important Web Analytics techniques for measuring performance and continuously improving results on your website.

Now turn to Part IV to learn how to create successful websites for the seven most common online business models.

Part IV

How To Build A Winning Website For Your Business Model

To Brand Or Not To Brand
The Pets.com Story

Everyone's favorite personality from the Dot-Com boom was undoubtedly the feisty Pets.com sock puppet. You might remember the precocious white puppy holding a microphone. He played the role of a roving newscaster delivering a comically dog's-eye commentary on everyday "human" life. We hardly noticed the hairy arm, wearing a wristwatch, reaching off the edge of our TV screens. Of course, that was part of the joke, just like the ending to each commercial, "Because pets can't drive!"

Pets.com started in early 1999, before any of the national pet store chains had an online presence. They announced their arrival by investing heavily in TV and radio ads. Their sock puppet was an instant hit! Pundits hailed Pets.com as one of the winners in the "New Economy." Like many other online stores at the time, Pets.com believed the way to success was to build a brand and gain market share as quickly as possible – no matter the cost. It was an article of faith in the Dot-Com industry that profits would eventually follow if you spent enough to build the brand. The high water mark of this strategy came when a host of startups spent millions of dollars to place TV ads on the 2000 Super Bowl. Pets.com reportedly spent $1.2 million dollars for their spot. And it was a funny commercial! The sock puppet was more popular than ever.

Then the post-holiday shopping numbers came in. Pets.com fell far short of its projected earnings. Building the brand through general advertising was not going to make it profitable after all. They had invested too heavily in their award-winning TV ads and not enough in determining the true sources of their return on investment. Awareness of their brand, and love for their mascot did not translate into a large enough base of loyal customers. The situation worsened as "bricks and mortar" stores like PetCo and PETsMART began to figure out the new online sales channel. They would be able to draw their loyal customers away from Pets.com to their own online stores.

Then, insult was added to injury. The Pets.com dog received a nasty letter from rival sock puppet, "Triumph the Insult Comic Dog," famous for his appearances on the Conan O'Brien Late Night TV show. Triumph, with his cigar and crude remarks threatened to sue. Well, as it turns out, pets not only can't drive, they don't take crap from insult comic dogs either. The Pets.com dog sued first. In what was perhaps the most surreal moment in the Dot-Com drama, two sock puppets faced off, in a mock trial, on the Conan O'Brien show. Pets.com was the unquestioned loser in the court of public opinion. The sock puppet kept his chin up for a few more months. Pets.com was put to sleep later that same year.

The closing act to the drama came the following year, during the 2001 Super Bowl. eTrade, a survivor in the Dot-Com crash ran a commercial spoofing the old 70's Save the Earth commercial where an Indian walks through a landscape covered in litter. In the eTrade ad, a chimpanzee walked through a landscape littered with Dot-Com mascots and logos. In the closing shot, he looks down on a discarded Pets.com sock puppet and sheds a tear.

Why did some companies, like eTrade, succeed online when others, like Pets.com, failed?

The chapters that follow will answer that question.

In Part I, you learned how to define your online business model and put together an Internet Marketing Plan. The chapters in Part IV dig deeper into what goes into building a successful Internet Marketing program for seven of the most common online business models. You will learn how to align your business model with the Internet Marketing features and services most likely to produce positive results for your company. In the process, you will also learn some common Internet Marketing techniques and how they can support your overall business objectives.

The seven online business models discussed in Part IV are:

Chapter 15   eRetail Websites
Chapter 16   Free Online Services Websites
Chapter 17   Content Websites
Chapter 18   Small Business Websites
Chapter 19   Consumer Goods Manufacturer Websites
Chapter 20   Business-to-Business Websites
Chapter 21   Nonprofit Organization Websites

These seven business models are prototypical examples. Your business may not fit exactly into one of these seven categories. That is okay. The foundational principles for successful Internet Marketing are contained in these seven business models. If your business is a little different, the concepts discussed here can be applied to your business model as well.

The important thing to remember is that no business fits into a cookie cutter mold. Even if you do find yourself in one of these categories, you still need to map out exactly what your business model and strategy is. Then use the examples here as guidelines to be applied, not as a formula to be followed.

Chapter 15

Building A Successful eRetail Website

In this chapter, you will learn . . .
- How to define the online business model for an eRetail website
- How to measure success for an eRetail website
- How to design a successful user experience for an eRetail website
- The tactics used by successful eRetail websites

Catalog Fulfillment Gone Electric
The PCMall Story

In 1995, PCMall went live as one of the early entries in the new online shopping marketplace. This eRetailer does not have the name recognition some of its famous cousins enjoy. Nevertheless, PCMall has been consistently successful and has even spun out a number of other online businesses. In 1987, two brothers Frank and Sam Khulusi started Creative Computers. The mail order catalog business sells computer hardware and software. Early in the 1990s, they realized that the World Wide Web presented a perfect channel for expanding their direct mail business. The idea was born for PCMall and MacMall. Two versions of their online store would appeal to their two target audiences.

The reason for their persistent success is the same as the reason for their lack of name recognition. The Khulusis understood the mail order business model. Creative Computers had built relationships with manufacturers and a distribution infrastructure. They knew how to calculate exactly what it costs to supply and deliver each product they sold. This is an all-important metric for mail order profitability. They also understood that the key to mail order success is very different from retail stores. Retailers focus on *building a brand* through general advertising. Catalogers focus on *building a list* of customers who can continue to be promoted to. By realizing they were in a mail order business, PCMall avoided the trap of burning capital on general advertising to gain awareness for their online store. Instead, they focused on gaining customers who would yield a profitable return on each item sold.

Along the way, the Khulusis set up a number of new Dot-Com businesses. They even tried their hand at creating an *incubator,* called IdeaMall, to fund new Dot-Com ventures. Of their five most notable start-ups, two succeeded and three failed. That is pretty good odds. uBid, a successful online auction site was sold for a nice profit before the Dot-Com crash. eCost, a discount computer eRetailer has also been a success. ToyTime and Kabang were both online stores that closed down along with hundreds of other eBusinesses as the bubble began to burst. eLinux was rolled back into the PCMall store. By 2002, they realized that having an incubator was not as glamorous as it was hyped up to be. They turned their focus back to the original core, the PCMall business.

There is nothing flashy about PCMall. What it does have, though, is practical business sense and the ability to make a mail order business work online. PCMall succeeded because they understood a lesson all eRetailers must know. An online store is an electronic mail order catalog. Even though they are called online "stores," they are really online catalogs. Failure to understand the difference can prove fatal.

In this chapter, we will walk through the steps successful eRetailers go through to create a winning website.

Understanding The eRetail Website

Some of the Internet's most familiar websites are the online stores. There are two types. The first type only sells through one sales channel, the Internet. These are known as *pure play* Internet businesses. They include stores like Amazon.com. Other online stores are multi-channel retailers. They have traditional sales outlets and supplement them with the online sales channel.

Almost every major retailer falls into this category, and a large percentage of smaller ones.

When online shopping first became "the next big thing," there was a lot of talk about making the online experience seem like you were entering and walking around in an actual store. The thinking was, a customer is entering a "virtual store," so they should feel as if they are actually walking into the front door of a store when they enter your website. This represented a basic misunderstanding many had at the time. Shopping online is not like going into a store. What it is a like, however, is shopping from a mail order catalog. It was this inability to recognize online shopping as mail order catalog shopping that led to some of the dramatic failures, like Pets.com.

Dimensions of the eRetail Online Business Model

In Part I, you learned an easy way to begin defining your online business model. You start by choosing from among seven basic dimensions that form the foundation of all online businesses (see Figure 15.1). This quick and easy approach will allow you to implement a set of features and tactics aimed at achieving the goals of your business or organization.

> **Seven Dimensions To Online Business Models**
>
> ✓ 1. eCommerce
>   2. Business Development
>   3. Lead Generation
>   4. Brand Development
>   5. Customer Relations
>   6. Information Delivery
>   7. Cost Savings

Figure 15.1

An eRetail website is primarily following an *eCommerce* business model. Everything done on the website is to support generating sales through the website. As you read on, you will discover how to have a successful online store.

"Luke, I Am Your Father"

At its core, eRetail is a *direct marketing* business model. An online store is an electronic mail order catalog. More than any other online business model, eRetail follows classic direct marketing practices. The foundation is the online catalog. Customers must be able to easily find the items they are looking for. Then they must have an easy and convenient way to place their orders. On this foundation, features are added with the goal of increasing the volume of sales to each customer.

This would have been a shock to many entrepreneurs starting eRetail businesses in the Dot-Com boom. There was so much youthful zeal and pride. These entrepreneurs truly believed they were doing something so new it required creating an entirely new economy to understand it. They described themselves as tech-savvy Davids who were going to slay the old economy Goliaths. Well, stogy old Direct Mail certainly fits the bill as "old economy." I imagine a young, innovative entrepreneur who always pictured himself as the Luke Skywalker character in this high-tech adventure. After wrestling for years to build a new kind of business, he looks up to see Direct Mail, who he knows for killing the rainforests by always filing his mail box with ads he doesn't want. Then Direct Mail reaches down to him, and says, "Luke, I am your father."

Today, this is not such a big shock. We now know it was not really David versus Goliath after all. Really, it was the age old story of new ideas improving on tried and true models. A brief description of how those tried and true direct mail campaigns earn revenue will show what all online stores are trying to accomplish.

A Direct Mail Primer

In Chapter 7, we reviewed the basics of direct mail for its application to email practices. This section will review that discussion and show how the same principles also apply to the eRetail online business model.

There are two basic types of direct mail campaign. The classic mail campaign is aimed at generating immediate sales. These are usually sent to a large list of both customers and prospects. They have a promotional offer aimed at eliciting an immediate response. This type of direct mail campaign is typically called a *targeted marketing campaign*.

The second type is a *customer communications mailer*. These are sent to existing customers and are usually offered as a service, or value-added benefit to the customer. Customer communication mailers include things such as service reminders from your car dealership, birthday cards from your favorite restaurant, or notification of sales from your favorite department store. These mail pieces also contain a call to action and usually an offer. But, it is a soft sell. The goal is to keep you as a satisfied customer and incentivize you to keep purchasing from the company. The return from customer communication mailers goes beyond immediate sales. It also includes the future purchases you make as a loyal customer, plus the positive word-of-mouth they generate among your friends.

Both types of direct mail campaign include the same five basic elements.

1.   The List

Direct mail starts with a *list*. The direct mail list is the group of people who receive your marketing message. These people are selected by using a targeting method that chooses people or businesses who are most likely to respond to your message.

2.   Opening the Envelope

After receiving the message, recipients in the mail group must *open the envelope*. This is the first hurdle. You can probably think of many mail pieces you have thrown away without opening. We all do it every day. To overcome this, direct marketers have devised many methods aimed at getting people to open their envelopes.

3.   The Marketing Piece

If your recipient does open the envelope, they will see your *marketing piece*. This piece will always contain a *marketing message* and a *call to action*. It will usually also contain a *promotional offer* to incentivize people to respond to the *call to action*. In the case of a mail order catalog, the entire catalog is the marketing piece.

4.   The Response

The next hurdle is for recipients to *respond* to your marketing piece. This could entail calling a 1-800 phone number, returning a business reply card, or many other possible actions. Not surprisingly, this is called a *response*. Recipients who go the extra step of responding are called *responders*.

5.   The Conversion

The final hurdle is for responders to actually make a purchase (or carry out some other desired end result). When they do, it is called a *conversion*. In some cases, the conversion takes place as part of the response. The call to action could be, for example, "Return this card and start your subscription to Today's Internet Guru." In cases like this, the act of responding is also the conversion event.

Direct mail success is measured in terms of response rates and conversion rates.

Like Father, Like Son

Now we will see how an eRetail website follows the exact same process as the classic direct mail campaign.

1.   The Lead

First, potential customers are exposed to your business. They may see your link in search engine results, see a banner ad on a special interest website or are exposed to your marketing message in any number of other online venues. The group of people who enter your target keywords in a search engine or view target websites you advertise on are equivalent to the direct mail list. They are targeted by the interests they display in their online behavior.

2.   The Click-Thru

The first hurdle you cross is for those web users to actually click on your link or banner ad. This is the same as opening your envelope.

3. The Landing Page

When they do "open your envelope," they are sent to a page on your website. That first page is equivalent to the promotional piece they pull out of the envelope. It is called the *landing page*.

4. The Response

A promotional mailer typically has one, or maybe two calls to action. On an eRetail website, there are many calls to action. Any one can result in a response. Most importantly, shoppers are presented with product assortments for them to purchase. Once they add a product to their shopping cart, they are taking an important step towards making the purchase.   Other responses include such things as opting-in to your email list or creating a wish list.

5. The Conversion

Finally, when a purchase is made, you have a conversion.

eRetail success is measured in terms of response rates and conversion rates.

Typical eRetail Goals

Once you have defined your online business model, the next step is to determine what goals will lead to success. These goals set the compass heading for your website.

There are basically three goals to the typical eRetail business model. These three will lead to maximizing online sales through the website. They are:

(1)   Convert interested shoppers into buyers
(2)   Convert buyers into repeat buyers (also known as "loyal customers")
(3)   Maximize the total purchases made by each loyal customer

Of course, this is a prototypical list. As you go through this process, you will need to define goals specific to your own online store.

Measuring Success For An eRetail Website

Now you have set the compass heading for your website, by understanding your online business model and setting effective goals. This will let you develop a set of tactics and site features to reach those goals. Before you can do that, however, you must determine how you are going to measure success on your website. This section will show you how to calculate Return on Investment (ROI) for the eRetail website.

The eRetail website earns revenue from sales transactions on the website. ROI for the website is attained in two ways: First, by gaining *immediate sales*. Second, by increasing the *lifetime value* of a customer. Higher lifetime values can be obtained by increasing the frequency of purchase or by increasing the average amount spent per visit. In other words, by increasing the total amount of revenue earned from a given customer. The key to understanding eRetail ROI is therefore found in two formulas which represent these two ways of realizing revenue (see Figures 15.2 and 15.3). *These two formulas for calculating ROI are inherited from eRetail's direct mail roots. They are the basis of all direct marketing programs.*

ROI from Immediate Sales

The first ROI formula is the classic direct response return on investment. In economic terms, sales on an eRetail website are directly comparable to sales resulting from a direct marketing promotion. That is to say, the return on investment derived from website activity aimed at generating immediate sales is calculated in the same way as ROI from a direct mail campaign. The classic direct response ROI formula is used (Figure 15.2).

When an eRetail site adds features or online marketing campaigns with the goal of driving immediate sales, the direct response ROI formula shows whether the investment is worth it.

Direct Response Return on Investment (ROI)

(AVG. PROFIT PER SALE) – (COST PER CONVERSION)

This formula is calculated using the
following formulas:

$$\begin{bmatrix} \text{COST PER} \\ \text{CONVERSION} \end{bmatrix} = \frac{\text{COST PER IMPRESSION}}{\text{CONVERSION RATE}}$$

$$\begin{bmatrix} \text{CONVERSION} \\ \text{RATE} \end{bmatrix} = \frac{\text{\# SALES}}{\text{\# IMPRESSIONS}}$$

Figure 15.2

To calculate ROI from immediate sales, you first determine the *cost per conversion*. You can do this by making the following calculations:

➤ Measure the total number of site visitors coming from the campaign or users of the online feature you are measuring (these are called *impressions*).

➤ Measure the total number of sales resulting from those impressions (these are called *conversions*).

➤ Calculate the *conversion rate* obtained from the campaign, or feature, by dividing the number of sales by the number of impressions. (The conversion rate is the percentage of impressions that result in a conversion).

For example: assume you receive 10,000 visits from your paid search listings on Google. If 200 of these result in a sale, you will have a 2% conversion rate from Google paid search.

➢ Next, calculate your cost per impression.

In the Google example, assume you paid $0.50, on average, for every click to your website. Your cost per impression is $0.50.

➢ Finally, you can determine your cost per conversion by dividing the cost per impression by the conversion rate.

In the Google example, your cost per conversion would be ($0.50 / 0.02) = $25.

Another way to think of this is, at a 2% conversion rate, you need to get 50 impressions to generate one sale. At $0.50 per impression, your cost per conversion is ($0.50 * 50) = $25. (These two formulas are the same.)

In addition to calculating your cost per conversion, you must also calculate (or at least estimate) your *profit per sale*. If your profit per sale is greater than you cost per conversion, then you are making a profit.

A common mistake is to calculate ROI using revenue from sales instead of profit. This will overestimate your ROI and can result in a net loss.

ROI from Increasing Customer Loyalty

The second formula is customer lifetime value. There are many variations of the lifetime value formula. Figure 15.3 shows a very simplified version of the formula. In it, we simply use sales volume and profit margin to measure the value each customer represents to your company for one fiscal year.

Annualized Lifetime Value
(# SALES PER YEAR) * (AVG. PROFIT PER SALE)

Figure 15.3

Lifetime value is calculated for each customer. The basic idea is simple. Measure how many purchases a customer makes each year. Calculate the profits earned from those purchases. That tells you how much each customer contributes to the bottom line. As noted, this is a very simple form of a lifetime value calculation. A complete formula includes estimated number of years remaining as a customer and estimated growth or decay rate in expenditures with your company. Then a discount rate is applied to annualize the net value. The simple form is used here because it makes the point more clearly. Plus, in many cases, a simple formula will suffice to obtain a basic measure of success or failure for a new site feature or service. The goal is to increase profits earned from each customer. This can be obtained by increasing total volume of purchases per year, average amount spent per purchase, or both for each customer using the feature.

When an eRetail site adds features or services aimed at increasing customer loyalty, the annualized lifetime value calculation is used.

These two direct marketing formulas reveal a wide range of possibilities for eRetailers in employing Internet Marketing tactics. The most important variable is profits per sale. Related to this are two major factors that must be considered when choosing features and services for an eRetail website. These are the average size of purchase and profit margin expected to be gained from purchases. For a company selling big ticket items with large profit margins, small gains in loyalty can yield large profit gains. Tactics aimed at building long term customer relationships with your customers may yield big results. On the other hand, companies with a small inventory of popular novelty items may find it more profitable to pursue tactics aimed at increasing immediate sales. The specific mix of features chosen will vary, but the basic economics underlying success or failure are rooted in these two traditional direct marketing formulas.

Designing The eRetail User Experience

We have now defined the eRetail online business model, identified typical goals and shown how to measure the success of your website. The next step is to design a user experience for your customers that successfully achieves the goals of your online business model.

Many businesses make the mistake of trying to build a website before taking the time to figure out what the website is there to accomplish. That is always a set-up for poor results. Only after mapping out a user experience that will lead to successfully achieving your business goals should you put your web designer to work creating the look and feel for your website.

This section will walk through a typical user experience that successful eRetail websites create to generate sales through the website.

The Goal of Website Design

The primary purpose of a website is to meet the needs and wants of customers coming to the site in a way that maximizes the attainment of Internet Marketing goals. The easiest way to understand what a website is trying to accomplish is to think of it as a funnel. At the wide end, tactics are employed to reach out to customers, appeal to their interests and entice them to enter your website. From this point onward, every action a user takes should be moving them down the funnel, towards the ultimate outcome(s) you want to achieve from your website.

When customers come to the eRetail website, they are seeking to make a purchase. The outcome the eRetail store hopes to achieve from the site visit is that they will indeed make a purchase. Sounds good so far. Both customer and store have the same goals. There is a difference though. Customers may have a specific item in mind that they want to buy. In some cases, the customer may not expect to buy anything at all during the visit, but is just "window shopping." The store, on the other hand, not only wants customers to find the items they are interested in, but also wants them to both buy additional items and become repeat shoppers on the website. Figure 15.4 shows how the eRetail website accomplishes these three goals.

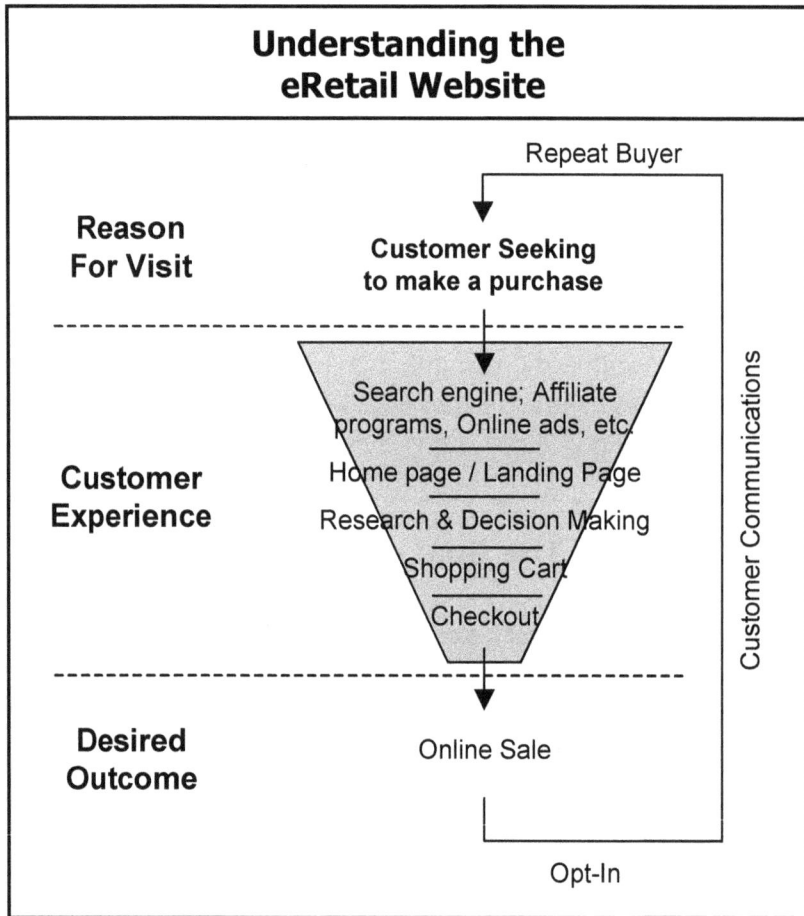

Understanding the eRetail Website

Repeat Buyer

Reason For Visit — **Customer Seeking to make a purchase**

Search engine; Affiliate programs, Online ads, etc.

Home page / Landing Page

Research & Decision Making

Shopping Cart

Checkout

Customer Experience

Customer Communications

Desired Outcome — Online Sale

Opt-In

Figure 15.4

There are basically five steps in the path from interested shopper to buyer. It starts with the initial contact and ends with the sale. At every one of these steps, the customer could have the opportunity to move forward in the process, abandon the visit or opt-in for future communications and loyalty incentives.

Now let us look at the five steps in the typical eRetail user experience.

The eRetail User Experience

1.   First Contact

In general, a small percentage of shoppers come directly to the eRetail website to make their purchase. Instead, they are doing something else online and have to be enticed into coming to your site. They may be searching for a product and click on a link to your store. They may be reading an article on a special interest website and view a banner ad. They may be reading their email and respond to a special offer from your website. *The eRetail website must aggressively recruit potential shoppers to the website.*

2.   The Landing Page

Most customers have to be enticed to come to the website, and do not usually come specifically ready to make a purchase. For this reason, the first thing they see when they "land on" your website is critically important. This is called the *landing page*.

In most cases, the company's home page will not do a very good job of this. Therefore, the eRetail business spends a lot of time optimizing the pages that customers land on when they come to the site. Customers will typically be directed to a particular product or category page deep in the website, that corresponds to what they have been searching for. Or else, they will be placed on a specially designed landing page targeted to their interests.

The landing page has to immediately appeal to your customers plus draw them down the path you want them to take, ultimately leading to a purchase and/or an opt-in for future communications.

3.   Research and Decision Making

If the landing page is successful in keeping the customer on the website, that is when the actual shopping process begins. There are many things that can and do go on during this process. These will be discussed in more detail later in this chapter.

The critical factor to consider when designing the website is to allow customers to successfully make their purchase decision and complete the sale without abandoning the site before they finish.

4.   The Shopping Cart

A critical step in any shopping visit on an eRetail site is the shopping cart. Anyone who has shopped online is familiar with them. This is where a customer puts their items before the final checkout. A smoothly functioning shopping cart is essential to a successful website. At a minimum, customers must be able to easily add and remove items from the cart. They should also be able to see the total costs. Most customers will also want a way to find out how much their shipping costs are likely to be. *If a customer is frustrated with trying to use your shopping cart, or cannot figure out their total cost they are very likely to leave the site and try shopping at your competitor.*

5.   Checkout

The final step in the shopping visit is the checkout. You may feel as if you are home free at this point. Don't! This is one of the places where good design is most critical. Many customers abandon their visit at checkout. There are always going to be customers who go through the process just for research and never intended to complete the sale. There is nothing you can do about these. But there are also a lot of customers who may be abandoning the checkout page because of things you can fix. If customers find high shipping costs or expected a discount and find they are not qualified to receive it they are likely to leave. If customers find the total price is too high and have a hard time removing items from their order before completing the purchase, they may leave. In these cases, they might never come back.

The key to a successful checkout is to make sure there are no surprises for the customer when they reach the checkout page. If surprises cannot be avoided, they should be able to easily go back and modify their order.

On most websites, the checkout process is also where new users register for the website. This is another place where a poor experience can cause customers to abandon the website. On the other hand, the site registration step also provides a great opportunity to opt-in customers to future communications and special offers.

Now, let us look at the specific things done on eRetail websites that make them successful.

eRetail Roadmap To Success

The final step before you actually build your website is to map out the specific objectives and tactics that will lead to successfully achieving your goals. In Part I, we called this your *roadmap to success*. The tactics in your "roadmap" are the building blocks that will create a winning user experience on your website.

Figure 15.5 presents a set of objectives and tactics common on eRetail websites. They are laid out according to the four levels of customer intimacy described in Chapter 2. A quick survey of the objectives and tactics shown here will give you an idea of what goes into a successful eRetail website.

These tactics are prototypical examples. They should be used as guidelines to give you an idea of what your website can accomplish. However, you will have to determine specific objectives and tactics that match the unique aspects of your business and the needs of your customers.

Typical eRetail Objectives and Tactics

	Objectives	Tactics

Interest	Optimize traffic from all available online channels	1. Use all methods which yield positive ROI to drive traffic to the website, including:
		
		  a. Search Engine Optimization & Search Engine Marketing
		
		  b. Get listed on shopping websites
		
		  c. Advertise on special interest websites
		
		  d. Set up an affiliate program and recruit affiliate partners
		
		2. Optimize landing pages

	Be competitive in the marketplace	3. Offer competitive pricing, product assortment and quality
Trust	Create a secure, reliable and generally positive user experience	4. Effective online catalog with search 5. Secure & reliable transactions and a privacy policy 6. Up-to-date information 7. On-time delivery and return policy 8. Responsive customer service 9. Provide a user-friendly shopping cart and account management features 10. Easy opt-out ability for all email
Satisfaction	Assist with the shopping process, so research & decision-making can take place on the site.	11. Product information, specs, pictures 12. Product reviews, ratings & buyer guides 13. Product recommendations
Loyalty	Provide customizable shopping features, so customers utilize site as a shopping resource and not simply a place to buy	14. Customizable site features

	Use targeted email to cultivate customer relationships resulting in repeat purchases and referrals	15. Create a large opt-in email list and use email to generate repeat sales
	Utilize viral marketing to transform loyal customers into a marketing asset	16. Include Forward-to-a-friend links on all content (reviews, buyer guides, pricing, special offers, etc.)

Figure 15.5

The next section goes into detail about the how these tactics work together to make the eRetail site successful. If you do not want to dig this deep into the details, feel free to turn ahead to the next chapter.

The Roadmap Unfolded:
Typical eRetail Tactics

In this chapter you have learned what successful eRetail websites are trying to accomplish and how to design a website that meets those objectives. Revenue generated from the eRetail site is realized through a sale on the website. All of the tactics are aimed towards getting the customer to complete sales without abandoning the session. The financing for onsite features comes from the profit margins of incremental sales they generate. Some of these features are costly to implement and may not yield sufficient increased sales to warrant using them on your site. They are included here so you know what the possibilities are and have some familiarity them.

The following table contains a detailed description of the tactics presented in the Roadmap to Success table (Figure 15.5). It provides nuts-and-bolts examples of the type of things implemented on successful eRetail websites. You can use this information as a framework for developing your own website. However, there is no substitute for defining the details of your own online business model and mapping out a set of tactics that will meet your own organizational goals.

Building Interest

With the eRetail website, successful interest building can be thought of as bringing customers two steps forward in the sales process. The first is successfully outreaching to customers while they are off of your website, resulting in a click to your site. The second is that they continue shopping on your website after their first impression.

Utilize all profitable methods to drive traffic	The core of the eRetail business model is generating traffic and converting traffic to sales. The first part of this is to use every method at your disposal to get traffic to your website. In Part II, you learned the key ways businesses use to generate traffic. You will very likely use all of these with the eRetail website. Part III then showed you how to evaluate each of your traffic sources to optimize the profitability of your traffic management program.
Optimize landing pages	With eRetail, the first impression is the most important. Since you are literally "trolling" the Internet for traffic, most of your customers will not know what they should expect when they get to your site. With the eRetail website, clicking on a link in a search engine or on a banner ad is equivalent to opening the envelope of a direct mail piece. If they do "open the envelope," then the first web page they see is equivalent to the promotional ad they find in the envelope. It *absolutely must* be appealing to the customer and entice them to continue. For this reason, eRetail websites spend a lot of time developing custom landing pages that are targeted to the different traffic sources. They also optimize the pages on the website to make sure search engine links drop customers on content pages they are most interested in. *Sending traffic to the home page is the least effective way to begin a shopping visit. Developing custom landing pages and deep linking to product or category pages is a must.*
Competitive pricing, product assortment and quality	This tactic probably should go without saying. The Internet is a very competitive "Bazaar" for online shoppers. For almost any product they want, dozens of competing stores are only a mouse click away. People have to like what they see when they browse your product selection. That means products they want at prices they are willing to pay.

Building Trust

Once customers decide to continue shopping on your website, they must feel confident that they will have a positive experience. Shopping online promises ease and convenience. Shopping online is also risky. To be competitive, all eRetail stores should have the following tactics in place.

Online catalog with search	The foundation for eRetail websites is an online catalog. There should also be a search engine allowing customers to use keywords to find what they are looking for. Customers must be able to find the products they are interested in and see pictures of them. The catalog must also be linked to a standard suite of eCommerce features. These include a shopping cart and checkout.
	For a small store, with a small product assortment, you can get away without a search engine (not recommended). In this case, extra care must be taken to make sure category pages and menus are intuitive and easy to navigate.
Secure & reliable transactions and information handling	Customers must know their online transactions and private information will be kept secure. Identify theft is a big problem online. Customers are very sensitive to it and will abort a shopping visit if they do not see proof that they are safe. This means using a trusted third-party vendor to handle your transactions. You should not process credit card transactions yourself, the way you would at your physical location. Customers know identity thieves can steal information while it is being sent to your computer. You must use a trusted secure transaction service and clearly display their logo.
	Customers are also concerned that you might mishandle their information and allow your computer systems to be "hacked." Worse still, they are afraid that you might not be ethical and may sell their private information. You must be aware of this and allay these fears. One important way to do this is through your privacy policy.
	Every website must have a privacy policy. Although most customers will never look at it, your privacy policy is an extremely important part of your website. *If a customer files a lawsuit against your business, the courts will look at your privacy policy to decide your case. You must be very careful to craft a policy statement that assures your customers of their safety and your good intentions, but also does not hold you liable for more than you can actually do.*

Up-to-date information	A third deal-buster for your online store is out of date information. If customers come to your store and find products listed that are no longer available, or promotions that are no longer current, they will lose confidence in your business. They may still buy something on that visit, if you have the best price. But they are likely to think that if you do not maintain your own information you may be just as lax with their private information. This can make them afraid to shop with your store. Also important is informational content on your website. If you have articles posted on the home page about last year's products, customers will not really take your store seriously.
User-friendly shopping cart & account management	If you make it past the first three hurdles, and your customer actually tries to shop and buy something on your site, you have to make it easy for them. People hate inconvenience on a website more than almost anything. Your shopping cart, registration process and account management features must be user-friendly and meet their needs. With the shopping cart, customers must be able to easily add and remove items. They must also be able to view their total price. It is more difficult to calculate shipping costs and taxes in the shopping cart. However, some indication of what the total costs will be should be included. This same ease of use must also carry over to the checkout page. The account management features are often called something like, "My Account." This is where the user can see things like their order status and order history. Most importantly, it includes their shipping address and opt-in status for any special features or email newsletters. The biggest usability issue to watch for here is to make it easy for customers to change their information or opt-out.
On-time delivery and returns	After a customer actually goes all the way and makes a purchase from your website, you must be able to deliver on time. Customers will not shop again at a website that sent their order late. If there is a potential problem with delivery times for a given item, you need to let the customer know before they complete the sale. If the order takes a long time, but they were told up front, most customers will give you another shot. You must also make it easy for customers to return products they are not satisfied with. Have a clearly worded return

	policy on the website. Make sure your customer service representatives are well versed with your return procedures. The quickest way to turn a customer into an enemy is to upset them when they are not satisfied. At all costs make sure this does not happen.
Responsive customer service	Unless you have a very large store, you will probably not need a large customer service staff. But you must have at least someone who is responsible for customer service. You must respond to all emails within 24 hours. If you have someone who answers the phone, which you should, they must be friendly and responsive to your customer's needs.
Easy opt-out	The final trust-breaking mistake some online stores fall into is to make it hard, or impossible for customers to opt-out of email. The rule is simple. Everybody hates Spam. If you are sending Spam, customers will not buy from you. If a customer tries to opt-out of an email and cannot, it is Spam.

Building Satisfaction

After you have captured your customers' interest and won their trust, then they will be responsive to additional functionality that adds a "Wow" factor to your website. The tactics in this group are commonly used on eRetail websites to help customers in the shopping process. However, unlike the tactics we discussed above, these are not essential to the website. They are extras that can help generate additional sales and win over repeat customers. But they can be costly to implement. So care must be taken to demonstrate a positive return on your investment for any of these features you decide to implement.

There are two general outcomes that this set of features are trying to achieve. First, you want to keep the customer on your website while they are making the buying decision. If they do not have enough information to feel comfortable making a purchase, they will go looking for that information. If they cannot find it on your website, they may never come back. Second, you want to encourage them to buy things they were not thinking of before they came to your website.

Robust product information	It is essential that you have pictures, pricing and a product description for all products on your website. Still, this may not be enough for customers to make a purchase. You may also want to include more detailed product specifications, usage guidelines, or other information about the product to help the customer decide if this is what they really want.

Product reviews, customer ratings and buyer guides	There are often competing products meeting the customers' needs and they want to be able to choose which is right for them. You may add features such as product reviews or customer ratings, to help them find the best products. You could also create buyer guides for popular types of products. Features like these represent a significant investment in creating content. However, if successful, they will increase conversions on the site. Customers are more likely to make a purchase if they are better equipped to find what they are looking for. These features, if well implemented, will also cause customers to keep coming back to the website. They will find your site a useful shopping resource and may even add it to their "Favorites" list. This is sometimes called making the website "*sticky*."
Product recommendations	It is common for eRetailers to use some sort of product recommendations. Products are presented to the user that they were not originally considering. These recommendations aim to increase the overall volume of purchases the customer makes during the visit. There are a number of devices an online retailer can choose from to deliver such recommendations. All of these tools use targeting technology to identify the customer's likely interests and generate some type of recommendation. Recommendations will typically be displayed in either a list of recommended items or dynamically positioned promotional content.

Building Loyalty

The final set of tactics are aimed at getting customers to keep returning to your website and buying more. The basic idea behind these tactics is to get the customer to participate with you in creating the shopping experience. If possible, you also want your customers to send other people to your website.

Customizable site features	Customizable site features are basically telling your customers, "Go ahead and make our website your own personal shopping assistant." Amazon.com is the master at this. At Amazon, a customer can turn the entire home page into their own personal shopping website. You may not be able to go that far, but you can set up features on the website that users can customize to help them meet their shopping needs. There are some fairly easy customizable features

	you can provide. Perhaps the easiest is to let customers save the contents of their shopping cart to view later. That way, if they are not ready to make a purchase, they can come back and continue where they left off. You can also let them choose from a set of special interest categories, and have an area on the home page where new or popular products in those categories are displayed. Other customizeable features include allowing customers to set up a gift registry or wish list. These allow customers to tell their friends exactly what they want to receive for their birthday, the holidays or other special days.
	The great thing about customizable features is they are the ultimate win-win. The customer wins because they get just the information they want. But you win even more, because they are telling you exactly how to target them for promotional content and offers
Opt-In email	Opt-in email serves a dual purpose. On the one hand, creating an email list allows your existing customers to become an additional traffic source. You will continue to send them promotional messages to drive traffic to your website. Customers can self-select promotional emails or newsletters they want to receive. This can be done as part of your customer registration or you can simply let customers enter their email addresses to receive email. If you make sure to include offers that are of interest and value to your customers, they will see these emails as a value added. This is a good way to generate new sales from your existing customers. On the other hand, if you do not have anything of value to offer, your customers are likely to see these emails as Spam and get offended.
	If you decide to take this further, you can use email to interact with your customers one-on-one. Through such things as birthday offers, reminder messages, or personalized recommendations you cultivate a loyalty relationship with your existing customers
Forward-to-a-friend	The final eRetail tactic is both powerful and inexpensive. If customers like what they find on your website, give them a way to tell others about it. You can do this by providing Forward-to-a-friend links on every page and email message. Generating business from this type of "word of mouth" marketing is called *viral marketing*.

Conclusion

In this chapter, you have learned how to be successful selling products online through an online store. In the next chapter, you will learn how to be profitable sending traffic and sales leads to other businesses online.

Now turn to the Free Online Services website.

Chapter 16

Building A Successful Free Online Services Website

In this chapter, you will learn . . .
- How to define the online business model for a Free Online Services website
- How to measure success for a Free Online Services website
- How to design a successful user experience for a Free Online Services website
- The tactics used by successful Free Online Services websites

Arbitrage At The Infomediary
The BizRate.com Story

BizRate.com (now called Shopzilla) started as a school project. Farhad Mohit was a graduate student at the University of Pennsylvania's Wharton School of Business. He convinced his professor, Dr. David Reibstein, to help transform his class assignment into a business. Then, in 1996, along with friend and fellow Penn student Henri Asseily, they started a company. It began in the garage of Farhad's parents' Southern California home. The idea was to bring some sanity to the new world of online shopping that had become like the Wild West of the online frontier. They recruited online stores who let them serve customer satisfaction surveys at checkout. Then they sent, to willing customers, a follow up survey after the products had arrived. BizRate quickly became recognized as the Consumer Reports of online shopping. Stores clamored to get the BizRate seal of approval.

The original business model was to earn revenue as a research company. However, they soon realized the people who would benefit most from this information were online shoppers themselves. So, they revised their business model. The new goal was connecting in-market buyers with qualified sellers. October 1999 was dubbed "Red October." That month, BizRate.com staff worked around the clock to launch a new comparison shopping portal in time for the holiday shopping season. Shoppers could search for stores that had the best price, customer service and on-time delivery. By the 2000 holiday season, BizRate.com had become one of the Top 10 most visited retail websites on the Internet (according to Media Metrix).

The new business model was straightforward enough: spend less to get traffic (clicks in) than you charge to send traffic to merchant sites (clicks out). BizRate earned the difference by adding value to the experience. Customers qualify themselves by searching for the specific products they are in the market for. Then, by viewing BizRate's research findings, the shopper will find a store they can have confidence buying from. Both merchants and shoppers benefit. But revenue on clicks is counted in pennies. To be successful, they had to be vigilant to hold every business unit accountable to delivering a positive profit margin on click-thrus. That meant making painful decisions. Pet projects had to be cut which added user services at a cost that could not be recouped through increased clicks or higher click-thru rates. It paid off. By the 2002 holiday shopping season the company had become profitable. Profit margins have continued to grow, year after year, since then.

The lesson BizRate.com learned is a basic truth all Free Online Service providers must know. As cool and useful as the website is to its users, ultimately the value of the service is that it is a source of traffic to other sites willing to pay for sales leads.

In this chapter, we will walk through the steps successful Free Online Services companies go through to create a winning website.

Understanding The Free Online Services Website

When you look for something on the Internet, you probably start by entering a keyword or phrase into a search engine. You may have a free email account with them also. When you want to buy something, you may go to a comparison shopping site, like Shopzilla, to find the best price or customer satisfaction record. You plan a party and send invitations through an online invitation service. You need a job and post your resume online. None of these "pure play" websites charges you for the service. So how do they make money?

Dimensions of the Free Online Services Online Business Model

In Part I, you learned an easy way to begin defining your online business model. You start by choosing from among seven basic dimensions that form the foundation of all online businesses (See Figure 16.1). This quick and easy approach will allow you to implement a set of features and tactics aimed at achieving the goals of your business or organization.

The primary dimension for Free Online Services is *lead generation*. These websites offer a free service that draws people to their website. Once there, those people become qualified

Seven Dimensions To Online Business Models

1. eCommerce
2. Business Development
✓ 3. Lead Generation
4. Brand Development
5. Customer Relations
6. Information Delivery
7. Cost Savings

Figure 16.1

sales leads for other businesses. The Free Online Services website makes money by charging businesses for access to qualified leads. As you read on, you will discover how to be successful offering a free online service.

The Lead Game

The basic business model behind Free Online Services is *Lead Generation*. People with a direct marketing background recognize this as a variation of the old list business. The goal of the lead game is to collect information about customers on your list that will make them valuable to companies who want to sell something to them. A quick look at a typical "old school" list business will paint a picture of what all lead generation businesses are trying to do.

The Polk Company is the granddaddy of all list businesses. They have been in the lead generation business for over 125 years. Polk used to have the largest targeted direct mail list available, with over 165 million mailable names (before they sold it to Equifax). Their specialty is an extensive database of automotive information. The following simple example is typical of how Polk makes money from their list.

Information on the Polk list tells us that a certain person is a middle-aged woman, earning a high income. Let us call her Janet. Knowing this information about Janet makes her lead a good prospect for various products. You can probably think of some commercials and ads that are targeted to her. How much do you suppose a company would pay to deliver a message to say 100,000 people fitting this description? What if we also know that 40,000 of these have owned Asian import cars before? How much do you think Lexus or Acura would pay to deliver a message to that group? Now let us also say that 5,000 of this smaller group filled out a survey saying they are in the market to buy an import luxury car in the next four weeks. Would these 5,000 highly qualified leads be worth more than the 100,000 somewhat qualified leads? Absolutely!

This is what Free Online Services websites are trying to do.

A Source of Qualified Traffic

For online businesses, leads are delivered as traffic to paying websites. There are a number ways to convert online leads into revenue. The easiest to understand, and most common, is to charge partner websites for leads who click-thru to their websites. In this chapter, we will discuss this type of lead model. It should be kept in mind that the same principles presented here will also apply to other methods of delivering leads to paying partners.

Two other lead generation models are also fairly common. The first is when customers enter information about themselves with the expectation that others will search the database and locate their information. This is how job search, real estate and dating websites work. Another model is for users of the website to post a call to action that others will respond to. In this case, the user posting the information pays a commission when a transaction occurs. This is how online auctions, like eBay, and B2B exchanges work.

For most Free Online Services, the sales lead is delivered to the paying client when the site user clicks on a link and is sent to the client's website. This is called a *redirect* from the free service's website to a client's website. When a customer clicks on the client's link, that results in a redirect to the client. But before the customer is actually put on the client website, the redirect is recorded for future billing.

If you have an online invitation service, you are hoping companies like party supply stores or concert ticket services will pay top dollar to put an ad on your site. If you have a comparison shopping site, you are hoping stores will pay top dollar for customers who have already gone through the effort of researching a product and then clicking on a link to their store. Search engines charge more to get your "sponsored link" displayed higher in the search results list. People are more likely to click on the top links. All of these examples are ways to use targeting to increase the value of sales leads generated through your website.

Notice this business model is very different than eRetail. Like night and day really. Revenue is generated by how much money companies are willing to pay for your sales leads, not from how much is actually spent by the consumer.

Typical Free Online Services Goals

Once you have defined your online business model, the next step is to determine what goals will lead to success. These goals set the compass heading for your website.

An important key to understanding how to reach your goals is to realize that this business model is a balancing act between meeting the needs of your site users and the needs of your partners who are paying for the leads.

There are four basic goals for the typical Free Online Services website.

(1)   Convert interested browsers into site users
(2)   Transform site users into qualified sales leads, by using their site activity to direct them to partner sites where they will be likely to convert
(3)   Earn the highest possible revenue per lead
(4)   Convert site users into repeat users who continue to redirect to paying partner sites

Of course, this is a prototypical list. As you go through this process, you will need to define goals specific to your own website.

Measuring Success For A Free Online Services Website

Now you have set the compass heading for your website, by setting effective goals. This will let you develop a set of tactics and site features to reach those goals. Before you can do that, however, you must determine how you will to measure success on your website. This section will show you how to calculate Return on Investment (ROI) for the Free Online Services website.

The key to calculating ROI for the Free Online Services website is to realize that information about consumers using the service is the real product. Information gained from their activity on the website is used to add value to the paying customers. The true customers are companies willing to pay for the sales lead. Profit margins on goods actually purchased only have an indirect impact. Companies expect to use that profit margin to fund their own internal initiatives. They will not be likely to give a large percentage of it to buy the lead. For this reason, the lead generation business model is a very small profit margin business. It requires a very large traffic volume to succeed. In the struggle to become profitable, many Free Online Services have sought to supplement their lead revenues by offering paid services or by licensing their technology.

With Lead Generation, ROI is obtained by sending leads to partner sites for a fee. The key formula behind the lead generation business model is found in Figure 16.2

If you look carefully, you will see that the formula in Figure 16.2 tells us there are three components to this business model:

➢ First, bring traffic (visits) to your site.

➢ Second, through activity taking place on the site, transform that traffic into leads who click-thru (redirect) to paying partners.

➢ Third, have a sales strategy to make sure you are getting paid for those redirecting leads.

To generate positive return (i.e. profits), you must earn more for leads you sell than you pay for leads you buy. Some of the most dramatic Dot-Com failures were those who got this formula wrong. They paid too much for traffic to the site (often in TV ads). They either overestimated or failed to estimate potential revenues from leads redirecting to partners. Some invested heavily in online features that did not translate into significant increases in revenue per lead. Those same features may have been profitable on eRetail sites with a direct marketing business model driven directly by profits from online sales. But they were not the right tactics for a lead generation business model.

$$\boxed{\begin{array}{c}\textbf{Profit Per Lead}\\[8pt]\hline\\ \text{(REVENUE PER REDIRECT)} - \text{(COST PER REDIRECT)}\\[8pt] \text{This formula is calculated using the}\\ \text{following formulas:}\\[12pt] \left[\begin{array}{c}\text{COST PER}\\ \text{REDIRECT}\end{array}\right] = \dfrac{\text{COST PER VISIT}}{\text{REDIRECT RATE}}\\[20pt] \left[\begin{array}{c}\text{REDIRECT}\\ \text{RATE}\end{array}\right] = \dfrac{\text{\# REDIRECTS}}{\text{\# VISITS}}\end{array}}$$

Figure 16.2

Designing The Free Online Services User Experience

We have now defined the Free Online Services model, identified typical goals and shown how to measure the success of your website. The next step is to design a user experience for your customers that successfully achieves the goals of your online business model.

Many businesses make the mistake of trying to build a website before taking the time to figure out what the website is there to accomplish. That is always a set-up for poor results. Only after mapping out a user experience that will lead to successfully achieving your business goals should you put your web designer to work creating the look and feel for your website.

This section will walk through a typical user experience that successful Free Online Services websites create to generate leads through the website.

The Goal of Website Design

The primary purpose of a website is to meet the needs and wants of customers coming to the site in a way that maximizes the attainment of Internet Marketing goals. The easiest way to understand what a website is trying to accomplish is to think of it as a funnel. At the wide end, tactics are employed to reach out to customers, appeal to their interests and entice them to enter your website. From this point onward, every action a user takes should be moving them down the funnel, towards the ultimate outcome(s) you want to achieve from your website.

The key to understanding the Free Online Services website is to see the service being offered as a means to an end. It is not the end in itself. The free service must offer a benefit to its users; otherwise they will not continue to use it. But the larger purpose of the service is to give customers the opportunity to self-identify characteristics about themselves that will make them qualified leads for other businesses.

There are basically three steps in the process of taking customers from potential site users to qualified leads. This process is shown in Figure 16.3

Now let us look at the three steps in the typical Free Online Services user experience.

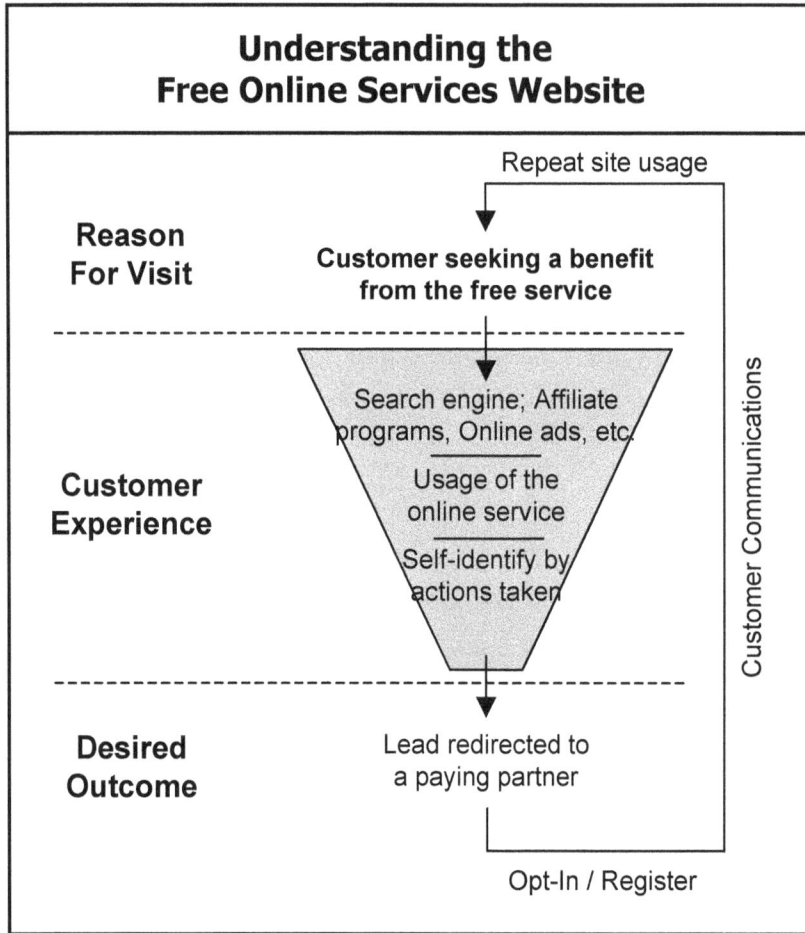

Understanding the Free Online Services Website

Repeat site usage

Reason For Visit

Customer seeking a benefit from the free service

Customer Experience

Search engine; Affiliate programs, Online ads, etc.

Usage of the online service

Self-identify by actions taken

Customer Communications

Desired Outcome

Lead redirected to a paying partner

Opt-In / Register

Figure 16.3

The Free Online Services User Experience

1.   First Contact

Free Online Services websites are similar to eRetail sites in their need for traffic. Both business models revolve around getting as much traffic as possible. They need to pursue every available method to drive traffic to the website. However, since the profit margin for these websites is much, much lower than for eRetail, they must be even more vigilant about making sure all traffic buys are profitable.

2.   Usability and Benefits of Service

Once you have enticed users to your website, the next step is to get them to actually use your service and like what it does for them. Since there are so many varieties of online service, it does not make sense to try and describe specific methods here. The general point is, "Your service must work for the customer."

3.   Segment Users into Targeted Buckets

The final step in the funnel is to transform site users into targeted leads. Activities on the website are designed to transparently place users into targeted buckets. Search engines do this automatically through the topic being searched. Other online services could allow users to choose different service options based on lifestyle or service need. For example, an online invitation service could give different options for corporate users and personal users. This creates two targeted lists. Personal users may then choose between party invites and concert invites. At each step, the list becomes more targeted.

For the lead generation business model, a click to a paying partner is the payoff device. All of the tactics will be designed to drive customers to these links. The paths users take through the site should be evaluated to make sure there are not too many steps between the user activity and the payoff device. Otherwise, revenue is lost by allowing users to leave the site before being presented with the option to leave through a paying link.

This brings us to one final consideration for Free Online Services. A delicate balance must be reached between providing a top quality service to the consumers using your site and the paying partners receiving the sales leads. Both are customers and both are stakeholders in the process. Exceptional value must be provided to both in a win-win proposition to keep them participating in your business. Only by doing this can your business also experience a win in the form of sustainable profits.

Now let us look at the specific tactics Free Online Services websites use to become successful.

Free Online Services Roadmap To Success

The final step before you actually build your website is to map out the specific objectives and tactics that will lead to successfully achieving your goals. In Part I, we called this your *roadmap to success*. The tactics in your "roadmap" are the building blocks that will create a winning user experience on your website.

Figure 16.4 presents a set of objectives and tactics common on Free Online Services websites. They are laid out according to the four levels of customer intimacy described in Chapter 2. A quick survey of the objectives and tactics shown here will give you an idea of what goes into a successful Free Online Services website.

The Free Online Services model has two sets of customers. The users of the service are one set of customers. The website must satisfy them, so they continue using the service and responding to lead generation opportunities. The partner companies who pay for the sales leads are the other set of customers. The website must continue to provide them with a reliable source of leads that convert to sales (or otherwise convert). A successful strategy must balance the needs of both sets of customers while also delivering profits to the business. *You must create a win-win-win.*

Practically speaking, this means you must have objectives and tactics targeted to both sets of customers. This can be confusing. The Objectives and Tactics table, in Figure 16.4, has been structured to make this easier to follow. For each of the four levels of customer intimacy there is a single objective, with corresponding tactics, for each of the two customer sets.

These tactics are prototypical examples. They should be used as guidelines to give you an idea of what your website can accomplish. However, you will have to determine specific objectives and tactics that match the unique aspects of your business and the needs of your customers.

Typical Free Online Services Objectives and Tactics

	Objectives	Tactics
Interest	Aggressively drive traffic to the website	1. Utilize all profitable methods to drive traffic to the website
	Recruit paying partner sites	2. Actively outreach to potential partners
		3. Participate in affiliate programs
		4. Participate in ad-server networks
Trust	Provide a user-friendly and secure user experience	5. User-friendly navigation, user interface, help, instructions/tutorials,
		6. Privacy policy and secure information handling
	Ensure competitive pricing of leads – so partner sites realize positive profits	7. Auction/ Bid pricing for leads
Satisfaction	Online services meet or exceed user expectations	8. Ensure that site users get the results they want. This includes, Search / Browse returning relevant and accurate information
		9. High quality content, meeting user needs and/or expectations
	Effectively target users based on their onsite activity to deliver highly converting leads to partners	10. Based on search criteria: User finds specific information and clicks on links to partner sites. Is qualified by having actively searched for it
		11. Based on user-provided information: User registers for the service and provides information about themselves used for targeting
		12. Based on viewed content: User chooses to view content or use services that reveal their interests
Loyalty	Use opt-in email and viral marketing techniques to generate additional site usage	13. Create an opt-in email list and send communications promoting additional usage of the site
		14. Include Forward-to-a-friend opportunities in all email communications and appropriate site content

	Maintain communications with partner sites providing results, & recommendations for improvement, resulting in continued and increased lead purchases	15. If purchasing keywords, automatically recommend additional popular variations 16. Provide reporting of program results (in email and/or onsite) and include recommendations for modifications to improve their results

Figure 16.4

The next section goes into detail about the how these tactics work together to make the Free Online Services website successful. If you do not want to dig this deep into the details, feel free to turn ahead to the next chapter.

The Roadmap Unfolded:
Typical Free Online Services Tactics

In this chapter you have learned what successful Free Online Services websites are trying to accomplish and how to design a website that meets those objectives. With the Free Online Services website there are two sets of customers. The immediately obvious customers are the users of the service. The less obvious, but more important customers are the partners who pay for sales leads. The successful website must have objectives and tactics targeted towards both groups.

With the Free Online Services website, you are a traffic middleman. You are buying traffic from other websites who will be qualified leads to your website. Then you, in turn, are adding some value to those leads by what you learn about them on your site, and selling them as qualified leads to another site. Your profits come from how much you can charge for that value added information. This typically is not much per lead. For all tactics employed in the Lead Generation model, we start by estimating the revenue per click. This is our ceiling. Everything the website does is aimed at paying less to get traffic than you earn by selling the leads.

The following table contains a detailed description of the tactics presented in the Roadmap to Success table (Figure 16.4). It provides nuts-and-bolts examples of the type of things implemented on successful Free Online Services websites. You can use this information as a framework for developing your own website. However, there is no substitute for defining the details of your own online business model and mapping out a set of tactics that will meet your own organizational goals.

Building Interest (site users)

Since revenue from a single site visit is extremely small, building interest among site users is all about driving traffic to the website at as low a cost as possible. Of course, you must also have a service that people will use.

Utilize all profitable methods to drive traffic	This business model revolves around redirecting traffic from your site to other websites who will pay for the qualified sales lead. To be profitable, you must have a high volume of site users to direct to paying partner sites. That means driving traffic to your site is the most important factor in your ultimate success. Traffic is bought primarily by strategic placement of listings on search engines. That is the most cost-effective traffic source. Search Engine Marketing is at the heart of the Free Online Services business. Additionally, much Search Engine traffic can be obtained at close to zero cost if you do a good job of optimizing your web pages for search engines to find them. For this reason, Search Engine Optimization is also a critical interest building tactic for attracting site users to these websites. Beyond this, you will need to cautiously evaluate other online traffic sources and advertising options based on how good a fit they are for your website.

Building Interest (partners)

Building interest with partners typically involves a combination of an in-house sales staff (who are basically selling online ad space) and participating in third-party networks who do this for you.

Actively outreach to potential partners	This tactic is not so much a tactic of the website as of the business itself. The key point to be aware of here is that if you want to be successful with a Free Online Services website, you have to have a sales strategy to sell your leads to business partners. The specifics will vary depending on the service you are offering. But you will need a staff to be responsible for planning and outreaching to potential business partners. You will also need an area of your website dedicated to partner recruitment and support. This area is often named something like: "Merchant Services" or "Advertising Partners."
Participate in affiliate programs	All websites need traffic. Many of them set up affiliate programs that will pay any site who can send traffic to them. An important tactic for a website who is in the business of sending traffic to paying businesses is to find every available affiliate program who will pay for your leads. This is especially important for services that generate search results of websites that site users will redirect to. This is, in a sense, easy money. You do not need to do any selling, you just sign up for their affiliate program and get paid when a user on your site clicks on their link.
Participate in ad-server networks	Finally, redirecting leads from your website to another site who will pay for it is very similar to a magazine selling ad space in locations that potential customers will see. The space on your site where the site user sees your partner's link or ad is basically advertising real estate. It is the same as space reserved for ads in a magazine. There are companies who specialize in buying and selling that real estate so you and your partners do not have to deal with the hassle. These are called *ad server networks*. If you want to sell ad space on your website on a Cost-Per-Click (CPC) or Cost-Per-Thousand (CPM) basis, then an ad-server network might be the right answer.

Building Trust (site users)

Once users come to your website, then you must gain their trust. They must feel confident that if they use your service they will get the results they want without suffering any harmful consequences. This simply means the service must work for the user and must be safe. Most of us have had experiences where we use an online service and then discover we are being bombarded with Spam or have gotten a virus on our computer. Your customers will be afraid of the same thing happening to them. They will also be afraid of entering any personal information onto your website. You must allay those fears.

User-friendly navigation and user interface	Usability is a key to success for any website. All online business models must succeed with this tactic. If a customer finds it hard to do what they are trying to do on your website, they will just leave. With a free online service, your website is basically a software application the customer is using. You must take special care to make sure it is easy for them to use. This means doing usability tests when designing the user interface. It also means including easy to access instructions and help.
Privacy policy and user security	If customers can use your service but do not trust their security, they will not come back. You must be vigilant to ensure the bad guys are not piggy backing on your website. Of course, you must not violate the trust of your customers by selling their email addresses to Spammers. But you must also make sure nobody else is sneaking into your system and doing it without your knowledge. There is one outdoor enthusiast magazine I subscribed to whose email newsletter was infested with viruses and spyware. They were not trying to infest my computer. But they were not careful to keep their email servers from being hacked by someone who would.

In addition to being vigilant to protect the security of your customers, you must also post a written privacy policy. You must clearly tell what you will do with your customers' information and how you will protect their privacy. Your privacy policy has significant legal ramifications as well. *If a customer files a lawsuit against your business, the courts will look at your privacy policy to decide your case. You must be very careful to craft a policy statement that assures your customers of their safety and your good intentions, but also does not hold you liable for more than you can actually do.* |

Building Trust (partners)

With the business partners who will be buying your leads, winning trust is all about secure transactions and competitive pricing. The specifics of how you go about this will depend on the nature of your service and how leads will be delivered.

Auction / bid pricing for leads	One tactic used by websites who are charging for click-thrus from search result listings is to set up a bid pricing mechanism for your leads. If you allow partners to buy your leads directly off of your website, you may want to provide some kind of bid pricing method. It is basically like an auction, where partners select keywords and bid for how much they will pay for a redirect. Depending on their bid, the link to their site will be listed higher or lower in the search results listings. If you are handling transactions on your website, you must use a third party vendor to ensure the security of the transaction. This is the same as for the eRetail site.

Building Satisfaction (site users)

Now users have decided to give your service a try. The next level of intimacy is that they like what they found. The specific ways you will accomplish this will, of course, depend on the kind of service you are offering. In general, it comes down to results and quality. As with the eRetail site, you may want to add bells and whistles to your site to delight your customers. There is too much variety among services to attempt to cover these here. The one critical factor to remember is you must evaluate all such tactics against your revenue per lead ceiling, to make sure you are remaining profitable.

Relevant search / browse results	For most online services, users will be searching or browsing for some kind of information as a key part of the service. This is obvious for a search engine. It is also true for job placement sites, real estate sites, dating sites and product review sites. The list goes on. The first key to satisfying your users is to make sure they get what they are looking for when they search or browse your site. This could mean having advanced search features to focus their results. It could mean providing additional information in the search results page to help them make sense of what they are seeing. It always means investing in a quality search engine tool that will deliver relevant results. *In other words, do not go cheap on your search engine.*

High quality content	The second thing that will satisfy your site users is the quality of the content they find after the search or browse results are returned. This also is less a tactic of the site itself and more a tactic of the business. Nevertheless, it is critical to the website's success.

Building Satisfaction (partners)

For your partners, satisfaction comes down to just one thing – do the leads convert? To achieve this, your service must be designed to effectively target site users based on their onsite activity. There are three major ways websites do this.

Deliver targeted leads based on user search criteria	The first way to target your leads is simply to let them search for what they are interested in. Once they have completed their search, you will display links to partners that they can choose from. They automatically are targeted, because they search for something they are interested in and then make the effort to further investigate what your partner has to offer.
Deliver targeted leads based on user-provided information	The second way leads are targeted is for the site user to provide information for you. In this case, the partner will also do the searching. The value to the users is the win-win to be gained from being connected with a partner. So site users will give enough information about themselves to allow partners to find them. An obvious example of this is the dating website. This model is slightly different, since users have to pay to receive the benefits of the service. What is actually happening on these sites is members are both users and partners. They enter information about themselves to become qualified leads for someone searching for them. They are also paying a fee, as a partner, to be able to access other qualified leads on the site. Another well known type of service using this technique is the job placement website.
Deliver targeted leads based on viewed content	The third way leads can be targeted is based on the content users choose to view. This is the advertising model. Magazines and television stations use this model to sell ad space next to content that viewers are interested in. Websites can also do this. In general, this is a much less effective model than either of the previous two targeting methods.

Building Loyalty (site users)

Building loyalty to your free service will depend on the nature of that service. In general, there are services that people sign up for and there are others that people use on an as-needed basis. In the first case, customers enter into a relationship with your website by registering. There may be opportunities to build up loyalty by personalizing their online experience or otherwise making the service an integral part of one of their personal needs or goals. In the second case, it is much harder to get customers to return on their own accord. In both cases, repeat usage is gained primarily by making your users' lives easier. If it works for them, they will keep using it. For both types of service, you can also use email to generate repeat and referral traffic.

Opt-in email	As with the eRetail business model, site users can be given the option to sign up for opt-in email newsletters. These newsletters in turn drive traffic back to the website, thus increasing the total volume of sales leads redirecting through the site. Plus they may contain sponsored links directly to partner sites. If paid services are offered, then emails can be used to up-sell users to these revenue generating services.
Forward-to-a-friend	Forward-to-a-friend emails can work very well for the Free Online Services website. If customers like what they find on your site, give them a way to tell others about it. You can provide Forward-to-a-friend links on every page and email.

Building Loyalty (partners)

In many cases, your partners will be making their online media buy through third-party companies either handling the purchase for them or the sale for you. In this case, there is not much you can do to generate loyalty, except to deliver quality leads at a competitive price. If partners are purchasing directly through your website, you can nudge them along in the process.

Automatically recommend program improvements	Partners who purchase leads directly from your website are registered users of the site, just like eRetail customers. You can use email to keep in contact with them and recommend improvements to their program or promote complementary services.
	One feature you can include to increase total volume of leads purchased by partners is to dynamically recommend other lead options. For example, a pay-for-placement search engine could recommend additional popular keywords.

Conclusion

In this chapter, you have learned how to successfully create a service that transforms site users into targeted sales leads. You have also learned to be profitable by sending those leads to other businesses online. In the next chapter, you will learn how to create a winning Content website.

Now turn to the Content website.

Chapter 17

Building A Successful Content Website

In this chapter, you will learn . . .
- How to define the online business model for a Content website
- How to measure success for a Content website
- How to design a successful user experience for a Content website
- Tactics used by successful Content websites

Mining The Virtual World
The About.com Story

Scott Kurnit's vision of the Internet was one of people connected in a worldwide network of shared interests. Others focused on the technology or on the data flowing along the Information Superhighway. Scott focused on the humanity. His vision was for a place where hundreds of experts wrote about thousands of topics. Web users would be connected to expert guidance on the topics they are interested in. It could be learning a foreign language, building a website, or growing mushrooms. Scott called it the "Human Internet."

In 1996, Scott and a group of entrepreneurs started recruiting expert "guides" from countries all over the world. Then, in April 1997, The Mining Company went live. Their tagline was, "We dig the web so you don't have to." By 1999, The Mining Company, renamed to About.com, had become one of the top 10 most visited Internet properties. They had over 500 expert guides writing on over 50,000 topics.

The About.com website is easy to navigate. This is a critical factor in their success. When you find one topic you are interested in, there are many ways to find other related topics on the About.com network. The sub-site for any given topic is hosted by a guide who has authored articles, tutorials or other useful information. The rest of the page is filed with links to other useful resources. The feeling is that About.com, and their guides, are *recommending* a host of other related resources and information. This is where they make their money. Spread throughout About.com's content pages are also millions of links to related content and resources on other websites. Many, if not most, of these links are *monetized*. About.com gets paid when you click.

In 2005, About.com was purchased by the New York Times for a reported $410 million. It continues to be one of the most visited sources of content on the Internet. According to Neilsen-Net Ratings, one out of every five people on the Internet uses About.com.

In many ways, About.com is the ultimate content website. Their pioneering efforts teach lessons that every Content website must follow. About.com realized that content on the Internet is most effective when it is focused on a highly specific interest. Then, once people find content of interest, they must be able to easily navigate through the site to other related information. Most importantly for those seeking to earn revenues from their website content, viewers of highly targeted content are also highly qualified leads for online ads. By placing links and ads within the context of website content, viewers will see it as useful resources rather than as intrusive advertising. As long as these links are worth clicking on, people will keep returning to the site and keep clicking on the ads.

In this chapter, we will walk through the steps successful Content providers follow to create a winning website.

Understanding The Content Website

You can look up almost anything on the Internet. You might want to know about poverty in Africa or real estate values in Texas. You can find it on the Internet. You may want expert advice on high protein diets or how to adopt a pet. When you search for topics like these, you are likely to find a number of websites filled with helpful information at no cost to you. No survey of typical websites would be complete without the Content website. These are websites whose mission is to deliver information as a public service to a target population. They are a big part of what we all love about the Internet.

Dimensions of the Content Website's Online Business Model

In Part I, you learned an easy way to begin defining your online business model. You start by choosing from among seven basic dimensions that form the foundation of all online businesses (Figure 17.1).

This quick and easy approach will let you implement a set of features and tactics aimed at achieving the goals of your business or organization.

Seven Dimensions To Online Business Models

1. eCommerce
2. Business Development
✓ 3. Lead Generation
4. Brand Development
5. Customer Relations
✓ 6. Information Delivery
7. Cost Savings

Figure 17.1

The primary dimension of the Content website is *Information Delivery*. These websites offer a free service that provides information of relevance to a target audience.

Many Content websites also seek to earn revenue by serving ads on their content pages. This adds a *Lead Generation* dimension to the online business model.

Subsidized vs. Monetized Content

In general, Content websites do not earn revenue directly by delivering content. Rather, the content is in support of some other organizational goals. There are two common variations of the Content website. First are those providing some type of not-for-profit public service. In these cases, there is no organizational goal to earn income directly from the content itself. Instead, content is providing a public service that indirectly supports other goals. Information delivery is *subsidized*. Second are those who provide information which attracts site visitors who then become qualified leads for other websites. By displaying ads within the content pages, these websites earn revenue from their content. These websites are *monetized*.

Subsidized Content Websites

The first type of Content website are pure Information Delivery websites. Many government agencies and nonprofit organizations provide extensive amounts of free information online. In cases like these, the goal is to support the mission of the agency to promote the public good.

Some for-profit businesses may also provide public service information. For example, an insurance company may create a Content website with health and wellness information. In these cases, the goal is not to earn money directly, but to disseminate information. In the case of the insurance company providing health and wellness information, they may be seeking an indirect benefit of generally improving the wellness of their customers, and thus reducing claims payouts. More typically, the company will be seeking an indirect benefit of improving their brand image. This would be the case for an alcohol company providing information against drunk driving and underage drinking.

Monetized Content Websites

Many Content websites seek to earn revenue from their web pages. This is called *monetizing* the website. Creating Content websites for the purpose of earning ad revenue has become something of a cottage industry among individuals seeking to make extra money online. Some earn their entire livelihood this way.

The basic idea is that the same people who are searching for information about a topic are also buying products and services related to that topic. If you have a Content website, or blog addressing a certain issue, you can make extra money by serving ads related to that issue. Ads can come in the form of online advertisements, paid search listings, or participation in affiliate programs. (All of these are discussed in Part II.)

On the other hand, some people look for affiliate programs with high payouts. A website creator will find affiliates that are selling into a niche audience who will also be interested in useful information that she is able to provide. Then she creates Content websites specifically with the intent of earning money through the affiliate programs targeted to that niche market.

Typical Content Website Goals

Once you have defined your online business model, the next step is to determine what goals will lead to success. These goals set the compass heading for your website.

The Content website typically has two goals:

(1)   Successfully deliver desired content to information consumers
(2)   Generate revenue by targeted ads on content pages

Of course, this is a prototypical list. As you go through this process, you will need to define goals specific to your own website.

Measuring Success For The Content Website

Now you have set the compass heading for your website, by setting effective goals. This will let you develop a set of tactics and site features to reach those goals. Before you can do that, however, you must determine how you are going to measure success on your website. This section will show you how Return on Investment (ROI) is calculated for the Content website.

Calculating ROI for Subsidized Content Websites

In general, to calculate ROI, you start with a measure of monetary return from a given action. You then count the actions in question and calculate a monetary return per action. This cannot be done if there is no direct monetary return, as with the subsidized Content website.

To calculate success for this type of website, you need to devise a measure, not of revenue earned, but of effectiveness of information delivery. For example, if your agency is trying to build awareness for a specific issue, such as homelessness in your city, then you may want to measure number of unique visitors to your website or number of click-thrus to food banks. If your agency provides statistics for researchers, you may measure successful downloads of data files or aborted visits because users were not able to find the information they needed. The specific success metrics will depend on what your organization is trying to accomplish. Part III describes how to use Web Analytics to measure the effectiveness of content on the website.

Calculating ROI for Monetized Content Websites

ROI for monetized Content websites is exactly the same as for Free Online Services, described in Chapter 16. A content website is itself a free service. Revenue is earned by qualifying traffic as being interested in the topic addressed on the site. Companies selling products and services to people with that interest will pay for leads from your website. This is the Lead Generation model.

With Lead Generation, ROI is obtained by sending leads to partner sites for a fee. The key formula behind the lead generation business model is found in Figure 17.2.

Profit Per Lead

(REVENUE PER REDIRECT) – (COST PER REDIRECT)

This formula is calculated using the following formulas:

$$\left[\begin{array}{c} \text{COST PER} \\ \text{REDIRECT} \end{array} \right] = \frac{\text{COST PER VISIT}}{\text{REDIRECT RATE}}$$

$$\left[\begin{array}{c} \text{REDIRECT} \\ \text{RATE} \end{array} \right] = \frac{\text{\# REDIRECTS}}{\text{\# VISITS}}$$

Figure 17.2

If you look carefully, you will see that the formula in Figure 17.2 tells us there are three components to this business model:

➢ First, bring traffic (visits) to your site.

➢ Second, through activity taking place on the site, transform that traffic into leads who click-thru (redirect) to paying partners.

➢ Third, have a sales strategy to make sure you are getting paid for those redirecting leads.

To generate positive return (i.e. profits), you must earn more for leads you sell than you pay for leads you buy.

Designing The Content Website User Experience

The key to a successful Content website is simply that people are able to find what they need and get it in a format they can use. The user experience starts with customers being able to find your website when they are looking for information you provide. It ends with them successfully viewing or downloading useful information or clicking a link to additional resources. If your website is monetized, they will find links and ads to other websites who are willing to pay for the click. The process is shown in Figure 17.3.

Many businesses make the mistake of trying to build a website before taking the time to figure out what the website is there to accomplish. That is always a set-up for poor results. Only after mapping out a user experience that will lead to successfully achieving your business goals should you put your web designer to work creating the look and feel for your website.

The Goal of Website Design

The primary purpose of a website is to meet the needs and wants of customers coming to the site in a way that maximizes the attainment of Internet Marketing goals. The easiest way to understand what a website is trying to accomplish is to think of it as a funnel. At the wide end, tactics are employed to reach out to customers, appeal to their interests and entice them to enter your website. From this point onward, every action a user takes should be moving them down the funnel, towards the ultimate outcome(s) you want to achieve from your website.

This section will walk through a typical user experience that successful Content websites create to effectively deliver information and generate monetized click-thrus through the website. Now let us look at the steps in the typical Content website user experience.

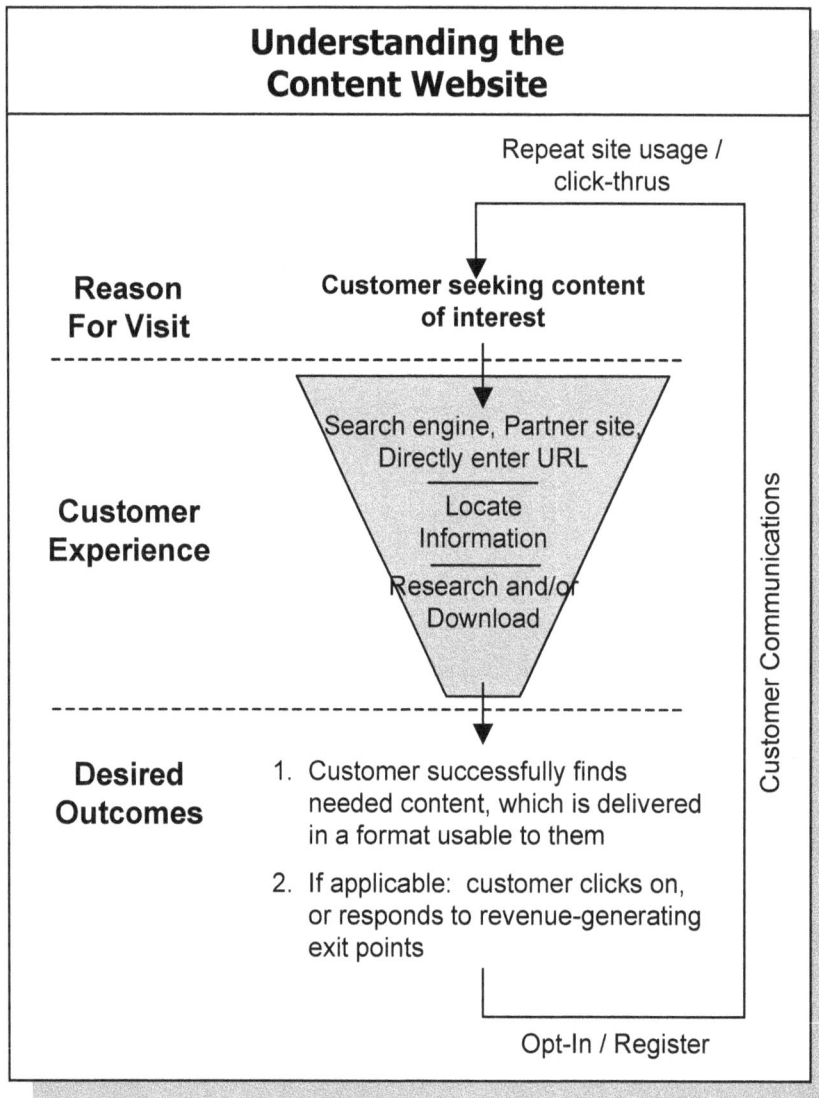

Figure 17.3

The Content Website User Experience

1.   First Contact

For the Content website, the most important way you will reach out to your potential site users by letting them find you when they are looking for a resource you have. This boils down mostly to optimizing your website for search engines. Identify all of the words and phrases people may type into search engines related to the information services you offer. Then make sure search engines will find your site when those keywords are entered. A second way to reach out to your potential site users is to get the word out about your website on partner websites. If there are online magazines or special interest websites that cater to interests related to your cause, try to get them to place your link on their websites. If your website is the online component of a larger public outreach program, then you will include reference to the site on your offline materials.

Monetized content websites will also rely on Search Engine Marketing.

2.   Navigation and User Interface

Once users get to your website, they have to be able to find what they want. This is the first hurdle. If they cannot find the information in the first few seconds on the site, there is a good chance they will abandon the session and look somewhere else for it.

The most important way to address this issue is by taking time to map out your menu choices on the top and left navigation. This does not add any technical costs to website development. But it will involve some human costs in the time taken to map out your onsite menus. The hierarchy of menus and items in them is known as your site's *taxonomy*.

Another critical component to many Content websites is a robust onsite search capability. People should be able to enter search terms into a search engine on your website and find information they are looking for. Search engine technology, however, can be costly to buy. Many nonprofit agencies cannot afford to spend that much on their website. For this reason, having an easy to navigate taxonomy is all the more important.

3.   **Researching on Your Site**

The reason users are most likely on your website in the first place is to research an issue of importance to them. The information they find obviously must meet their needs. This means having information that is truly relevant and accurate. But it also means presenting it in a way that is accessible to the user. When users look for information on the Internet they scan first, then they read on if they find what they want.

Users on your website will spend a few seconds on a given web page and quickly look over the high level information to see if it has what they need. They will look at headlines and menu items. If it has what they need, then they look a little deeper to get some high level details. They will look for bullet points, or maybe read the first few lines of text. If they still feel they need more, then they will actually read the paragraphs of written text. This is called *scanning*. Well-crafted Web content will accommodate this practice.

4.   **Information Delivery**

Your site users need to receive the information in a format most usable for them. In a large number of cases, they will want to download information and take it with them. The format of the download will be different for different websites. The important concept to remember is to find out what your target audience will be using your information for and how they will want to use it. Then deliver it in a method that is most conducive to those uses.

There are many options for delivering content. The most common is to create a "print friendly" version of the HTML page the user is viewing. A typical web page has a variety of content elements including images, tables and text. If you expect your site users to print your information, you can let them view it on a separate page that removes HTML formatting and peripheral content. This will be easy for them to print and easy to save to their computers.

A second, very common method of delivering content is to allow downloads of white papers and articles in PDF files. These are created to be displayed in Adobe Acrobat or similar software. They have the advantage of being very small and easy to download. Also, longer articles, that people do not want to take the time to read online, can be downloaded and read later at their leisure.

A third very popular information delivery method is the audio or video download. There are many varieties. With the popularity of MP3 players, a very popular download method has become the "Pod-cast" (named for the Apple iPod). This is basically a download that can be saved onto the user's iPod, or other MP3 player.

Websites that include statistical information can allow the files to be downloaded as spreadsheets or comma-delimited text files that can be used in MS-Excel or other spreadsheet programs. This one is my personal favorite. I have spent many frustrating hours reformatting tables of numbers that were only available as unformatted text documents or HTML web pages. If you have a website with statistical information, you may have had this experience. Please do not put your site users through this torture.

5.   Click-Thru on Monetized Ads

Finally, if your website is pursuing a Lead Generation business model, the most critical step in this whole process is generating click-thrus on ads placed on your content pages. It is not enough for people to just click-thru on your ads. You also need them to convert to sales when they get to the target site. Most Content sites today place ads from affiliate programs or paid search listings. Affiliate programs offer higher payouts, but are usually monetized on a pay-for-performance basis. That means you get paid only if the site user converts to a sale. Even if you are serving cost-per-click ads, you still need to be concerned about conversions. Your advertisers will not continue serving ads on your website if they do not produce conversions.

There are three key factors that contribute to the success of your monetized content pages: relevance, context and pre-selling.

➤ **Relevance:** The ads you serve on your pages must be *relevant* to the content on that page. The closer you match what your content is saying with the products and services being presented, the more interested your site visitors will be in the ads.

➤ **Context:** Even if the ads are relevant to the content on the page, still they may not get the visitors' attention. To increase click-thrus, the ads should be presented within the *context* of the content. In the simplest sense, this means placing ads directly next to the content where a relevant topic is being discussed.

➤ **Pre-Selling:** The content on your web page is preparing site visitors to buy the products or services they will find once they click on the ad.

For example, if you have a consumer electronics website, you might serve an ad for the latest digital camera. You will be more effective placing that ad on a page discussing digital cameras than on one discussing satellite radio. It is *relevant* to the page content. You can increase your results by placing the ad directly next to the paragraph where digital cameras are being discussed. That is, by placing it in *context*. You will further increase the conversion rates that take place after users click on the ad by talking about the benefits of that specific camera within the body of the article. That is *pre-selling*.

Content Website Roadmap To Success

The final step before you actually build your website is to map out the specific objectives and tactics that will lead to successfully achieving your goals. In Part I, we called this your *roadmap to success*. The tactics in your "roadmap" are the building blocks that will create a winning user experience on your website.

Typical Content Website Objective and Tactics

	Objectives	Tactics
Interest	Ensure that web searchers find the site when searching for topics covered	1. Search engine optimization 2. If it yields profitable ROI, search engine marketing
	Get links from related websites	3. Personally contact related websites to post links to your site
Trust	Ensure that customers have a positive online experience that allows them to easily find the information they want	4. Scannable page content 5. User-friendly navigation and interface, with short path to information sought by user 6. Functional onsite search 7. Freshness and accuracy of content
Satisfaction	Provide user-friendly information delivery	8. Printable version of text pages; Data downloads in MS-Excel or text file; Video/audio downloads in multiple formats
	Maximize click-thrus to monetized cross-links	9. All links and ads on the page presented in context, to complement the main body of content
	Ensure quality of target websites and resources	10. Human approval and periodic review of all websites and offsite content linked to from the site (both monetized and non-monetized)
Loyalty	Use targeted email to cultivate customer relationships resulting in repeat visits and monetized click-thrus	11. Create an opt-in email list and use email to deliver monetized or non-monetized content and generate repeat visits
	Utilize viral marketing and syndication to increase the reach of site content	12. Include Forward-to-a-friend links on all content and emails 13. Create eBooks or other viral objects from valuable content 14. RSS feed to distribute your content

Figure 17.4

Figure 17.4 presents a set of objectives and tactics common on Content websites. They are laid out according to the four levels of customer intimacy described in Chapter 2. A quick survey of the objectives and tactics shown here will give you an idea of what goes into a successful Content website.

These tactics are prototypical examples. They should be used as guidelines to give you an idea of what your website can accomplish. However, you will have to determine specific objectives and tactics that match the unique aspects of your business and the needs of your customers.

The next section goes into detail about the how these tactics work together to make the Content website successful. If you do not want to dig this deep into the details, feel free to turn ahead to the next chapter.

The Roadmap Unfolded:
Typical Content Website Tactics

In this chapter you have learned what successful Content websites are trying to accomplish and how to design a website that meets those objectives. The basic consideration for a Content website is to make sure people find the information they need as effectively as possible. In the process, links and monetized ads must be placed within the context of page content, so site users find them useful and click on them.

The following table contains a detailed description of the tactics presented in the Roadmap to Success table (Figure 17.4). It provides nuts-and-bolts examples of the type of things implemented on successful Content websites. You can use this information as a framework for developing your own website. However, there is no substitute for defining the details of your own online business model and mapping out a set of tactics that will meet your own organizational goals.

Building Interest

Building interest with the Content website is mostly a matter of being found on search engines and getting linked to from other related websites. People will be searching for information related to the topic(s) your website addresses. You must be found by them.

Search engine optimization	Search engine optimization is essential for any website. Most people will find a content website while they are searching for information about a particular topic of interest. They will find your website if it appears in their search listings. Optimizing the content on your web pages to be found by search engines is the most important thing you can do to get traffic to your content website.
Search engine marketing	Paying for sponsored links on search engines (known as search engine marketing) is simply paying to get your search results listings displayed to people searching for the topics your site addresses. If you are monetizing your website with paid links, this will be an important part of your strategy. The key is to pay less for traffic from search engines than you earn from clicks to the ads on your website.
Get linked to	Content websites form a natural information network. Each of the websites offering content related to the issues your site addresses will benefit by being linked to from other related sites. It also helps them to have links on their site to other related sites. In this way, web users can find one site and continue to follow links to more and more content of interest. You should get your website linked in to this network of sites related to the issue(s) you address. Having links from other websites is also an important factor in being listed on search engines.
	For a content website, the first place to start when seeking links from other sites is to perform your own searches on the topic related to your website. Then personally contact the website owners for all the sites you find that are complementary to your own. Offer to place links to their site on your own website and ask them to place links in return. Also offer suggestions about places on their website that will generate the most clicks to your website.

Building Trust

With the Content website, building trust means people can find what they are looking for and are not disappointed when they find it. This basically comes down to good site design and quality of content.

Scannable page content	The most important consideration for a Content website is scannable page content. When people are looking for information on the Internet, they are impatient. They will scan the first web page they find on your site and decide in a few seconds if it has what they want. If not, they will go on to the next site. The content on your website must not only be useful, it must be presented in a way that makes it easy for people to find the parts that they want to use.
User-friendly navigation	User-friendly navigation is an important key to success for any website. For the content website, it is critical. You must have easy to follow menus with categories that make sense to your users. This is a matter of usability. Site users must be able to intuitively understand what they need to click next to get to where they want to go.
Site search	If your website has more than just a very small number of pages, you should have onsite search. People are used to using search to find what they need on the Internet. They will expect to do the same when they come to your website.
Freshness and accuracy of content	The last three tactics all are meant to help people find what they are interested in. Once they find it, they must like what they find. All information posted must be accurate and up to date. If it is not, visitors to your website will assume the whole site is unreliable. They will not come back. Taking the time to regularly update your site content is a must.

Building Satisfaction

Satisfaction on the Content website comes mainly from making it easy for site visitors to access and use the information you provide.

User-centric information delivery	One of the most frustrating experiences when doing research online is to find what you need, but then have a hard time getting at it. There are many variations to this frustrating experience. You have probably experience some of them.

	You find an article you need and want to keep a copy. But the page is full of graphics and ads that waste the color ink cartridges in your printer. You have to cut and paste the text of the article into a document and delete the ads. It is much easier when the site includes a link to display a "print friendly" version of the page, without the graphics
	You find just the perfect table of numbers that shows the trend you need for. But there is no option to download it. You have to cut and paste the text into a separate document. Perhaps it allows you to download it as a text file, but you need to put it into a spreadsheet. If you have numerical data on your website, consider how your site users will need to use it. Then deliver it in a format they can easily use.
	Your website might have articles, eBooks, video downloads, audio downloads, charts or graphs. Always think about how the end user will be using your information. If you make it easy for them, they will keep coming back to your website.
	If your website provides news of interest, you can deliver a daily factoid directly to the BlackBerry or PDA of your site users. If your website provides music reviews, you can create downloadable ring tones for their cell phones. There really is no limit to how user-centric you can get with your information. Most of the technologies for delivering content are relatively inexpensive to implement.
Cross-links in context of page	For many Content websites, the reason for the site to exist is to earn revenue from clicks on monetized ads. These ads are typically some sort of banner ad or text link. To be effective, and seen as valuable to the site user, these must be presented within the context of the content being viewed.
	The same is true for non-monetized links. Any resource that your website links to should be presented in a way that makes intuitive sense to the user. This way, the entire website is seen as supporting the goals of the site user.
Ensure quality of links	Not only must the quality of your site content be maintained, you must also ensure the quality of content your site links to. Site users view a content website as a public resource. Links displayed on content pages will be viewed as recommended resources. When users click on those links and find useful content, that reflects positively on your site. If not, it calls into question the reliability of your site as a resource.

Building Loyalty

Loyalty for a Content website basically means site users come to see your content as a resource they rely on and will pass along to their friends or colleagues. Web content is naturally suited to being delivered through the Internet. You do not need to rely on people coming back to your website, although you will want them to do that also. You can deliver content directly to users and make it easy for them to pass it along to others.

Opt-in email	Opt-in site users to a free newsletter. This gives you the opportunity to deliver your site content directly to a large group of people who are interested in what your website has to offer. If they like what you send them, they will follow links back to your website and forward your newsletter to friends and colleagues.
Forward-to-a-friend	Include Forward-to-a-friend links on articles, or other useful content found on your website. This will make it easy for people to send your site content to others. They will not only find your content valuable, but are likely to come to your website to find more of the same.
Create viral objects	If you have valuable content, you can package that content to be passed along. This is the essence of viral marketing. You can create eBooks, white papers, video clips, or any number of other items that can be sent through email. Then make these available to your site users, with an easy way for them to forward it along. Include some promotional copy and a link to your website. This will spread the word about what your website is offering and bring new users to your website.
Create an RSS feed	RSS is basically a way to push out headlines and short blurbs directly to your site users' computers. They can click on links in the feed and be sent to the full content on your website. If you have content that will be regularly updated, you can use an RSS feed to keep your users up to date on information they care about. This will keep them coming back to your site, and make your content a part of their daily lives.

Conclusion

In this chapter, you have learned how to be successful delivering information online and earning revenue by serving ads on a Content website. In the next chapter, you will learn how to create a successful Small Business website.

Now turn to the Small Business website.

Chapter 18

Building A Successful Small Business Website

In this chapter, you will learn . . .
- How to define the online business model for a Small Business website
- How to measure success for a Small Business website
- How to design a successful user experience for a Small Business website
- The tactics used by successful Small Business websites

Finding Customers In A Digital Haystack
The Decision Software, Inc. Story

Jeff Fowler owns the marketing database company Decision Software, Inc. (DSI). In 1999, their flagship product was a campaign management system Jeff designed. It was called "TopDog." Since then they have replaced it with a new product, MarketWide. DSI was a small company, with only nine employees. Still, TopDog outperformed similar software offerings by the largest vendors in the Database Marketing business. Plus, their expert staff and nimble approach to problem solving allowed DSI to create a fully working prototype system, with the client's own data, in the same time it took their larger competitors to write a sales proposal. If DSI could just get in front of a potential customer, their superior product and skilled engineers would win the business. The biggest challenge Jeff faced was getting those initial visits.

DSI had set up a Web Analytics software to monitor the performance of their website. Jeff knew that the software did not only report on clicks to their web pages. It also reported the names of businesses who were visiting the DSI website. He figured if someone from a potential client was visiting the site and checking out products then they were probably in the market for a marketing database solution. He did not wait for them to call. He looked up the company phone numbers and made his sales pitch. As a result, Jeff not only got the sales visits, but DSI won a number of new clients. A typical client installation would run in the hundreds of thousands of dollars. That simple act of checking the traffic logs for their corporate website resulted in a pretty big windfall.

In the small action of checking web traffic logs and scheduling sales visits, the Decision Software, Inc. website accomplished the main purpose of all small business websites. It generated sales leads that convert into new customers.

In this chapter, we will walk through the steps successful small businesses go through to create a winning website.

Understanding The Small Business Website

Many small businesses lack the resources, or do not feel the need to build an elaborate website. Instead, they put up a basic website with information about their company and a way to contact their sales staff and customer service. The basic Small Business website is essentially the same thing as a very elaborate Yellow Pages ad. You are "hanging out your shingle" on the Internet, so people can find your business. These websites can be built for a few thousand dollars or less. Often, ROI is never measured. Rather, the relatively low cost is just considered a necessary business expense.

Dimensions of the Small Business's Online Business Model

In Part I, you learned an easy way to begin defining your online business model. You start by choosing from among seven basic dimensions that form the foundation of all online businesses (see Figure 18.1). This quick and easy approach will allow you to implement a set of features and tactics aimed at achieving the goals of your business or organization.

The primary dimension for a Small Business website is *Business Development*. The website is there to capture sales leads.

The Small Business website is also the main, or only place where your business is represented online. For everyone looking online for information about your company, the website is the standard by which the business is judged. For this reason, all Small Business websites also have a *Brand Development* dimension.

Seven Dimensions To Online Business Models

	1.	eCommerce
✓	**2.**	Business Development
	3.	Lead Generation
✓	**4.**	Brand Development
	5.	Customer Relations
	6.	Information Delivery
	7.	Cost Savings

Figure 18.1

Making a First Impression

For a small business, the website is first, and foremost the virtual "shingle" they hang out to let people find them online. It is the first impression many potential customers will have of the business. Since many, if not most of a small business's customers will do research online at the start of their purchase process, that first impression must put the best foot forward.

This comes down to three basic things.

1.　　A Professional Appearance

Potential customers will judge the business by the presentation they find on the website. If the website is professional and shows attention to detail, then customers will assume the business does the same. If the website is confusing and hard to navigate, customers will assume they will have a frustrating experience with the business also. The Small Business website must, above all other things, make customers feel confident that they can trust doing business with this company.

2. Communicate the Brand Identity

Besides being confident in the quality of the company, potential customers will also size up what the company is all about by that first impression. Every business has an identity they want to present to the public. This is their *brand*. The most important purpose of a brand identify is to create an emotional bond with customers. Companies craft the presentation they make to their customers to reflect what the relationship with the business will be like. The website is the first contact many customers will have with the business. It is the first opportunity to present that brand identity and begin forming an emotional bond with potential customers.

Consider two small, fictitious architectural firms. One, Fabulous Homes, Inc., specializes in high-end, artistic designs for home renovations. They are expensive. They only use the best materials and spend time customizing their designs to match the homeowner's dreams. Customers will be able to show off their homes for decades to come. The second firm, Practical Homes, Inc., specializes in quality homes at an affordable price. They have designed a variety of standard home footprints that can be slightly modified to meet the specific details of the property. Their customers are typically small development companies. These are both architectural firms specializing in designing single family-homes. However, their brand identities are completely different. The websites they build should reflect those differences.

Fabulous Homes, Inc. will probably have a very artistic look to their home page. They will have elaborate fonts for their subject headings and stylized lines outlining content areas. They may even have a Flash element introducing the website with an artist's rendering of a beautiful home being drawn as the user watches.

Practical Homes, Inc. will have a more down-to-business look and feel to the site. They will still have some artistic elements, because they are an architectural design firm. However, those elements will be presented within a more businesslike interface. There probably will not be a Flash entry screen, because business users typically do not have time to sit through a movie before they get to the website.

3.   Draw Them into the Purchase Process

While the website is making the initial impression, it must also be drawing the site visitor into the purchase process. In other words, the initial imagery and presentation should not only present the brand identity, but also convey a message enticing the site visitor into beginning a customer relationship with the business.

Let us return to the Fabulous Homes, Inc. example. Consider the following two messages that could be displayed on their home page.

"Licensed Architects Specializing in Home Design"
"Let Us Build Your Dream Home"

Both of these messages communicate what the firm does. But only the second one builds on the emotional bond of their brand to draw customers further into the purchase process.

Guiding Customers to a Purchase Decision

Once the Small Business website has made a good first impression, then the site user will begin pursuing their reason for coming to the website. They may be doing research before beginning the purchase process. They may be comparing companies. They may be looking for a product to purchase. They may be comparing prices. The website must be built with an awareness of what potential customers will want to do when they come to the site. Then it can guide them through a process most likely to result in a sale. This will be different for each business, depending on the nature of the product and the target market.

Let us return once more to the Fabulous Homes, Inc. example. The senior partner, Joe Fabulous, conducted some market research to find out what his customers needed before they would be ready to hire his firm. He did this by simply calling some of his current and past customers and asking for their input. Joe found out that most customers had to be convinced in four areas before making their final decision:

✓ *Education*:
They need to learn about custom home design, to make sure it is right for them.

✓ *Visualization*:
They need to see examples of similar homes, to picture the end result.

✓ *Imitation*:
They need to hear testimonies from other homeowners, to know that Fabulous Homes is a company they will be happy with, and can boast about.

✓ *Validation*:
They need to be assured that Famous Homes uses only the best products and is recognized for delivering quality results.

Fabulous Homes, Inc. designed their website to lead site visitors through each of these four decision criteria. They did this in two ways.

First, they designed their site navigation to feature five tabs at the top of the page. One content area was dedicated to each of the four key considerations. A fifth was dedicated to general company information.

✓ Learn About Custom Homes
✓ Visit Our Dream Homes
✓ Hear From Happy Customers
✓ See Our Industry Awards
✓ About Us

Customers could visit each of these content areas at their leisure. No matter which issue was of concern to them during the particular site visit, it would be easy for them to find the assurances they needed to continue in the purchase cycle.

In addition to designing the site navigation around the four considerations of the purchase process, Fabulous Homes also created an online guide that led prospective customers through each of these four issues. They could view the tutorial as a streaming video movie on the website. They could click through it as HTML pages, starting in the "Learn About Custom Homes" section. They could download it as a movie file that they can watch on their computer later. Customers could also request a DVD to be sent to their homes.

Fabulous Homes identified what it would take to transform a site visitor into a client. Then they designed their website around the needs of the customer in a way that would lead customers to the desired result, a sale.

Capturing Sales Leads

In the previous discussion, we showed how a website needs to lead a curious customer from interest to desire. Still, desiring to do business with a company requires no effort or risk on the customer's part. Going the next step requires initiating a conversion. Many people are reluctant to do this, even if it is the best thing for them to do. The website has to entice them to make that step. There are many ways to accomplish this. Three practices are fundamental.

- ✓ Provide a phone number
- ✓ Provide an incentive
- ✓ Provide a needs assessment form

Let us continue with our story. If the site design and content does its job, customers will receive enough assurance that they want to pursue a custom home and will feel confident that Fabulous Homes, Inc. is a company they might want to have design it for them. This is all great. Still, many customers will abandon the site visit and not go any farther. The website has to make it easy for them to take the plunge and actually begin a dialogue with the company. This is where capturing sales leads comes in.

To bring site users into a dialogue with the company, Fabulous Homes, Inc. used a combination of the three tactics mentioned above. Every content page concluded with a call to action, inviting the customer to contact the company for a free consultation. This call to action included a phone number and a link to a needs assessment form. This is a very low-effort, low-risk step for a site visitor to take. Still, many customers will not respond to a call to action like this. It makes the customer do all the work without really offering anything in return. "Well," a business owner might argue, "we offer a free consultation." Most people do not consider a free sales call as much of an incentive. Even if they really want to talk to the company, there is just some kind of instinctual reluctance people feel. Joe Fabulous knew this was human nature. He also knew that it does not take much of an incentive to motivate a customer to take such a small step.

Once again, Joe relied on the customer research he had done. Since most of his customers were wealthy, they would not be particularly moved by some inexpensive giveaway. Instead, Joe decided to offer something related to what the company was all about, but that also would mean something to his potential customers. They decided that for every in-person consultation, Fabulous Homes, Inc. would donate a tree to the local "Green Spaces" organization that converted abandoned lots into neighborhood parks. Now they had completed the process of initiating a customer relationship through the website. They had created a lead generation device that would motivate potential customers to respond while also supporting the brand identity of a classy company that makes homes and neighborhoods beautiful.

To take it one step further, Fabulous Homes also created a graphical treatment of the call to action. They included it on the home page and along the right side of each content page. This would give every page a right hand border that offered potential customers the opportunity to save a tree and beautify a neighborhood.

Typical Small Business Website Goals

Once you have defined your online business model, the next step is to determine what goals will lead to success. These goals set the compass heading for your website.

The basic small business website typically has three goals:

(1)   Generate sales leads
(2)   Support customer loyalty by providing easy online access to customer service
(3)   Support the brand

Of course, this is a prototypical list. As you go through this process, you will need to define goals specific to your own website.

Measuring Success For The Small Business Website

Now you have set the compass heading for your website, by setting effective goals. This will let you develop a set of tactics and site features to reach those goals. Before you can do that, however, you must determine how you are going to measure success on your website. This section will show you how Return on Investment (ROI) is calculated for the B2B website.

The return on investment (ROI) from leads generated through the Business Development lead generation process can be measured as shown in Figure 18.2. You would basically calculate the average profit earned from a converted sales lead. Then you would calculate the conversion rate for sales leads generated through the website. Finally, you would calculate the total costs to generate a lead through the website.

However, it should be cautioned that converted sales leads is not the only return generated from the Small Business website. There is also an important branding component to the website. This is actually the bigger justification for these small websites. If you do not have a website at all, or if your website is not very good, it will actually cause you to lose customers.

Now let us look at the process for calculating ROI for leads generated through the Small Business website.

ROI for Business Development

Calculating ROI for Business Development with a small business is very similar to ROI for sales through an eRetail website. It is based on conversion of sales leads generated through the website. In fact, you will use the same method shown in Chapter 15 for calculating ROI from immediate sales on the eRetail site to calculate the return from your efforts to generate leads to your business. The only real difference is in the steps which go into taking a customer from a user on the website to a converted sale.

With the Small Business website, you are capturing sales leads that will be closed by a salesperson. Whereas, the eRetail site closes the sale during the user session, the Small Business site begins the sales process. A quick look at the process will clarify what you will be measuring.

1.   Website Response

The first step in the process is to convert site visitors into sales leads. With eRetail, site visitors are converted directly to sales. We calculated a *conversion rate* at this point. With the Small Business site, a sale will not be made until later in the process. At this point, we are measuring *responses* to marketing materials on the website. In general, there are three response devices customer can respond to on the website. They can call a phone number, fill out an online form, or send an email. To measure how effective your website is at eliciting responses you will simply divide the total number of responses by the total number of site visitors (also called *impressions*). This is called the *response rate*.

2.   Conversions

In the next step, a salesperson will follow up on the sales leads (also called *responders*) and hopefully close the sales. When an actual sale takes place, that is considered a *conversion*. You can calculate two different conversion rates. To measure the conversion of sales leads to sales, you would divide total conversions by total responses. To measure conversion of site visitors to sales, you would divide total sales by the total number of site visitors (impressions).

This second measure can be used to directly calculate your ROI. To do this, you will measure your cost per impression in the same way as the eRetail site. You will add up all your costs to generate leads to the website and then divide the total number of site visitors by this number to get a cost per impression. With the eRetail site, however, we included all of the website costs in the calculation of total costs. With the Small Business site, you will only measure costs associated with the parts of the website which generate sales leads. The other, development and maintenance costs will be counted towards the Brand Development ROI.

3.   Profit Per Sale

The third step is to measure your profit per sale. Once again, the basic concept is exactly the same as for the eRetail site. You will calculate (or estimate) your total profit per sale, not including your web costs. The difference between the Small Business and eRetail models is found in the nature of the sale. There are many types of small business. Some are very similar to the eRetail model and make sales directly (these should refer to Chapter 15 for an in-depth discussion of eRetail websites). Some are retail stores. Others are B2B businesses or service businesses that require a longer sales process. In these latter cases, the total revenue earned from a single sale may be realized over a period of time. For example, many B2B sales include contracts for services or products to be delivered over a number of months, or years. You must estimate the entire expected value of the sale, rather than just the immediate revenue generated. Similarly, the costs per sale must include the costs incurred by the salesperson in addition to general production and marketing costs.

Once you have completed this process, you can calculate ROI for your online Business Development efforts. At this point, the formula is exactly the same as for eRetail, as shown in Figure 18.2

Only after your website has become successful in generating sales, should you pursue a traffic generation strategy, as described in Part II.

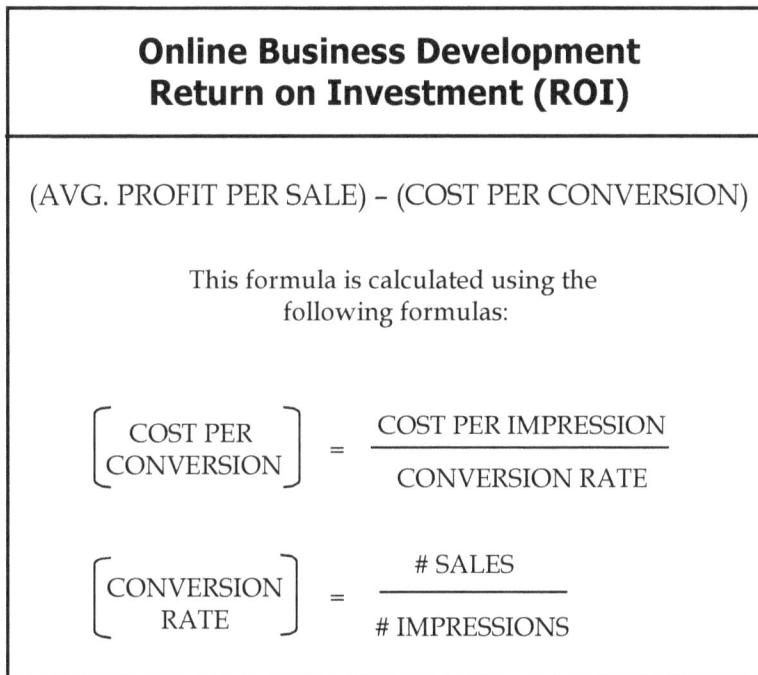

Online Business Development
Return on Investment (ROI)

(AVG. PROFIT PER SALE) – (COST PER CONVERSION)

This formula is calculated using the
following formulas:

$$\left[\begin{array}{c} \text{COST PER} \\ \text{CONVERSION} \end{array} \right] = \frac{\text{COST PER IMPRESSION}}{\text{CONVERSION RATE}}$$

$$\left[\begin{array}{c} \text{CONVERSION} \\ \text{RATE} \end{array} \right] = \frac{\# \text{ SALES}}{\# \text{ IMPRESSIONS}}$$

Figure 18.2

Designing The Small Business Website User Experience

The key to a successful Small Business website is to convince customers that your business is right for them, starting with their first impression on the home page. Then, in as few mouse clicks as possible, get them to fill out a lead form or call your phone number.

Many businesses make the mistake of trying to build a website before taking the time to figure out what the website is there to accomplish. That is always a set-up for poor results. Only after mapping out a user experience that will lead to successfully achieving your business goals should you put your web designer to work creating the look and feel for your website.

This section will walk through a typical user experience that successful Small Business websites create to initiate customer relationships and capture sales leads through the website.

The Goal of Website Design

The primary purpose of a website is to meet the needs and wants of customers coming to the site in a way that maximizes the attainment of Internet Marketing goals. The easiest way to understand what a website is trying to accomplish is to think of it as a funnel. At the wide end, tactics are employed to reach out to customers, appeal to their interests and entice them to enter your website. From this point onward, every action a user takes should be moving them down the funnel, towards the ultimate outcome(s) you want to achieve from your website.

Figure 18.3 shows the flow of a successful user experience.

Next, let us look at the steps in the typical Small Business website user experience.

The Small Business Website User Experience

1.   First Contact

In general, people coming to the Small Business website will first come from search engines or be referred directly to your website. Since budgets are typically small, the first step is to optimize your web pages for search engines. Once you have demonstrated that you are successfully converting site visitors to sales leads, then you can begin pursuing other online traffic generation methods (see Part II).

Figure 18.3

2. Home Page and Content Pages

The first impression on any website is always of critical importance. Web users will only give a web page a few seconds before they decide if they will stay or move on. You must capture their attention and win over their interest within a couple of glances at your site. For the Small Business website, traffic is often sent directly to the home page. Budgets are usually too small to support an ongoing initiative to build targeted landing pages. It is of utmost importance that the home page wins over potential customers.

A common mistake is neglecting to spend enough time designing an effective home page. The home page must positively reflect your brand. It must also quickly draw customers into the actions you want them to take on the website. This can only be done by taking some time to map out what information you want your customers to reach and what actions you want them to take. Then you can design the home page to appeal to your customers' interests while drawing them to the information and actions you want them to find.

If you are planning to direct customers to lower level pages on the website, or to custom built landing pages, you will want to spend time designing these pages to be as effective as your home page.

As a note of caution, some freelance web developers and small design shops love to create Flash animation "welcome" screens for the websites they build. Unless you specialize in something related to the creative arts, this is usually not a good idea for a business website. Customers researching companies they want to do business with do not want to waste their time watching video animation before they find the information they need. Just take them directly to a very professional looking home page where they can easily find whatever information they need. That is the best way to make a great first impression.

3.   Navigation and Useful Content

Once you have successfully brought a customer to your website and kept their interest, then you must make sure they do not get frustrated and leave. As with all websites, having an easy to navigate taxonomy is critical.

It is also important to identify the information customers will need in order to make the decision to enter the sales process with your company. Then make sure you have this information presented on your website in a way that is easy for them to find and navigate through. For example, you could build your website with four main tabs on the top navigation: a section for product descriptions, one for company information, one for client relations and customer testimonials and a fourth for customer service contacts.

4.   **Lead Generation**

The final step in the user experience is to get site visitors to initiate a contact with your company. This could be by calling your phone number or by submitting a lead form on the website. The ultimate goal of your website is to get as many sales leads as possible. To accomplish this, you need to structure your website content so every path through the site leads to a contact opportunity, or has a prominently displayed call to action with a phone number or a link to the lead form.

The Small Business website is there to generate sales leads for the business and to make sure the company can be found online. There are ultimately two critical factors for success. First, you must design your navigation and web pages so customers are drawn towards opportunities to respond to a call to action, resulting in a sales lead. Second, you must ensure that your website reflects your offline branding and presents a level of quality and professionalism that will not hurt your brand.

Small Business Website
Roadmap To Success

The final step before you actually build your website is to map out the specific objectives and tactics that will lead to successfully achieving your goals. In Part I, we called this your *roadmap to success*. The tactics in your "roadmap" are the building blocks that will create a winning user experience on your website.

Small Business Website Objectives and Tactics

	Objectives	Tactics
Interest	Ensure that web searchers find the site when searching for your company, products or services you offer	1. Search engine optimization 2. If yields profitable ROI, search engine marketing or set up an affiliate program
	Ensure that customers seeking company or product information, or customer service can find your company	3. Put website URL in offline ads, collateral materials, product specs, etc.
Trust	Provide a positive user experience that engenders trust and a willingness to continue in the sales process	4. Optimize content on home page and landing pages to make best first impression 5. User-friendly navigation and user interface for the website 6. Ensure privacy of customer information
Satisfaction	Provide content to help customers make their purchase decision, and choose your company	7. Information customers will need when evaluating potential companies to do business with, in a way that is easy to find and of top quality appearance. Typical info includes: ✓ Product/services info ✓ Company info and exec. bio's ✓ Customer list & testimonials ✓ Community involvement & awards ✓ Contact Us & customer service 8. Deliver sales lead submission opportunities as part of content that is of service to the customer, such as: needs assessment form, downloadable white papers, etc.
Loyalty	Use opt-in email to retain customers and generate additional sales	9. Periodically send follow-up email to the opt-in list, checking on satisfaction and with promotional offers and/or recommended enhancements to their products/services

Figure 18.4

Figure 18.4 presents a set of objectives and tactics common on Small Business websites. They are laid out according to the four levels of customer intimacy described in Chapter 2. A quick survey of the objectives and tactics shown here will give you an idea of what goes into a successful Small Business website.

These tactics are prototypical examples. They should be used as guidelines to give you an idea of what your website can accomplish. However, you will have to determine specific objectives and tactics that match the unique aspects of your business and the needs of your customers.

The Roadmap Unfolded:
Typical Small Business Website Tactics

In this chapter you have learned what successful Small Business websites are trying to accomplish and how to design a website that meets those objectives. The basic considerations for a Small Business website are to make customers feel confident that doing business with your company will be a good thing for them and to initiate a conversation with them.

The following table contains a detailed description of the tactics presented in the Roadmap to Success table (Figure 18.4). It provides nuts-and-bolts examples of the type of things implemented on successful Small Business websites. You can use this information as a framework for developing your own website. However, there is no substitute for defining the details of your own online business model and mapping out a set of tactics that will meet your own organizational goals.

Building Interest

Building interest with the Small Business website involves reaching out to prospective customers to draw them into the process of becoming a sales lead.

Search engine optimization	Most people will find a Small Business website while they are searching for information about a products or services they are interested in. They will find your website if it appears in their search listings. In some cases, they will know about your business and type your company name, or a variation of it into the search engine. Surprisingly, for some businesses with fairly typical sounding names, their website does not show up when their own business name is entered. Optimizing the content on your web pages to be found by search engines is the most important thing you can do to get traffic to your Small Business website. Search engine optimization is discussed in Chapter 6.
Search engine marketing	Paying for sponsored links on search engines, known as search engine marketing, is simply paying to get your search results listings displayed to people searching for the topics your site addresses. If your website is successful in generating sales leads, this will often be an important part of your strategy. A variation of search engine marketing is to pay to have your company name included in online yellow pages and business directories. Search engine marketing is discussed in Chapter 6.
Start an affiliate program	An affiliate program is a way to pay other websites a commission on sales to leads they send to your website. If you are able to clearly associate sales with visits by customers on your website then you may want to consider starting an affiliate program. Affiliate programs are discussed in Chapter 9.
Offline presentation of URL	For all businesses who have offline collateral, it is a good idea to include your website URL. Many people will feel reluctant to make a phone call to a business they are interested in. It is just inconvenient for them. But they will visit the website. If you have done a good job of designing your website to convert visitors into sales leads, a visit to your website will take them one step closer to a sale.

Building Trust

With a Small Business, the website is initiating the first contact with a prospective customer. This would otherwise take place with a human being. Building trust depends on the professionalism of the customer's experience with your "virtual salesman," the website. This includes the tone and presentation of what, in essence, is your sales pitch to the online customer. It also includes the usability and appearance of your website and online services.

Home page and landing pages	Usability and quality of content is essential for any website. With the Small Business website there is an even stronger microscope on these aspects of user experience. Potential customers are evaluating whether they want to do business with your company. They will assume their experience with your website will be the same as the experience they will have with your company if they decide to do business with you. The first contact your business makes with potential customers will often be through the home page, or the landing page a search engine places them on. These pages must be designed to make the best impression and to draw the customer further along in the sales process.
User-friendly navigation	All websites must have user-friendly navigation. For the Small Business website, site design should be built around leading the customer to a purchase decision. That means helping them find all of the information they need before they feel comfortable taking the next step with your business. Site navigation must be designed to make this process intuitive. A poorly designed set of menu options or content tabs can confuse your customers and cause them to leave the site before they find out what you have to offer.
Ensure privacy of customer information	Ensuring the privacy and security of customer information is critical any time such information is collected on a website. One important way to do this is through your privacy policy. Every website must have a privacy policy. Although most customers will never look at it, your privacy policy is an extremely important part of your website. *If a customer files a lawsuit against your business, the courts will look at your privacy policy to decide your case. You must be very careful to craft a policy statement that assures your customers of their safety and your good intentions, but also does not hold you liable for more than you can actually do.*

Building Satisfaction

With the Small Business website, satisfaction is gained mainly by guiding them through the process of making a purchase decision. The easier and more intuitive this is, the happier they will be. This will also bring them closer to additional sales for the company.

Content to aid purchase decision	There is no "one size fits all" approach to content on your Small Business website. You must put yourself in your customers shoes. What do they need to make their purchase decision? Then you must do everything you can to have what they need on your website. You should have a professional presentation that convinces them you will take care of them better than your competitors.
	There are a number of things you can do on your website to help customers move forward in the sales process. Start with the beginning. What will someone need who is starting out his or her pre-purchase research? They may be looking for an overview of your company or your products/services. They may want to see things like: a company profile, profile of typical clients, and a partial customer list. Make this information easy for them to find.
	You may service different types of customer. Perhaps you have both business customers and individuals. You may offer a different service to homeowners versus renters. There are any number of ways you may divide your customer base. If this is the case, you may want to create content areas targeted specifically to these customer segments. Make it easy for them to see how your company meets their specific needs and wants. Do not make them have to sift through pages of information they do not care about.
Capture sales leads	The end result of a potential customer's experience with your website should be to begin a dialogue with your company. This may take more than one visit. Still, you ultimately want them to move from being an interested visitor to being a qualified sales lead. To do this, you must include devices on your website to capture lead information that can be followed up by a sales person.
	If your business allows transactions to take place directly on the website, then leading customers into the transaction process serves the same function as capturing a sales lead.

Building Loyalty

Loyalty for the Small Business website mainly comes down to maintaining contact with customers and potential customers. The best way to accomplish this online is with email.

Opt-in email	For a small business, personal communication makes a big difference. Email can be used to maintain relationships with existing customers and to keep prospective customers interested.
	It is a well known fact that dissatisfied customers usually do not express their dissatisfaction before they leave. They just stop doing business with you. On the other hand, one of the biggest factors contributing to customer loyalty is when a business responds well to a customer complaint. This presents a dilemma. How can you respond if they never tell you there is a problem? Email can be used to periodically ask your customers about their satisfaction with your company and give them an opportunity to offer comments. This makes a nice point of contact for happy customers. It also gives you the opportunity to rescue at-risk customers.
	You will also have potential customers who have expressed interest in your company, but have not yet made a purchase. You can use email to periodically send them special offers or otherwise maintain contact, keeping them in the sales pipeline. Of course, these emails can, and should also be sent to existing customers to give them an incentive to do more business with you.
	Before you undertake any email efforts, you must explicitly obtain permission to send marketing email to those whose email address you have obtained. This is called opting-in to your email program. Read Chapter 7 to learn about setting up effective Email marketing.

Conclusion

In this chapter, you have learned how to be successful initiating and building customer relationships through a Small Business website. In the next chapter, you will learn how to create a successful corporate website for a Consumer Goods Manufacturer.

Now turn to the Consumer Goods Manufacturer website.

Chapter 19

Building A Successful Consumer Goods Manufacturer Corporate Website

In this chapter, you will learn . . .
- How to define the online business model for a Consumer Goods Manufacturer website
- How to measure success for a Consumer Goods Manufacturer website
- How to design a successful user experience for a Consumer Goods Manufacturer website
- The tactics used by successful Consumer Goods Manufacturer websites

Interactive Skunk Works At A Car Company
The Toyota.com Story

1995 was an exciting year in the Direct Response Department at Toyota Motor Sales, USA. The little department of twelve people were developing Toyota's fledgling integrated marketing program. It was the beginning of a long string of successful innovations. One of the analysts on the team, Brian Williams, was responsible for acquiring a marketing presence with the online services, CompuServe and Prodigy. Early in the year, Brian told the group, "We have got to get onto this new service, America Online. It is still small but it's more user friendly and everyone is going to start using it." A week or so later, Brian started saying, "We need to start our own website."

In January 1995, most people barely knew what a website was. Jim Pisz, the department manager, had cultivated a kind of skunk works mentality in the little group. So Jim championed the Internet program and the rest of the team jumped on the idea.

A few months later, *www.toyota.com* was winning award after award as the best corporate website. But they still could not send email outside the company. It was a cumbersome process getting set up to send and receive messages with a couple of key vendors. It did not always work. Still, it was better than using overnight delivery, or more often having the vendors come and pick up documents in person.

Like the few other corporate websites existing at the time, *www.toyota.com* was mainly an information resource. It was designed to bring traffic to the website who would request a brochure and opt in to their direct mail list. To reach this goal, Toyota created a lifestyle magazine covering topics of interest to their target buyers. This was one of the earliest examples of what is now a common practice, building content pages to attract search engine traffic. It soon became obvious, though, that customers wanted to use the website for two-way communication with Toyota. They were using the comment field on brochure requests to give feedback and ask for help. You can imagine the surprise when request forms started coming in with calls for help on their current vehicles and comments about problems with the website. In fact, this was happening so often with corporate websites at the time that a new term was created. It was called, *forced email*.

Over the next few years, Toyota continued to add innovative features to their website. A "Dealer Locator" was added. This let in-market buyers be connected directly to a local dealership. An "Owners Only" area nurtured loyalty among existing customers. Yes, eventually they were able to send and receive email directly with their customers.

Toyota knew that the average American car buyer was going online. To protect and build their brand with these buyers, they would have to offer a superior online customer experience. To avoid missing the opportunity to make sales to potential customers, they had to effectively capture sales leads and move them forward in the sales process. To keep their loyal customers happy, they had to offer the convenience of online customer services. These are lessons that must be learned by every Consumer Goods Manufacturer as they develop an Internet Marketing strategy.

In this chapter, we will walk through the steps successful Consumer Goods Manufacturers go through to create a winning corporate website.

Understanding The Consumer Goods Manufacturer Corporate Website

The Consumer Goods Manufacturer is a producer of goods. They do not usually sell directly to the consumer. Instead, they focus on creating quality products that others will sell. This is the key to understanding the Consumer Goods Manufacturer website.

People develop an emotional bond with products they can depend on. Once they find a product they like, most people would rather not switch. They will even tell others about how good it is. Loyal customers become spokespersons for the products they trust. All successful branding is built around this little piece of human nature. Consumer Goods Manufacturer websites exist primarily to promote this experience among their customers.

Dimensions of the Consumer Goods Manufacturer Online Business Model

In Part I, you learned an easy way to begin defining your online business model. You start by choosing from among seven basic dimensions that form the foundation of all online businesses (see Figure 19.1). This quick and easy approach will allow you to implement a set of features and tactics aimed at achieving the goals of your business or organization.

There are typically two primary dimensions to the Consumer Goods Manufacturer website online business model: *Brand Development* and *Cost Savings*.

1. Brand Development

These websites have a different business model from any of the websites we have looked at so far. Their primary goal is to build and maintain *brand loyalty*.

Customers are likely to visit the Consumer Goods Manufacturer website either for customer service or information.

When customers get there, you must meet or exceed their expectations to prevent causing damage to your brand. When this is accomplished, then you have an opportunity to build additional intimacy in the customer relationship.

Seven Dimensions To Online Business Models

1.   eCommerce

2.   Business Development

3.   Lead Generation

✓ 4.   Brand Development

5.   Customer Relations

6.   Information Delivery

✓ 7.   Cost Savings

Figure 19.1

2.   Cost Savings

Another goal for the corporate website is to *reduce costs*. When product information and customer service can be provided online, you save money otherwise spent on more expensive resources, such as your call center and printed brochures.

Typical Consumer Goods Manufacturer Website Goals

Once you have defined your online business model, the next step is to determine what goals will lead to success. These goals set the compass heading for your website.

The following are typical goals for the Consumer Goods Manufacturer website.

Brand Development Goals

(1)   Positively support corporate and product brands

(2)   Increase customer loyalty by providing convenient online customer service

(3)   Direct interested shoppers to retail outlets with a higher likelihood to convert than before the site visit

(4)   Increase customer loyalty with op-in communications or other online services

Cost Savings Goals

(5)   Reduce costs by providing information and customer service electronically; thus reducing call center, print and postage costs.

Of course, this is a prototypical list. As you go through this process, you will need to define goals specific to your own website.

Hybrid Websites

Before we move on, there are two more considerations to make mention of for the Consumer Goods Manufacturer website.

First, some corporate websites double as eRetail websites, selling the goods that they manufacture. For these hybrid sites, the eRetail portion of the site has the goals described for eRetailers in Chapter 15. The rest of the corporate site, however, still has the goals described in this chapter. These two sets of goals must be balanced.

Second, manufacturers often distribute their products primarily through channel partners, such as retail department stores. The corporate website serves not only the end consumer but also the channel partners. In this case, part of the website might serve as a business to business (B2B) website. Chapter 18 describes the B2B Supplier website.

Measuring Success For A Consumer Goods Manufacturer Corporate Website

Now you have set the compass heading for your website, by setting effective goals. This will let you develop a set of tactics and site features to reach those goals. Before you can do that, however, you must determine how you are going to measure success on your website. This section will show you how Return on Investment (ROI) is calculated for the two primary dimensions of the Consumer Goods Manufacturer website.

ROI for Brand Development

Measuring ROI for Brand Development is very difficult. There are many factors that do not lend themselves to easily being measured.

The corporate website is only one component of a larger branding strategy. Its biggest role is to prevent loss of customers. This is not easily put into numbers. A corporate website may be used for some proactive measures. These include things like channeling sales leads to retail outlets and providing online promotional offers to incentivize retail sales. Corporations also will often use the website as a part of larger integrated marketing campaigns. ROI for these specific activities can be measured using the same two formulas shown in Chapter 15 (Formulas 15.2 and 15.3).

It would be a mistake, however, to assume the ROI generated from these efforts is a true reflection of the value of the website.

Ultimately, the most significant return you get from the corporate website comes down to this: A large percentage of your customers use the Internet to research and communicate with companies they buy products from. What is going to happen if they cannot find your company or products online? What would happen if they do find it, but are not impressed by what they see? *In other words, having a good corporate website is a critical need to prevent your market share from being captured by competitors who have a better website than yours.*

A second, hard to measure, source of ROI is the results from customers receiving customer service through the website. It is the same issue. For customers who want the convenience of online customer service, you risk losing customers by not offering those services on your website. However, the bigger reason for companies to put customer service online is because of the cost savings. That part can be measured, as we are about to see.

ROI for Cost Savings

Customers today have learned to be impatient. If they can avoid waiting on hold to get service over the telephone, they will. This creates a win-win opportunity. Companies can significantly reduce costs by providing help to their customers online. Customers often come to the corporate website looking for information or services that otherwise would likely require a telephone call or a package of printed materials being sent in the mail. Websites can also be used to accomplish administrative tasks like processing rebates or warranty claims. All of these things are more expensive to perform offline.

You may be spending a lot of money at your call center by simply giving answers to questions your customers could look up themselves, if it was easy for them to do so. If this is the case, you can put a Frequently Asked Questions (FAQ) section on your website. Or, put your user manuals online.

ROI From Cost Savings

(OFFLINE COST OF SERVICE) - (ONLINE COST OF SERVICE)

Figure 19.2

ROI from cost savings is a straightforward proposition. It can be expressed in the formula shown in Figure 19.2.

Designing The Consumer Goods Manufacturer Corporate Website User Experience

We have now defined the Consumer Goods Manufacturer website online business model, identified typical goals and shown how to measure website success. The next step is to design a user experience for your customers that successfully achieves the goals of your online business model.

Many businesses make the mistake of trying to build a website before taking the time to figure out what the website is there to accomplish. That is always a set-up for poor results. Only after mapping out a user experience that will lead to successfully achieving your business goals should you put your web designer to work creating the look and feel for your website.

This section will walk through a typical user experience that successful Consumer Goods Manufacturer websites create to support their brand, build customer loyalty and reduce costs.

The Goal of Website Design

The primary purpose of a website is to meet the needs and wants of customers coming to the site in a way that maximizes the attainment of Internet Marketing goals. The easiest way to understand what a website is trying to accomplish is to think of it as a funnel. At the wide end, tactics are employed to reach out to customers, appeal to their interests and entice them to enter your website. From this point onward, every action a user takes should be moving them down the funnel, towards the ultimate outcome(s) you want to achieve from your website.

To understand the Consumer Goods Manufacturer website we turn to the funnel a user travels through between their initial interest and the desired outcomes you hope will result from their visit. With this model, users will typically take one of two paths through the website, as shown in Figure 19.3.

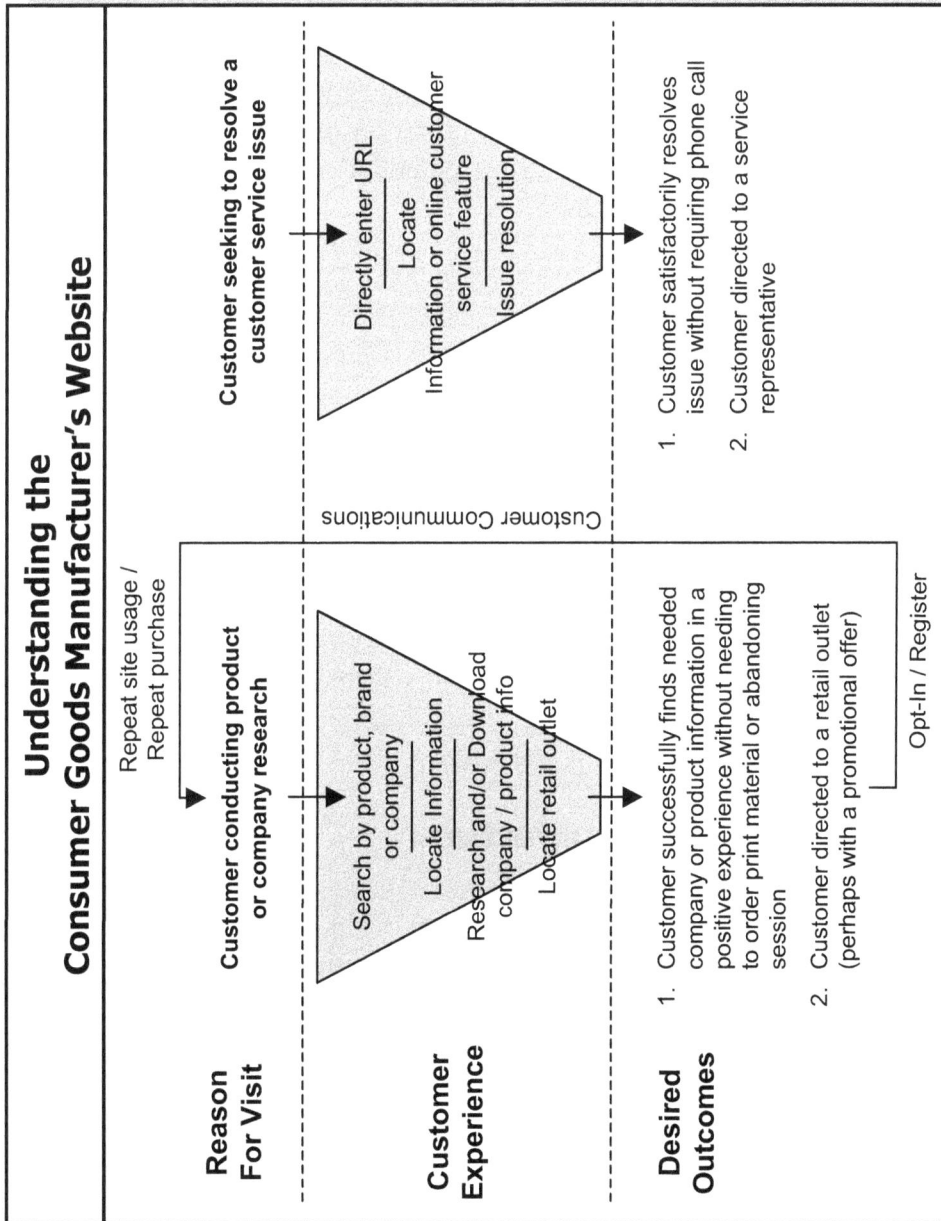

Understanding the
Consumer Goods Manufacturer's Website

Reason For Visit

Repeat site usage / Repeat purchase

Customer conducting product or company research

Customer seeking to resolve a customer service issue

Customer Experience

Search by product, brand or company

Locate Information

Research and/or Download company / product info

Locate retail outlet

Directly enter URL

Locate

Information or online customer service feature

Issue resolution

Customer Communications

Desired Outcomes

1. Customer successfully finds needed company or product information in a positive experience without needing to order print material or abandoning session

2. Customer directed to a retail outlet (perhaps with a promotional offer)

Opt-In / Register

1. Customer satisfactorily resolves issue without requiring phone call

2. Customer directed to a service representative

Figure 19.3

Brand Development Path

In the first path, customers visit the website seeking information about your company or products. There are two outcomes you will typically hope for. The first is to improve the overall reputation of your brand, resulting in future sales. The second is to direct potential customers to a retail outlet where they will make a purchase.

Customer Service Path

The second path is customer service. In this path, customers are seeking to resolve an immediate service issue. The desired outcome is that their issue be resolved resulting in continued satisfaction and loyalty to your business.

Each of these paths supports both brand development and cost savings goals. In both cases, the customer's ability to get what they came for will either build up or hurt your company's brand. Also, both paths include delivery of information and services in a less costly manner than other offline delivery methods.

The Consumer Goods Manufacturer Website User Experience

Both of the paths customers take on the Consumer Goods Manufacturer website follow the same basic steps through the funnel.

1.   First Contact

In general, customers coming to the Consumer Goods Manufacturer's corporate website already have an interest in your products or brand. They are already looking for you. You want to make sure it is easy for them to find you. If they are looking for information or services that can be provided at a lower cost online, you also want to make sure they find their way to the online alternatives.

2.   Information Search

Now you have successfully attracted prospective customers to your website and existing customers to your online services. The next step is to make sure they can find what they are looking for. You must have user-friendly navigation and onsite search. This is the next step where you can lose customers. If they are frustrated trying to use your website, they will leave.

3.   Self-Service Activity

Both of the user paths through your website involve some kind of self-service activities. Some users on the Brand Development path will download information or locate a retail outlet for your products. Customer service customers will use your online customer service features. At the minimum, this will require them to locate your phone number. It may include such activities as searching for FAQs or interacting in an online chat session with your customer service representative.

The basic business model for a Consumer Goods Manufacturer website is *brand development* and *cost savings*. The foundation for an effective corporate website is to make sure people get their immediate needs met when they come to your home page. Those needs are for information and customer service. Identify the payoffs customers are looking for on your site. Are they looking for detailed product specifications? Are they looking to order replacement parts? Maybe they need instructions from your product user manuals. They might need information about recalls, directions to repair centers or retail outlets. Maybe they just want the phone number to a customer service representative. Whatever the needs are for your customers, map out a simple path for them to reach their payoff, in as few mouse clicks as possible. If these basic needs are not met, your website (or lack thereof) will damage customer loyalty by the frustration that results.

Once your customers' basic needs are met, you are at ground zero. You are not shooting yourself in the foot. But you are not necessarily increasing loyalty yet either. Now you can build upon the foundation to increase loyalty and build intimacy in the customer relationship.

Consumer Goods Manufacturer Corporate Website Roadmap To Success

The final step before you actually build your website is to map out the specific objectives and tactics that will lead to successfully achieving your goals. In Part I, we called this your *roadmap to success*. The tactics in your "roadmap" are the building blocks that will create a winning user experience on your website.

Figure 19.4 presents a set of objectives and tactics common on Consumer Goods Manufacturer websites. They are laid out according to the four levels of customer intimacy described in Chapter 2. A quick survey of the objectives and tactics shown here will give you an idea of what goes into a successful Consumer Goods Manufacturer website.

These tactics are prototypical examples. They should be used as guidelines to give you an idea of what your website can accomplish. However, you will have to determine specific objectives and tactics that match the unique aspects of your business and the needs of your customers.

Typical Consumer Goods Manufacturer Website
Objectives and Tactics

	Objectives	Tactics
Interest	Ensure that customers find the website when searching for company name, brands or products	1. Search engine optimization and online directory listings 2. Put URL in offline ads, collateral materials and product labels/specs
	Direct customers seeking product information or customer services to lower cost online alternatives	3. Promote website on call center messaging, brochures, user manual, etc.
Trust	Ensure that customers have a positive online experience that positively supports the image of the brand	4. User-friendly navigation and interface, with short path to information/services sought by user 5. Freshness and accuracy of content 6. Easy to find customer service options 7. Responsive customer service 8. Design elements complementary to offline branding elements
Satisfaction	Provide services to help customers make their purchase decision while still on the site	9. Enhanced product information
	Direct interested customers to retail outlets to make a purchase	10. Directory of retail outlets (with links to websites)
	Provide automated customer service options (to reduce offline costs)	11. Self-serve information and customer service resources 12. Online chat with customer service representative
Loyalty	Use outbound email and a company log to build customer relationships	13. Opt-in email 14. Loyalty rewards 15. Company blog
	Convert customer service cases to loyal customers by going the extra mile	16. Customer service follow up survey & timely response to poor results

Figure 19.4

The next section goes into detail about the how these tactics work together to make the Consumer Goods Manufacturer website successful. If you do not want to dig this deep into the details, feel free to turn ahead to the next chapter.

The Roadmap Unfolded:
Typical Consumer Goods Manufacturer Corporate Website Tactics

In this chapter you have learned what successful Consumer Goods Manufacturer websites are trying to accomplish and how to design a website that meets those objectives. The most important thing a Consumer Goods Manufacturer website must do is make sure customers' needs are met. When customers go to the website, they want to find a company and products they can fall in love with. It is the purpose of the website to let them do just that.

The following table contains a detailed description of the tactics presented in the Roadmap to Success table (Figure 19.4). It provides nuts-and-bolts examples of the type of things implemented on successful Consumer Goods Manufacturer websites. You can use this information as a framework for developing your own website. However, there is no substitute for defining the details of your own online business model and mapping out a set of tactics that will meet your own organizational goals.

Building Interest

In general, customers coming to the Consumer Goods Manufacturer website already have an interest in your products or brand. They are already looking for you. You want to make sure it is easy for them to find you. If they are looking for information or services that can be provided at a lower cost online, you also want to make sure they find their way to the online alternatives. The tactics in this section are designed to accomplish this.

Search engine optimization and online directory listings	With the Consumer Goods Manufacturer corporate website, people will often look for you by entering your company name or a product name in a search engine, online business directory or online yellow pages. The most important interest building tactic, therefore, is to optimize your website pages and pursue a search engine marketing strategy that ensures anyone who is looking for you can find you.
URL in offline materials	For the corporate website, it is also important to view the website as one piece of a larger integrated marketing strategy. You will also be communicating with your customers with print materials, advertisements and direct marketing campaigns. All of these other media are opportunities to present your website URL to customers.
Promote website in call center messaging and offline information resources	One of the key goals of the corporate website is to provide information and customer service at a lower cost than offline alternatives. To maximize your cost savings investment, you will need to intercept customers while they are pursuing these services and direct them to the website. One typical method is to include a message promoting the website on all automated telephone answering messages, especially the on-hold message for customer service. You can also include your URL in user manuals and product fact sheets.

Building Trust

The key to building trust on the Consumer Goods Manufacturer website is to make sure customers find what they are looking for on your website, without becoming frustrated or disappointed.

User-friendly navigation and user interface	User-friendly navigation and user interface is a critical need for every website. This is especially important when the purpose of the website is for customer to quickly find what they are looking for.
Freshness and accuracy of content	If customers are able to find the content they are looking for, then that content must be accurate and up to date.
Responsive customer service	Responsive customer service is, of course, essential to any business. In addition to having a good customer service program, there are two things that should be considered non-negotiable for your website. Whenever a customer sends an email to customer service or submits an online form, the website should auto-generate an acknowledgement of having received the online form or email. It should also include a message telling the customer what kind of response they should expect. Second, there should never be more than 24-hour turn around for emails and submitted forms (less than 2 hours preferable).
Complement offline branding	Another important factor is to build an overall sense of comfort and trust with your corporate brand. Companies spend a lot of time developing branding elements that support their corporate image. These must be consistently implemented on the website. Colors, logos, font treatments and the like should all be consistent with your offline branding efforts.

Building Satisfaction

On the Consumer Goods Manufacturer website, satisfaction is gained by going the extra mile. If you help them in their process, you will create a win-win for both of you. They may be looking for information to make a purchase decision, looking for a retail outlet, or seeking customer service. The farther along you can move them in the process, the more satisfied they will be. You will also be that much closer to a sale. By automating these processes on the website, you will also yield significant cost savings.

Enhanced product information	If a customer comes to your website looking for information about one of your products, they are probably either trying to decide if they should buy it or looking for information about how to use it. Of course, you want them to buy it and be able to use it in the way that gives them the most satisfaction. The corporate website should have the most in-depth information available for your products. Complete user specifications should be available for each product. User manuals, instructions, safety messages and the like should be easily accessible on the website.
	Two other popular features on corporate websites are product comparisons and product reviews. Customers are already using the Web for this. Some companies offer it on their own website. That way, at least it is happening in their environment. If all else is equal, customers are likely to stay with the company providing the service. Plus, it is possible to show them special offers or other incentives that the customer might not find on another site.
	Finally, some websites allow users to customize the product offerings. Automakers let customers pick their color and other options. Then they direct the customer to a dealership with that car in stock. Features like these take away reasons customers might have for buying elsewhere and increase their satisfaction and trust in your company.
Directory of retail outlets	Customers are interested enough in your brand to look up your products online. Make it easy for them to take the next step and buy. Provide a directory of retail outlets. Include in this directory a search feature, allowing customers to enter their zip code and find the nearest outlets.
	This feature can also be important if customers will need to locate a retail outlet to obtain warranty repairs or replacement parts for your products.

Self-serve information and customer service resources	Customers hate to wait on the telephone. Your website should make it very easy for them to perform a variety of tasks that they will find unpleasant on the phone. This includes things like finding FAQs about customer service issues, filing complaints, or submitting warranty or rebate claims. If they can easily do these things on the website, they will be happy and you will win by reducing costs.
Online chat with customer service personnel	One final feature that many companies are offering now is online chat for customer service. This has become very easy. There are a number of companies who can facilitate this on a cost per chat session basis. This can greatly reduce your customer service costs because one representative can have multiple chat sessions open at the same time. On a phone call, a representative is 100% dedicated to a single client for the duration of the call.

Building Loyalty

Loyalty for the Consumer Goods Manufacturer site involves bringing your customers into a relationship with the company. This is true "*brand loyalty.*" Consumer Goods Manufacturer customers want to have an emotional attachment with brands they love and trust. The ultimate purpose of your website is to help them discover that kind of relationship with your brand. Tactics in this section provide incentives to your customers to make repeat purchases, but are also aimed at making your customers feel like part of your brand family.

Opt-in email	The features we've discussed up to this point all are needed to build customer interest, trust and satisfaction. We have not yet begun using the website to build relationship. A typical practice is to engage customers in an ongoing dialogue. Customers can opt into a company newsletter. Basic questions asked when the customer opts in can be used for targeting messages to their interests. Email can be sent offering product update information and promotions for complementary products or upgrades.
	Of course, all such communications must be made easy for the customer to opt-out of. Otherwise they may feel like they are being spammed, and loyalty can be damaged.
Loyalty rewards	There are other ways to move farther up the pyramid of online needs that promote long term loyalty. Customers can

	be invited into an "inner circle" of privileged customers. Many companies give rewards for passing offers along to their friends and family or for repeat purchases. Allowing customers to earn points for such loyal actions is the essence of loyalty rewards programs, such as frequent flier miles. You could also periodically ask privileged customers to participate in product research surveys. This is a valuable source of intelligence for Marketing and R&D. Plus, it is the kind of inclusion that turns happy customers into raving fans.
Company blog	Many companies today include a company blog on the corporate website. This is a very easy and low-cost way to stay in communication with loyal customers. Besides information about products and services, the blog is a good place to celebrate contributions made to your industry or the communities you serve. A blog is also a good place to inform customers about potential problems that could hurt your company image or customer satisfaction.

Business blogs are discussed in detail in Chapter 12. |
| *Customer service follow-up* | A final thing you can do for your customers that will yield big loyalty returns is to simply follow up after a customer service inquiry. You can auto generate emails or prompt phone calls from your call center at a specified time after the service issue is closed. By simply asking your customers if they were satisfied with the response they received, and then acting on any dissatisfaction, you can take your customers from merely being satisfied to being apostles for your brand. |

Conclusion

In this chapter, you have learned how to build a corporate website for a Consumer Goods Manufacturer. You will be able to build a website that supports your company's brand and also contributes cost savings to the business. In the next chapter, you will learn about the most complex online business model discussed in this book.

Now turn to the B2B website.

Chapter 20

Building A Successful B2B Website

In this chapter, you will learn . . .
- How to define the online business model for a B2B website
- How to measure success for a B2B website
- How to design a successful user experience for B2B websites
- The tactics used by successful B2B websites

Unlimited Customer Care At A PC Near You
The ABC Uniform Story*

ABC Uniform Services (ABC) was a latecomer to the Internet. This is not unusual for Business-to-Business (B2B) suppliers who make their bread and butter through in-person relationships with clients. The ABC Corporation is a multi-billion dollar managed services company and one of the largest employers in the United States. Still, ABC Uniform Services, the largest of three uniform divisions had only a small eBrochure in place of a corporate website.

ABC had successfully built a client base of over 200,000 business customers earning over $1 billion in revenue from uniform rental and laundry services. They had not needed the Internet to build the business. In a time of fierce competition and increasing fuel costs, investing in the Internet seemed like a luxury. But ABC was also strategically integrating their uniform divisions. They wanted to provide a single face to the customer. The two other uniform divisions, maintaining the RuggedWear and ABC Gear brands, had mail order catalogs selling to businesses and government agencies. They

---

* The actual name and certain details of this Business-to-Business company have been changed to safeguard proprietary company information.

had long since created online stores to supplement their catalog business. However, there was no integrated outreach to the customer.

In 2005, three senior executives, representing the three uniform divisions, championed an inter-divisional, ABC Uniform task force to create a best-of-breed corporate presence on the Internet. The task force began tackling the challenges of creating a website tailored to the needs of business clients.

From the start, it was agreed the website must reflect the company's mantra of Unlimited Customer Care. Business customers must feel like their needs are being taken care of when they come to the website. This could prove difficult for a service organization with clients as large as WalMart and as small as the local corner deli. To reach this goal, a Web strategy was devised consisting of four pillars.

> *Reach out to rental services customers.* Rental services customers would typically sign up for a multi-year managed services contract. It was not a quick sale. The new website would focus on generating needs assessment forms to be forwarded to local account executives. Plus, content pages were built to educate potential customers and capture search engine traffic.

> *Create an integrated online store.* An integrated online storefront was created that would serve both rental and retail sales customers. The goal was to increase retail revenue from rental customers and to expose rental service options to retail customers.

> *Present customized business solutions.* A separate area was created to present package solutions for vertical industries and specialty markets. In addition, micro-sites were created for their two largest specialty markets, Auto Dealerships and Restaurants. The entire website would promote consultative solutions for each customer.

> *Create an integrated account services area.* A customer services area was created where both rental and retail customers could manage aspects of their account and access customer service.

In September 2006, after a year and a half of planning and development, the new website went live with functionality representing each of the four pillars

It was a long, slow journey for a service business accustomed to providing in-person care to their business customers. In the process, ABC Uniform Services learned the lessons all B2B Suppliers must learn to be successful online. Business customers are typically in a long term relationship with their suppliers. A B2B website is about supporting relationships throughout the client lifecycle. At the start of the sales cycle, the website provides education and captures sales leads. Existing customers are provided with support services and opportunities to make additional purchases. Finally, customers with different needs do not receive a "one size fits all" approach. All customers can find website content that meets their needs.

In this chapter, we will walk through the steps successful B2B Suppliers go through to create a winning website. This chapter focuses on larger B2B companies. However, principles can be applied to businesses of any size. Chapter 18 provides an in-depth discussion of Small Business websites.

Understanding The B2B Website

B2B relationships are all about partnerships. Companies rely on goods and services provided by their suppliers to be successful. When they look for a company to do business with, they want a partner who will understand their goals and help them deliver results, quarter after quarter. The B2B website exists to initiate and maintain partner-ships like these.

Dimensions of the B2B Supplier's Online Business Model

In Part I, you learned an easy way to begin defining your online business model. You start by choosing from among seven basic dimensions that form the foundation of all online businesses (see Figure 20.1). This quick and easy approach will allow you to implement a set of features and tactics aimed at achieving the goals of your business or organization.

All B2B websites have *Business Development* as the primary dimension to their online business model. There are two other dimensions many B2B Supplier websites will also have.

It is very common for B2B sites to have a *Cost Savings* dimension, similar to the Consumer Goods Manufacturer website.

Additionally, the B2B website may have a *Customer Relations* dimension where they engage in an ongoing interaction with customers through the website. A

Seven Dimensions To Online Business Models
1.   eCommerce
✓ 2.   Business Development
3.   Lead Generation
4.   Brand Development
✓ 5.   Customer Relations
6.   Information Delivery
✓ 7.   Cost Savings

Figure 18.1

B2B Supplier website that includes all three of these dimensions is the most complex of all the websites covered in this book. For many small B2B businesses, this chapter will be more than you need. Chapter 20 describes the Small Business website.

Typical B2B Website Goals

Once you have defined your online business model, the next step is to determine what goals will lead to success. These goals set the compass heading for your website.

The following are typical goals for the B2B Supplier online business model.

Business Development Goals

(1)   Convert site visitors into qualified sales leads, ultimately into sales
(2)   Positively support corporate and product brands

Cost Savings Goals

(3)   Reduce costs by providing account management services, company information and customer service electronically; thus reducing processing, call center, print and postage costs.

Customer Relations Goals

(4)   Increase customer loyalty and volume of products/services per customer by offering online account management services

(5)   Generate sales through cross-sell/up-sell promotions delivered to current customers

(6)   Increase customer loyalty by providing convenient online customer service

Of course, this is a prototypical list. As you go through this process, you will need to define goals specific to your own website.

Measuring Success For The B2B Website

Now you have set the compass heading for your website, by setting effective goals. This will let you develop a set of tactics and site features to reach those goals. Before you can do that, however, you must determine how you are going to measure success on your website. This section will show you how to calculate Return on Investment (ROI) for the B2B website.

ROI for Business Development

Calculating ROI for the Business Development dimension is very similar to ROI for sales through an eRetail website. It is based on conversion of sales leads generated through the website. In fact, you will use the same method shown in Chapter 15 for calculating ROI from immediate sales on the eRetail website to calculate the return from your efforts to generate leads to your business. The major difference is in the steps which go into taking a customer from a user on the website to a converted sale.

With the B2B website, you are capturing sales leads that will typically be closed by a salesperson. Whereas, the eRetail site closes the sale during the user session, the B2B site begins the sales process. A quick look at the process will clarify what you will be measuring.

Once you have completed this process, you can calculate ROI for your online Business Development efforts. At this point, the formula is exactly the same as for eRetail, as shown in Figure 20.2

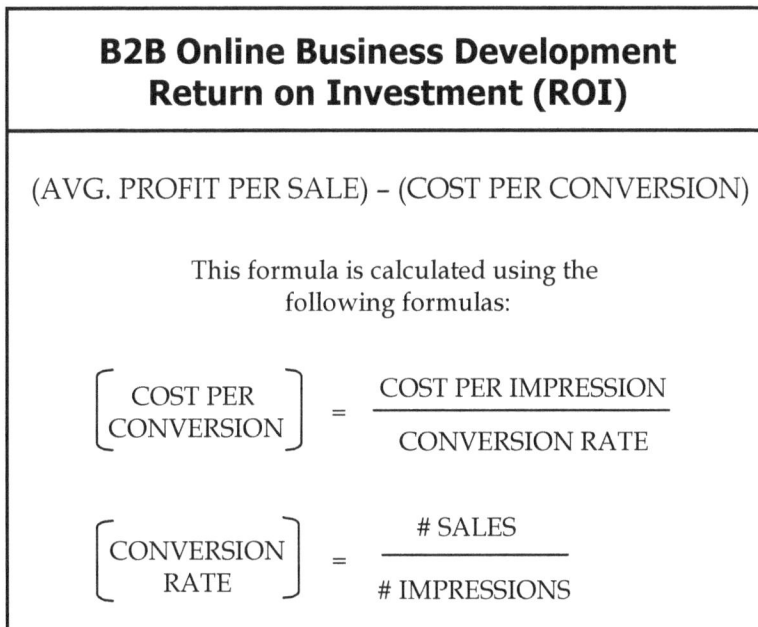

B2B Online Business Development
Return on Investment (ROI)

(AVG. PROFIT PER SALE) − (COST PER CONVERSION)

This formula is calculated using the
following formulas:

$$\left[\begin{array}{c} \text{COST PER} \\ \text{CONVERSION} \end{array}\right] = \frac{\text{COST PER IMPRESSION}}{\text{CONVERSION RATE}}$$

$$\left[\begin{array}{c} \text{CONVERSION} \\ \text{RATE} \end{array}\right] = \frac{\text{\# SALES}}{\text{\# IMPRESSIONS}}$$

Figure 18.2

---

1. Website Response

The first step in the process is to convert site visitors into sales leads. With eRetail, site visitors are converted directly to sales. We calculated a *conversion rate* at this point. With the B2B site, a sale will not be made until later in the process. At this point, we are measuring *responses* to marketing materials on the website. In general, there are three response devices on a website. Customers can call a phone number, fill out an online form, or send email. To measure how effective your website is at gaining responses simply divide the total number of responses by the total number of site visitors (also called *impressions*). This is called the *response rate*.

2. Conversions

In the next step, a salesperson will follow up on the sales leads (also called *responders*) and hopefully close the sales. When an actual sale takes place, that is considered a *conversion*. You can calculate two different conversion rates. To measure the conversion of sales leads to sales, you would divide total conversions by total responses. To measure conversion of site visitors to sales, you would divide total sales by the total number of site visitors (impressions).

This second measure can be used to directly calculate your ROI. To do this, you will measure your cost per impression in the same way as the eRetail site. You will add up all your costs to generate leads to the website and then divide the total number of site visitors by this number to get a cost per impression. With the eRetail site, however, we included all of the website costs in the calculation of total costs. With the B2B site, you will only measure costs associated with the parts of the website which generate sales leads. The other, development and maintenance costs will be counted towards the Cost Savings or Customer Relations ROI.

3. Profit Per Sale

The third step is to measure your profit per sale. The basic concept is exactly the same as for the eRetail site. You will calculate (or estimate) your total profit per sale, not including your web costs. The difference between the B2B and eRetail models is found in the nature of the sale. With the B2B sale, the total revenue earned from a single sale may be realized over a period of time. For example, many B2B sales include contracts for services or products to be delivered over a number of months, or years. You must estimate the entire expected value of the sale, rather than just the immediate revenue. Similarly, the costs per sale must include the costs incurred by the salesperson in addition to general production and marketing costs.

ROI for Cost Savings

ROI from Cost Savings is exactly the same as for the Consumer Goods Manufacturer website. Online delivery of information and customer service is less costly than offline alternatives. Additionally, there are potentially great savings to be realized from online account management services. You will simply estimate the costs to deliver each of these services offline and subtract the actual amount you spend to deliver the same services online. You may be saying to yourself, "Well, that is easier said than done." Unfortunately, this is often true. So, give it your best effort.

ROI From Cost Savings

(OFFLINE COST OF SERVICE) - (ONLINE COST OF SERVICE)

Figure 18.3

ROI for Customer Relations

ROI for online Customer Relations is primarily realized by increasing the lifetime value of customers who use the online services. You will implement customer focused features and services on your website with the goal of increasing the total amount of revenue earned per customer. The basic formula is the same lifetime value calculation shown in Chapter 15.

Annualized Lifetime Value
(# SALES PER YEAR) * (AVG. PROFIT PER SALE)

Figure 18.4

Customer Relations features on the website serve a dual purpose. On the one hand, they reduce costs. On the other hand, they can increase sales. To measure the success of these features, you will identify certain key metrics you are trying to increase. Then you will monitor changes to these metrics. Some metrics will measure the Cost Savings ROI. Typical cost savings metrics include such things as: average account processing costs per customer or number of transactions performed online. Other metrics will measure the Customers Relations ROI. Metrics you may measure include, average annual revenue per customer or number of sales orders placed through the online features.

Designing The B2B Website
User Experience

We have now defined the B2B Supplier's online business model, identified typical goals and shown how to measure the success of your website. The next step is to design a user experience for your customers that successfully achieves the goals of your online business model.

Many businesses make the mistake of trying to build a website before taking the time to figure out what the website is there to accomplish. That is always a set-up for poor results. Only after mapping out a user experience that will lead to successfully achieving your business goals should you put your web designer to work creating the look and feel for your website.

This section walks through a typical user experience that successful B2B websites create to cultivate customer relationships through the website.

The Goal of Website Design

The primary purpose of a website is to meet the needs and wants of customers coming to the site in a way that maximizes the attainment of Internet Marketing goals. The easiest way to understand what a website is trying to accomplish is to think of it as a funnel. At the wide end, tactics are employed to reach out to customers, appeal to their interests and entice them to enter your website. From this point onward, every action a user takes should be moving them down the funnel, towards the ultimate outcome(s) you want to achieve from your website.

There are many similarities between the B2B website and the eRetail website. In both cases, the company's primary goal is to generate sales through the website. There are also many similarities to the Consumer Goods Manufacturer website. Customers come to the site primarily for information or customer service. There are however, two major differences between these two business models and the B2B Supplier website. The first is the sales and customer relations process. They are more elaborate for business clients than for retail customers. Second, B2B Suppliers are typically not just selling a product, but a vendor relationship.

With a B2B Supplier, the primary function of the website is to funnel customers and potential customers into the sales process. If they are already in the sales process, then the function of the website is to keep them moving forward in that process. If they are existing customers, the website should give them reason and opportunity to continue increasing their business with your company. The user experience for a B2B website is shown in Figure 20.5.

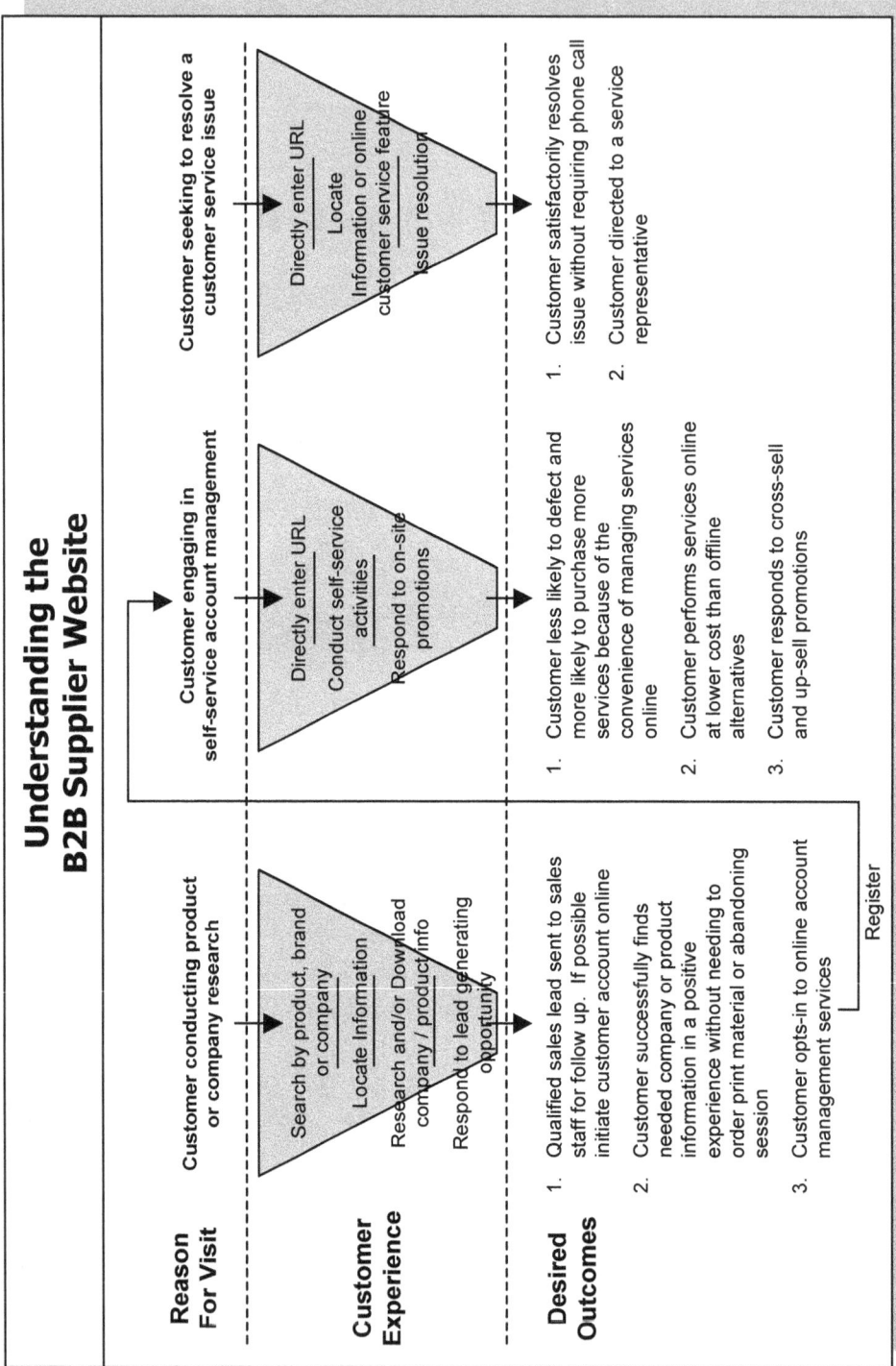

Understanding the B2B Supplier Website

Reason For Visit

Customer conducting product or company research

Customer engaging in self-service account management

Customer seeking to resolve a customer service issue

Customer Experience

Search by product, brand or company
Locate Information
Research and/or Download company / product info
Respond to lead generating opportunity

Directly enter URL
Conduct self-service activities
Respond to on-site promotions

Directly enter URL
Locate Information or online customer service feature
Issue resolution

Desired Outcomes

1. Qualified sales lead sent to sales staff for follow up. If possible initiate customer account online
2. Customer successfully finds needed company or product information in a positive experience without needing to order print material or abandoning session
3. Customer opts-in to online account management services

Register

1. Customer less likely to defect and more likely to purchase more services because of the convenience of managing services online
2. Customer performs services online at lower cost than offline alternatives
3. Customer responds to cross-sell and up-sell promotions

1. Customer satisfactorily resolves issue without requiring phone call
2. Customer directed to a service representative

Figure 18.5

With the B2B website, there are three possible customer paths customers can take through the site. They correspond to the three reasons customers have for visiting the site. These are shown in Figure 20.5. There are multiple outcomes the company desires to achieve from each of these user paths. The user experience must bring customers into the path most appropriate to them, while producing the desired outcomes most appropriate to that particular site visit.

The first key to understanding what the successful B2B website is doing is to understand what these outcomes are.

Business Development Path

The first path is the business development path. Customers come to your website seeking information about your company or products/services. This means it is very likely they are in the process of making a purchase decision. The ultimate outcome you are hoping for is a sale. There are four ways a visit can result in sales for your company.

1.   Sales Lead

With a B2B site, the next step in the sales process is often for the customer to speak with a sales representative. The specific outcome you want to achieve from the site visit, in this case, is that they will become a sales lead. Visitors can convert to sales leads by calling your phone number, submitting an online form, or sending email asking for a follow up contact.

2.   Online Sale

In some cases, you may be able to sign up new customers directly through the website. Perhaps smaller sales can be concluded online where more complex sales require a sales person.

3.   Move Customers Further Down the Sales Pipeline

Customers may be early in their decision making process and conducting preliminary research. They may not yet be ready to speak to a sales person. A third way to support future sales is to provide a positive user experience which helps move these customers further along in the sales process, and points them in the direction of your company. You could provide free downloads of helpful white papers or an opt-in newsletter to keep your business top of their mind, and get their contact information for future communications.

1.   Opt-In for Self-Serve Features

Finally, if you offer self-service account management features through your website, you will want to sign up customers to these services. The more time customers spend interacting with your business online, the more likely they are to make additional purchases in the future. This is the topic of the next customer path.

Customer Relations Path

The second path through your website is the Customer Relations path. Customers who have signed up for self-service account management features come to the website to use them. There are three outcomes self-service features can accomplish for your business.

1.   Cost Savings

The major reason companies usually have for setting up these automated services is they can provide substantial cost savings for the company. Orders, invoices, reports and change requests can all be processed electronically. These are all things that would otherwise require the time of salaried employees, not to mention potential savings in paper and postage costs.

2.   Increase Loyalty

Online account management provides a convenient and trusted method for customers to do business with your company. If customers get in the habit of using these services, they are likely to want to shift more and more of their business to your company. It makes life easier for them. They will also be less likely to defect to a competitor, because they will have to go through the hassle of setting up a new method of managing their services with the new vendor. This is sometimes called creating a *barrier to exit*.

3.   Cross-Sell

Finally, with customers spending a considerable amount of time interacting with your website, you have the opportunity to present them with promotions and special offers for additional products/services. As registered users of your online service, you will also be able to deliver promotional offers in email messages (assuming they have opted-in, of course).

Customer Service Path

The third path through your website is the Customer Service path. As with any business, you will have customers who come to your website seeking to resolve customer service issues. The B2B website has the same desired customer service outcome as the Consumer Goods Manufacturer website.

1.   Customer Satisfaction and Loyalty

The desired outcome is that their issue be resolved, resulting in continued satisfaction and loyalty to your business.

All three of the customer paths through your website contain opportunities to support the cost savings goals of the B2B online business model.

The B2B User Experience

Now let us look at the user experience that will achieve the desired outcomes. All three of the paths through the B2B Supplier website follow the same basic steps through the funnel.

1. **First Contact**

The B2B Supplier's online business model is the most complex of all those we discuss in this book. As a result, the customer outreach is also the most involved. You will use tactics that have already been discussed in previous chapters. But you must put them all to use. As with the eRetail site, you will implement search engine optimization and all profitable traffic generating methods to drive potential sales leads to your website. Like the Consumer Goods Manufacturer website, you will make sure your website can be found in online directories and any other place your customers or prospects will be searching for you by name, brand or products. Finally, you will be promoting your onsite account management services both onsite and offsite. Offsite, you will promote the site in collateral material, in your on-hold telephone messages and in the sales process itself.

2. **Information Search**

Now you have successfully attracted prospective customers to your website and existing customers to your online services. The next step is to make sure they can find what they are looking for. You must have user-friendly navigation and, if you have a large website, onsite search. You must also design your content pages so customers can, at a glance, find what they are looking for. This is the next step where you can lose customers. If they are frustrated trying to use your website, they will leave.

3. **Self-Service Activity**

All three of the user paths through your website involve some kind of self-service activities. The Business Development path requires customers to conduct research and find a method to contact your company. The Customer service path requires interacting with the online customer service features or at least to find the phone number. The onsite account management features are the most extensive self-service activities requiring the customer to interact with web-based software. The website must make it easy and intuitive for customers to complete these activities to their satisfaction.

4. Response Action

Finally, in the Business Development and Customer Relations paths, customers are incentivized to respond. Customers in the Business Development path must respond to some type of implicit or explicit call to action resulting in a sales lead response. For users who have not yet registered for onsite account management services, the choice to do so requires responding to a call to action on the site. You may also include additional promotional messages on the website which users can respond to. In all of these cases, the website must be successful, not only in bringing customers to view the call to action, but they must actually respond to it.

B2B Roadmap To Success

The final step before you actually build your website is to map out the specific objectives and tactics that will lead to successfully achieving your goals. In Part I, we called this your *roadmap to success*. The tactics in your "roadmap" are the building blocks that will create a winning user experience on your website.

Figure 20.6 presents a set of objectives and tactics common on B2B websites. They are laid out according to the four levels of customer intimacy described in Chapter 2. A quick survey of the objectives and tactics shown here will give you an idea of what goes into a successful B2B website.

These tactics are prototypical examples. They should be used as guidelines to give you an idea of what your website can accomplish. However, you will have to determine specific objectives and tactics that match the unique aspects of your business and the needs of your customers.

Typical B2B Supplier Objectives and Tactics

	Objectives	Tactics
Interest	Generate traffic that converts into sales leads	1. Utilize all profitable methods to generate traffic to the website and ensure that customers looking for the business will be able to find it
	Sign up customers for automated account management services	2. Promote online self-service features on the website and include in the sales process
	Direct customers to lower cost information/service options	3. Promote website on call center message, brochures, user manual, etc.
Trust	Provide a positive user experience that engenders trust and a willingness to continue in the sales process	4. User-friendly navigation and user interface for the website and online services
		5. Deliver sales lead submission opportunities as part of content that is of service to the customer, such as: needs assessment form, downloadable white papers, etc.
		6. Ensure privacy of customer data
Satisfaction	Provide content to help customers make their purchase decision, and choose your company	7. Corporate information businesses will need when evaluating potential partners in a way that is easy to find and of top quality appearance
		8. Online ordering, RFP submission
Loyalty	Create an online services user experience that increases loyalty and generates additional sales	9. Online customer service
		10. Automated account management features
		11. Onsite promotion of additional products/services
	Use opt-in email to retain customers and generate additional sales	12. Periodically send follow-up email to opt-in list, checking on satisfaction and including promotional offers and/or recommended enhancements to their service program

Figure 18.6

The next section goes into detail about the how these tactics work together to make the B2B website successful. If you do not want to dig this deep into the details, feel free to turn ahead to the next chapter.

The Roadmap Unfolded:
Typical B2B Tactics

In this chapter you have learned what successful Business-to-Business websites are trying to accomplish and how to design a website that meets those objectives. The basic considerations for a B2B website are similar to the Consumer Goods Manufacturer website. Identify what payoffs your customers are looking for when they come to your website. Then make sure they reach their goal as effectively as possible. In the process, the B2B website must provide a level of professionalism that makes potential customers want to do business with you.

The following table contains a detailed description of the tactics presented in the Roadmap to Success table (Figure 20.6). It provides nuts-and-bolts examples of the type of things implemented on successful B2B websites. You can use this information as a framework for developing your own website. However, there is no substitute for defining the details of your own online business model and mapping out a set of tactics that will meet your own organizational goals.

Building Interest

Building interest with the B2B website involves reaching out to prospective customers to draw them into the process of becoming a sales lead. It also involves reaching out to existing customers to get them to sign up for online services and utilize online customer service.

Optimize all profitable traffic sources	The B2B site must employ the same tactics as the Consumer Goods Manufacturer website to ensure that customers who are searching for you will find you. You must, therefore, optimize your website pages and pursue a search engine marketing strategy that ensures anyone who is looking for you can find you. Besides the major search engines, you may also want to get listed in online business directories, such as Business.com, and online yellow pages, such as Superpages.com.
	In addition, you will be generating revenue for the company by converting visitors to the website into qualified sales leads. You must also pursue an aggressive program employing some or all of the traffic driving methods discussed in Part II.
Promote self-service features	If implemented properly, self-service account management features on the website are a significant source of revenue for the company. Once you have worked all the kinks out, you will want to promote them aggressively. This can include opting customers into them during the sales process. You will probably want to promote the services on the website and in your offline collateral materials. You could also offer an incentive to customers in email or direct mail promotions.
Promote website in call center messaging and offline information resources	The B2B website has the same cost savings objectives as the Consumer Goods Manufacturer website. You will pursue the same means to direct customers towards using the online services. This could include promoting the website on automated telephone answering messages, especially the on-hold message for customer service. You can also include the URL in user manuals and product fact sheets.

Building Trust

A B2B website is initiating the first contact with new customers and conducting account services for existing customers. These would otherwise take place with a human being. Building trust depends on the professionalism of the customer's experience with your "virtual salesman" and "virtual account executive". This includes the tone and presentation of what, in essence, is your sales pitch to the online customer. It also includes the usability and appearance of your website and online services.

Usability and professionalism	Usability and quality of content is essential for any website. With the B2B website there is an even stronger microscope on these aspects of user experience. Potential customers are evaluating whether they want to do business with you. This often means entering into a strategic partnership with your company. They will assume their experience with your website will be the same as the experience they will have with your company if they decide to do business with you.
Capture sales leads	To capture B2B sales leads, you must look at the unique dynamics of the sales and customer relations processes for your specific business. Is the sales process handled by a corporate sales staff? Then product specification pages should contain sales contact information. Maybe include a request for information (RFI) form that is automatically forwarded to the appropriate sales manager. A free download could be offered that requires the customer to provide his, or her contact information. All of these options bring the potential customer into the sales cycle and connect them with the people in your company responsible for moving them forward in the process.
Ensure privacy of customer information	Ensuring the privacy and security of customer information is critical any time such information is collected on a website. One important way to do this is through your privacy policy.
	Every website must have a privacy policy. Although most customers will never look at it, your privacy policy is an extremely important part of your website. *If a customer files a lawsuit against your business, the courts will look at your privacy policy to decide your case. You must be very careful to craft a policy statement that assures your customers of their safety and your good intentions, but also does not hold you liable for more than you can actually do.*

Building Satisfaction

As with the Consumer Goods Manufacturer website, satisfaction on the B2B website is gained by going the extra mile with your customers. Whatever your customers are trying to accomplish when they come to your website, take them as far as possible along that process. This will satisfy, or even delight the customer. It will also bring them that much closer to additional sales for the company.

Quality of content	There is no "one size fits all" approach to the content you need on your B2B website. You must put yourself in your customer's shoes. What do they need to make their business decision? Do everything you can to have that on your website. Focus on having a professional presentation that will convince them that you will take care of them better than your competitors. There is just one caveat. When you need human interaction to complete the sale you may not want to give them all the information they need. You want to give them just enough to convince them to continue a dialogue with a sales representative.
	There are a number of things you can do on the website to help customers move forward in the sales process. Start at the beginning. What will people need who are starting out their research of potential partners? They may be looking for an overview of your company and products/ services. They may want to see things like: company financials, size of company, profile of typical clients, and a partial customer list. Make this information easy for them to find.
	You may service a variety of industries or offer a variety of different services that cater to different companies. If this is the case, you may want to create content areas targeted to these customer segments. Let them see how your company meets their specific issues. Do not make them sift through pages of information they do not care about.
	In all cases, make it extremely easy and enticing to contact a sales representative.
Online ordering or request for proposal submission	Many companies have started handling their bid process online. In some cases, this may take place through a third party "B2B exchange." In other cases the company's procurement department will handle it themselves. Vendors often hate having to participate in this process. It is designed to drive prices down and often removes the human salesperson from the process. If you differentiate yourself

through the quality of your service and not your low price, these online bids will likely be disadvantageous for you. Nevertheless, if your customers want you to provide these services, you should participate.

Another convenience many companies want is to place their wholesale orders online. With the B2B provider, this is often a more complicated process than the eRetail site. The business client may need to configure a bulk order to be delivered to multiple locations. You may need to calculate negotiated discounts or volume discounts dynamically. If you offer a service, such as a limousine or catering service, customers may want to simply place their order through your website. Offering this convenience can keep customers coming back because it is so easy to work with you.

Building Loyalty

Loyalty on the B2B website is build around a mutually rewarding, interactive relationship with your customer. In other words, you make their life easier by helping them manage parts of the customer relationship online. They can submit and resolve customer service issues through the website. They can manage their account online. They can research products and services easily. While they are doing this, you can send them customer communications and promote additional products and services to.

Online customer service	Customers often go to B2B websites for customer service. Create opportunities for customers to resolve their customer service issues online. This is a win-win. Customers get faster service and your business saves money.
	Care must be taken here to make sure customers still have ready access to human beings to help them if that is what they want. For the B2B Supplier, your business is providing a service. A balance must be reached between the cost-saving opportunities of online customer service and the level of service expected by your customers to keep them loyal.
Automated account management features	Business clients typically represent higher revenues and profits per customer than retail customers. So a greater investment may be justified for your online customer relationship features. Order and billing status may be made available online. Perhaps a linkage could be established with your sales force automation software. Account managers could be automatically notified when clients perform

	certain actions on the website, such as browsing a new product. You may want to create a personal web page for each client with things like customized order submission forms, account staff contact information and links to key reports relevant to the client's account. Features like these make your customers' lives easier and create a barrier to exit, because they would lose the convenience if they defect to a competitor.
Onsite promotions and communications	Self-serve account management and customer service brings your customers to your website. While they are there, you can reserve real estate on the web pages to promote additional products and services. You can also use that space to ask them to take a short online survey about your website or your services. These types of surveys demonstrate to your customers that you care about them and value their input. Once a customer has logged on to your website, to manage their account, you can target promotions for additional products and services based on their unique account profile. These are all ways to turn the user's visit into a dialogue with the company.
Opt-in email	It is a well known fact that dissatisfied customers usually do not express their dissatisfaction before they leave. They just stop doing business with you. On the other hand, one of the biggest factors contributing to customer loyalty is when a business responds well to a customer complaint. This presents a dilemma. How can you respond if they never tell you there is a problem? Email can be used to periodically ask your customers about their satisfaction with your company and give them an opportunity to offer comments. This makes a nice point of contact for happy customers. It also gives you the opportunity to rescue at-risk customers.
	You will also have potential customers who have expressed interest in your company, but have not yet made a purchase. You can use email to periodically send them special offers or otherwise maintain contact, keeping them in the sales pipeline. These emails can also be sent to existing customers, to give them an incentive to do more business with you.
	Before you undertake any email efforts, you must explicitly obtain permission to send marketing email to those whose email address you have obtained. This is called opting-in to your email program.

Conclusion

In this chapter, you have learned how to balance the multiple needs of a B2B website. This has been the most complex of all the online business models we discuss in this book. You will be able to successfully generate sales leads for your business. You will be able to satisfy your customer service needs. You will be able to offer online account management services that build loyalty and result in significant cost savings for your business. In the next chapter, you will learn how to create a successful Content website.

Now turn to the Content website.

Chapter 21

Building A Successful Nonprofit Organization Website

In this chapter, you will learn . . .
- How to define the online business model for a Nonprofit Organization Website
- How to measure success for a Nonprofit Organization website
- How to design a successful user experience for a Nonprofit Organization website
- The tactics used by successful Nonprofit Organization websites

Creating A Window Of Hope
The Peacock Foundation Story

In 1987, Michael Peacock was a passenger on Northwest Flight 255 when it crashed on a freeway outside of the Detroit airport. The crash left only one survivor, a two year old child. Her mother had saved her life by acting as a human shield from the flames. Michael left behind a wife, Catherine, and two daughters, nine year old Lisa and twelve year old Amy. Ten years later, Catherine Peacock was taken in an automobile accident. Lisa responded by dedicating her life to helping children suffering from grief, loss and trauma. Out of her own process of healing, the Peacock Foundation was born.

Lisa realized that for children suffering after a trauma, their worst enemy is the natural defense mechanism that closes themselves off from the people in their lives. They may blame themselves. They may feel there is something wrong with "me." Above all, they cannot acknowledge the source of their pain. They try to close it off, and close themselves off in the process. But, their grief does not go away. Some children lash out in violence. Some become problem children in school. Most exhibit anti-social behavior of some type.

All of this puts them at great risk, as they become teenagers. Many will end up in jail or in abusive relationships. It is a vicious cycle. It is a cycle that can only be broken when a child is able to take the first step of opening up about the trauma they have experienced.

That is where the Peacock Foundation comes in.

The children are not able to open up to their teachers, parents or classmates. But, they can open up to animals. Lisa brings exotic animals into a group counseling session and lets the children interact with them in a controlled setting. Each animal has a lesson to "teach" the children about healthy social interaction. The chinchilla teaches the children about caring for others. The snake teaches about fear, anxiety and protection. Week after week, the children meet new animals. With each visit, they also learn how to express themselves. They find themselves interacting, not only with the cute and friendly animals, but also with the other children in the group and their teachers.

There is no miracle cure for a child's broken life. But, there is a first, vital step of being able to let people in. The other children in the group become a peer support network for one another. The teachers and parents (when they have parents who are able to participate) are part of the process also.

Anyone who has experienced trauma in life and who loves children can immediately see the incredible gift the Peacock Foundation brings to these children. Still, it is not immediately obvious to the general public. The Peacock Foundation consists of Lisa and a team of dedicated volunteers. Together they create a window of hope for children who could not see that a path to healing was possible. For its first four years, Lisa was able to self-fund the organization with her own savings. However, the need surpassed her own ability. She needed a way to ensure the financial viability of the organization into the future. More than that, she had a vision for expanding services to more children. She wanted to recruit more volunteers, hire paid staff and add counselors.

But how could she do this for a cause that people do not understand and that produces results which cannot be measured?

Part of the answer was to re-design the Peacock Foundation website. It had been a basic informational site with Lisa's personal story and a few pages about the animals and services offered. It needed to become a vehicle for getting the word out and for recruiting partners to help meet the needs.

The first step was to identify those who would be willing to help. These are the people who the website would be designed to reach. Lisa and her board realized it would be people who have experienced grief, loss or trauma themselves. These people would feel an immediate emotional bond with the children who are going through an experience they still feel deeply in their own hearts. A second group would be small businesses in areas where the Peacock Foundation provides services. These businesses will want to help meet the needs of the communities they serve.

The second step was to define the message. The new purpose of the website would be to build that emotional bond with partners and potential partners. What should the website convey to accomplish this. To answer the question, they identified five stages to the healing process:

- ✓ Able to acknowledge your trauma
- ✓ Provided with a safe way to express your emotions
- ✓ Develop a community to assist in the experience of healing
- ✓ Develop the skills to navigate through interaction within community
- ✓ Able to help others in their healing

Realizing the importance of the fifth stage in the healing process was the breakthrough. For people who have gone through grief, loss or trauma in their lives, the healing process is not truly complete until they are able to reach out and help others become healed. The Peacock Foundation had discovered a new dimension to their mission. They would be able to help people work through their own healing by giving them an opportunity to help in the healing of broken children.

The messaging and imagery of the website would be designed around a call to action: "Create Hope For A Traumatized Child."

At this point, the website came alive in the minds of Lisa and the Board of Directors at the Peacock Foundation. They had a vision of what it could accomplish. Next, they set out to define volunteer opportunities and cost per child served. This information would be used to define different levels of partnership involvement. They created an online partner application and educational materials about the program. They developed an email strategy for opting-in partners and potential partners. The people on this email list would become the front line for creating awareness of the needs. All of this would revolve around the new vision for the website. They were building a network of partners who would work together to provide children with a window of hope.

As of the writing of this book, the Peacock Foundation is in the process of rolling out its newly re-designed website.

Understanding The Nonprofit Organization Website

Nonprofit organizations are part of the unseen glue that holds society together. When they are successful, nobody notices. They just quietly meet needs the general public would rather not think about. A website is often an important part of meeting those needs.

Nonprofit organizations come in all shapes and sizes. They range from international service organizations, like the Red Cross, to individuals with a heart to help, like Lisa Peacock and the Peacock Foundation. There are museums with multi-million dollar endowments. There are homeless shelters who rely on daily food donations from local businesses. Wherever there is a need, there is someone with a heart to help. Their organizations are as varied as the needs they meet and the people they serve. Still, all nonprofit organizations have two things in common. They all meet needs that others might not perceive or understand. They also all depend on the help of partners to meet those needs. The Nonprofit Organization website is built around these two factors.

Dimensions of the Nonprofit Organization Online Business Model

In Part I, you learned an easy way to begin defining your online business model. You start by choosing from among seven basic dimensions that form the foundation of all online businesses. This quick and easy approach will allow you to implement a set of features and tactics aimed at achieving the goals of your business or organization.

Seven Dimensions To Online Business Models

1.   eCommerce
✓ 2.   Business Development
3.   Lead Generation
✓ 4.   Brand Development
5.   Customer Relations
✓ 6.   Information Delivery
7.   Cost Savings

Figure 21.1

There are typically three dimensions to the Nonprofit Organization online business model: *Information Delivery, Business Development (a.k.a. Partner Development)*, and *Brand Development (a.k.a. Awareness)*.

1.   Information Delivery

Nonprofit organizations often use their websites to disseminate information or to provide resources related to the issues they address. The website may also serve as a resource center for members of the population being served. Therefore, *Information Delivery* is often the major dimension of this online business model.

2.   Business Development (Partner Development)

Nonprofit organizations also will typically use the website to recruit new members/partners or to receive donations. This is not quite the same thing as a business recruiting new customers. However, the basic process is the same as the *Business Development* dimension.

Because nonprofits are building ongoing relationships with partners who will volunteer and/or make donations, this dimension is more accurately called *Partner Development*.

3.   Brand Development (Awareness)

Another major purpose of the Nonprofit Organization website is to promote awareness of the issues being addressed by the organization. In some cases, there is also an activist or community involvement component to the organization. The website is often used to motivate action on behalf of the cause. These website uses are not exactly the same as a business building awareness for their brand. However, using the website as a vehicle to promote awareness is essentially the same thing as the *Brand Development* dimension. Since nonprofits are not building a brand, but creating awareness for a public need, this dimension is more accurately called *Awareness*.

Typical Nonprofit Organization Website Goals

Once you have defined your online business model, the next step is to determine what goals will lead to success. These goals set the compass heading for your website.

The following are typical goals for the Nonprofit Organization website.

Information Delivery Goals

(1)   Provide information and resources empowering those seeking to help with the cause
(2)   Provide information and resources to the population being served
(3)   Connect service recipients with access to services

Business Development (Partner Development) Goals

(4)   Recruit volunteers, members and/or donors
(5)   Opt-in supporters to email and/or other partner communications

Brand Development (Awareness) Goals

(6)   Create awareness of the issue(s) and motivate action.

Of course, this is a prototypical list. As you go through this process, you will need to define goals specific to your own organization.

Hybrid Nonprofit Organization Websites

The website for a nonprofit organization, as discussed above, is basically a hybrid between the subsidized content website (discussed in Chapter 17) and the small business website (discussed in Chapter 18). A more complete understanding of how to create a successful website can be gained by reviewing these chapters.

There are also cases where a nonprofit organization will use the website for other uses, described elsewhere in this book. The following two are especially common.

An Online Store on the Website

In some cases, a nonprofit organization will want to sell things through their website. There are a variety of reasons for doing this. Some nonprofits subsidize their activities through retail sales of some sort. Others have books and other resources for sale. Museums have bookstores or novelty shops. The list goes on.

If you are planning to sell things through your website, there are companies who make it easy to set up an online store. They will handle the eCommerce processing such as online transactions, secure data exchange and eCommerce web pages for the eRetail store. This is the easiest, and probably the safest way to go about it.

From the perspective of your online business model, adding an online store is basically adding an eRetail component to your website. The goals and tactics are essentially the same as those discussed in Chapter 15.

Providing an Outsourced Service to Government Agencies

Some nonprofit organizations offer services that are subcontracted out to government agencies, or otherwise work in conjunction with them. Organizations like homeless shelters, food banks or free health clinics often work together with local and regional government agencies. They may offer overflow services for public agencies who exceed their service capacity. Some organizations are partially funded through government grants and are accountable to meeting certain requirements.

In cases like these, the nonprofit organization is acting like a Business-to-Business (B2B) supplier, with the government agency as their client. The website might handle some of the outreach and administrative aspects of these public-nonprofit partnerships. Although this is different in many ways from a B2B supplier, from the perspective of an online business model, the organization is basically adding a B2B supplier component to their website. For more information, turn to Chapter 20.

Measuring Success For The Nonprofit Organization Website

Now you have set the compass heading for your website, by setting effective goals. This will let you develop a set of tactics and site features to reach those goals. Before you can do that, however, you must determine how you are going to measure success on your website. This section will show you how Return on Investment (ROI) is calculated for the Nonprofit Organization website.

ROI for Information Delivery and Awareness

In general, to calculate ROI, you would start with a measure of monetary return from a given action. Then you count the actions in question and calculate a monetary return per action. This cannot be done if there is no direct monetary return, as is the case with much of what nonprofit organizations are trying to accomplish with their websites. In other words, a store can measure profits per sale but how do you calculate the benefit of somebody practicing better pre-natal care because they saw your website?

To calculate the success of this type of website, you would need to devise a measure, not of revenue earned, but of effectiveness of information delivery or awareness efforts. For example, if your organization is trying to build awareness for a specific issue, such as child nutrition, then you may want to measure number of unique visitors to your website or number of downloads of your eBook on low cost, healthy meals for children. If you provide data sheets for advocacy groups and researchers, you may measure successful downloads of data files or aborted visits because users were not able to find the information they needed. Perhaps you are promoting volunteerism in your community. You may measure click-thrus to the websites of local service organizations. The specific success metrics will depend on what your organization is trying to accomplish. Part III describes how to use Web Analytics to measure the effectiveness of content on the website.

ROI for Partner Development

Calculating ROI for Partner Development is similar to ROI for sales leads through a Small Business website. It is based on conversion of leads generated through the website. However, with a nonprofit organization, there is not always a direct monetary return resulting from a new partner. In many, if not most cases, nonprofit organizations are seeking a non-monetary return. Some common non-monetary benefits gained from Partner Development efforts include:

✓ Volunteer service
✓ In-kind donations
✓ Newsletter subscriptions (to meet awareness goals)
✓ Increasing member roster (to support lobbying efforts)
✓ Board membership

In these cases, you must estimate the value of a new enrollment. In other words, you must answer the question, "How much is it worth spending to gain a new partner?" Even if this number is a guess, it will give you a target to measure against. Then you can compare what you are actually spending.

In some cases, the only goal is to receive donations. In this case, ROI can be measured directly. Still, care must be taken to set up a measurement that is appropriate for your organization.

ROI for Monetary Donations

Calculating ROI for donations is <u>not</u> the same as ROI from sales. With sales, you are earning a profit per sale, which can be measured. Donations do not yield profits. Therefore, you cannot base ROI on a profit margin calculation. One method to measure ROI from donations is to evaluate your Internet Marketing costs *in terms of a percentage of the donation amount*. Consider the following example.

> ABC Community Services is a nonprofit organization that provides services to senior citizens and low-income households in a number of mid-sized cities. They have a policy of applying no less than 90% of all donations towards program costs. That leaves 10% for administration and marketing costs. Let us assume the organization has streamlined their operations. Administrative costs account for only 8% of donations. That leaves 2% which can be used towards marketing. They spend 1% of their total donations on print materials and outbound phone calls. We are now left with 1% of donations that can be spent for online recruitment. This can be used as the breakeven amount for measuring the success of Partner Recruitment efforts on the website. If the average donation amount is $100, then they can spend $1.00 per new partner on website recruitment costs.

For many organizations, a calculation like this might be overkill. What if ABC Community Services only provided services to one community? In this case, they may just have a small budget for all website activity. They include this under general administrative costs. They might, for example, have a $1,500 website budget which covers: website hosting, content updates, email campaigns and secure transaction processing for donations. In this case, the organization would not calculate an ROI per donor. They would simply try to optimize the results from all online efforts, working within their budget.

Designing The User Experience For A Nonprofit Organization Website

We have now defined the Nonprofit Organization online business model, identified typical goals and shown how to measure the success of your website. The next step is to design a user experience for your customers that successfully achieves the goals of your online business model.

Many businesses make the mistake of trying to build a website before taking the time to figure out what the website is there to accomplish. That is always a set-up for poor results. Only after mapping out a user experience that will lead to successfully achieving your business goals should you put your web designer to work creating the look and feel for your website.

The Goal of Website Design

The primary purpose of a website is to meet the needs and wants of customers coming to the site in a way that maximizes the attainment of Internet Marketing goals. The easiest way to understand what a website is trying to accomplish is to think of it as a funnel. At the wide end, tactics are employed to reach out to customers, appeal to their interests and entice them to enter your website. From this point onward, every action a user takes should be moving them down the funnel, towards the ultimate outcome(s) you want to achieve from your website.

This section will walk through a typical user experience that successful Nonprofit Organization websites create to effectively deliver information and build partner relationships through the website.

To understand the Nonprofit Organization website we turn to the funnel a user travels through between their initial interest and the desired outcomes you hope will result from their visit to your website. With this model, users will typically take one of two paths through the website. These are shown in Figure 21.2.

Information Delivery Path

The first path is the Information Delivery path. Partners, service recipients or the general public will view your website as a resource. They each have information needs they hope to have met on the website. For members of your target population, they will come to your website seeking such things as access to services, instructions on use of services, directions to your facility. Partners may use your website as an information resource, to receive aids for their own outreach efforts, or just for the latest stories about the impact your organization is having. The general public will find your website while they are looking for information or resources related to the issues you serve. They may find you on a search engine or find a link on a related website. In all three of these cases, the website must quickly and easily take them to the information they need. Those resources must also be easy for them to use when they find them.

Partner Development Path

One of the truly great things about nonprofit organizations is that everybody wins. People who volunteer and give always benefit. The act of helping others is often an incredibly meaningful experience for your partners. Sometimes it gives them the ability to give back where they had a need in their own past. Sometimes it is a part of the healing process they are going through themselves. Sometimes it just helps cement the human bond between the giver and the community, or society at large. It is always a good thing to give people the opportunity to lend a hand.

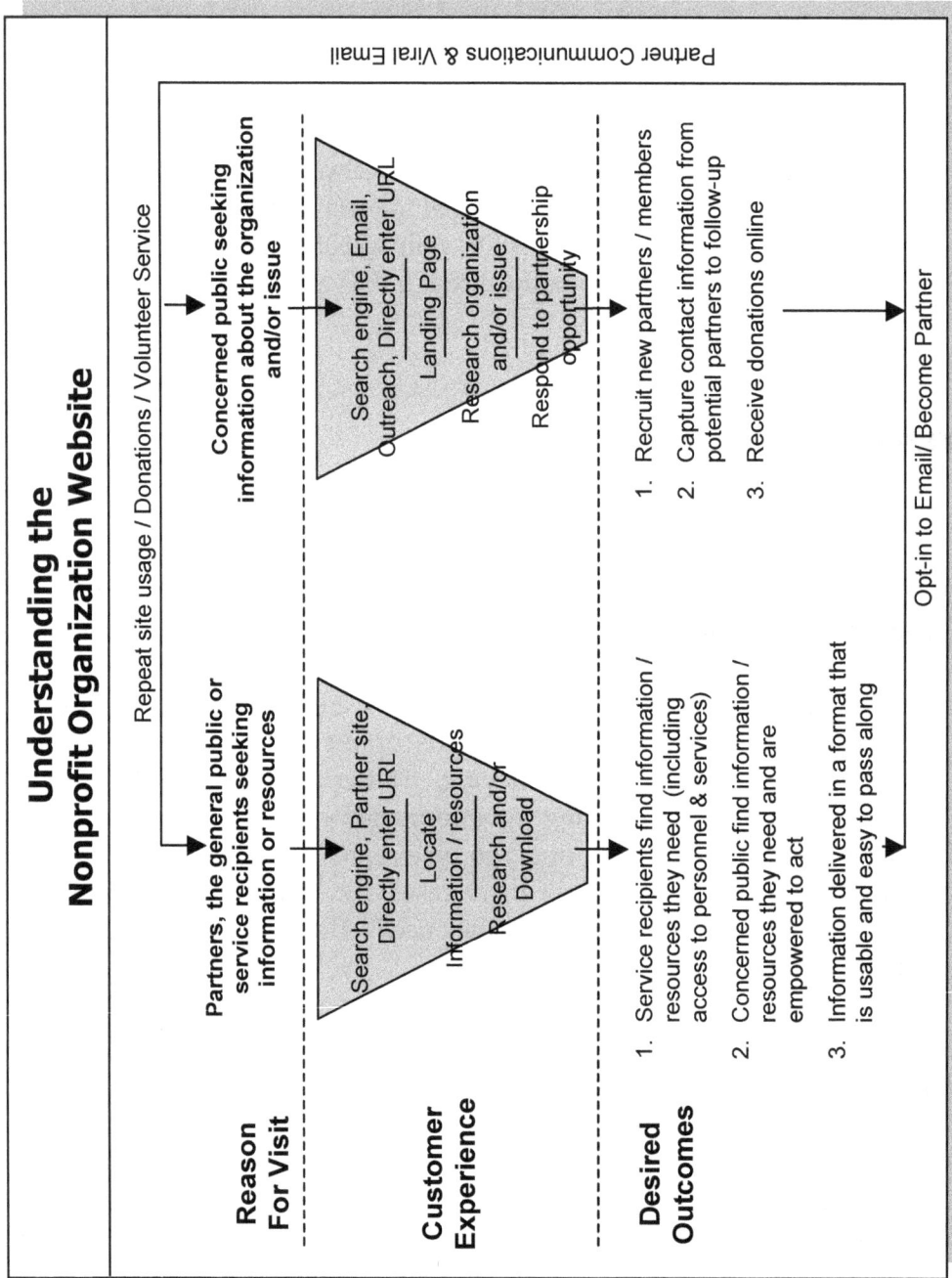

Understanding the
Nonprofit Organization Website

Partner Communications & Viral Email

Reason For Visit

Repeat site usage / Donations / Volunteer Service

Partners, the general public or service recipients seeking information or resources

Concerned public seeking information about the organization and/or issue

Customer Experience

Search engine, Partner site, Directly enter URL
Locate
Information / resources
Research and/or Download

Search engine, Email, Outreach, Directly enter URL
Landing Page
Research organization and/or issue
Respond to partnership opportunity

Desired Outcomes

1. Service recipients find information / resources they need (including access to personnel & services)

2. Concerned public find information / resources they need and are empowered to act

3. Information delivered in a format that is usable and easy to pass along

1. Recruit new partners / members

2. Capture contact information from potential partners to follow-up

3. Receive donations online

Opt-in to Email/ Become Partner

Figure 21.2

The second path through the Nonprofit Organization website is the Partnership Development path. Concerned members of the public will come to your website seeking information about your organization or the issue(s) you address. They may have people in their lives who need services like those you provide. They may have been personally affected by the type of circumstances you address. They may have been made aware of the issue by a friend, a TV commercial or another website. In any case, they have searched for information and found your website. The job of the website is not merely to give them information. It is to create a connection where they can find a way to contribute to meeting the needs they have begun to recognize. That may just be by finding information they can use in their own lives. But, it may also be that they can help you meet the needs the organization feels passionate about. The website should give them the opportunity to do so by partnering with your organization.

Many people who work with nonprofits genuinely dislike asking people for help. Even more, they dislike asking for money. The reality is, your organization is doing something worthwhile. You are not asking for a handout. You are giving people the opportunity to become more complete human beings by being part of the unseen glue that holds together the broken pieces of our world.

The Nonprofit Organization Website User Experience

The following steps provide a guideline for mapping out a user experience on your website. These steps support both the Information Delivery and Partner Development paths user may take through the website.

1.   First Contact

For a Nonprofit Organization website, the most important way you will reach out to your potential site users is by letting them find you when they are looking for a resource you have. This boils down mostly to optimizing your website for search engines. Identify all of the words and phrases people may type into search engines related to the information services you offer. Then make sure search engines will find your site when those keywords are entered. A second way to reach out to your potential site users is to get the word out about your website on partner websites. If there are other nonprofit organizations or special interest websites that cater to interests related to your cause, try to get them to place your link on their websites. Finally, if your website is the online component of a larger public outreach program, then you will include reference to the site on your offline materials.

Only pursue other, more costly, online traffic generation methods (such as Search Engine Marketing) if you have the available budget or if you plan to conduct a recruitment campaign through the website. Then be sure to measure the performance of those efforts to make the best use of your marketing budget.

2.   Home Page and Content Pages

The first impression on any website is always of critical importance. Web users will only give a web page a few seconds before they decide if they will stay there or move on. You must capture their attention and win over their interest within a couple of glances at your site. For the Nonprofit Organization website, traffic is often sent directly to the home page. Budgets are often too small to support an ongoing initiative to build targeted landing pages. Because of this, it is of utmost importance that the home page is able to effectively reach out to potential partners.

A major goal for the Nonprofit Organization website is to create a bond between the organization and the concerned public (including potential and current partners). This will first be an emotional bond. Loyal partners to your organization are bonded by an empathy with the needs addressed by the organization and their own need to help. The home page must be designed so the first impression serves to nurture that bond. Time should be taken to define a core message speaking to this bond between your organization and partners. Then, craft the text and choose the images for your home page to reflect that message.

A common mistake is to neglect to spend enough time designing an effective home page. The home page must positively reflect your cause. It must also quickly draw site visitors into the actions you want them to take on the website. This can only be done by taking some time to map out what information you want your site visitors to reach and what actions you want them to take. Then you can design the home page to appeal to their interests while drawing them to the information and actions you want them to find.

If you are planning to send people directly to lower level pages on the website, or to custom built landing pages, you should spend time designing these pages to be as effective as your home page.

As a note of caution, some freelance web developers and small design shops love to create Flash animation "welcome" screens for the websites they build. Unless your organization specializes in something related to the creative arts, this is usually not a good idea. People doing research online do not want to waste their time watching video animation before they find the information they need. Many will leave before the cool Flash movie finishes playing. Just take them directly to a very professional looking home page where they can easily find whatever information they need. That is the best way to make a great first impression.

3.   Navigation and User Interface

Once users decide they want to stay on your website, they have to be able to find what they are looking for. This is the first hurdle. If they cannot find the information in the first few seconds on the site, there is a good chance they will abandon the session and look somewhere else for it. Unfortunately, many Nonprofit Organization websites are built with a very small budget and cannot afford to bring usability experts into the design process. As more and more information gets added, it can get buried under hard to navigate links and menu choices.

The most important way to address this issue is by taking time to map out your menu choices on the top and left navigation. This does not add any technical costs to website development. But it will involve some human costs in the time taken to map out your onsite menus. The hierarchy of menus and items in them is known as your site's *taxonomy*.

Another critical component to many information websites is a robust search capability. People should be able to enter search terms into a search engine on your website and find the information they need. Search engine technology, however, can be costly to buy. Many nonprofit agencies cannot afford to spend that much on their website. For those agencies, having an easy to navigate taxonomy is all the more important. That is the only way users will find what they need.

4a.   Researching on Your site

The reason users are most likely on your website in the first place is to research an issue of importance to them. The information they find must meet their needs. This means having information that is relevant and accurate. But it also means presenting it in a way that is accessible to the user. When users look for information on the Internet they scan first, then they read on if they find what they want.

Users on your website will spend a few seconds on a given web page and quickly look over the high level information to see if it has what they need. They will look at headlines and menu items. If it has what they need, then they look a little deeper to get some high level details. They will look for bullet points, or maybe read the first few lines of text. If they still feel they need more, then they will actually read the paragraphs of written text. This is called *scanning*. Well-crafted web content will accommodate this practice.

4b.   Information Delivery

Your site users need to receive the information in a format most usable for them. In a large number of cases, they will want to download information and take it with them. The format of the download will be different for different websites. The important concept to remember is to find out what your target audience will be using your information for and how they will want to use it. Then deliver it in a method that is most conducive to those uses.

There are many options for delivering content. The most common is to create a "print friendly" version of the HTML page the user is viewing. A typical web page has a variety of content elements including images, tables and text. If you expect your site users to print your information, you can let them view it on a separate page that removes a lot of the HTML formatting and peripheral content. This will be easy for them to print and easy to save to their computers.

A second, very common method of delivering content is to allow downloads of white papers, articles and eBooks in PDF files. These are created to be displayed in Adobe Acrobat or similar software. They have the advantage of being small and easy to download. Also, longer articles, that people do not want to take the time to read online, can be downloaded and read later at their leisure.

A third very popular information delivery method is the audio or video download. There are many varieties. With the popularity of MP3 players, a very popular download method has become the "Pod-cast" (named for the Apple iPod). This is basically a download that can be saved onto the user's iPod, or other MP3 player.

Finally, websites that include statistical information can allow the files to be downloaded as spreadsheets or comma-delimited text files that can be used in MS-Excel or other spreadsheet programs

5a. Partner Recruitment

The final step in the user experience is for the site visitor to initiate a partnership with your company. This could be by a partnership form on the website, by calling your phone number or by making a donation (see 5b). To accomplish this, you will need to structure the content on your site so key paths through the site lead to a partnership opportunity. Web pages should have a tasteful, yet prominently displayed call to action with a link to the partnership form, donation page or a phone number.

In addition to partnership and donation opportunities, the website should also include opportunities to sign up for your opt-in email list. Typically, this will be done by providing an email newsletter that they agree to receive. This is also a way to initiate a relationship with concerned people who do not want to become partners or donors. Through email communications, you can build awareness, and provide resources. If handled well, many people on the email list, will eventually participate in your organization at some level.

5b.   Accept Online Donations

If your website is going to accept online donations, you must offer a secure method to process the transactions. Except for very large organizations, this should be handled by a third party that specializes in secure online transactions. The risk is too great to try and handle it yourself. Identity theft is a very large problem. Your organization must be able to guarantee the privacy of personal information submitted through the Internet. If you cannot, you take on the liability if anything happens with the information customers submit to your website. For this very reason, companies have been set up who will process that transaction for you. In addition to eliminating the risk, it also will reassure your potential donors. They may not be, and should not be willing to send credit card information to a website that does not use a trusted source to ensure the security of their personal data.

Nonprofit Organization Website
Roadmap To Success

The final step before you actually build your website is to map out the specific objectives and tactics that will lead to successfully achieving your goals. In Part I, we called this your *roadmap to success*. The tactics in your "roadmap" are the building blocks that will create a winning user experience on your website.

Figure 21.3 presents a set of objectives and tactics common on Nonprofit Organization websites. They are laid out according to the four levels of customer intimacy described in Chapter 2. A quick survey of the objectives and tactics shown here will give you an idea of what goes into a successful Nonprofit Organization website.

These tactics are prototypical examples. They should be used as guidelines to give you an idea of what your website can accomplish. However, you will have to determine specific objectives and tactics that match the unique aspects of your organization and the needs of your target audiences.

Typical Nonprofit Organization Website
Objectives and Tactics

	Objectives	Tactics
Interest	Ensure that web searchers find the site when searching for topics covered	1. Search engine optimization 2. If part of a budgeted outreach, search engine marketing
	Get links from related websites	3. Post with online directories & personally contact related websites
Trust	Effective home page	4. Optimize home page content around building partner relationships
	Ensure that site visitors have a positive online experience that allows them to easily find the information they are interested in	5. Scannable page content 6. User-friendly navigation and interface, with short path to information sought by user 7. Functional onsite search (if applicable) 8. Freshness and accuracy of content
Satisfaction	Provide user-friendly information delivery	9. Printable version of text pages; Data downloads in MS-Excel or text file; Video/audio downloads in multiple formats
	Provide usable and reliable links to additional resources	10. Links to other resources easy to find and of guaranteed quality
	Partnership opportunities built into the context of content on the website	11. Present partnership and donation opportunities tastefully, but prominently
Loyalty	Use targeted email to cultivate customer relationships resulting in greater awareness and repeat visits	12. Create an opt-in email list and use email to deliver useful information, build awareness of your organization and generate repeat visits
	Utilize viral marketing to increase the reach of site content	13. Include Forward-to-a-friend links on content and emails 14. Create eBooks or other viral objects from valuable content

Figure 21.3

The next section goes into detail about each of the tactics shown in Figure 21.3. If you do not want to dig this deep into the details, feel free to turn ahead to the next chapter.

The Roadmap Unfolded:
Typical Nonprofit Organization Website Tactics

In this chapter you have learned what successful Nonprofit Organization websites are trying to accomplish and how to design a website that meets those objectives. The basic consideration for a Nonprofit Organization website is to create an emotional bond with people who will be willing to help meet the needs the organization addresses. The website must also make sure people find information or resources they need as effectively as possible. In the process, the Nonprofit Organization website presents opportunities to volunteer, donate or otherwise participate in the cause.

The following table contains a detailed description of the tactics presented in the Roadmap to Success table (Figure 21.3). It provides nuts-and-bolts examples of the type of things implemented on successful Nonprofit Organization websites. You can use this information as a framework for developing your own website. However, there is no substitute for defining the details of your own online business model and mapping out a set of tactics that will meet your own organizational goals.

Building Interest

Building interest with the Nonprofit Organization website is mostly a matter of being found on search engines and getting linked to from other related websites. People will be searching for information related to the issue(s) your website addresses. You must be found by them.

Search engine optimization	Search engine optimization is essential for any website. Most people will find a Nonprofit Organization website while they are searching for information about an issue of concern to them. They will find your website if it appears in their search listings. Optimizing the content on your web pages to be found by search engines is the most important thing you can do to get traffic to your website. Search engine optimization is discussed in Chapter 6.
Search engine marketing	Paying for sponsored links on search engines (known as search engine marketing) is simply paying to get your search results listings displayed to people searching for the topics your site addresses. If you have a marketing budget to pay for advertising to bring people to your website, this will be an important part of your strategy. Search engine marketing is discussed in Chapter 6
Get linked to	Websites form a natural information network. Each of the websites offering content related to the issues your site addresses will benefit by links from other related sites. It also helps them to have links on their site to other related sites. In this way, web users can find one site and continue to follow links to more and more content of interest. You should get your website linked in to this network of sites related to the issue(s) you address. Having links from other websites is also an important factor in being listed on search engines. For your Nonprofit Organization website, the first place to start when seeking links from other sites is to perform your own searches on topics related to your website. Then personally contact the website owners for all the sites you find that are complementary to your own. If it is appropriate for your website, offer to place links to their site on your own website and ask them to place links in return. Make sure you also offer suggestions about places on their website that will generate the most clicks to your website.

Building Trust

With the Nonprofit Organization website, building trust means people develop a connection with your organization and find it easy to locate information and resources they care about. This basically comes down to a well thought out home page and landing pages, plus generally good site design and quality of content.

Make a connection with the site visitor	With a Nonprofit Organization website, trust begins with an emotional bond between your organization and the site visitor. This is true for any website, on some level. It is at the heart of a Nonprofit Organization website. You should take time to determine the things that will make people feel an affinity to your cause and your organization. Then design the presentation and messaging of your home page and content pages to reflect those things. This is the impression people will associate with your organization.
Scannable page content	The most important consideration for the usability of a content-rich website is scannable page content. When people are looking for information on the Internet, they are impatient. They will scan the first web page they find on your site and decide in a few seconds if it has what they want. If not, they will go on to the next site. The content on your website must not only be useful, it must be presented in a way that makes it easy for people to find the parts that they want to use.
User-friendly navigation	User-friendly navigation is an important key to success for any website. If your website is presenting information and resources for the public, it is critical. You must have easy to follow menus with categories that make sense to your site users. This is a matter of usability. Site users must be able to simply look at the web page and intuitively understand what they need to click next to get to where they want to go.
Site search	If your website has more than a small number of pages, you should look into having onsite search. People are used to using search to find what they need on the Internet. They will expect to do the same when they come to your website.

Building Satisfaction

Satisfaction on the Nonprofit Organization website comes mainly from making it easy for site visitors to access and use the information you provide.

User-centric information delivery	One of the most frustrating experiences when doing research online is to find what you need, but then have a hard time getting it. There are many variations to this frustrating experience. You have probably experienced some of them.
	If your website contains articles or other content that users will want to print, it is much easier when the site includes a link to display a "print friendly" version of the page, without graphics and HTML code.
	If you have numerical data on your website, consider how your site users will need to use it. Then deliver it in a format they can easily use.
	Your website might have white papers, eBooks, video/audio downloads, charts or graphs. Always think about how the end user will be using your information. If you make it easy for them, they will keep coming back to your website.
	If your website provides news of interest, you can deliver a daily factoid directly to your site users' PDA or wireless device. There really is no limit to how user-centric you can get with your information. Most of the technologies for delivering content are relatively inexpensive to implement.
Ensure quality of links	The Nonprofit Organization website often will serve as a resource center for issue(s) addressed by the organization. Site users will hope to find links to related information and resources that can be found both on the website and on other websites. These should be provided in a manner that complements the site navigation and is intuitive to the user.
	You must ensure the quality of content you link to. Users will view the links displayed on content pages as recommended resources. When users click on those links and find useful content, it reflects positively on the quality of your site. If not, it calls into question the reliability of your site.

Tasteful presentation of partnership and donation opportunities	An important purpose for the Nonprofit Organization website is to recruit partners and donors. This must be presented on the website in a way that is prominently built into the context of the website. That way, site visitors will be drawn to the opportunities to participate. However, it must also be tasteful, and not appear to be a pushy sales pitch. Otherwise, people may be turned off by your organization.

Building Loyalty

Loyalty for a Nonprofit Organization website basically means people feel an affinity towards your organization and want to spread the word about you to others. It also, often will mean that they view your website as a valuable resource. They may come to rely on the information you provide and want to pass it along to people they know.

Web content is naturally suited to being delivered through the Internet. You need not rely on people coming back to your website, although you will want them to. You can deliver content directly to users and make it easy for them to pass it along to others.

Opt-in email	Opt-in site users to a free newsletter. This gives you the opportunity to deliver content directly to a large group of people interested in what your website has to offer. If they like what you send them, they will follow links back to your site and forward your newsletter to friends and colleagues. Email marketing is discussed in Chapter 7.
Forward-to-a-friend	Include Forward-to-a-friend links on articles, or other useful content found on your website. This will make it easy for people to send your site content to others. They will not only find your content valuable, but are likely to come to your website to find more of the same.
Create viral objects	If you have valuable content, you can package that content to be passed along. This is the essence of viral marketing. You can create eBooks, articles, video clips, or any number of other items that can be sent through email. Then make these available to your site users, with an easy way for them to forward it along. Include some promotional copy and a link to your website. This will spread the word about what your organization is all about and bring new users to your website. Viral marketing is discussed in Chapter 10.

Conclusion

In this chapter, you have learned how to successfully build awareness for your cause, deliver information and recruit partners through a Nonprofit Organization website.

This is the final chapter. Turn now to the Concluding Thoughts

Concluding Thoughts

Doing Good While Doing Well
The Salesforce.com Story[*]

A common theme among many of the businesses that succeeded through the Dot-Com boom, and then crash, has been a genuine customer-centric philosophy and a social conscience. There was a little bit of hippie in many of those entrepreneurs, even if it was an obsessively driven, over-achieving type of hippie. It was not only in the "bring your dog to work" days, or the free chair massages, or the famous blue jean and t-shirt business attire. For many, the Dot-Com revolution was a heartfelt movement to make the world a better place. No collection of Internet Marketing stories would be complete without showing this side of the drama that unfolded in those years. It continues today. Marc Benioff and Salesforce.com is just one out of countless stories of business leaders, and employees, who are genuinely trying to use the Internet and their business platform to make a positive difference in the world we live in.

In 1999, Marc Benioff launched Salesforce.com with a vision to re-invent the software industry. It was a bold vision. Still, Marc had no lack of confidence. Before this, he had spent thirteen years holding various senior management positions at Oracle, one of the world's largest software companies. However, his vision was to do the exact opposite of what had made Oracle so successful.

Oracle was legendary for installing humongous, enterprise solutions on-site at their clients' facilities. This required companies to invest large sums of money in hardware, software and staff to help keep it all running. Marc thought businesses should not have to bother with all of that. Salesforce.com would maintain all of the software at their own facility.

[*] This story is adapted from Marc Benioff's book, "The Business of Changing the World" (2007).

Clients would simply pay a subscription fee to use it. The initial product was a contact management system helping salespeople cultivate relationships with their customers and prospects. It required no hardware or software at the client's site. The clients simply logged in through the Internet and started inputting their data. To Marc, this represented the "end of software." Businesses of all sizes would be empowered with access to the kind of computing solutions previously reserved for large corporations. In the process, they would realize cost savings and efficiency gains. It is a trend that has continued to gain momentum. At the same time, Salesforce.com has continued to grow and win industry awards.

Setting businesses free from the shackles of in-house hardware and software was not the end of Marc's vision. While at Oracle, he had also spent time setting up a major corporate philanthropy initiative. He knew first hand the impact companies could have in meeting the needs of the world. It is not merely a win-lose proposition where shareholders give away profits as a handout to the needy. Everybody wins when a company helps the communities they serve. Those communities become stronger markets for the company's products. Their people become better employees. Of course, the company wins positive public relations points.

Once again, Marc was not satisfied. He was convinced it could be done better. He set out to found his own company on a more holistic model where philanthropy would be "integrated" into the very fabric of the corporate culture. Shortly after launching Salesforce.com, a nonprofit organization was also launched, Salesforce.com/foundation. The new organization had a mission. In Marc's words, it was to "provide access to technology to youth in underserved communities and funding for youth entrepreneurship and education programs globally." The two organizations were joined at the hip through their 1-1-1 model of corporate philanthropy. One percent of equity (shares of stock), one percent of corporate profits and one percent of employee time would all be donated to the nonprofit organization. As Salesforce.com grew so would Salesforce.com/foundation. Their employees would all be along for the ride through paid time to dedicate towards community service.

At this point, it was no longer Marc's baby. He had unleashed the energies and creativity of the entire Salesforce.com staff towards making a difference in the world. Stories now abound of employees innovating not only software solutions but also community service solutions. As a result, the company is stronger. Employees are fulfilled and motivated by a corporate culture they can believe in. The individual employee, the communities served, and the company are all winners.

The employees at Salesforce.com, and countless other unsung heroes, teach a lesson that motivated many of the pioneers of the Dot-Com revolution and continues to motivate business leaders today. Doing business in the Twenty-first Century has been forever changed by innovations ushered in through the Internet. The Internet has created opportunities for companies to make the world a better place through innovative application of new technologies. However, an even more profound change has come from a realization that philanthropy and profits are not conflicting company goals. In fact, the more closely the two are tied together the more successful a company, its employees and the communities they do business with will be. As you pursue your own Internet Marketing projects, opportunities will abound to use the new technologies and new business models to make a positive impact in the markets and communities you serve.

What You Learned In This Book

This book has equipped you with the key skills and knowledge you need to be a successful Internet Marketer. It has taken you from soup to nuts, from a high level overview to practical nuts-and-bolts implementation.

In Part I, you learned how to put together an Internet Marketing plan for your business. Starting with strategy, you learned how to define your online business model and how to map out goals and objectives to meet the needs of your business model. Moving on to tactics, you learned how to define your target market and how to choose the right online features and marketing activities to reach your goals.

In Part II, you learned the practical techniques for bringing traffic to your website. This is the common denominator behind all successful websites.

You must get people to your website. These chapters provided step-by-step instructions for being successful with: search engines, email, online advertising, affiliate programs, viral marketing and blogs. Plus, a bonus chapter included a guide for making money by serving ads on your website or blog.

In Part III, you learned how to measure the performance of your website by using Web Analytics software. You learned what Web Analytics is and how it works. More importantly, easy to follow guidelines showed you how to set up advanced reporting that can be used to drive continual increases in the profitability of your website.

In Part IV, you learned how to create successful websites for the seven most common online business models. You learned that all websites are not created equal. Quite the opposite. Each online business model has its unique dimensions that determine what will be needed to make the website successful. By learning what it takes to make each of these seven business models successful, you will be able to apply the concepts to be successful with any website or web-based business.

Besides providing you with practical instruction about how to be successful with Internet Marketing, this book has also given real-world lessons from companies that pioneered many of the skills and strategies you have learned. These brief stories at the start of each chapter act as a history lesson, of sorts. The hope is that stepping into the shoes of those who have gone before will provide valuable insights into what Internet Marketers are still trying to accomplish today.

Time To Write Your Own Story

Now it is time for you to write your own Internet Marketing story. This book has presented the strategies, tactics and practical how-to guidelines for using the Internet to make your business or organization successful. Along the way, you have learned the lessons from some of those who pioneered the Internet Marketing terrain. Whether you are a beginner or a seasoned professional in the field, I hope this book has been of help. If this has been an introduction for you, let me welcome you to the ranks of Internet Marketing professionals.

Appendix A:
Online Resources For Internet Marketers

www.about.com

This is one of the original content websites. It contains articles and how-to tutorials by content area experts on thousands of topics, many related to Internet Marketing.

www.associateprograms.com

This website by Allan Gardyne is loaded with articles and tutorials related to affiliate programs. A great reference for those participating in or setting up their own affiliate programs.

www.clickz.com

This is one of the original websites supporting the Internet Marketing community. It contains news and instructional articles written by experts in their respective fields. Their archive goes back to the hay day of the Dot-Com revolution.

www.dma.org

The website for the Direct Marketing Association. There are many resources on this website for both Direct Marketing and Internet Marketing. Most importantly, you will find the DMA guidelines for email marketing which are essential for anyone planning to use email for their business or organization.

www.emarketer.com

Online magazine eMarketer dedicated to measuring and reporting on Internet industry trends and stats. Filled with articles and research reports, most require a subscription but many are free.

www.fcc.gov

The website for the US Federal Communications Commission. This website includes information related to the regulation of cell phones and wireless devices.

It should be consulted by anyone planning to deliver email or other content to wireless devices.

www.forrester.com

The website for industry leading Forrester Research. Filled with research reports on various topics including Interactive Marketing. Most reports are paid however there are a few free ones.

www.ftc.gov

The website for the US Federal Trade Commission. This website contains information related to the CAN-SPAM Act which regulates email marketing. It should be consulted by anyone planning to use email for their business or organization.

www.howstuffworks.com

Full of tutorials and how-to articles on all sorts of topics, from ham radios to HTML. There are many good Internet Marketing tutorials on this site.

www.iab.net

The website for the Internet Advertising Bureau (IAB) an association dedicated to supporting the Internet Advertising industry. The website includes industry standards and guidelines, research reports and news along with other resources supporting the industry.

www.internetbasedmoms.com

This website is dedicated to home-based Internet businesses by, as the title says, moms earning extra income for the household. It offers some very useful tutorials for any small business using the Internet to reach their customers.

www.jupiterresearch.com

The website for industry leading Jupiter Research. Has many paid reports covering various Internet related topics in addition to other industries.

www.marketingpower.com

This is the website for the American Marketing Association. It has many authoritative articles covering a variety of Internet Marketing topics.

www.searchenginewatch.com

This website provides tons of resources supporting all things related to search engines. It is an essential resource for anyone pursuing search engine marketing (SEM) or search engine optimization (SEO).

www.tamingthebeast.com

This website has many useful how-to articles written by Michael Bloch on a variety of Internet Marketing subjects.

www.technorati.com

The leading search engine for blogs. This also offers a small library off free open source tools for the tech-minded blogger.

www.useit.com

This is the website of Web Usability guru Jakob Nielsen. Jakob is one of the foremost usability experts in the industry. His website is filled with useful how-to articles related to making your website deliver an effective user experience.

www.w3schools.com

Filled with many excellent tutorials covering Internet technology, mostly back-end application languages such as HTML, .NET and XML.

www.webmonkey.com

This is one of the original websites offering free tutorials for Internet related topics. It has mostly technical tutorials and much of the content is dated now, but still a useful resource.

www.website101.com

Full of tutorials and how-to articles on all things Internet. Articles are written by practitioners in their respective fields and organized into topics by the site editor.

www.wikipedia.org

This is a free-for-all encyclopedia. Volunteers post entries on every topic under the sun. You will find tons of useful and interesting information, but there is little quality control over the accuracy of information on Wikipedia posts so use at your own risk.

Appendix B:
References

AbayomiPaul, Tinu (2005). Increase Traffic to Your Blog from Search Engines The Top 5 Tips. Retrieved Nov. 10, 2006, from http://website101.com/RSS-Blogs-Blogging/

Angel, Gary. (2006). Functionalism and Web Analytics. Retrieved Nov. 10, 2006, from http://www.webpronews.com/expertarticles/expertarticles/wpn-62-20060809FunctionalismandWebAnalytics.html

Balardvale Research. (2004). Market Trends – Web Analytics: History and Future. Retrieved Nov. 10, 2006, from http://www.ballardvale.com/free/WAHistory.htm

Bloch, Michael. Viral Marketing & the Internet. Retrieved Nov. 10, 2006, from http://www.tamingthebeast.net/articles/viralmarketingt.htm

Bloch, Michael. Viral Marketing Tips. Retrieved Nov. 10, 2006, from http://www.tamingthebeast.net/articles/ViralMarketing..htm

Bloch, Michael. Email Marketing Ethics and Spam Reporting. Retrieved Nov. 10, 2006, from http://www.tamingthebeast.net/articles/EmailMarketingEthicsSpamReporting.htm

Blood, Rebecca. (2000). Weblogs: a History and Perspective. Retrieved Nov. 10, 2006, from http://www.rebeccablood.net/essays/weblog_history.html

Boutin, Paul. (2001). Search Engine Optimization – Free!. Retrieved Nov. 10, 2006, from http://www.webmonkey.com/webmonkey/01/23/index1a.html?tw=e-business

Brain, Marshall. How E-mail Works. Retrieved Nov 10, 2006, from http://www.howstuffworks.com/email.htm

Brain, Marshall. How Web Advertising Works. Retrieved Nov 10, 2006, from http://computer.howstuffworks.com/web-advertising.htm

Bresh, Scott. Your Web Traffic and Your Bottom Line – Visitors and Pageviews. Retrieved Nov. 10, 2006, from http://website101.com/web-traffic-analysis-statistics/index.html

Bruner, Rick E. (2005). The Decade in Online Advertising: 1994-2004. DoubleClick, Inc.

Bruton, Linda J. (2004). Why Marketers Should Blog & Why It Took Me So Long To Blog. Retrieved Nov. 10, 2006, from http://website101.com/RSS-Blogs-Blogging/

Carrigan, Shaun. Using Email Newsletters as Marketing Tools. Retrieved Nov 10, 2006, from http://www.marketingpower.com/content17625.php#

Collins, Shawn. (2000) History of Affiliate Marketing. Retrieved Nov. 10, 2006, from http://www.clickz.com/showPage.html?page=832131

Collins, Shawn. (2000) This Year's Model. Retrieved Nov. 10, 2006, from http://www.clickz.com/showPage.html?page=819911

Davis, Mischelle. Introduction to Email Marketing. Retrieved Nov 10, 2006, from http://www.marketingpower.com/content14223.php#

Direct Marketing Association. (2005). E-mail Delivery Best Practices. Direct Marketing Association

Doyle, Noah. Principles of Email Marketing. Retrieved Nov 10, 2006, from http://www.marketingpower.com/content1286.php#

Dun, Decian. Affiliate Marketing Overview. Retrieved Nov 10, 2006, from http://www.marketingpower.com/content1030.php#

Franklin, Curt. How Internet Search Engines Work. Retrieved Nov. 10, 2006, from http://www.howstuffworks.com/search-engines.htm

Gamse, Philippa. Mining for Gold...In Your Web Traffic Logs. Retrieved Nov. 10, 2006, from http://website101.com/web-traffic-analysis-statistics/index.html

Gamse, Philippa, Top 7 Reasons to Review Your Web Traffic Analysis. Retrieved Nov. 10, 2006, from http://website101.com/web-traffic-analysis-statistics/index.html

Gamse, Philippa. Unlocking the Keys to Your Web Site Traffic Analysis. Retrieved Nov. 10, 2006, from http://website101.com/web-traffic-analysis-statistics/index.html

Gardyne, Allan. (2006). Affiliate Program Tutorial. Retrieved Nov. 10, 2006, from http://www.associateprograms.com/articles/188/1/Affiliate-Programs-Tutorial

---

Gardyne, Allan. (2005). How to Get Reciprocal Links. Retrieved Nov. 10, 2006, from http://www.associateprograms.com/articles/48/1/How-to-get-reciprocal-links

Gardyne, Allan. (2005). One-Way Links Explained. Retrieved Nov. 10, 2006, from http://www.associateprograms.com/articles/43/1/One-way-links-explained

Gardyne, Allan. (2006). The Million Dollar Affiliate. Retrieved Nov. 10, 2006, from http://www.associateprograms.com/articles/438/1/An-interview-with-the-million-dollar-affiliate

Harris, Tom. How Affiliate Programs Work. Retrieved Nov. 10, 2006, from http://money.howstuffworks.com/affiliate-programs.htm

Harris, Tom. How Banner Ads Work. Retrieved Nov. 10, 2006, from http://money.howstuffworks.com/banner-ad10.htm

Hering, James. (2003). The Next Gator Iteration. Retrieved Nov. 10, 2006, from http://www.clickz.com/showPage.html?page=3113061

Hespos, Tom. (2001). The Scum of the Web. Retrieved Nov. 10, 2006, from http://www.clickz.com/showPage.html?page=934701

Housley, Sharon. (2005). Innovative Business Use of RSS as a Technology. Retrieved Nov. 10, 2006, from http://website101.com/RSS-Blogs-Blogging/

Intrapromote. (2001). The Proof is in the Pass-Along: A Viral Marketing Tutorial. Retrieved Nov. 10, 2006, from http://www.intrapromote.com

Jensen, Mallory. (2003). A Brief History of Weblogs. Columbia Journalism Review. Retrieved Nov. 10, 2006, from http://www.cjr.org/issues/2003/5/blog-jensen.asp

Johari, Sanjay. It Makes Sense to Add Google Adsense Ads to Your Blog. Retrieved Nov. 10, 2006, from http://website101.com/RSS-Blogs-Blogging/

Johnson, Janet. Corporate Blogging Made Simple. Retrieved Nov. 10, 2006, from http://www.marketingpower.com/content28649.php#

Kingdon, Mark. (2006) Blog Advertising: A Quick Tutorial. Retrieved Nov. 10, 2006, from http://www.clickz.com/showPage.html?page=3623011

Klais, Brian. How to Select an Email Marketing Vendor. Retrieved Nov 10, 2006, from http://www.marketingpower.com/content17642.php#

Krakoff, Patsy and Wakeman, Denise. Top 10 Blog Writing Tips. Retrieved Nov. 10, 2006, from http://website101.com/RSS-Blogs-Blogging/

Krakoff, Patsy and Wakeman, Denise. 16 Ways to Drive Traffic to Your Blog. Retrieved Nov. 10, 2006, from http://website101.com/RSS-Blogs-Blogging/

Lacy, Sarah. (2005). Analyzing Google's Analytics Strategy. Retrieved Nov. 10, 2006, from http://www.businessweek.com/technology/content/nov2005/tc20051115_111104.htm

Lewis, Sage. Site Statistics – What they Should be Telling You and Probably Aren't. Retrieved Nov. 10, 2006, from http://website101.com/web-traffic-analysis-statistics/index.html

Loh, Roger. 7 Benefits of Building Niche Blogs. Retrieved Nov. 10, 2006, from http://website101.com/RSS-Blogs-Blogging/

Maci, Fernando. Is Anyone Visiting My Website?. Retrieved Nov. 10, 2006, from http://website101.com/web-traffic-analysis-statistics/index.html

Maslow, Abraham. (1943). "A Theory of Human Motivation" in *Psychological Review*, 50:370-96

McElwain, The Hits that Matter Most - CR. Retrieved Nov. 10, 2006, from http://website101.com/web-traffic-analysis-statistics/index.html

McKenna, Regis. (1991). Relationship Marketing: Successful Strategies for the Age of the Customer. Perseus Books

Messer, Stephen D. Managing a Successful Affiliate Marketing Program. Retrieved Nov 10, 2006, from http://www.marketingpower.com/content16579.php#

Messer, Stephen D. Maximizing Return from the 80-20 Rule. Retrieved Nov 10, 2006, from http://www.marketingpower.com/content16577.php#

Morrissey, Brian. (2003). News Publishers, Gator Settle Suit. Retrieved Nov. 10, 2006, from http://www.clickz.com/showPage.html?page=1581401

Nielsen, Jacob. (2005). Weblog Usability: The Top Ten Design Mistakes. Retrieved Nov. 10, 2006, from http://www.useit.com/alertbox/weblogs.html

Nielsen NetRatings. (2006). Nielsen NetRatings Search Engine Ratings. Retrieved Nov. 10, 2006, from http://searchenginewatch.com/showPage.html?page=2156451

OConnor, Jason, Web Analytics Murder By Numbers. Retrieved Nov. 10, 2006, from http://website101.com/web-traffic-analysis-statistics/index.html

Parker, Pamela. (2003). Gator Becomes Claria. Retrieved Nov. 10, 2006, from http://www.clickz.com/showPage.html?page=3113061

Peppers, Don and Rogers, Martha (1993). *The One to One Future, Building Relationships One Customer at a Time*. Doubleday

Philips, Steve. Driving Site Traffic. Retrieved Nov. 10, 2006, from http://www.marketingpower.com/content1302.php#

PriceWaterhouseCoopers. (2006). IAB Internet Advertising Revenue Report: Second Quarter 2006. PriceWaterhouseCoopers LLP

Sakalosky, Mark. (2002). Gator: Problem or Solution. Retrieved Nov. 10, 2006, from http://clickz.com/showPage.html?page=1547791

Sakalosky, Mark. (2003). Golden Rule, Updated. Retrieved Nov. 10, 2006, from http://www.clickz.com/showPage.html?page=3077661

Saunders, Christopher. (2001). IAB Blasts Gator.com as Unfair, Deceptive. Retrieved Nov. 10, 2006, from http://www.clickz.com/showPage.html?page=874141

Sullivan, Danny. (2002). Search Engine Submission Tips (formerly: A Webmaster's Guide to Search Engines). Retrieved Nov. 10, 2006, from http://searchenginewatch.com/showPage.html?page=webmasters

Summary.net. Web Analytics Tutorial. Retrieved Nov.10.2006, from http://www.summary.net/manual/tutorial

Tillinghast, Tig. (2001) An Affiliate Marketing Primer. Retrieved Nov. 10, 2006, from http://www.clickz.com/showPage.html?page=842381

Vargas, Elizabeth. (2004). People of the Year: Bloggers. Retrieved Nov. 10, 2006, from http://abcnews.go.com/WNT/PersonOfWeek/story?id=372266&page=1

Waldrop, Sheri. Email Marketing Tutorial by Sheri Waldrop. Retrieved Nov. 10, 2006, from http://www.internetbasedmoms.com/ezine-publishing/email-marketing-rules.html

WebSideStory. (2004). Web Analytics – It's Surprisingly Simple. Retrieved Nov. 10, 2006, from http://www.websidestory.com

Wikipedia. (2006). Web Analytics. Retrieved Nov. 10, 2006 from http://en.wikipedia.org/wiki/Web_analytics

Wikipedia. (2006). Web Banner. Retrieved Nov. 10, 2006 from http://en.wikipedia.org/wiki/Web_banner

Wingate, Kim. Tracking Single Page Conversions. Retrieved Nov. 10, 2006, from http://website101.com/web-traffic-analysis-statistics/index.html

Wirken, Dany. (2006). The Pitfalls of Business Blogging. Retrieved Nov. 10, 2006, from http://www.chauy.com/2006/08/the-pitfalls-of-business-blogging#more-477

Appendix C:
Index